Memories of the Slave Trade

Memories of the Slave Trade

Ritual and the Historical Imagination in Sierra Leone

Rosalind Shaw

The University of Chicago Press
Chicago and London

Rosalind Shaw is associate professor of Anthropology
at Tufts University. She has co-edited two previous
books and has published many articles in professional
journals.

The University of Chicago Press, Chicago 60637
The University of Chicago Press, Ltd., London
© 2002 by The University of Chicago
All rights reserved. Published 2002
Printed in the United States of America
11 10 09 08 07 06 05 04 03 02   5 4 3 2 1

ISBN (cloth): 0-226-75131-7
ISBN (paper): 0-226-75132-5

Library of Congress Cataloging-in-Publication Data

Shaw, Rosalind.
    Memories of the slave trade : ritual and the
  historical imagination in Sierra Leone / Rosalind
  Shaw.
       p.   cm.
    Includes bibliographical references (p.   ) and
  index.
    ISBN 0-226-75131-7—ISBN 0-226-75132-5
  (paper)
    1. Witchcraft—Sierra Leone. 2. Slave trade—
  Sierra Leone.   I. Title.

  BJ1584.S5 S53   2002
  306′.09664—dc21

                              2001004442

In memory of my mother, Manon Elissa Shaw

Contents

Illustrations

Acknowledgments

At times even I was not convinced that I would finish this book. Once I began writing it in 1993, the book took on a life of its own, becoming a greedy entity that constantly asked for more, growing bigger and bigger as it demanded new chapters here, additional development there. Now, at last, it is quieter, and I have learned that I do not necessarily have to indulge its each and every wish. Writing this book has been a difficult experience; despite the astonishing beauty of Temne divination and cosmological ideas, the material I explore is often painful, and it is given an even sharper edge by Sierra Leone's present circumstances. Many Sierra Leonean friends—some of whom I have known for over twenty years—have died, disappeared, or become sick, impoverished, and traumatized during ten years of war, even as they have inspired me with their courage and resourcefulness.

My acknowledgement of debts, therefore, begins with them. My biggest debt is to Michael Sanasi Kalokoh, my first research assistant in 1978 and my close friend and advisor ever since, without whose knowledge, kindness, and unflagging professionalism my work could not have got off the ground. Profuse thanks are also owed to Fala Mansaray and Filo Turay, my research assistants in 1989 and 1992 respectively. I will never forget the generosity of my hosts who allowed me to become part of their lives and households: in Petbana Masimbo, the late Pa Kaper Bana, the late Pa Alfa Koroma, Pa Moses

Kalokoh, and Pa Abdulai Kalokoh; in Matotoka, Paramount Chief Bay Kafari III and Pa Yamba Kore; and in Freetown, Hajja Khadi Tejan-Kamara and Mrs. Latifa Dyfan. Hajja Khadi told me in 1978 that she would be my mother in Sierra Leone, and some of the happiest memories of my life are from the times I spent in her compound, talking with her over cassava-leaf *plasas* as she supervised the cloth-dyeing work of her children and grandchildren. Nor can I ever repay the diviners and Muslim specialists who taught me so much; those with whom I worked most closely were the late Pa Alfa Koroma (Petbana Masimbo), Pa Santigi Tarawali (Petbana Masimbo), Pa Biyare Seri (Mafonke and Makeni), Ya Mari Gbla (Matotoka), Pa Fode Gbla (Mayan), Ya Mabinti Kamara (Koidu), the late Pa Ahmadu Fonah (Rokirfi), the late Ya Yebu Kane (Malal and Mabont), the late Pa Yamba Nhoni Kamara (Freetown), Ya Bay Kolone (Freetown), and Pa Ibrahim Sankoh (Wellington). I also benefited from my conversations with countless people in Petbana Masimbo, Makeni, Matotoka, Magburaka, Freetown, and Koidu who are too numerous to be named here, but I would like to express particular thanks to the late Yan Safi, Mr. Myers, Ya Nandewa, and Kadiatu Kamara.

My Ph.D. research at the School of Oriental and African Studies was funded by the (then) Social Science Research Council of the U.K.; I also received an Emslie Horniman Scholarship and assistance from the University of London's Central Research Fund for my 1977–78 fieldwork in Sierra Leone. I am grateful to the Institute of African Studies in Fourah Bay College, University of Sierra Leone, for affiliation and for the generous provision of an office in July and August 1978. I gratefully acknowledge funding for my fieldwork in 1989 from the Carnegie Trust for the Universitites of Scotland and the University of Edinburgh's Centre for African Studies. My 1992 fieldwork was generously funded by the Wenner-Gren Foundation for Anthropological Research and by a Faculty Research Grant from Tufts University. Fellowships at the Bunting Institute and at the Harvard Women's Studies in Religion Program in 1992–93 gave me the time and reading opportunities to rethink my material through the lens of history and memory. And in 1994, fellowships from Harvard University's Center for the Study of World Religions and Northwestern University's Institute for Advanced Study and Research in the African Humanities allowed me to write the beginnings of this manuscript.

During my Ph.D. research at the University of London's School of Oriental and African Studies, David Dalby generously gave me Temne language instruction, lent me his unpublished Temne-English dictionary, and gave me letters of introduction for my fieldwork in Sierra Leone. Likewise, my thesis would have been difficult to complete without John Middleton's and David Parkin's encouragement and their insights into ritual and meaning.

Over the years, many others have shared their ideas and given me invaluable feedback; they include Mark Auslander, Ralph Austen, Sandra Barnes, Robert Baum, Jennifer Cole, Jean and John Comaroff, Toyin Falola, Mariane Ferme, Christopher Fyfe, Cecil Magbaily Fyle, Eric Gable, Rosalind Hackett, Kris Hardin, Adrian Hastings, Michael Herzfeld, Michael Jackson, Charles Jędrej, Ogbu Kalu, Ivan Karp, Cory Kratz, Michael Lambek, Wyatt MacGaffey, Mike MacGovern, Mohamed Mahmoud, D. A. Masolo, Kay Moseley, the late Donatus Nwoga, Joseph Opala, Stephan Palmie, Keith Ray, Loretta Reinhardt, Paul Richards, Ellen Schattschneider, Ben Soares, Marilyn Strathern, Charles Stewart, Alison Sutherland, Brad Weiss, and Richard Werbner. Special thanks go to my most generous critics, Misty Bastian and Adeline Masquelier, for their unfailing insight. I have benefited enormously from the careful readings and comments I received from participants at the annual Satterthwaite Symposium, founded by Richard Werbner; the 1993 conference on "African Philosophy as Cultural Inquiry" in Nairobi organized by Ivan Karp and D. A. Masolo; the 1997 conference on "Magic and Modernity" organized by Birgit Meyer and Peter Pels at the University of Amsterdam; and the 2000 Symposium on Perspectives in Contemporary Anthropology organized in Guerneville, California by Brad Weiss.

I am especially grateful to Alice Clemente, David Beach, and Jeanne Penvenne for their translations of the excerpts from Fernandes 1951 [1506–10]; to Mohamed Mahmoud for his translation of the Temne-Arabic diagrams in chapter 4; to Bill Hart for bringing my attention to the Nylander engraving I have used for the front cover; and to Maggie Bruno, Judy Jacobs, and Peggy Casey for their help, patience, and tolerance of my many requests. I owe a great deal to Susan Ostrander for her advice and phone calls at a crucial point in this manuscript's gestation, and to Michael Herzfeld and Jane Huber for an editorial collaboration that transformed my writing.

I have also learned much from my students, especially those in my seminar on "Memories of the Slave Trade." And finally, I am most grateful to the University of Chicago Press's anonymous readers for their careful reading and invaluable suggestions, to T. David Brent for his patient encouragement, and to Richard Allen for his perceptive questions and superb editing.

Above all, I wish to acknowledge my late mother, Manon Elissa Shaw, for sensitizing me to other ways of thinking and living, for encouraging and supporting my work in Sierra Leone, and for providing an example of independence of spirit from which I will always draw strength.

Note on Temne Orthography

I have phoneticized Temne words according to International Phonetic Alphabet conventions. Vowels are pronounced as follows:

a as in *bad*
ɑ as in *up*
e like the *e* in *ecru*
ɛ as in *get*
ə like the *e* in *camel*
i as in *eel*
o like the *o* in *low*
ɔ as in *dog*
u as in *June*

The homorganic nasal *ŋ* is pronounced like the *ng* in *thing;* if followed by a *b* or *p*, however, it is pronounced *m*.

Introduction

Speaking through an interpreter, in Temne, he began by saying that the slave business was finished and that therefore it should not be spoken about. Edward Ball, *Slaves in the Family*

When Edward Ball, the descendant of slave owners in South Carolina, traced the history of the white and African American sides of his family, he found that his ancestors had bought some of the human cargo of slave ships from Sierra Leone (1998: 420). He concluded his search with a trip to Sierra Leone, visiting the ruins of the main slave factory on Bunce Island in the estuary of the Sierra Leone River and interviewing descendants of African slave traders. Most of these descendants were awkward, and sometimes irritated and eva- sive, at being confronted with the aggressively interrogative style of a Western journalistic interview, featuring such statements as "Your ancestor was a slave dealer" (423). Although Ball managed to persuade members of the ruling family in the old slave-trading port of Port Loko to perform a ritual of atone- ment with him at the water's edge (443–45), the overall impression he gives is that Sierra Leoneans do not like to be reminded of the slave trade. The claim is sometimes made that Africans deny their own responsibility for the slave trade, and on the whole Ball's interviews appear to support this.

The condition of the important historical site of Bunce Island strengthens

1

the impression that the slave trade is forgotten or denied in Sierra Leone. There, the overgrown ruins of the slave factory once owned by the Royal African Company have been left to decay since the early nineteenth century, when the island was abandoned (plate 1). An American anthropologist, Joseph Opala, conducted several years of archaeological and archival research on Bunce Island (Opala 1977), but none of the successive Sierra Leonean governments since independence has attempted to preserve and restore it in order to develop it as a commemorative site. This neglect forms a stark contrast to the attention and resources given to other slave-trading sites in West Africa. The Maison des esclaves on the Senegalese island of Gorée, for example, has been designated a UNESCO world heritage site (see Hinchman forthcoming); the slave castle of Cape Coast in Ghana has recently been the focus of an integrated development project funded by USAID and the Government of Ghana, with support from the Smithsonian Institution (Mullen Kreamer forthcoming); and the road from the town of Ouidah, in Benin, to the beach where slaves were loaded into ships was developed as a commemorative project called La route de l'esclave, with support from UNESCO (Law forthcoming).[1]

But if we are attentive to forms of remembering different from those of verbally discursive admissions and projects of public memory, we find that beyond Bunce Island's abject silence as a commemorative site, and beyond the awkward silences of Ball's interviewees, the slave trade is not forgotten in Sierra Leone. If, as Ball was told, "the slave business . . . should not be spoken about" (1998: 439), there are other ways of remembering the past than by speaking of it. In this book, I explore some of these other ways in the Temne-speaking communities I knew in northern Sierra Leone.

Divining Memory

In the beginning there was a river. The river became a road and the road branched out to the whole world. And because the road was once a river it was always hungry. Ben Okri, *The Famished Road*

Okri's chimerical image of a road that once began as a river, that links those upon it with the "whole world," and that is, in addition, an insatiable consumer of human life, suggests the kinds of connections between world-historical processes and "magical" capacities (particularly those deriving from all-devouring roads and rivers) with which I am concerned here. This is an exploration of ritual, memory, and modernity on the West African side of the Atlantic world.

We are by now familiar with arguments that "much of what has been taken to be timeless tradition is, in fact, the paradoxical effect of colonial rule" (Dirks 1992a: 8)—constructions, for example, of caste in India (Dirks 1992b) and of "Bushmen" in the Kalahari desert (Wilmsen 1989). For globalization, as Gupta and Ferguson observe, is "a shared historical process that differentiates the world as it connects it" (1992: 16), generating a diversity of practices and identities that are often taken to be defining emblems of "a culture." In this book, I seek to push back such historical outcomes to a time several centuries before colonial rule. Specifically, I shall argue that certain ritual practices and images among Temne speakers in northern Sierra Leone may be understood as memories of temporally removed processes (cf. Munn 1990) created by an Atlantic commercial system that spanned three continents.

These ritual practices and images include those of the spirit landscape, techniques of divination, diviners' visionary experiences, the negotiations of diviners' clients, cosmologies of witchcraft, practices of witchfinding, colonial stories of "human leopards," and phantasmagoric rumors about malefic ties between diviners and postcolonial leaders. While pernicious images of diviners ("witch-doctors"), divination, and witchcraft have long been integral to Western "inventions of Africa" (Mudimbe 1988), these areas of ritual and cosmology have all, I will argue, been shaped by the experience of the Atlantic slave trade. They not only unsettle binary notions of "traditional ritual" and "modern processes," but also—as I suggest below—require us to extend our understandings of modernity.

This book is also about divination, which, as all anthropologists know, is concerned with moments of danger. Such crises as sudden death, problematic childbirth, illness, and collapsing granaries erupt above and beyond "ordinary" predicaments, demanding action that departs from that of everyday practice. But an exploration of Temne divination *(ka-thupəs)* entails a broader focus than that on the crises precipitating the consultation of diviners; it also requires attention to certain dangers perceived in the very nature of divination itself. These dangers are mapped within divination techniques, experienced during diviners' initiatory visions, and represented as inherent in the persons of diviners *(aŋ-thupəs)* themselves. They are also seen in the imputed motives of diviners' clients—especially women on the one hand and members of postcolonial business and political elites on the other—who are suspected of using diviners to harm others covertly. How, though, can these understandings of divination, diviners, and clients be viewed as memories of the Atlantic slave trade?

There is a growing literature on the embedding of histories in meanings and practices that are not discursively "historical" in the manner of oral narratives and written accounts of the past. James, for instance, examines how Uduk on the Sudan-Ethiopian border reveal through their ritual practice an implicit "moral knowledge" of an earlier existence as hunters—a "deposit" of past events and actions that is not verbally recalled and that, following Foucault, she calls an "archive" (1988). As the literature on embodiment has grown both in scale and significance, scholars have recognized that the past is remembered not only in words but also in images and nondiscursive practical forms that go beyond words. "For the poetics of history," as Comaroff and Comaroff write, "lie also in mute meanings transacted through goods and practices, through icons and images dispersed in the landscape of the everyday" (1992: 35).

In acknowledging this point we have, of course, to beware of drawing an oversimplified dichotomy between the verbal and the nonverbal. It has long been apparent that, far from being literalistic, linear chronicles, oral narratives are more often complex condensations of cultural and historical meanings in images and metaphors. Schoffeleers (1992), for example, demonstrates how narratives of the Mbona cult in southern Malawi fix historical processes in images rather than in literal narrative content: the warfare and social upheavals set in motion by Portuguese militarization and enslavement in Zambesia around the turn of the seventeenth century, he argues, are encoded both in narrative images of a martyr, Mbona, and in the ceremonial cycle and ritual geography of Mbona's cult.

How may memory be present in nonverbal forms and practices? Here Bourdieu's conception of history and practice would seem relevant:

> The *habitus*—embodied history, internalized as a second nature and so forgotten as history—is the active presence of the whole past of which it is the product. As such, it is what gives practices their relative autonomy with respect to external determinations of the immediate present. This autonomy is that of the past, enacted and acting, which, functioning as accumulated capital, produces history on the basis of history and so ensures the permanence in change that makes the individual agent a world within the world. (Bourdieu 1990: 56)

For Bourdieu (in this instance at least) the habitus does not, as many critics have charged, entail merely a closed cycle of repetitive change. Although much of what Bourdieu writes does indeed convey a sense of unproblematic reproduction, this is not a fair overall assessment of his understanding of the historical nature of the habitus. The latter is a product of "the whole past," "accumulated" and therefore *continually* constituted by historical events and processes even as those events and processes are transformed by integration into the habitus.

At first sight, Bourdieu's habitus might seem an unproductive concept for contexts characterized by dislocation and rupture. Thus De Boeck argues that in Congo, during "both the colonial and postcolonial periods it was/is no longer possible unproblematically to (re)produce habitus, and therefore history; and for the same reason it is not possible in either context to forget about habitus as history" (1998: 31). But although De Boeck eloquently captures a sense of the loss of a "harmonious memory environment" (33), of the rupture of the postcolonial present from a past world of cohesiveness and familiarity, in fact the habitus as the "active presence of the whole past" (Bourdieu 1990: 56) encompasses past dislocation just as much as past stability. Furthermore, we cannot assume that the precolonial past was significantly less marked by rupture and crisis than the present. Before we throw out the concept of habitus in favor of an analytic frame that privileges fragmentation alone, let us consider how, far from being lost through experiences of disruption, dislocation, destruction, and even apocalypse, the habitus feeds on these and takes them into itself. Instead of being inimical to reproduction, then, rupture *becomes* part of what is reproduced.

To put this another way, a theory of practice is historical not only because, as Ortner puts it, it "concerns the ways in which a given social and cultural order mediates the impact of external events by shaping the ways in which actors experience and respond to those events" (1989: 200). A theory of practice is also a theory of memory that suggests a different way of "remembering" the past, in which not only everyday choices (marriage strategies, ethnic identifications, and alliances [Tonkin 1992: 109–11]) but also violently dislocating transregional processes (conquest, colonialism, migration, war, wage labor) are rendered internal, are (literally) incorporated into people and their social and cultural practice. The Comaroffs have stressed, for instance, that attempts at social transformation entail bodily reform and the remaking of everyday habits, from colonial housing and sanitation schemes to the work-discipline of the daily timetable in Christian missions—projects in which the body is implicitly recognized as a mnemonic entity (Comaroff and Comaroff 1992: 70). "From this perspective," they note, "history involves a sedimentation of micropractices into macroprocesses" (38).

This formulation can also be reversed. History, in addition, involves the sedimentation of macroprocesses into micropractices, especially during processes of conquest, colonization, dislocation, and turmoil. As Kleinman and Kleinman observe:

> Bodies transformed by political processes not only *represent* those processes, they *experience* them as the lived memory of transformed worlds. The experience is of memory processes sedimented in gait, posture, movement, and all the other corporal components which together realize cultural code and social dynamics in everyday practices. The memorialized experience merges subjectivity and social world. (1994: 716–17)

Thus expressions of thirst in healing rituals of Tshidi Zionist churches in apartheid South Africa, for example, tied together symptoms of bodily affliction, experiences of an oppressive social world, and memories of drought as a sign of political and moral disruption (Jean Comaroff 1985: 75, 201). In a rather different translation of colonial process into ritual praxis, acts of European conquest in the Putumayo region of Amazonia have, according to Taussig, "become objectified . . . as magically empowered imagery capable of causing as well as relieving misfortune" (1987: 367), thereby crystallizing history as sorcery. Likewise, successive alien rulers of what is now northern Sudan live on in the form of *zar* spirits that possess women's bodies, both afflicting and empowering their human hosts (Boddy 1989), while in western Nigeria, strongly politicized images of male "mounting" (of both horses and women) deriving from the eighteenth-century Oyo empire are drawn upon in Oyo Yoruba spirit possession today (Matory 1994). Further north, European military postures and gestures in colonial Niger are caught mimetically by Hauka spirits who possess Songhay men's bodies, as well as by, Stoller suggests, certain postcolonial Nigerien political leaders with links to the Hauka (Stoller 1995). And in northwestern Madagascar, members of the Antankarana royal descent group who drowned while evading pursuit by the Merina in the nineteenth century return as *trumba* spirits during an annual bathing ritual, repeating the moment of their death in their agonized contortions as they enter living Antankarana bodies (Lambek 1996: 245–46).

The foundational study for explorations of ritual as memory is, of course, Paul Connerton's pathbreaking work, *How Societies Remember* (1989). Here Connerton develops the notion of habit memory, "the capacity to reproduce a certain performance" (1989: 22), with respect to commemorative rituals

through which participants reenact the past in explicitly mnemonic performances (41–71). In commemorative rituals, the past is not only remembered
cognitively but also embodied; it is through such embodiment, moreover, that
these rituals "work for their participants" and "are . . . persuasive to them" (71).
Connerton goes on, however, to make a problematic distinction between
the incorporation of the past through techniques, proprieties, and ceremonies
of the body, and the inscription of the past through such media as written
texts, computers, audiotapes, and cinema (72–79). Although, as Stoller argues
(1995: 30), Connerton's categorization may give us a useful counterweight
to the privileging of textual metaphors in the history of hermeneutics, the
dichotomy thereby produced of body versus text and of incorporation versus
inscription is suspiciously reminiscent of Enlightenment oppositions of mind
and body, reason and passion, intellect and emotion. Several scholars have,
moreover, criticized Connerton by drawing attention to cultural practices that
either collapse his opposition altogether (Battaglia 1992; Middleton 1996)
or reconfigure it in terms of complementarity (De Boeck 1995). Connerton's
characterization of habit-memory as "the capacity to reproduce a certain performance" (1989: 22) may, however, point us in a more fruitful direction.

Practical Memory and Reproduction   Here I wish to turn to Giddens's distinction between discursive and practical consciousness. "Discursive consciousness," according to Giddens, "connotes those forms of recall which the actor
is able to express verbally," while "practical consciousness involves recall to
which the agent has access in the *durée* of action without being able to express
what he or she thereby 'knows'" (1984: 41–49). Extending this to memory,
we may identify a distinction between discursive and practical memory that
is not based on a simple dichotomy between body and text. Rather than pre-
suming a privileged opposition between embodiment and inscription deriving from a Western history of ideas, we are instead directed to the experiences,
understandings, and intentions of cultural actors themselves. We can thus distinguish between, on the one hand, the reflexive sensibilities of discursive
memory in explicit, intentional narrative accounts of the past and, on the
other hand, the more tacit apprehensions of practical memory, "forgotten as
history" (Bourdieu 1990: 56) precisely because they are embedded in habits,
social practices, ritual processes, and embodied experiences.

I do not, however, wish to replace the fixed opposition of "incorporation"
versus "inscription" with yet another. Instead, we can view discursive memory
and practical memory as two poles of a continuum that does not entail a zero-

sum conception of particular cultural forms as located exclusively at one or another of these extremes. Connerton's example of commemorative rituals is a good one: such rituals are based partly on discursive memory in that their performers explicitly and intentionally reenact the past (1989: 45). Yet such ceremonies, Connerton emphasizes, involve more than cognitive competence. The participants are "habituated" to their performance through what Connerton calls a "bodily substrate" (71), thereby drawing on practical as well as discursive memories of how to embody their past.

Attention to such processes requires a recognition of practical, nondiscursive forms of memory as having at least as much importance as those that are discursively "about" the past. Through the practical knowledgeability of cultural actors, historical events are incorporated into the environment of practices, meanings, and values that these actors produce. Bourdieu's sense of a "forgetting" of the past as discursively available history, but by the same token a "remembering" of it as "second nature" (1990: 56), thereby directs us to an understanding of practical memory in terms of the articulation of historical events with processes of social and cultural reproduction. This articulation, however, is by no means unproblematic.

Practical memories, we should note, are just as likely to consist of painful, difficult traces of the past as they are to embody the harmonious familiarity and facility that Connerton describes. Memories of the slave trade in West Africa are a case in point. As Austen (2001) notes, discursive oral accounts of the slave trade are relatively rare in West Africa, a fact that he attributes to the morally and socially problematic nature of the trade. In many parts of West Africa, the "work" of discursive memory is often similar to that which Cole describes for a Betsimisaraka town in east Madagascar:

> For the people of Ambodiharina, to remember is to draw a connection or link between themselves and the particular person or practice they remember. It is to recognize and thereby create the power of the persons who are remembered. Considered as a whole, Betsimisaraka theory holds that to remember is more than simply to recall a specific event or fact. It means defining their place and position in the world, asserting links with particular people and places while rejecting others. (Cole 1998: 616)

In most cases, the violence of the slave trade and the moral difficulties it entailed would preclude its being an attractive choice for the drawing of such connections: this is why Edward Ball's questions about the slave-trading past in Sierra Leone were often met with awkward responses.[2] Baum, who is exceptional in having been able to collect discursive accounts of the slave trade among Diola-speakers in Senegal, writes of the extended testing he underwent before Diola went beyond their initial statements that "slavery . . . [had] never existed" (1999: 16).

In contrast to this discursive near-silence, however, there are elaborations of less discursive and more oblique contemporary ideas that evoke, through profoundly disturbing images, some of the terror and moral problems that trouble memories of the slave trade: Congolese witches who transport the souls they steal across the Atlantic to work in U.S. factories (MacGaffey 1986: 62); sorcerers in Cameroon who turn their victims into zombies and force them to labor in plantations (Geschiere 1997); and vampire cowrie shells (the former currency of the slave trade in West Africa) that suck blood and grow on human corpses (Isichei forthoming). In the following chapters, I explore other such stories, together with more practical memories in ritual form, in which the slave trade is forgotten as history but remembered as spirits, as a menacing landscape, as images in divination, as marriage, as witchcraft, and as postcolonial politicians.

History, Change, Reproduction   Given that disjuncture, rupture, and instability currently enjoy analytic privilege, a focus on memory as reproduction raises problematic issues of the historical continuity of social and cultural forms. Both anthropologists and historians have been justifiably wary of the presumption of continuity, of taking for granted any apparent "sameness" in particular social and cultural forms at different points in time. In a statement on current thinking concerning culture, power, and history, for instance, Dirks, Eley, and Ortner acknowledge that in some cases, "long term cultural configurations have, indeed, been very stable," but add that "we now realize that this is a peculiar state of affairs, requiring very sharp questioning and investigation" (1994: 3). This wariness is compounded by anthropologists' desires to distance themselves from earlier studies of a timeless "ethnographic present" in places that were, in fact, in the midst of colonial dislocations and metamorphoses at the time of study.

Yet the primacy given to disjuncture is not without its own shortcomings. Much hinges on how we understand "stability": if the latter is cast simply as a static state, then Dirks, Eley, and Ortner's statement above that stability "is a peculiar state of affairs, requiring very sharp questioning and investigation" is straightforwardly self-evident. But if we understand the apparently stable in terms of processes of recurrence and reproduction, we move away both from the image of inert passivity and from the concept of persistence as the opposite of change. Given that neither the historical transformation of a particular locality nor the individual innovations of social actors are ever ex nihilo creations, reconstruction necessarily entails reproduction. As Dirks himself writes of postcolonialism, for instance, "the sedimented effects and legacies of colonial power are now attested to by a great variety of writings . . . from Fanon to Rushdie, that reveal the extent to which colonialism lives on in postcolonial societies and psyches" (1992a: 7). People do not respond as tabulae rasae when they construct and confront transformative events and political processes; rather, experiences of those events and processes that become sedimented as memory are themselves mediated and configured by memory. From such a position we can recast persistence, recurrence, and reproduction as integral parts of transformation and innovation rather than as their antitheses.

Issues of historical persistence and reproduction during times of transformation and dislocation are of particular consequence for this book, given that the Atlantic and internal slave trades in Sierra Leone spanned more than four hundred years. Both anthropologists and historians tend to avoid histories that extend over several centuries:[3] historical anthropology, for example, tends to be focused on the colonial era. At the same time, as world-systems theory has been replaced by studies of transnationalism and globalization, the time-depth of such studies has also shrunk (as the term "transnationalism" itself tells us) to the era of nation-states and their border crossings. Focusing on colonialism alone and consigning what came before it to a homogenized "precolonial" past replicates earlier, ahistorical studies by pushing the temporal blind spot back one hundred years or so. I am not suggesting that we need fewer analyses of colonialism, transnationalism, or recent memory; nor am I advocating that we resurrect world-systems theory. But we often forget that in many parts of the world the colonial era was relatively short and was commonly preceded by other kinds of transregional connections that were not only as significant as colonialism but also shaped colonialism itself. By examining memories of the slave trade through a history of Sierra Leone that reaches back long before either of its two colonial eras in the nineteenth and twentieth centuries, I wish to draw attention to the ways in which both colonial and postcolonial processes may themselves be understood through memories of earlier transregional processes.

A focus on cultural memories of the slave trade as extending beyond the historical transformations that succeeded this trade, however, rubs uncomfortably against the axiom that the origin of an idea, a word, a story, or a practice cannot "explain" its later meanings (White 2000: 15–19). This axiom refers to unproblematized derivations of social and cultural phenomena from earlier forms, somewhat in the manner of nineteenth-century social theorists' hypotheses on the origins of religion, patriarchy, classification, and the incest taboo—hypotheses that Evans-Pritchard (1965) characterized as "just-so stories." My aims in this book, however, are different: my argument is about memory, not origins. To argue (as I do in chapter 9), for example, that popular Sierra Leonean rumors about politicians who commit ritual murder are cultural memories of colonial "human leopard" rumors, and that the latter can themselves be understood as memories of the slave trade, is not to "explain" the first two as nothing but updated versions of rumors of white cannibalism on slave ships. Nor is it to suggest that the cultural meanings of stories about white slavers' ingestion of Africans were the same as those of stories about nineteenth-century chiefs' and twentieth-century politicians' uses of human organs to prepare medicine for economic or political success. Late-twentieth-century politicians, nineteenth-century chiefs, and eighteenth-century slave traders belonged to different social worlds and were involved in different relationships with those around them. Yet these worlds and relationships did not arise sui generis: peoples' experiences of postcolonial politicians, I argue, are historically mediated by memories of those who profited from the colonial legitimate trade, while experiences of the latter were themselves historically mediated by memories of those who profited from the Atlantic slave trade. Understandings of relationships of extraction can both be new stories *and* draw upon prior relationships involving the "consumption" of human beings.[4]

As should be clear from the transformations I outline in the next chapter for Sierra Leone during the Atlantic slave trade and the century of colonial legitimate trade that replaced it, this region has been anything but timeless and static. But the metamorphoses and upheavals in question have themselves been part of the reproduction (and often the intensification) of the processes with which I am most concerned in this book: the development of a landscape of terror and capture; the exchange of commodified people for imported money and goods; and the growth of new kinds of leaders whose power and wealth were derived from this exchange. During massive changes that took place during the nineteenth century, after the Atlantic slave trade was abolished (see chapter 1), the three above-mentioned processes not only endured but actually escalated, fed by an expanding *internal* slave trade that was engendered by the new British Colony's legitimate commerce. Although this internal slave trade was prohibited when the British Protectorate was imposed in 1898, and internal slavery was abolished in the Sierra Leone Protectorate in 1929, these assumed new forms under colonial rule and postcolonial domination. Even before the outbreak of the rebel war that has ravaged Sierra Leone since 1991, the landscape of the late twentieth century did not lose its terror (see chapter 2). "Big men" (especially national politicians), moreover, are rumored to have (secretly, ritually) exchanged human beings for wealth and power, while money and Western commodities are often linked to the image of an invisible city of witches whose affluence is built upon the theft of human lives. Such aspects of global capitalism and postcoloniality as high-tech international communication and transport, imported commodities, the diamond business, galloping inflation, avaricious politicians, a "kleptocratic" state—and, over the past ten years, a violent rebel war so devastating that it has made even the appearance of a state difficult to sustain—are experienced in terms of images and practices that, I shall argue, are practical memories connecting present and past experiences of predatory commercial flows.

Beyond "The Politics of the Past in the Present"   Further issues raised by a study of memories from the distant past derive from assumptions about "the politics of the past in the present" that are usually attributed to Maurice Halbwachs (1992). What is remembered from the past, the argument goes, depends on the interests and concerns of those in the present, such that every generation detaches the memories in question more and more irrevocably from the original events and processes. Memory moves in only one direction: forward.

This latter approach has been an important and productive interpretive strategy, originating partly as a critique of naive readings of oral testimonies as if the latter give us direct, literal, and unmediated access to the past. Yet what began as a useful critique is all too often used by Halbwachs's successors as an axiom, thereby rendering the argument tautologous and exacerbating its problematic neofunctionalism: whenever the past appears in the present, it "must" only be serving present interests and concerns. That this may close more doors than it opens is clear, however, from Barber's extraordinary study of a genre of Yoruba praise-poetry called *oriki:*

> Each corpus of *oriki* . . . contains a multiplicity of items from different historical moments, accumulated over long periods. This historical variegation in *oriki* usually remains invisible and uncommented on. The items from different his-

torical moments are not usually arranged in chronological order, nor are the most ancient units separated from the newest ones; they may be performed in virtually any order and combination. (Barber 1991: 26)

These panegyrics are not straightforward historical "accounts"; those who use them invoke the past to evoke particular states of being in persons and lineages. Yet neither are oriki simple reflections of present interests: Barber argues that their awkward juxtapositions keep the past alive without necessarily "fitting" it to the task at hand (1991: 34). Oriki are thus profoundly historical without being either discursive narratives about the past *or* utterances whose significance is limited to the politics of the present.

What about the slave trade, however? Given that the Atlantic slave trade was brought to an end in the nineteenth century and that domestic slavery in the Sierra Leone Protectorate was abolished in 1929, how can it be legitimate to argue that current ritual practices or images are memories of the slave trade rather than embodiments of more recent or contemporary concerns? In answer, I turn to four striking cultural memories of the slave trade from other parts of West Africa. Although these materializations of the slave trade are enmeshed in contemporary concerns, they cannot be reduced to present interests alone.

First, in the Casamance region of Senegal, Diola lineage spirit shrines *(hup-ila)* underwent profound metamorphoses during the Atlantic slave trade—which, on this part of the West African coast, endured until the late nineteenth century (Baum 1999). Custodianship of these shrines, which had formerly been vested in lineage elders, came to be given to those who had captured and sold a slave, thereby making wealth the basis for spiritual authority. In addition, a new kind of shrine was developed by and for those who had committed the serious moral transgression of selling a child from their own community: this was "the shrine of the rice granary" *(hupila hugop)*, concealed within the household's granary to evade detection and established in order to protect the family from harmful retaliation by the spirit-shrine of the family from which the child in question was taken. Today, bearing witness to the ritual power ascribed to slave trading, many hupila shrines in Diola villages include wooden fetters in their composition. And the memory of certain families' transgressions in selling their own community's children is maintained by secret sacrifices that their descendants must still offer to this perennially hungry shrine, without which they run the risk of being wiped out by the avenging hupila of their long-dead victims. In this latter instance, as Werbner argues for postcolonial memories (1998: 2–3), such intractable traces of the past in bodies, homes, ritual space, and social relations are unwelcome and problematic rather than being mere projections of present desires back in time.

Second, in what is now southern Benin and Togo—the site of the former kingdom of Dahomey, whose economy in the eighteenth and early nineteenth centuries was based upon the capture and sale of slaves—wooden carvings called *bocio* often depict men and women as slaves whose arms, legs, necks, and mouths are bound with cords, chains, shackles, and muzzles (Blier 1995). These bound bocio are powerful ritual objects that (among other things) deflect attack away from their owner, as well as enabling the latter to attack others by disempowering them. Do these objects relate to present concerns? Yes—their owners use them in pursuit of their own current agendas. Can they also be viewed as material memories of the slave trade? Yes—it is on the capture and binding of slaves in this region's past that the forms of power and disempowerment that the bocio so vividly embody are patterned.

For the third instance we stay in the same area. In southern Togo, members of Ewe Vodu ritual communities consider themselves to be indebted to the spirits of the northern slaves whom their forbears acquired and often married (Rosenthal 1998). Thus the descendants of slave owners now honor the spirits of their ancestors' slaves, paying off their debts for these slaves' labors and for their contribution to the community's lineages by establishing shrines and offering their own bodies for the slave spirits to possess and enjoy. Their ethnographer was advised that white Americans too should establish shrines for the New World slaves their ancestors had once owned: "Why should you not pay your debts to the slave spirits in the way we Ewe do? You would be better off for it" (Rosenthal 1998: 153). Again, these embodiments both speak to current concerns *and* materialize memories of "bought people" and of the trade through which they came.

Finally, in northern Togo, the area from which many of the slaves incarnated in Ewe vodu ceremonies were taken, the body of a slain foreigner lies in the sacred forest of the Kabre-speaking village of Kudwe (Piot 1999: 37–38). Two different stories circulate about this corpse: according to one version, it is that of a German soldier who stole sorghum during the colonial "pacification" of the region; according to the other version, it is that of a slave raider from a warrior group known as the Samasi. "It is not difficult to imagine why Kabre might conceptually equate the predations of the slave trade with colonization, and thus one predator with another," Piot observes of these divergent narratives (1999: 38). In Kudwe, then, memories of late-nineteenth-century colonial conquest seem to have been shaped just as much by older memories of eighteenth-century slave raiding as the latter have by later memories of colonization: each is remembered through the lens of the other. Thus the supposedly unilineal direction of memory revision from the past to the present in "presentist" arguments is disrupted by the reversed and two-way temporality of these Kabre memories.

As with all functionalist arguments, explanations in terms of the politics of the present do not begin to confront the historical experience congealed in the wooden fetters and secret sacrifices of the Diola hupila hugop, the chains and shackles of the bound bocio figures of Southern Benin and Togo, the ecstatic debt-repayment of vodu possession, and the ambiguous corpse buried in Kudwe's sacred forest. Whatever else these highly charged objects and embodiments accomplish, they also condense memories of the slave trade. At the same time, as in the divergent Kudwe stories about the foreign corpse as slave raider and colonizer, and as in the "historical variegation" of Yoruba oriki (Barber 1991: 26), such memories may combine events and processes from different historical moments. Such is their chronological heterogeneity that, drawing on Vansina's term "palimpsest traditions" (1974: 320), we could call them palimpsest memories. Thus in Sierra Leone experiences of postcolonial processes—including the rebel war—may be layered with memories of the Atlantic slave trade as well as those of the colonial legitimate trade that replaced it, thereby moving memory both forward and backward in time.

Memory and Modernities   If memories of the slave trade are not simply about the present, I would nevertheless argue that they are about modernity. Yet memory is often cast as antithetical to modernity: following Paul de Man, for instance, Connerton (1989: 61) claims that the core experience of modernity is that of a deliberate erasure of the past in pursuit of a desire for a continuously fresh start. This desire is often, after all, advanced as an explicit ideology to "make a complete break with the past" (Meyer 1998a). Connerton sees this process of willed forgetting as ultimately driven by the capitalist world market, for "capital accumulation, the ceaseless expansion of the commodity form through the market, requires the constant revolutionizing of production, the ceaseless transformation of the innovative into the obsolescent" (1989: 64).

Yet ironically, as Connerton also observes (1989: 61), this relentless pursuit of new departures is in fact highly dependent on the elaboration of memories of the past (see, again, Meyer 1998a). And further, it is easy to forget that the capitalist world market, together with many of the other processes associated with modernity, is itself several centuries old. In many parts of the world, the transformation into a universe of foreign commodities, capitalism, and transregional commercial flows dates back to the fifteenth century—as was the case for Sierra Leone's integration into an expanding Atlantic system. Thus not only does the modernist rhetoric of forgetting actually *require* the production of memories, but also modernity itself is hardly recent, and has been generating memories for some time. Experiences of turn-of-the-millennium forms of modernity are, I argue, mediated by layers of earlier historical experiences of modernity, reproducing these as memories that tie together past and present processes of "modern" transformation.

Such processes do not, moreover, comprise a single-tracked, homogeneous set of mechanisms that unfold in the same way anywhere and everywhere (see, e.g., Comaroff and Comaroff 1993; Rofel 1999). The idea that modernity is plural—that diverse visions and appropriations of modernity are constituted through particular regional histories—is not new (see, e.g., Sahlins 1988). It is important, however, not to view this plurality as a product of the articulation of local culture with monolithic global capitalist processes, in accordance with "a top-down model whereby the global is macro-political economic and the local is situated, culturally creative, and resistant" (Ong 1999: 4). While global processes are indeed differently appropriated (and resisted) through particular cultural logics, these processes are themselves "always already" cultural. Globalizing capitalist relationships, moreover, are also heterogeneous due to the disparities in power and positionality they generate: the Atlantic slave trade, for instance, was not "the same" process for a merchant in New England who provided ships and capital, an English slave-ship captain and his crew, an African merchant whose wealth derived from the sale of slaves, a member of an African community living with the possibility of attack and enslavement, and a slave undergoing the Middle Passage. Because of the different political-economic relationships they involved, the contrasting historical transformations they engendered on opposite sides of the Atlantic, *and* the manifold cultural meanings through which they were both appropriated and criticized in diverse locations, capitalist modernities took plural forms in different parts of the Atlantic world from the very beginning.[5]

West Africa's own modernities were developed through the globalizing processes that integrated this region into the Atlantic world. Thus even social and cultural practices in rural parts of Africa that appear at first glance to be the very antithesis of what is "modern" or "cosmopolitan" were often, as Piot emphasizes in his critique of the globalization literature, "forged during the long encounter with Europe over the last three hundred years and thus owe their meaning and shape to that encounter as much as to anything 'indigenous'" (1999: 1). Such practices—including apparently "traditional" forms of divination, as we shall see—often bear the traces of that encounter in unexpected ways.

Exploring modernity through West African memories of the slave trade may also require us to make other revisions to our understandings of modernity. While Gilroy (1993: 45, 71) argues that modernity in the Black Atlantic world was born of the experiences of the Middle Passage and of New World institutions of slavery, modernity in West Africa was instead born of globalizing commercial flows of foreign wealth, the growth of new elites based on that wealth, and various processes of enslavement through which, over the course of nearly four centuries, people were transformed into alienable commodities. In Sierra Leone, both the Atlantic slave trade and the colonial legitimate trade that followed it marked capitalist modernity as entailing the exchange of human life for wealth and power—a modernity whose very nature was, and is, witch-like (see De Boeck 1998: 29; Shaw 1997: 869). Memories of the slave trade from both eras, I argue, keep open a vision of the predatory nature of modernity that resonates all too strongly with the violence of Sierra Leone's rebel war. These memories often take ritual, "magical," and phantasmagoric forms, as in the image of Okri's hungry, all-devouring road invoked at the beginning of this introduction. Thus while on the European and American sides of the Atlantic, the economic logic of the slave trade helped construct a modernity that was defined (for those who were white, affluent, formally educated, and male) in terms of "rationality," in this part of the West African Atlantic the imperative to produce slaves helped construct a contrasting memory of a vampiric modernity through images of the very occult forces that modernity was supposed to have superseded.

Agency's Allure   Finally, the Atlantic slave trade raises critical issues of African and European agency. In the 1960s and 1970s, many Africanist historians reacted against ideas that European slave traders had duped Africans by plying them with trinkets. These historians underscored African political agency (e.g., Curtin 1975), but in so doing they tended to downplay the deleterious effects of the Atlantic slave trade on African warfare, internal slavery, and demography. Some even made a case for the alleged benefits the slave trade brought by stimulating state formation (e.g., Fage 1969).[6] Historical studies of the Atlantic trade have, however, undergone profound transformations since then.

More recently, African agency both during and after the slave trade has been accented through attention to emergent elites, as in Matory's remarkable study of Brazilian ex-slaves who constructed a transatlantic Yoruba nation in both Nigeria and Bahia (1999). This interest in elites is also popular among those writing about the agency of the colonized and the missionized: it is from elites, after all, that we are most likely to find named personal actors with clear projects preserved in archival sources. Yet important as such studies are, it would be unfortunate if a focus on named elite actors were to *displace* interpretations of the everyday (and often less verbally discursive) actions of ordinary people whose names are recorded only in the rarest cases.

Another strategy for highlighting African agency in the slave trade is to look for acts of direct resistance. Rathbone (1996), for instance, puts together an intriguing survey of such activism in West Africa, demonstrating that slave revolts and runaway slave communities were by no means limited to the New World and the Middle Passage. In Sierra Leone a leader called Captain Tomba from "some country villages that opposed [the slave traders] and their trade at the River Nunez" (Atkins 1735, quoted in Rathbone 1996: 186–87), was particularly intractable when captured as a slave, and later led a shipboard mutiny. Slaves held in the slaving fort on Bance [Bunce] Island mounted an insurrection armed only with their irons and chains (Rathbone 1996: 186); a slave ship that entered the river Nunez in 1825 encountered residents who refused to load it (187); and, after a mutiny on a Danish ship in the Rokel river estuary in 1788, the slaves who escaped founded a free settlement called "the Deserters' Town" in the hills of the Sierra Leone peninsula (193). Yet even such fascinating glimpses as these tell us little about the everyday tactics through which people lived with the contingencies that the Atlantic commerce generated.

Three decades after Curtin's arguments about African agency, broadly similar debates (updated for current theoretical sensibilities) are still flourishing. In both anthropology and history, agency appears to have expanded into the privileged moral space formerly held by resistance: as "the romance of resistance" (Abu-Lughod 1990) has waned, the allure of agency has blossomed. Like resistance, agency necessarily operates in a recursive relationship with structure and power (Giddens 1984)—a relationship from which agency is now, however, frequently cut loose (Karp 1995). This detachment of agency from power and structure seems to be in part a reaction against earlier analyses of the lives of human subjects as overdetermined. Yet this reaction is in many ways just as problematic as the analyses against which it is cast as a critique: currently, as Comaroff and Comaroff put it, "an almost Althusserian overdetermination has been replaced by a Derridean indeterminacy" (1997: 15). At its most crude, this reaction takes the form of reiterations that people are not "passive objects" but "active subjects," are not "victims" but "agents," and are not "subjugated" but "authors of their own histories." Such formulaic declarations are disturbingly resonant of a dominant North Atlantic discourse of unfettered individualism and freedom of choice—a discourse that "continually pulls us away from systemic understanding and inclines us toward constructions that emphasize individual freedom, choice, power, ability" (Bordo 1993: 30).

Foucault's reformulation of relations of power has been particularly important in refining the more simplistic of these responses. Yet while his arguments have freed us from zero-sum notions of power as imposed solely from above, enabling us to see operations of power and resistance as widely dispersed through everyday practices (e.g., Foucault 1979), these arguments have also had an insidiously levelling effect on analyses of dominance. The Foucauldian vocabulary of "dispersal" suggests an even distribution of interchangeable particles in a uniform space (analogous, for instance, to gas molecules in a glass jar, or pollen grains across an open field)—an image that effectively erases distinctions among different kinds and degrees of power and agency. As Bordo argues in relation to such erasure in feminist analyses, "to struggle effectively against [culturally entrenched] forms it is first necessary to recognize that they *have* dominance, and not to efface such recognition through a facile and abstract celebration of 'heterogeneity,' 'difference,' 'subversive reading,' and so forth" (1993: 30). It is, of course, crucial to recognize, for example, that capitalism has been differently appropriated in heterogeneous cultural worlds, that European colonization was converted to the local agendas of the colonized, that women inventively deploy patriarchal ideas and images for their own purposes, and that those who are subject to even the worst forms of oppression "have agency too." But if we stop there, we risk collapsing distinctions among contrasting kinds of agency that are associated with contrasting kinds of power. The agency of those who deploy "weapons of the weak," and of those who creatively appropriate signs and processes of dominance "from below," for example, are each very different from the agency of those whose authority allows them to act upon the world through control of an apparatus of domination.

What is potentially insidious here, as both Asad (1993) and the Comaroffs (1997: 18) point out, is that when we celebrate the agency of those who have been the objects of transregional European enterprises (via colonization, missionization, or the Atlantic slave trade) without adequately distinguishing the very different agency of colonizers, missionaries, or slave traders, we risk writing neorevisionist histories. During the slave trade in Sierra Leone, the Europeans who bought slaves and offered money, firearms, and other imported goods in exchange; the chiefs and wealthy traders who sent out warriors, and who seized and sold debtors and convicted witches; the warriors who raided for slaves; the diviners who controlled the ritual techniques through which people were convicted of witchcraft and other wrongdoings; and those who were themselves sold as slaves all "had agency." But it would be absurd to stop at this point, thereby downplaying crucial differences among the capacities of people with very different kinds and degrees of power. Given that "people are never only active agents and subjects in their own histories," as Asad puts it, "the interesting question . . . is: In what degree, and in what way, are they agents or patients?" (1993: 4).

The Duality of Incorporation   In anthropology, the fetishizing of agency (Spyer 1997: 515) has for some time now been part of standard responses to analyses of such globalizing European initiatives as capitalism and colonialism. The most notable of these responses were initially made in the 1980s, in reaction to world-systems theory. Sahlins (1988) argued, for instance, that far from homogenizing the worlds of local peoples, Western capitalism has itself been appropriated and subsumed by local cultural logics in various parts of the world. Similarly, Ortner criticized political-economic analyses in which history is treated "as something that arrives, like a ship, from outside the society in question" (1984: 143), and she directed anthropologists against making the assumption that "much of what we see in our fieldwork and describe in our monographs must be understood as having been shaped in response to [the capitalist world system]" (143). People, she affirmed, are not just "passive reactors to and enactors of some 'system,' but [are] active agents and subjects in their own history" (143).

World-systems theory is now long gone. But some of the more recent scholarship on colonialism, globalization, and modernity replays Ortner's and Sahlins's 1980s critiques of world-systems arguments about "the juggernaut of capitalism" (Ortner 1984: 143). In this scholarship, the fact that cultural actors use their own ideas and practices to appropriate transnational forms is often used as the basis for either-or dichotomies of agency *versus* hegemony, of the domestication of Western forms *versus* the critique of these

Western forms, as if these were mutually exclusive alternatives.[7] In their recent criticism of the ethnography of modernity, for example, Englund and Leach (2000) discuss stories from the Rai Coast of Papua New Guinea about "liver thieves" employed by Europeans who kill local people in order to sell their organs overseas. On the one hand, the authors observe, such stories might be seen as expressing anxieties about the extractive nature of globalization. But on the other hand, the stories can be understood in terms of Rai Coast villagers' notions of personhood and wealth, and of the productive violence of affinity and exchange. Thus by first setting up a binary opposition between these two ethnographic interpretations, then proceeding to explicate the latter, the authors assume that they have necessarily refuted the former (2000: 230–33).

When, as in the Rai Coast stories, new forms of foreign wealth are bent and stretched to fit local cultural practices and moralities, such domestication is often determined to be an unambiguous process of incorporation. But there is much more involved than a single process whereby foreign wealth becomes a "wholesome" local cultural entity. First, the bending and stretching of foreign wealth is often accompanied by a reciprocal bending and stretching of the cultural practices and moralities into which it is assimilated; and second, even in its locally digested form, this wealth may nevertheless be framed by a moral discourse that identifies it as problematic or ambivalent. This co-transmutation of absorber and absorbed, and the back-and-forth movement between desire, imitation, and appropriation on the one hand, and critical commentary on the other, each constitute what I call the duality of incorporation.

Let us explore this by revisiting the Diola spirit-shrines of the Casamance region of Senegal that I briefly introduced earlier. During the Atlantic trade, emerging Diola Esulalu slave-trading elites of the eighteenth century were able to avoid witchcraft accusations by distributing their new wealth through sacrifices at Esulalu spirit-shrines (Baum 1999: 118–28). They thereby ritually incorporated this wealth into local concepts of prosperity. Yet this ritual domestication of the slave-trade wealth had profound consequences for Esulalu sacrifice, spirit-shrines, and ritual authority: in the mid-eighteenth century a new shrine (*hupila hudjenk*, "the shrine of the fetters") spread through Esulalu communities, and wealth—displayed and distributed through the "inflationary" sacrifice of increasing numbers of animals—replaced spiritual charisma as the basis for the selection of shrine elders. In the meantime, other spiritual powers began to attack those who became "very rich," undermining their capacity to have children (120); wealthy Esulalu slave owners of the nineteenth century are now remembered as having lost their heirs through disease and accidents because Emitai, the high god, disapproved (160). Thus while the Atlantic trade's wealth was incorporated into Diola ritual, Diola ritual was reciprocally "Atlanticized." This wealth was unevenly digested, moreover, and became the focus of an uneasy, ambivalent relationship with other aspects of Diola cosmology and morality: the slave-trade wealth was both domesticated *and* criticized, admired *and* castigated.

Clearly, to focus only on the critique of new wealth and other foreign imports while downplaying their appropriation and incorporation would be to succumb to the same binary logic as that of arguments celebrating domestication and discounting domination. I do not, moreover, wish to be read as disparaging the many important and brilliant studies by those who choose to emphasize creativity rather than disruption, symbolic control rather than colonial domination, dynamic cultural resilience rather than contradiction. "Of course," as Ortner writes, "oppression is damaging, yet the ability of social beings to weave alternative, and sometimes brilliantly creative, forms of coherence across the damages is one of the heartening aspects of human subjectivity" (1995: 186). But at the same time, these social beings' experience of the damage is just as deserving of our attention as the creative forms of coherence they weave across it. In fact these forms of coherence are often ways of reconfiguring and remembering such damage.

By examining Temne divination through the lens of ritual memory, I seek to explore forms of coherence through which diviners, clients, and others both remember the terror of the slave trade *and* turn that terror into creative ritual forms. I thereby seek to trace an alternative history of the slave trade—a history of moral imagination (Beidelman 1986; Hunt 1999: 11) told primarily in the language of practical memory through places and practices, images and visions, rituals and rumors.

In chapter 1 I trace the incorporation of that part of the upper Guinea coast that the Portuguese called "Serra Lyoa" into an expanding Atlantic system. Both the European presence on Sierra Leone's coast and rivers and the export trade in slaves developed from the late fifteenth century, reaching a peak in the eighteenth century. Although the export slave trade was prohibited by the British in the early nineteenth century, the internal trade in slaves expanded when the British established the Colony of Sierra Leone and promoted the legitimate commerce. This traffic in human commodities generated an escalation in warfare, raiding, and indebtedness, shaping conflict in the region and driving the emergence of new, problematic forms of wealth and leadership.

Chapter 2 concerns the transformation of the ritual landscape during the slave trade, over the course of which local spirits appear to have changed from useful neighbors to marauding raiders. I argue that these spirit raiders, together with protective techniques of enclosure and concealment, on the one hand, and stories of violence as located within the land itself, on the other, crystallized the slave-raiding past within the late-twentieth-century memory-scape.

Techniques of divination are the subject of chapter 3. Derived from techniques spread over a large part of the Islamic world, these forms of divination testify to enduring transregional cultural flows. At the same time, through the meanings that Temne diviners infuse via their modes of interpretation and their origin stories, these techniques are made to "remember" a local and regional history. Through their designation as Muslim and their Mande vocabulary, on the one hand, they materialize eighteenth- and nineteenth-century Islamic transformations in the region. And through Temne diviners' readings of a symbolism of roads, crossroads, towns, violence, and concealment, on the other hand, these techniques are also made to draw upon elements of the slave-trading past as a source of ritual efficacy.

In chapter 4 I explore the historical layering of different forms of knowledge that diviners I knew negotiated in their lives and visionary experience. These diviners' relationships with their tutelary spirits, I argue, converted past practices of seizure and enslavement for indebtedness into ritual power and knowledge, refashioning contractual relationships between "landlords" and "strangers" that developed during the slave trade. Through another layer of knowledge—that deriving from eighteenth- and nineteenth-century processes of Islamicization—divinatory skills were masculinized, and women's divinatory knowledge was rendered "backward" and potentially sinister. In the more reformed Islamic climate of the late twentieth century, however, the formerly prestigious literate knowledge of Muslim diviners was itself placed beyond the bounds of Islamic propriety in the eyes of many urban Sierra Leonean Muslims. But while the hegemony of a twentieth-century Western education once made divinatory skills appear antithetical to development and progress, the catastrophic failure of Sierra Leone's economy and infrastructure during the 1980s and 1990s effectively reversed this. With the consequent deepening of impoverishment, the collapse of the school system, and the emergence and entrenchment of the rebel war, ritual knowledge has come to acquire a renewed salience.

Chapters 5 and 6 are explorations of gender, marriage, and women's ritual practices in terms of social memory. In chapter 5 I argue that dominant representations of married women as potential channels of dangerous incursion into their marital homes reconfigure the ambiguities of marriage during the warfare and raiding of the Atlantic and legitimate trades. These representations both shape and are shaped by women's consultations of diviners, which I examine in chapter 6. Women form the secret majority of diviners' clients, and their ritual consultations take place within the context of dominant social memories of wives as vehicles for the entry of threatening external forces.

In chapter 7 I turn from private to public divination—a ritual form that was intimately connected to the Atlantic slave trade. Through public witchfinding, people were convicted as witches and could then be sold as slaves: effectively, therefore, this oracular process transformed persons into consumable commodities. But at the same time, those Africans and Europeans who profited from the slave trade, accumulating wealth through the consumption of human value, were widely rumored to be the biggest witches of all. In contemporary images of an invisible witch city, the slave trade has been "remembered" through images of modernity and of globalization as fundamentally predatory, witch-like processes.

Chapter 8 also concerns associations between the consumption of human life and past transregional circulations of wealth, goods, and people. Toward the end of the nineteenth and the beginning of the twentieth century, human leopard scares erupted in which chiefs and traders were accused of ritually murdering slaves, children, and other dependents, extracting their victims' organs in order to create medicines that would bring them wealth and political power. In these accusations, I argue, mnemonic stories of European cannibalism during the Atlantic trade were refashioned to comment on the predatory nature of the colonial legitimate commerce.

In chapter 9 I conclude with relationships between diviners and "big persons," especially national politicians and top civil servants. In popular critiques of postcolonial power, leaders are often depicted as having gained their positions and wealth through evil ritual practices prescribed and secretly implemented by diviners. Diviners who seek prestigious clients, accordingly, have to negotiate such disadvantageous representations. These rumors about politicians and diviners draw heavily upon the human leopard accounts of the colonial era, connecting postcolonial power and its abuses with memories of the threats that "modern" forms of wealth and leadership can pose to social morality and reproduction.

The Atlanticizing of Sierra Leone

What shall I say of the ports, particularly of the one in the Bay of Serra Leoa, which is so suitable for docking ships? Here the foreigners regularly careen, build and repair their ships. The port gives them refuge by protecting them and defending them from fierce storms, and they repay this by leaving their names as a memento. They carve them on the flat stones and the boulders of the famous Harbour of the Watering-place and on the trunks of trees there. Thus they offer perpetual thanks to the place for the kindness in the aspects of nature with which they were received. Manuel Alvares, *Ethiopia Minor and a Geographical Account of the Province of Sierra Leone*

But at a certain time a man was born, who was a wicked person, and a violent person: he was also a great man, he had plenty of money, and many slaves, and plenty of cattle, and many servants; who did not care for any one, and did just as he pleased, and troubled all his people: he became the author of death in the world. C. F. Schlenker, *A Collection of Temne Traditions, Fables and Proverbs*

The upper Guinea coast (sometimes called the Windward Coast or the Rice Coast) on the West Atlantic edge of Africa comprises the Casamance region of Senegal, Guinea-Bissau, Guinea, Sierra Leone, and Liberia. It is a mostly flat, swampy length of coast except for the hills of the Sierra Leone peninsula,[1] and it is crossed by numerous rivers whose navigable stretches were channels for trade and transport for centuries prior to the arrival of Europeans (Brooks 1993: 49). Inland, the rivers flow through savanna and forests from a range of mountains that protected the upper Guinea coast from invasion and conquest by the medieval Ghana and Mali empires to the northeast. The coast's inhabitants were—and are—rice farmers: the Casamance in the northern part of this region was, in fact, a "secondary cradle" of the development of African rice, *Oryza glaberrima* (Rodney 1970: 20). With a few exceptions, peoples organized themselves into small political units headed by chiefs and kings. They spoke languages classified as "West Atlantic"—a language family distantly related to the Bantu languages of Central, East, and Southern Africa, and whose southern cluster has been subcategorized as "Mel" (Dalby 1965). On the coast of Sierra Leone were Bullom-speakers and, further inland, speakers of Temne *(ka-themnε).*[2] Both peoples lived in villages, each village having a king (*Bee* in Bullom; *Obe* in Temne) who was paid no tribute but was owed farm and building labor, assistance in war (provided that a council of elders agreed the war was just), and special parts of wild animals killed in his domain (Fernandes 1951 [1506–10]: 80–93).[3]

Well before the coming of Europeans in the fifteenth century, the peoples of the region were organized into trade networks that connected different parts of the coast and rivers of upper Guinea and linked them to long-distance trade routes controlled by Mande-speaking peoples to the northeast (Brooks 1993: 79–96). At the other end of these Mande trade routes, in the urban centers of the Mali Empire and its satellite states, there was considerable demand for the salt that the coastal communities of upper Guinea produced. There was also a demand for forest commodities such as kola nuts and malaguetta pepper, for which Mande elites had developed a taste (Brooks 1993: 80). "The best *cola,*" wrote Manuel Alvares, a Jesuit priest who lived in Sierra Leone for ten years in the early seventeenth century, "is so appreciated by the heathen that it is carried by Mandinga merchants as far as Mecca; and there is no heathen sacrifice in which it does not play a part" (1990 [c. 1615], 2, chap. 1: 9). One of the principal kola-producing areas was the Temne-speaking region, which straddled what is now northern Sierra Leone and southern Guinea-Conakry (Brooks 1993: 83); in fact the word "kola"—together with its North American offspring "cola"—is a loanword from the Temne term *ak-ɔla.* In exchange for kola, the iron products of Mande smiths, cotton cloth, gold from the Mali Empire, and exotic trans-Saharan imports flowed into the upper Guinea coast (Brooks 1993: 82). Through the coastal and riverine flows of this trade, Mel-speaking peoples—Temne, Bullom, Baga, and Landuma—adopted "Sapi," the language of a Landuma group, as a common commercial language (Hair 1967; Brooks 1993: 80) that became the basis of a collective identification for Mel-speakers.

When Europeans arrived on this coast, then, they did not suddenly propel untouched and isolated African localities into the wide, cosmopolitan world: a translocal sphere of commercial relations was already in place, and it intersected with a trans-Saharan trade that linked three different continents. Instead, the growth of European trade brought about the integration of the upper Guinea coast's existing commercial system with new kinds of transregional circulations (see Gupta and Ferguson 1992). This new integration was, however, to transform the region in unprecedented ways.

In 1462, the Portuguese explorer Pedro da Sintra charted the coast of Sierra Leone, naming it "Lion Uplands" *(Serra Lyoa)* because the sound of the waves crashing on the rocks reminded him of the roaring of lions (or, in another version of this origin story, because he thought the peninsula's hills had a lion's shape). Four years later, Portuguese settlers in the Cape Verde islands to the northwest were given a charter by the Portuguese crown that granted them exclusive license to trade on the West African mainland. When, however, they proceeded not only to trade but also to reside on the mainland, establishing themselves as private traders—and thereby undermining the crown's attempted monopoly on trade—the crown made successive but largely futile attempts to legislate against their settlement. The Portuguese authorities called the settlers *lançados,* those who had "thrown themselves" among Africans. As the numbers of these European residents grew, and as they intermarried with their African hosts, a Luso-African trade language developed, taking the place of the former lingua franca, Sapi. This new creolized language of commerce came to be spoken throughout trading communities on the coasts and rivers of upper Guinea, as well as in the Cape Verde islands (Dalby 1970–71); remnants of it can be heard in Temne as Portuguese loanwords today (Turay 1976).

Some of the Portuguese lançados, who came to be called *tangomaos,*[4] not only married African women but also observed local ritual practices and had their bodies inscribed with the tattoos worn by their hosts. Such marks of African affiliation were deeply disturbing to the missionary Alvares's predecessor, Father Baltasar Barreira, who recorded his discouragement at such "backsliding" by baptized Portuguese Christians:

The *tangomaus* . . . are a sort of people who, although Portuguese by nation and Christian by religion and baptism, nevertheless live as if they were neither Portuguese nor Christian. For many of them go naked, and in order to get on better with the heathen of the land where they trade by appearing like them, they score their whole body with an iron blade, cutting until they draw blood and making many marks which, after they have been anointed with the juice of certain plants, come to resemble various designs, such as figures of lizards, snakes or any other creatures they care to depict. (Hair 1989: document 4, pp. 3–4; quoted in Brooks 1993: 191)

Body decoration was not the only form of Sapi material culture in which these European settlers participated. Admiring the ivory-carving skills of craftsmen in Sierra Leone, the lançados commissioned hybrid African forms of European dinner table objects: delicate, intricately decorated ivory cups, spoons, and salt-cellars that are now famed as the "Afro-Portuguese Ivories." Alvares describes "spoons made of ivory, beautifully finished, the handles carved in interesting shapes, such as the heads of animals, birds or the *corofis* [Temne *aŋ-kərfi*, "spirits"], all done with such perfection that it has to be seen to be believed" (Alvares 1990, 2, chap. 2: 6).

But it was not primarily for the sake of this fine ivory tableware that the lançados and tangomaos established themselves on the upper Guinea coast. They exchanged iron bars, cotton fiber, woven textiles, and salt from Portugal and the Cape Verde islands for gold, ivory, kola, malaguetta pepper, animal hides, and—most lucrative of all—slaves. "The *tangomaus*," wrote Barreira, "make their way through the whole of Guinea in this way, trading in slaves and buying them wherever they can obtain them" (Hair 1989: document 4, pp. 3–4; quoted in Brooks 1993: 191).

These lançados would settle on river estuaries—especially that of the Sierra Leone River—and take their canoes up creeks and rivers to find the slaves and other trade goods that they would sell. Trading nuclei were situated at almost every estuary, while upstream, at the farthest navigable point of the river, trade from the hinterland was channeled through a complementary trade terminus (Rodney 1970: 79). Thus the rivers that had long been the highways of the upper Guinea coast effectively became extensions of the Atlantic ocean, penetrating several miles inland. And because they were foci for European trade and settlement, the rivers also attracted further African settlement: "In the sixteenth century and for much longer," Rodney notes, "European ships and commercial activity acted as magnets in drawing the African population of the Upper Guinea Coast even closer to the waterways, and especially to the estuaries" (1970: 80).

The Sierra Leone River estuary, to which European seafarers were drawn by the trade prospects, safe anchorage, fresh water supply, and large natural harbor, came to be known as "the Watering Place" (plate 2). In 1580, Francis Drake carved his initials on a stone at the Watering Place, like the other "foreigners" that Alvares describes as "leaving their names as a memento . . . on the flat stones and the boulders of the famous Harbour" (1990, 2, chap. 1: 18). Later, in 1607, *Hamlet* was performed there—during Shakespeare's own lifetime— by sailors on an English expedition to India (Hair 1978). Pirates also frequented the estuary, attracted not only by the prospects of plunder but also by "the Traders settled here, [who] are naturally their friends" (Johnson, in Fyfe 1964: 69). By the early 1700s these "natural friends" of the pirates were English private traders, many of whom were retired pirates themselves. Johnson goes on, for example, to describe John Leadstone, "an old Fellow who goes by the name of *Crackers*, who was formerly a noted Bucaneer, and while he followed the Calling, robb'd and plundered many a Man: he keeps the best House in the Place, has two or three Guns before his Door, with which he salutes his Friends (the Pyrates, when they put in), and lives a jovial life" (69).

By the eighteenth century, English merchants had replaced Portuguese traders in the domination of the slave trade. This was a time of unprecedented slaving and warfare: in mid-century, between 4,000 and 6,000 slaves were dispatched from Sierra Leone annually (Rodney 1970: 250–51). Men like "Crackers" were prominent in the slave trade at this time, despite efforts by the English crown to control the trade by granting a private company—the Royal African Company—a sole monopoly. Further up the estuary, at the farthest navigable point for slave ships, this company had a fortified slave factory on Bence Island (later "Bance," and today "Bunce Island"), which was taken over by the London firm of Grant, Sargent, and Oswald in the mid-eighteenth century (Opala 1987: 5). That firm's employees on Bence Island were provided not only with an English country house (whose drawing room window looked directly onto the main slave enclosure [Falconbridge 2000 (1802): 23]), but also with a two-hole golf course (Smeathman 1773, in Fyfe 1964: 70) "served by African caddies dressed in kilts especially woven in Glasgow" (Thomas 1997: 342). Slave ships from Bence Island often took their cargos to South Carolina, where profits from rice plantations created a demand for slaves from Sierra Leone: with their expertise in rice cultivation, slaves from the "Rice Coast" of West Africa, as the upper Guinea coast was known, fetched a higher price (Opala 1987: 1–6).

Causes, Consequences, Agency   Sierra Leone, then, was integrated into an Atlantic mercantile system linking three continents. What were the consequences for peoples such as Temne speakers? In Sierra Leone—as in other parts of Africa—most slaves were acquired through wars and raids. According to Rodney (1970: 102), warfare and raiding accelerated as a direct result of the slave trade, the sale of captives to slavers being initially a byproduct but subsequently a motive for conflicts and raids. This issue, however, has been the focus of much heated argument in historians' debates concerning the impact of the Atlantic trade on Africa.

Fage (1969), most notably, claims that the slave trade did not generate increased warfare and raiding. Focusing on the large West African kingdoms of Asante and Dahomey further east, he argues that the Atlantic trade was inconsequential because the European demand for slaves merely added a further option to patterns of foreign trade that were already developing—including a trade in slaves. He cites two West African rulers, King Kpengla of Dahomey (1774–89) and King Osei Bonsu of Asante (c. 1801–24), who told European visitors that they fought wars for political reasons, not for the "economic" motive of capturing slaves for the Atlantic trade (1969: 402). Yet it is clearly problematic to suggest that simply asking the question "why do you do this?" will elicit a single definitive answer unfettered by the positionality of speaker and questioner in a particular sociopolitical context. As Inikori (1982) points out, both of the rulers in question made their statements at times of strong abolitionist sentiment in Europe, and accordingly "it would seem somewhat naive to expect these rulers to admit that they waged wars simply to acquire captives, in the face of the moral condemnation of this type of activity at the time" (1982: 49).

The argument that the wars of the slave trade era were waged for internal political reasons rather than for the externally influenced economic motive of acquiring captives to sell has sometimes been presented as one that restores agency to Africans. For example, reacting against claims that African participants in the slave trade were duped by the allure of European goods and money, Curtin writes:

> Africa was supposed to be a savage continent made that way largely by the slave traders. As "savages," the Africans had been seen only as victims, never as men in command of their own destinies, having a serious role to play in their own history. . . . If they said that African states had had real and legitimate interests, which they pursued through diplomacy and wars—that they were not mere

puppets in the hands of the slave traders—the new Africanists could be accused of trying to shift the burden of guilt for the horrors of the trade from European to African heads. (1975: 153)

It seems curious, as Inikori again observes, to argue "that to explain political and social conflicts in economic terms diminishes the level of civilization in pre-colonial Africa" (1982: 46). It is also odd that "political" and "economic" interests were presumed to be mutually exclusive rather than mutually consti-tutive. In the context of the slave trade on the upper Guinea coast, as we shall see, new forms of wealth *enabled* new forms of leadership, new political inter-ests, and new sources of conflict that were both "political" and "economic." This is not a simple, unidirectional history of Western "causes" and African "consequences," but neither is it an unfolding of parallel but autonomous histories of European commerce and African politics: there are too many in-terweaving strands. Ultimately, discounting the influence of the Atlantic trade on warfare in the name of African agency represents little improvement over simplistic claims of omnipotent European guile if our aim is to understand multiple, complex forms of agency and power in the integration of West Africa into the Atlantic world.

Most contributions to these debates on the consequences of the slave trade for Africa have been focused on the large slave-trading kingdoms, whose fighters raided surrounding areas for slaves. Sierra Leone, however, was far from the slave-trading kingdoms of Asante and Dahomey to the east, and its often watery, forested environment provided an effective barrier to slave-trading Mande states further north and northeast.[5] Unlike the large slave-trading states, this region had no major political or geographical boundary separating those who raided and those who were taken as slaves: the small chiefdoms into which Sierra Leone was organized included both those who raided for slaves and those who could be captured by raiders. Conflicts be-tween (and within) these chiefdoms were both exacerbated by tensions gener-ated by the Atlantic trade and encouraged by the slave trade's agents, who often supplied arms to both sides in a dispute. The frequent wars that arose— wars that defy categorization as either "politically" or "economically" moti-vated—"received the full blessing of the slave traders and their agents who supplied arms and supported one section against another" (Ijagbemi 1968: 26). The leaders who fought wars and sold their captives to the slave traders who had supplied their weapons were not "mere puppets in the hands of the slave traders," but neither were they wholly "in command of their own destinies" (Curtin 1975: 153): this was an intersection of African *and* European agency.

In eighteenth-century Sierra Leone, some of the everyday consequences of the above means of production of slaves were, according to Rodney, as follows:

> "They never care to walk even a mile from home without firearms," wrote John Atkins in 1721. This testimony clearly points to a state of insecurity bordering on anarchy. Another graphic illustration of this was to be seen in the disloca-tion of villages in Sierra Leone, and their re-siting in almost inaccessible hide-outs, away from the main waterways and the slave-raiding chiefs. (1970: 259)

Thus the attraction that Sierra Leone's rivers had exerted in the sixteenth cen-tury, when the presence of European trade and traders encouraged African settlement on the waterways, was now reversed (Rodney 1970: 80). Like Ben Okri's (1991) man-eating "famished road" that was once a river, both Sierra Leone's river highways and its roads had become dangerous channels for pre-dation that ordinary people sought to avoid.

The history of the Atlantic trade, then, encompasses much more than the transatlantic movement of people and goods in slave ships, the demographics of its forced migrations, and the lives of those it claimed directly as captives. It also includes the vast hinterland of violence and terror among those who remained on the African side of the Atlantic and were never taken as slaves, but who lived for centuries with both the anticipation and the consequences of the warfare, raiding, and other means of enslavement that the Atlantic trade engendered and multiplied.

The consequences of enslavement were, moreover, different for men and women. In most parts of West Africa, a bifurcated system developed: from the seventeenth century, most slaves exported through the Atlantic trade were men, while most slaves retained for the internal African market were women. According to Manning, "European prices for men became slightly higher than for women (reflecting higher male productivity in a situation where men could be controlled), and African prices for women became higher than for men (reflecting their sexuality, their slightly greater productivity in domestic labor under conditions of a restricted market for slave produce, and the diffi-culty of controlling men under African conditions)" (1990: 130). This bifurca-tion, according to Manning, had an impact on the ratio of men to women in the parts of Africa from which slaves were taken. This imbalance, in turn, often increased women's agricultural workloads, given that in most areas of Western

Africa (including the upper Guinea coast) land is relatively plentiful but short-ages of labor—especially during bush clearing and at harvest time—are prob-lematic (Richards 1986). At the same time, the gender ratio facilitated polygy-nous marriage, enabling rulers and wealthy merchants in particular to marry large numbers of wives (Manning 1990: 131–32). As Manning points out, "the result . . . was to reflect and actually increase the power of these big men" (1990: 132), while the absence of supporting kin reduced the power and rights of wives who were slaves in such marriages (MacCormack 1983a: 273, 276–77). I shall argue in chapters 5 and 6 that certain dominant representa-tions of the supernatural dangers of wives within their husband's house-hold—as witches, as diviners' clients, or as drawing the dangers of bush-spirit incursion—may have been underlined and exacerbated by the expanding presence of female slaves in polygynous marriages.

Mande Transformations   Another set of strands that must be traced in the intersection of African and European agency in an Atlanticizing Sierra Leone is that of several inflows of Mande-speaking peoples who entered the upper Guinea coast between the sixteenth and the nineteenth centuries. These new-comers originated from the Mande heartland, the Sudanic region of West Af-rica to the northeast, which has been characterized since at least the tenth century by its organization into centralized kingdoms that controlled the trans-Saharan trade. Some of these migrants came to impose their rule, some came as Islamic ritual specialists and Qur'anic teachers, and some came to trade. With their interregional connections, these expert traders not only con-trolled the long-distance trade to the Sudanic interior but also—and impor-tantly—often became agents in the Atlantic trade as well.

In the second half of the sixteenth century, Portuguese observers described what they saw as an "invasion" (which historians have interpreted as a gradual imposition of domination [Jones 1981]) of Sierra Leone by a group known as the "Mane"—a Mande-speaking people who described themselves as hav-ing come from the Mali empire. This Mane "invasion" led to an escalation of slaving, according to Rodney: "The origins of the Mane wars were entirely independent of the presence of Europeans, but, as a by-product, they filled the holds of slave ships. Yet it is significant that the Mane invasions coincided with the activities of European slavers. Inevitably the Mane came to look upon the supply of slaves to Europeans as an end in itself" (1970: 102). Some Temne-speaking groups took their place in a centralized kingdom headed by the Mane ruler, Bay Farma, acquiring Mande techniques of warfare and

government in so doing. Portuguese accounts tell of a dramatic transformation among Temne-speakers and their neighbors as a result of Mane rule.
One writer characterizes them as formerly having been "given to feasts and
pleasures" and as "a weak and cowardly people" who, "with the discipline
of the Manes . . . have become excellent soldiers and . . . good captains" (de Al-
mada 1964 [1594]: 356 and 374, cited in Rodney 1970: 60). But Manuel Alvares, the early seventeenth century Jesuit missionary we encountered above,
lamented these changes, noting that everyday activities were disrupted by
the dislocations of Mane domination and slaving:

> The kings and foreign governors are to blame for the land being impoverished,
> since they pride themselves so much in being in charge of it, and since their
> sons, brothers and relatives are so troublesome to the natives that for this rea-
> son they neglect and abandon their crafts. If we manage to obtain a little fish,
> wine or meat, we have to do it secretly by night—so greatly do the inhabitants
> fear those greedy crows! (1990, 2, chap. 3: 6)

Later on in the seventeenth century, however, these Mane overlords were gradually absorbed by their Temne-speaking subjects.

It was also during the seventeenth century that Temne-speaking groups
moved east and northeast from the coast into the territory of their Loko-
speaking neighbors, pushing them north as well as absorbing them through
intermarriage. In their eastern movement, they also encountered and settled
among the Kuranko, another Mande-speaking group. The oral traditions of
many eastern Temne-speaking communities, in fact, claim that their chiefdoms were founded by Kuranko, who often continued as the rulers of these
new polities (Ijagbemi 1968: 1–23; Fyle 1981: 22–26).

Mande political hegemony grew in the eighteenth century, when certain
Mande-speaking groups entered Temne-speaking areas in order to control the
slave trade (Ijagbemi 1968: 24–25). It is important to bear in mind, however,
that Mande and Fula interregional commerce encompassed far more than the
slave trade. Howard (1997) has identified three patterns of commerce in the
late precolonial period. First, a large east-west trade brought livestock, shea
butter, rubber, gold, and ivory from such areas as the Upper Niger and Futa
Jallon, and exchanged these for kola, salt, slaves, and foreign imports in the
Sierra Leone region (Howard 1997: 27). Some of this trade passed through
Falaba, the capital of the Solima Yalunka kingdom to the northeast of the
Kuranko-speaking area and an important entrepot in the eighteenth and nine-

teenth centuries (Fyle 1979b). Second, a smaller north-south trade moved slaves, kola, and imported goods up and down the coast. And third, inland routes connected eastern and southern Sierra Leone with the Futa Jallon (Howard 1997: 27).

Yet although trade with the interior was in many ways a continuation of that which had flourished before the arrival of Europeans, it was also influenced by the links that had developed between Mande and Fula merchants and European and Euro-African traders in slaves since the sixteenth century (Howard 1997: 26). Thus "by the eighteenth century," Rodney argues, "the hinterland . . . had immensely strengthened ties with the Atlantic trading system, so that, paradoxically, even influences from the interior reflected contacts with Europeans" (1970: 223). In the late eighteenth century, Rodney continues, many of the termini of caravans from the interior were sites of European factories (227). Some Mande and Fula merchants, moreover, were agents of European slave traders on the coast (Ijagbemi 1968: 24–25), becoming nodal actors in the articulation of the Atlantic and interior trades.

One instance of the dovetailing of the European slave trade and Mande political and economic power was the Susu occupation of Port Loko in northwestern Temneland in the latter part of the eighteenth century. Port Loko, an important center of the slave trade at the head of a navigable creek, was jointly controlled by Temne and Loko groups (Loko-speakers having already been displaced by Temne-speakers [Ijagbemi 1968: 27]). In the mid-eighteenth century, Susu migrants wishing to control the slave trade seized the town and imposed their political system based on Muslim titles, headed by the Alimami ("the Imam"). Their Temne subjects responded, however, by increasing their allegiance to Islam, intermarrying with their conquerors, and learning Susu military techniques. Then in the early nineteenth century, Moriba Kindo, a Temne leader with powerful Susu kinship connections, requested and was granted the Muslim political title of Adikali ("the Qadi" or judge). After reversing the meaning of his new title, claiming that it was superior to the senior Susu title of Alimami, he led the overthrow of the Susu in 1816 (Ijagbemi 1968: 76–82). By thus transforming themselves into their Mande "invaders," and then turning this transformation to their own meanings and purposes, the Port Loko Temne overcame their invaders.

In other areas too, a "Mandeizing" of Temne-speakers took place. Yet although Temne-speaking communities in contexts of Mande-speakers' domination adopted Mande names (Sayers 1927), assimilated Mande cultural practices, learned Mande military techniques, and absorbed their Mande rulers themselves through intermarriage, they did not adopt a Mande language.[6] Whereas both Mende and Loko each seem to be products of a transformation from Mel-speaking to Mande-speaking peoples (Jones 1981), Temne-speaking communities appear to represent a reverse process in which Mel-speakers absorbed Mande groups. Through this process, the formerly "feast-loving" communities of Alvares's early-seventeenth-century account became militarized, Islamicized, and in many cases (but to a lesser extent than dominant Mande groups) involved as agents in the European slave trade. They thereby incorporated some of the very forces that threatened them in the era of the Atlantic trade.

"Big Persons" and the Violence of Debt   It was also during the seventeenth and eighteenth centuries that a new kind of leader arose on the upper Guinea coast: wealthy merchants who had become affluent and powerful through the slave trade. "They were," writes Rodney, "the most salient representatives of a powerful social formation, produced by physical and commercial contact between Europe and the Upper Guinea Coast, and serving the interests of European mercantilism" (1970: 200). In so doing, of course, they also served their own interests: these leaders exemplify the necessity of treating African agency as complex and multiple. Often the descendants of European traders who had married into chiefly families, some of these men bore names such as Caulker, Cleveland, Tucker, and Rogers. But unlike chiefs, whose obligations toward those in their chiefdoms kept their wealth circulating among their dependents, these affluent figures were more easily able to accumulate material riches. One such leader was Henry Tucker, a powerful figure in the Sherbro area to the south in the mid-eighteenth century:

> His riches set him above the kings and his numerous people above being surprised by war; almost all the blacks owes him money, which bring a dread of being stopt upon that account, so that he is esteemed and feared by all who has the misfortune to be in his power. He's a fat man and fair spoken, and lives after the manner of the English, having his house well furnish'd with English goods. . . . He dresses gayley and commonly makes use of silver at his table, haveing a good side board of plate. (Owen [1746–57]: 76; in Rodney 1970: 218)

People's "dread of being stopt" by those such as Tucker derived from the penalty the latter exacted for indebtedness: as Rodney points out, "debts were by then among the most common pretexts for ensnaring victims for the Atlantic slave trade" (218). The English traveler Winterbottom, writing fifty years later at the turn of the nineteenth century, describes the regulated processes by which the "catching" of debtors took place:

> The African law authorises the creditor to sieze the goods or person of his debtor, or even the goods or person of anyone belonging to the debtor's town, without a palaver [legal dispute]. . . . The creditor catches, as it is called (that is, seizes) some one belonging to the same town, or family, with the debtor on which the debtor endeavours to procure a palaver to adjust the matter; if not, the persons seized may be sold as slaves. (Winterbottom 1969 [1803]: 127–28)

During that century, the export of debtors as slaves by wealthy merchants eventually ceased; yet, as we shall see, the numbers and powers of the new leaders multiplied.

Colonial Trade and Trade Wars   The final set of strands to be traced here begin with the establishment of a British Crown Colony. In 1787, a settlement for freed slaves from Britain and the New World—the Province of Freedom— was founded on the Sierra Leone peninsula, within the land of the Koya Temne. Successive agreements made firstly with a Koya subchief called King Tom and secondly with the Koya regent, Naimbana, stated that the land should be ceded to the settlement "for ever." But as this was foreign to a long-established form of agreement between Temne "landlords" and European "strangers" in which land could be used but never alienated permanently, it is unlikely that King Tom and Naimbana understood the meaning of this new contract (Ijagbemi 1968: 57–61). As the Koya Temne became aware of what had happened, they grew embittered. Several disputes and attacks upon the settlement ensued, during one of which, in 1789, it was burnt down by King Tom's successor, King Jimmy. The land of the settlement was taken over in 1791 by a London-based company called the Sierra Leone Company, which rebuilt the town and named it "Freetown." In 1808, however, after the Sierra Leone Company suffered heavy financial losses, the British government took over the settlement, making it a Crown Colony ruled by a British governor. The founding of Freetown marked a watershed in British involvement with Temne-speaking communities, not only for the Koya Temne whose land was forcibly annexed with each subsequent dispute (often on the flimsiest pretext), but also for Temne chiefdoms in the hinterland.

In 1806, the British made the Atlantic slave trade illegal for all British sub-

jects and instead promoted what they termed the "legitimate trade" in products such as timber, camwood, palm oil, palm kernels, and groundnuts. Because this legitimate trade depended on slave labor within the interior for the
production and transportation of the goods they wanted, however, the British
allowed internal slavery to continue in the hinterland for more than a century,
until 1929 (Lenga-Kroma 1978: 76–78; 153ff.; Rashid 1999): slave raiding was
therefore intensified. Slaves were also smuggled north, to work on groundnut
farms on the coast of what is now the Republic of Guinea (Jones 1983: 83–85),
and to farm or fight for northern military leaders (Wylie 1977: 83–84).

In the last quarter of the nineteenth century, the demand for palm kernels
increased rapidly (Mitchell 1962: 205). While slaves could always be transported overland, palm products are heavy and bulky relative to their value:
this meant that rivers—which had always been important in the slave trade—
were now crucial for transportation (Jones 1983: 105). Consequently, in addition to the intensification of slave raiding, new "trade wars" were now fought
over access to trading centers on the rivers (Ijagbemi 1968; 1973). As Lenga-
Kroma describes for southern Temneland, "the result of this situation was the
occurrence of frequent wars, and nineteenth century Southern Temne country
was thus characterized by professionalism in warfare, making both life and
property insecure throughout the first three quarters of the century" (1978: 83).

During this period certain forms of leadership and government were maintained, while others were dislocated. Up to the nineteenth century, leaders in
the hinterland had founded settlements, cleared the bush to make farms, and
built up followings of supporters whose security in turn depended on the
ability of those leaders to protect them from slave raiding (Abraham 1975;
Bledsoe 1980: 63; Denzer 1971; Dorjahn 1960b; Murphy 1980: 201). These
leaders became the ancestors of the ruling lineages in a particular area, from
which chiefs were drawn.[7] In the nineteenth-century trade wars, however, the
authority of these rulers was undermined.

During the legitimate trade, the numbers of wealthy merchants who had
arisen as a new kind of leader during the Atlantic trade increased. This was the
kind of leader who formed the basis for the mid-nineteenth century Temne
narrative excerpted at the beginning of this chapter: "a wicked person, and a
violent person: he was also a great man, he had plenty of money, and many
slaves . . . and did just as he pleased . . . he became the author of death in the
world" (Schlenker 1861: 27). Some such traders, in fact, accumulated so much
wealth through this colonial commerce that they became more powerful than
chiefs and challenged chiefly authority by force when their interests were in

conflict (Ijagbemi 1968: 304). Because they kept bands of professional warriors to fight and raid others for them (having the necessary wealth to supply these warriors with food, weapons, and protective medicines), these leaders became known to the British as "war chiefs" (Ijagbemi 1973). Accordingly, chiefs from ruling lineages responded by maintaining permanent bodies of specialized warriors themselves: warfare thereby became professionalized. This, in turn, brought about an escalation of fighting, raiding, and plunder:

> These professional warriors would not know, and would not care to know, the cause they were fighting for, so long as they got the promised reward. When this did not materialize, they would get out of control and would attack and plunder indiscriminately. When there was a chief powerful enough, . . . he would be able to keep his warriors under control. But most Temne . . . chiefs at this period had been rendered powerless by the incessant wars, which in turn rendered them very vulnerable to attack. (Ijagbemi 1968: 278)

Moreover, "some of these warriors," according to Ijagbemi, "became very wealthy and powerful, so much so that they came to overshadow the civilian rulers altogether" (213). Thus while the Atlantic trade engendered the commodification of bodies on the upper Guinea coast, the legitimate trade extended the kinds of transactional relationships that had thus far characterized European commerce (Rodney 1970: 171–222) to the leadership and defense of chiefdoms themselves.

The Colony authorities in Freetown saw the conflicts of the latter part of the nineteenth century as "tribal wars," failing to see the commercial rather than "tribal" origins of these wars in the legitimate trade they had themselves promoted (Ijagbemi 1968: 303–4, 1973: 41; Lenga-Kroma 1978: 157). Ironically, it was they, in fact, who eventually created what they called "tribalism"—an embattled sense of ethnic identity—through their mishandling of the conflict between the landlocked Yoni Temne and those Mende-speaking communities that controlled the important southwestern tidewater trading centers of Bumpe and Ribi, to which the Yoni were denied access. By supporting the enemies of the Yoni even when these enemies attacked other Temne chiefdoms unconnected with Yoni, and by regarding Mende groups as "friends of the administration," the Colony's actions united the southern Temne rulers and "turned the conflict into a Temne/Mende war" (Ijagbemi 1968: 306). The conflicts culminated in the Colony's punitive Yoni Expedition of 1887—named "the white man's war" by Temne in the area—that left towns and villages (and often rice farms) in both Yoni and Masimera chiefdoms shelled, burned, and plundered (Ijagbemi 1968: 296–99).

Convinced after this conflict that they needed a more direct imperialist policy in order to safeguard their control of the interior trade, the Colonial government proclaimed the establishment of a British Protectorate over the hinterland of Sierra Leone in 1896. The governor did so before consultation with the chiefs, however, who found that their authority had been considerably eroded (Lenga-Kroma 1978: 178–202). There followed risings in 1898 called the "Mende Rising" in the south and the "Hut Tax War" in the north (due to its precipitation, in part, by the government's attempts to collect a house tax), led by a Temne war chief, Bai Bureh (Denzer 1971). The imposition of the Protectorate was thus the occasion for further warfare generated by British economic interests.

Memory and Truth   Temne-speaking communities do not appear to have suffered as much as did many other groups during the Atlantic trade itself, due to Temne participation as intermediaries. Ijagbemi writes of the eighteenth century, for instance, that:

> The wars that loom so large in Temne traditions were probably not as destructive as often made out. . . . The intention was to incapacitate, not to kill, and success in battle was reckoned on the number of captives and the amount of plunder. . . . As well entrenched middlemen [of the slave trade, the Temne] constituted, with the Mande traders among them, "the entrepreneurs in the business." Nevertheless, there was a lot of movement of peoples—exiles on the run from war-infested areas—to avoid capture and enslavement. (1968: 73–74)

Like Ijagbemi, most historians have been careful not to sensationalize the history of warfare in the region, mindful of colonial stereotypes that attributed this history to the "warlike savagery" of the "natives" (see Abraham 1976: 121–23). They have tended instead to adopt a "life goes on" approach stressing social reproduction and cultural continuity (e.g. Abraham 1976; Hair 1967; Ijagbemi 1968; Jones 1983; Lenga-Kroma 1978): warfare and raiding were part of the environment in which crops were grown, marriages were contracted, children were born, and rituals were performed. Even in the seeming chaos of the nineteenth-century trade wars, warfare—like agriculture—had a regular, seasonal character, with both wars and trade normally ceasing during the rainy season when preparation of the rice farms was resumed (Ijagbemi

1968: 267–68, 277–78). Yet the fact that warfare, raiding, and the knowledge that bodies could become commodities in exchange for wealth formed part of the everyday conditions of life for over four centuries was surely insidious in itself. Terror had become a taken-for-granted aspect of the environment in which people's lives unfolded.

In fact, certain Temne accounts of the past do depict catastrophe and ruin. In the mid-nineteenth century, the missionary Schlenker in Port Loko collected Temne narratives that included remembrances of the sixteenth-century Mane leader Bay Farma and of other powerful warriors who came after him. The account of Bay Farma is a litany of destruction: "He entirely expelled (the people) on the whole of the Rokel, and they all fled"; "He destroyed the whole country" (Schlenker 1861: 3). After Bay Farma, a warrior and slave-dealer named Korombo is again described as destroying "the whole Temne country," seizing, buying, and selling people as commodities on every step of his path of havoc:

> At the towns, where he slept, he asked for boys; he took them and bought them, and went and sold them. When he met with a woman in childbed, he took out cloths and palmwine . . . and gave (them) to the woman, and said: "When thy child is worth the amount, I shall sell it." He took out a gun, and gave it to the husband. They were not able to kill him; they chopped him, (but) the cutlass did not enter (his body); they shot at him with a gun, (but) the balls did not hit him; and he was able to fly. When he came to a town, he assembled the people, selected (a number of) them, and sold them. (Schlenker 1861: 5)

Korombo's actions transform patterns of sociality into commercial transactions that bring about social and physical death. Relationships between guest and host, husband and wife, parent and child, the continuity of a community through its children, and practices of gift-giving are all subverted, in this account, from ways of creating and renewing social relationships into ways of accomplishing their destruction through the commodification of bodies, the obliteration of persons, and the plunder of the family's and the community's means of reproduction. This linkage between powers of penetration, of impenetrability, and of extraordinary mobility recurs in accounts of the eras of warfare; such capacities (as we shall see in chapters 7, 8, and 9) are also attributes ascribed to powerful elite persons—"big persons" *(aŋ-fəm a bana)*—today.

We do not have to make literalistic readings of such accounts as empirical annihilation in order to take them seriously. Rather, we could approach such accounts as holding the kind of truth that Taussig finds in stories of the Putumayo atrocities in Amazonia:

> The meticulous historian might seize upon the stories and fragments of stories, such as they are, to winnow out truth from distortion, reality from illusion, fact from myth. A whole field opens out here for tabulating, typologizing, and cross-checking, but what "truth" is it that is assumed and reproduced by such procedures? Surely it is a truth that begs the question raised by history, in this case the history of terror. . . . Alternatively we can listen to these stories neither as fiction nor as disguised signs of truth, but as real. (1987: 75)

Rather than being viewed as distortions, narratives of the destruction wrought by such figures as Korombo may be read as articulating social memories of warfare, dislocation, and terror—memories that carry considerable moral meaning.

In the following chapters, I explore a history of the slave trade through such moral and ritual memories. Not only do these memories subsume the processes of the slave trade within a framework of cultural meanings and values; they also provide a basis for the critique of subsequent processes—the British Protectorate, the abuses of postcolonial politicians, and the depredations of the rebel war at the end of the twentieth century—and thereby fold together past and present experiences of capitalism, transregional flows, and violence.

Sierra Leone Sojourns I lived in Sierra Leone from September 1977 to December 1978, returning for a brief three week visit in 1981, and for visits of three months each in 1989 and 1992, and during June and July 2001. My initial study—Temne divination—opened up intimations of a long history through which ritual ideas and practices in particular localities were connected to translocal circulations. After an initial stay in Matotoka, the headquarters of Tane Chiefdom, I moved to Makeni, working with diviners there and in the surrounding villages, and spending the most time in the small town of Petbana Masimbo. There the diviner I worked with, the late Pa Alfa Koroma, was the great-grandson of a Muslim cleric from what is now Guinea, who (along with many other eighteenth- and nineteenth-century foreign Muslim "strangers" I discuss in chapter 3) had been invited to settle in order "to help with the chieftaincy." It was when I spent time with Pa Koroma and members of his household, asking questions, attending divination sessions (when clients gave permission), talking to clients, and watching Pa Koroma prepare medicines, that I first became aware that the majority of diviners' clients were women, most of whom kept their ritual consultations secret from their marital households.

Thus began my focus on knowledge, power, and gender in divination, which I pursued when I later moved to Freetown for three months, and then to Koidu, the capital of the diamond district, for one month, exploring divination among Temne migrants. During my stay in Freetown, I met the late Pa Yamba Nhoni Kamara, a diviner and Poro cult association official. He would talk for hours, boasting about his ritual powers, telling me about his life, complaining about Sierra Leone's politicians, and, as he grew older, debating about God and Islam. I knew Pa Yamba over the course of fourteen years and write about his ritual life-course in chapter 4.

I initially assumed that, as a white British woman in a former British colony, people would associate me with colonialism. They often did. But there was another association that I had not anticipated: the Temne-speaking diviners I worked with told me repeatedly that I looked like their tutelary spirits. At first, I thought that they were talking about a whiteness that simply indexes the "otherness" of spirits. No, they insisted, the spirits who helped them divine really did look like Europeans *(aŋ-potho)*. When I visited a diviner called Pa Abdul in Magburaka, in northern Sierra Leone, I found a painting on his wall apparently depicting two white Peace Corps volunteers in bell-bottoms and platform heels: these, he told me, were his tutelary spirits. Later, when I asked another diviner, Ya Mabinti, to teach me cowrie shell divination *(ta-faŋt)*, she insisted that as a white person, I already had a close link to these objects and their powers. *"You people are the owners of these cowries,"* she said. *"There's no need to teach you. You just don't understand how to 'play' (wɔl) with them. You can 'see' (kəli) cowries. You know. But you don't understand."* She was, of course, right about the historical connection between Europeans and cowries, which were brought from the Indian Ocean to West Africa to become "the shell money of the slave trade" (Hogendorn and Johnson 1986).

This is certainly not a case of white people being worshipped as deities: these diviners' spirits are not Durkheimean reflections of Europeans. They need to be viewed, as I argue in chapter 4, in the context of the long history of the slave trade, the European wealth it brought, and the relationships between European "strangers" and African "landlords" it entailed. But at the time of my first fieldwork in the late 1970s, I lacked the conceptual framework of historical anthropology that would have helped me understand the white spirits.

Following my 1977–78 fieldwork, I made a very short visit in 1981 (for three weeks), but was unable to return for another eight years. In 1989, I lived in Petbana for three months, mourning the loss of Pa Koroma, who had passed away six years earlier. I focused on competing forms of Islamic knowledge, and listened to the late Pa Kaper Bana, the subchief responsible for chieftaincy ritual in Bombali Sebora chiefdom, who wished to teach me about Petbana's ancestors. I also worked with new diviners in villages in the Makeni area, notably the late Pa Fonah, a former student of Pa Koroma's, and Ya Yebu, who was remarkable in being a woman renowned for her skills in Islamic forms of divination that were ordinarily a male preserve.

My next stay in Sierra Leone was in 1992, when I spent three months in Freetown. I worked closely with Pa Yamba and (where possible) his clients; through him I came to know Ya Bay Kolone, a woman who, in addition to being a diviner and healer, had been "seized" by spirits of every cult association and ritual office available to women. My focus at that time was on women's negotiations of marital relationships through divination. By that year, Sierra Leone's economic predicament had become so bad that even for enterprising market women, divination was one of the few means available through which women had recourse against problems in their marital homes.

Despite the wretched economic situation in Sierra Leone, that rainy season of 1992 was a time of desperate optimism. The army, starved of resources, had been unable to defeat the rebels in the war that had started the year before; the economy was in freefall; and Sierra Leone had just been placed last in the UN's global ranking for quality of life. Yet Freetown was celebrating a popular military coup led by twenty-seven-year-old Valentine Strasser, which had replaced the corrupt All People's Congress (APC) regime three months before I arrived. The capital was filled with young, armed soldiers who were being feted as emblems of national renewal. But at the same time, armed robberies multiplied despite a nightly curfew, when the army patrolled the streets: the conclusion that most people reluctantly drew was that some of the soldiers were responsible or were at least in league with the armed robbers. These soldiers' involvement in the robberies turned out to be an ominous sign of what was to come.

The following year, during fellowships at Harvard, I was able to read a number of historical sources on Sierra Leone dating from the fifteenth to the

nineteenth centuries. Though my reading, I became aware that the ritual practices and gender discourses I had come to know had a massive historical dimension in the centuries of the Atlantic and legitimate trades in that region.
This discovery transformed my project, enabling me to reconceptualize both
divination and gender discourses in terms of social memory.

In the rest of this book, some of the people I describe are themselves memories. Due to the rebel war that has devastated the country since 1991, more
than two-thirds of Sierra Leone's population has been either displaced, killed,
or mutilated. If there is any comfort at all to be derived from the history of
the slave trade—both Atlantic and internal—in Sierra Leone, it is that even
after several centuries of escalating raiding and warfare, capture and disappearance, ordinary Sierra Leoneans nevertheless managed to build moral
communities. Given their extraordinary courage and strength, perhaps this
miracle can be repeated again.

Spirit Memoryscape

Landscapes bear traces of violent histories in different ways. One is through the suffusion of a place by the lingering presence of past violence and suffering: "haunted" houses, pools, forests, and stretches of road that were sites of murder, raids, drowning, or car accidents (Aretxaga 1998: 39–40; Masquelier 1992; Steedly 1993: 145). Another is through experiences and practices that evoke the presence of a decimated population in an emptied landscape— the unquiet preconquest dead in South America, and displaced Aboriginal ancestors in Australia (Taussig 1987; Morphy 1995). In the countryside of the Makeni and Magburaka areas that I knew from 1977 to 1992, the landscape had never been emptied by major population displacements (during my 1992 visit, the year-old rebel war had not yet spread beyond the southeast), but it nevertheless held a diffused sense of menace that went far beyond the haunting of local landmarks. It was not merely that the bush beyond human settlements and farms was permeated by the presence of mobile and dangerous forces: this is not by itself an unusual spirit geography. But it was in the character of these forces and in the forms of defense used against them that, I suggest, transformations of the landscape during the periods of slave trade and legitimate trade were remembered.

When I arrived in Sierra Leone and moved into the town of Matotoka for my first period of fieldwork in November 1977, I noticed that people were

Figure 1. Temne-speaking area in Sierra Leone

careful to lock every door and window shutter at night. My neighbors, for their part, noticed that I fastened the windows of my room so that the latter remained locked to potential burglars but slightly open to any available night breezes. *"Your windows are open at night,"* worried neighbors warned me; *"that's dangerous. You should close them."* Theft was indeed relatively common, but at that point in Sierra Leone's history it was so rarely accompanied by violence that I felt a sense of personal safety I had never known back in London. My hosts and neighbors expressed such concern, however, that I slept with closed windows in Matotoka thereafter.

I found the same concerns when I later moved to Petbana Masimbo, the village in which I spent most of my 1978 and 1989 visits. In both Matotoka and Petbana, houses were not only protected with locks and bolts; most were

also ritually "Closed"[1] *(kaŋtha)* by medicines that locked them against penetration by bush spirits and witches (see Littlejohn 1960b; 1963). Hung just
inside the doorway (plate 3) or from the center of the rafters, these medicines—usually known as "the Closure" *(aŋ-kaŋtha)*—usually took the form
either of a bottle of Islamic medicine *(ma-nasi)* or of an Islamic amulet *(aŋ-
sɛbɛ)* made from a folded sheet of paper upon which Arabic verses and diagrams had been inscribed by a diviner *(u-mɔre* or *u-ləfa)*. Bush spirits *(aŋ-kərfi
ka aŋ-kaŋth)*, I was told, sometimes make incursions into unprotected houses
and have sex with sleeping women inside, blocking the women's reproductive
capacities or causing them to give birth to monstrous spirit children. Witches
(aŋ-ser), on the other hand, might enter a house and invisibly drain the blood
and internal organs from children. Farms are also ritually Closed against
witches to prevent the latter from invisibly stealing the growing rice, leaving
the farmer with a failed crop. It is Closure that makes the construction of
houses and the cultivation of farms possible by exorcising that part of the
land on which they are made, placing them under the care of the protective
town spirits, the ancestors, and God (K-uru or Allah), and thereby creating an
invisible cordon sanitaire that other spirits and witches cannot penetrate.

The human body is similarly protected. Young children, whose bodies are
seen as particularly vulnerable to invisible attack, are often Closed with amulets. *"A child with a cough at Braima's house had a cowrie shell and a sɛbɛ tied around
his left wrist, with a string from the shell attached to a ring around his finger. Braima
said he was sick, and that this was to protect him from spirit attack."* Adults, on the
other hand, are more likely to conceal an amulet by wearing it under their
clothes. "With the Temne," as Littlejohn notes, "the body is closed off like
farms and houses; all space being penetrable by evil, that occupied by the
body is no different from any other" (1963: 8).

Certain forms of sacrifice *(s-athka)* bring about a similar ritual containment of the house or body, sometimes with a bottle of medicine blessed by
the name of God and hung from the rafters of a house, or with an undervest
made of similarly blessed strips of red and white cloth (often soaked in protective medicine), worn under the clothes. It is the name of God that makes
these ritual objects "sacrifices," exorcising the space of the house, farm, or
body and placing its boundaries under the protection of God and the ancestors *(aŋ-baki)*.

In addition to the admonitions I received about locking my door and windows properly at night, I was also warned about walking near the edge of
town after dark. Anyone abroad at such a time ran the risk of being attacked—

and not only by fellow human beings. Several people told me of frightening near-encounters with spirits. *"I saw a spirit (ɔ-kərfi) on a bush road at night. The spirit was walking with a big light. I felt weak in my body. I was behind it. It looked like an ordinary man, but it wasn't an ordinary man."* (*"If it looked like an ordinary man, how did you know it was a spirit?"*) *"Because I felt weak in my body."*

Even during the day, both the bush and the roads that run through it could be menacing spaces. Neither looked menacing to my European gaze: the tarred or laterite roads, often with houses spread along them, seemed unremarkable to me, and the bush was secondary growth that was not usually very thick. But the threat was invisible: bush spirits sometimes "seize" *(wop)* people who enter their domain without ritual protection, causing children in particular to disappear into the forest forever. These spirits can seize adults too, making their victims crazy and disoriented *(pɔŋk)*, turning them into mad people who wander along the roads and through the bush with no settled sense of place. At that time, the peril of the roads inhered in the bush spirits and witches traveling along them at night, congregating at crossroads and attacking unlucky human travelers. Rivers, in turn, were the abodes of alluring but treacherous light-skinned mermaids *(ɛ-yaroŋ)* who could make a man rich, but ultimately at the cost of his marriage, children, sanity, and even life itself (Shaw 1995). And in deep parts of the bush, I was sometimes told, lived short, hostile people who emerged in times of violence—notably during elections—to attack anyone they saw. Certain events that draw the locality into the turbulence of regional and national politics seemed to call forth embodiments of violence from within the landscape itself. As time went on, I learned to see this landscape and its dangers historically.

Modes of Memory   But at first, my impression of most people's everyday memories of the slave trading and colonial past was very similar to that of Cole, when she first arrived at a Betsimisaraka town in east Madagascar and entered "a world in which people behaved as if colonialism had never happened: neither omnipotent nor resisted, the colonial past was simply absent—or so it seemed to me at the time" (1998: 611). Cole found that this was partly because, for Betsimisaraka, discursive memory is not simply a matter of storing and retrieving information, but a means of establishing and maintaining relationships between oneself and particular people—primarily the ancestors (1998: 616). This was also true of most discursive remembering (= *tamtamnɛ*) in the Temne communities I knew, in which people would often speak of their deceased parents and grandparents, call the names of the

ancestors *(aŋ-baki)* of their lineage or town when making a sacrifice, and respond to my questions about particular ritual practices with such words as
"the old ones met it when they were born." It was this mode of discursive memory,
coupled with my own initial focus on the present rather than the past, that
gave rise to my first impression of continuity in Temne ritual, despite the presence of Islamic elements woven into most of the ritual practices I saw, and
despite my knowledge that the slave trade and colonialism had been important parts of Temne history.

In fact, the violence of the slave trade and colonialism were remembered,
but not as part of everyday knowledge. Discursive narratives about these eras
were the province of senior men: not everybody had the right to tell them,
and as a young, female, and European "stranger," I did not have the right to
hear them. Later, when I returned to Petbana in 1989, the late Pa Kaper Bana,
the ritual subchief of Bombali Sebora chiefdom (of which Petbana is a part),
saw my return as confirmation that my interest in Petbana was more than
casual and decided that my right to know about its past had changed. He
started to instruct me, first by repeatedly listing the names of Petbana's ancestors on different occasions, and finally by narrating an apocalyptic story of
the slave-raiding past, locating this past in an earlier landscape that God
(K-uru) had physically buried beneath the present one. I conclude this chapter
with his story.

But the slave trade is not only recalled in the special (and elite) knowledge
of Pa Kaper Bana's narrative about God's transformation of the land. Rather
than being recalled in a story about the landscape, the slave trade is more
generally remembered in the dangerous invisible presences that pervade the
landscape itself, and in the protective ritual techniques that people use in
order to live in this landscape. Everyday Temne memories of the slave trade,
then, take mostly nondiscursive, practical forms. Through a similar incorporation of memories into the landscape and ritual practices, Cole argues of Betsimisaraka colonial memories, people integrated formerly foreign elements
into ancestral histories and rituals: they "bent and shaped new practices to
previously existing local schemas" (1998: 627). And as I hope to show, in the
process of incorporating the raiding and warfare of Sierra Leone's slave-trading
past as practical memories, the local schemas themselves were bent and
shaped as well. In the next section, I explore a transformation in the invisible
inhabitants of the landscape who, over the course of the slave-trade centuries,
seem to have undergone a moral metamorphosis into predominantly negative beings.

Banished Spirits, Vanished Chapels   Viewing the Temne spirits and ancestors who people the landscape through the lens of the slave trade runs counter to long-held views of African ritual outside that of the "world" religions as essentially stable. Ritual was, until relatively recently, "allowed a dynamic role in regulating repetitive processes" but "was not recognized as a means of making history" (Jean Comaroff 1994: 313). Such misreadings have been compounded in many studies of religion in Africa by the formulaic schematizing of "African Traditional Religion" in terms of a supposedly universal "supreme God" who presides over a lower tier of "local" beings such as "the lesser deities and spirits" and "the ancestors"—a scheme implicitly based on a Judeo-Christian template (Horton 1984; Shaw 1990). Even those who reject the primacy accorded to a Judeo-Christian model may nevertheless read an essential sameness into rituals and cosmologies from different times and places in Africa as long as the latter concern spirits and deities that can be characterized as "local." Studies of spirit possession have been an exception: possession is accorded a unique and privileged dynamism in the literature, perhaps because historical agents and processes are given such a vividly embodied and above all verbally discursive voice in the persons of possession spirits.[2] Yet the literature is comparatively silent on how history may be recapitulated in the changing attributes and actions of (arguably) more mundane spirits of the land who are not embodied and "voiced" through spirit possession.[3]

In Temne-speaking communities, local spirits have undergone a radical transformation in ways that seem to crystallize historical processes associated with the Atlantic slave trade. As was made clear to me in the warnings I received about night-time walks and open windows, most spirits (aŋ-kərfi) in the southern Temne towns and villages I knew from the late 1970s to the early 1990s were amoral and destructive beings who were properly external to human settlement. The exceptions were bush or river spirits with whom particular ancestors had forged special relationships: these spirits had thereafter become town, lineage, chiefdom, and cult association spirits, and usually inhabited an area of sacred bush on the outskirts of town. And just outside most towns and villages, the male Poro association and female Bondo association each had their areas of sacred bush that were closed to non-initiates. On a temporary basis, in addition, members of the Poro built a miniature house in the town for the Poro spirit during initiations, while members of the Bondo built a Bondo enclosure during girls' initiations. Southern Temne towns and villages, however, included few shrines alongside human dwellings.[4] Only two kinds of shrine were both permanent and relatively centrally located, and these did not house spirits but forces that were—or had been—human: they were an ancestor shrine ("the house of stones," *aŋ-boro mə-sar*) and a twin shrine ("the house of twins," *aŋ-seth ŋa ta-bari*). These shrines usually coexisted—unproblematically for some, uneasily for others—with an Islamic focal point provided by either an open praying-place or a mosque *(aŋ-misiri)*.

But in the early period of the Atlantic trade from the turn of the sixteenth to the early seventeenth century, the spirit landscape was quite different. Our earliest surviving, detailed account of Sierra Leone was written by Valentim Fernandes at the beginning of the sixteenth century. Fernandes is thought to have obtained his information primarily from an informant called Alvaro Velho, who lived on or near the coast of Sierra Leone for eight years, probably as a trader (Fernandes 1951 [1506–10]: 103; 175–76 n. 197). According to Fernandes (or Velho), the inhabitants of the region known as "Serra Lyoa" (the coastal area from the Isles de Los to Cape Mount) spoke two closely related languages: there were Bullom-speakers *("Boloes")* living on the coast and Temne-speakers *("Temjnis")* living further inland. In and around their villages were a myriad of shrines: "All the villages of *Serra Lyoa* have a single faith and are idol worshippers and believe that idols can help them and provide relief for their needs. And they have many idols" (1951: 82; trans. Alice Clemente). Fernandes goes on to describe some of them: a spirit called *cru* (K-uru, today denoting "God" in Temne) who was "common to all" and was enshrined in a tree in the center of each village; a spirit embodied in a clay image "done to resemble the sun" (84); a figure resembling a famous deceased warrior; gender-specific cult association spirits housed in shrines that only those of the appropriate gender could enter; and ancestors represented either by figurative sculpture ("for the honorable men" [88]), or by pieces of wood carved into a round shape.

In addition, anthropomorphic healing "idols" dwelled in compounds and houses, at close quarters with humans: "And for all the illnesses, they have corresponding idols to which the sick make sacrifices, a man who has a headache, another who has a stomachache, another a pain in the *lauoyras* and so on for all kinds of pain. And these three are sticks carved in the form of men. And they have these three idols in their gardens and some have idols in their houses" (88; trans. Alice Clemente). There were also "idols" that promoted the prosperity of individual households—their wealth in children, rice, and domestic slaves: "And they have other idols in covered chapels along the roadways as in hermitages where all can pray for whatever need they have, one that his wife be fertile or that his slaves may not escape or that their rice grow well" (88; trans. Alice Clemente).

This ritual landscape forms a marked contrast to that of the late twentieth century. Those from the Temne-speaking villages I knew from 1977 to 1992 would find the presence of single-sex cult associations familiar but would not recognize most of their names. They might also be disconcerted by the sheer number of shrines—especially in people's compounds and houses—and by all the anthropomorphic images in wood and clay kept within them. In addition to the differences between the names, practices, and ritual institutions of the early sixteenth and late twentieth centuries, however, there also seem to be deeper contrasts. The moral qualities of the "idols" that Fernandes describes appear to differ from those of twentieth-century spirits. Instead of being almost exclusively the denizens of the outside—or, at best, the margins— that they are now, many early-sixteenth-century spirits were established in compounds and houses, while others were enshrined along paths and roads. And instead of raiding their villages, stealing their children, making them infertile, and ambushing travelers, causing the latter to go insane, many of these "idols" from the very early days of the Atlantic trade lived side by side with people, healing them and promoting their prosperity. The very presence of so many shrines testifies to the fact that here were powers with which people could negotiate.

The presence of Portuguese and other Europeans as lançados—traders who "threw themselves" into African communities on the upper Guinea coast—did not dislodge the spirits from their numerous "chapels." The lançados lived as "guests" (*hospede;* Rodney 1970: 83–84) or "strangers" (Brooks 1993: 135–39, 167–96) under the protection of the African "hosts" or "landlords" upon whom they relied: they were not permitted to rent land for cultivation (Rodney 1970: 204), they were bound by African practices of exchange and judicial process, and many were integrated into relationships of obligation with their hosts' families through marriage (Brooks 1993: 137, 189). These settlers were dependent upon the communities in which they lived: far from wishing to undermine local ritual practices, they participated in these practices themselves.[5]

A century later, in 1615, Alvares is still able to describe little "chapels" all over the built environment, in a spirit landscape that appears little changed from that depicted by Fernandes:

> The niches and little huts in which they keep their idols are tidier than many chapels of the true saints in Europe. To sum up, all these heathen possess a portrait of their devil, in their house, in their room, in their courtyard, at their door, in the clearings and fields where they grow their crops, on roads, at the

sources of streams, in ports where they labour, and in their hearts: all (their idols are) devils. (Alvares 1990 [c. 1615], 2, chap. 5: 8)

So when—and why—did most spirits become denizens of the outside? And why did spirits' "portraits" and "chapels" disappear from Temne houses, rooms, courtyards, doors, clearings, fields, roads, ports, and hearts?

For Alvares the missionary, "all (their idols are) devils": was Christian missionization responsible for the disappearance of the "chapels" Alvares described in the early seventeenth century? Christian missions have not had sufficient impact in Temne-speaking areas, either in Alvares's time or since, to effect such a change. What about the process of Islamicization? Thayer (1983) argues that the strong presence of Islam in Susu communities to the northeast has led to the development of a more sharply defined moral dichotomy between town and bush than that which obtains in other parts of Sierra Leone. Was the translation of local spirits into largely negative beings, their banishment from the town to the bush, and the vanishing of their "chapels" part of an intensification of this dichotomized Islamic moral space in Temne-speaking areas? As we shall see in the next chapter, the power of Muslim migrants from the north was strongly felt in eighteenth and nineteenth century Temneland and was accompanied by a widespread (although selective) incorporation of Islamic ritual practices. Yet while agents of Islam were certainly important catalysts for ritual change, the Muslim ritual specialists who helped bring Islam to southern and central Temneland were extremely accommodating of Temne ritual practices and ideas (e.g., Skinner 1978; Turay 1971: 63–64). It seems unlikely, then, that Islamicization could by itself have been responsible for the transformation of spirits from close neighbors into external marauders. Some of the characteristics of present-day spirits may, however, yield clues.

In Petbana Masimbo, two town spirits protected the village and its inhabitants. Pa Kenoni, a "spirit of war" (ɔ-kərfi ka a-rəfa), inhabited a wooded area next to a coconut palm behind the houses and ancestor shrine (aŋ-boro-mə-sar) in Petbana's central nucleus, while his wife, aŋ-yarɔŋ, was a mermaid who lived in a pool behind a kolanut tree close by. Pa Kaper Bana maintained Petbana's relationship with these spirits until his death in 1991. When I returned to Petbana for my second period of fieldwork in 1989, he told me about the relationship between these spirits and the town's founding ancestors:

> *Those who started this town—Bay Rank and Bay Simbo Keti—met these spirits. Bay*
> *Sebora Nhoni* [the paramount chief] *met them too. Pa Manke. Kegbenki. Na Yeliru-*

nia, their sister. They own these spirits. They were both bush spirits. Pa Kenoni was the chief of war (ɔ-bay ŋa a-rəfa)—at that time, no warrior trying to hurt the town would succeed. Na Yelirunia saw aŋ-yarɔŋ. At that time, aŋ-yarɔŋ went all around the town, talking like a chicken. Then in the morning people found fish scales from her tail everywhere!

Not only did Pa Kenoni, "the chief of war," defend the town from human incursion in the past; he also maintained his defense of Petbana from the kind of intruders who (until the rebel war spread to the area in the late 1990s) were most salient in the late twentieth century—his fellow bush spirits, as well as witches. Twice a year, at harvest and bush-clearing time, Pa Kaper Bana offered a red cock (the color of war) with curly feathers to Pa Kenoni in the latter's area of bush, and gave a white chicken to aŋ-yarɔŋ at her kolanut tree. At the same time, he also gave a red cock and another chicken (of any color or sex) to the ancestors in the "house of stones" (aŋ-boro-mə-sar). Everyone in Petbana—with the exception of a few Muslims who had renounced all truck with the spirits—gave two cups of rice to Pa Kaper Bana for his ritual maintenance of the town's ties with its spirit hosts and defenders.

Like Pa Kenoni, the ancestors who protected the town did so—at least in part—as warriors. Earlier, when I returned to Petbana briefly in 1981, I found that the wife of the Poro association leader, Pa Yamba, had recently died after making a deathbed confession that she was a witch. Pa Yamba had then consulted a diviner, who prescribed a sacrifice *(as-athka)* to keep her witch-shade *(aŋ-mɔŋpila)* away from the house: he embedded seven tiny axes, each about an inch long, in a block of wood by the front door (plate 4). *"If her shade comes near,"* Pa Yamba told me, *"the ancestors will seize the axes and fight her off."* The ancestors' defence of the house, then, took the form of warfare in miniature, carried out with weapons appropriate to villagers protecting their endangered homes.

So while bush spirits raided towns and roamed the bush and roads, "seizing" unlucky and unprotected victims, and light-skinned water spirits bestowed money and commodities upon men in Faustian (and ultimately life-depleting) exchanges, the ancestors and town spirits defended the town as invisible warriors. I am not suggesting that bush spirits, town spirits, and ancestors had no other qualities and condensed no other meanings than those of warfare: these are complex, diverse, and multilayered beings. But I hope to have shown that bush and river spirits were not randomly wild. They seemed, in fact, to crystallize many of the attributes of those who raided or traded for slaves during the Atlantic and legitimate trades. Likewise, the ancestors and town spirits did not protect the town in an abstract, generalized manner, but did so in the very way in which the ancestors of countless towns did, in fact, defend their communities from attack by raiders while they were alive.

Thus the multiple possibilities of ambush, seizure, and incursion by spirits and (more intermittently) "short people" from the bush recapitulate patterns of attack prevalent in the eras of the Atlantic and legitimate trades. The ubiquitous and neighborly spirits of the early sixteenth and seventeenth centuries, whose "portraits" people carried "in their house, in their room, in their courtyard, at their door, in the clearings and fields where they grow their crops, on roads, at the sources of streams, in ports where they labour, and in their hearts," were not only banished to the bush in later centuries. They also turned rogue, transformed—with the exception of the domesticated town spirits—from cohabiting benefactors into largely destructive assailants. In their metamorphosis and their exclusion as external beings, they integrate the violence of the Atlantic and legitimate trades into place and space, turning the landscape into a memoryscape. Through them, I suggest, the perilous potential of the southern Temne landscape condenses historical experiences of raiding and warfare, siege and ambush, death and capture, down the centuries and beyond recorded number.

Closure and Darkness   But how did people live in such an environment, and how are their ways of living remembered? The violence of the slave-trade eras is, as we have seen above, evoked not only in the dangers of a memoryscape populated by marauding spirits but also in forms of ritual protection through which habitable human spaces are created and maintained. In the beginning of this chapter, I described how people protect themselves against incursion and seizure by spirits and witches through techniques of ritual Closure. These techniques, together with a further set of techniques known as Darkness *(aŋ-sum)*, recapitulate patterns of defence prevalent in the eras of the Atlantic and legitimate trades. The warnings I was given about closing windows and not venturing beyond the town at night likewise evoke the temporality of warfare, in which warriors usually attacked settlements at night (Abraham 1975: 129). Let me turn, then, to the techniques that confer protection against past and present forms of attack.

Closure creates a state of ritual impenetrability, while Darkness brings about ritual concealment. Each has a great deal in common with other techniques of ritual bulletproofing and invisibility in different parts of Africa. Yet in different regions, these techniques develop within particular local and regional histories. In Sierra Leone's past, the Atlantic and legitimate trades generated escalating imperatives for such forms of protection, constantly investing these practices with new salience. Any understanding of Temne practices of Closure and Darkness must begin, accordingly, with an appreciation of the ways in which space could be made (provisionally, but never absolutely) safe during the Atlantic and legitimate trades.

Historically, the prototype for protected space in this region has been the circular fortified town, encircled by one or more rings of defensive fences (and sometimes ditches) to repel attack. The Mane "invaders" who dominated Sierra Leone in the sixteenth and early seventeenth centuries built these towns as part of their military apparatus: when an English sea captain, Edward Fenton, visited Sierra Leone in 1582–83, he noted that "the Chiefest Town the K. of farme [the Mane ruler] hath is called Carrnorre. stronglie fortified with tymber: his forces be 10,000 persons with Bowes and arrowes, swordes and Targetts" (Taylor 1959: 103). Such fortifications were also used by local peoples as a defence against Mane "Bowes and arrowes, swordes and Targetts," as Alvares describes thirty years after Fenton: "How completely they [the Mane] carried out the oath they had taken to be the burial ground of their enemies! . . . (See,) now they clash and break down the stockades!" (1990 [c. 1615], 2, chap. 13: 5). Further south, in the Cape Mount area, Dapper tells us in 1668 that "the farmers have built their houses and dwellings in . . . fenced villages, or rather fortresses, in order to flee there in times of need" (quoted in Jones 1983: 169).

Concealment was another important form of defence. Alvares depicts one community's strategy in evading discovery by the Mane: " The fearful respect these savages have for the conquering (Manes) has made them so careful and cunning that, in order to conceal the path to their secret villages, they walk it backwards" (1990, 2, chap. 2: 2). He goes on to give an account of resistance among the Limba, describing their concealment in underground hiding-places: "They are astute and clever, and inclined to be warlike, hence their villages have underground places, in which they live with all the necessities of life when besieged. This is how they have preserved their independence (and avoided conquest by) the Mane" (1990, 2, chap. 2: 3). "Were these accounts just rumors?" a positivist historian might ask, skeptical about the existence of villages whose inhabitants lived underground or walked backwards. Yet even if they were, rumors are never "just" rumors. As White puts it, "the purpose of gossiping, rumormongering, and even talking is not to deliver information but to discuss it" (2000: 176): rumors tell us a great deal about the issues and concerns that are important to those who tell them. What is clear from Alvares's account is that concealment was a very salient concern during this conjunction of Mane domination and European trade nearly four centuries ago.

As the warfare associated first with the Atlantic trade and then with the legitimate trade intensified, the number of stockaded towns increased (plate 5). During the late-nineteenth-century trade wars, "fear of sudden attack hung constantly over many towns and villages; for there was no knowing where the warriors might strike next. People moved together and built strongly fortified centers (Ro Banka, in Temne) for their own defence" (Ijagbemi 1973: 40). They would leave these fortified towns during the day to go to their farms and would return to their protected interiors at night or when under attack. Some such towns were especially elaborate, as Fairtlough, the District Commissioner at Kwalu (in the south) describes:

> As a rule live trees are growing around the town at intervals of about three feet apart. They fill up these spaces with big slabs of wood, and lace them together with creepers and bush-ropes, making a solid wall about two feet thick, and from fifteen to eighteen feet high. On the top of this they place brushwood projecting outwards so as to prevent scaling. That is the inside fence; a solid mass. The next fence is rather more open and not nearly so thick: long poles and live trees in some cases. They make a sort of trellis with brushwood on the top. The third or outside fence is higher still. . . . In the spaces between the fences they dig holes and put sharpened stakes, supposed to be poisoned, in the bottom of them, and cover the whole over with loose brushwood. Outside on the paths leading up to the town they put sharpened bamboo splinters, poisoned.[6]

Those who constructed stockaded towns often used concealment as well as fortified enclosure as a form of defence. Nineteenth-century observers describe many such towns that were barely discernible from the outside, while those within them used a watchtower and a system of "loopholes" to see out. The English traveler Rankin, for example, found that the town of Magbele was "a fortified town" whose defence consisted not only of its surrounding wall but also "in the narrow paths approaching it through the forest, winding in many curves, and allowing the advance of a single man only at a time. They are generally blocked by vegetation. . . . The town is completely hidden from sight at a distance of a few yards" (1836: 237–38). Many Temne villages today still bear the name *ro-Mankane*, "the hiding place."

Like stockaded towns, warriors' bodies could also be fortified by a protective boundary. When Rankin was in Magbele, he saw Temne body armor that consisted of impressive radiating spikes:

> The war-dress of the Timmanee warrior has never been described: it is unique. As capture, and not slaughter, is the object of war, defensive armour is adopted accordingly. . . . Now, to avoid the iron grasp of the cunning adversary, who, hidden by a neighbouring tree, or beneath the fallen branches by the path-side, is ready to spring forward, seize the wanderer from behind, and throw him, the Timmanee arms himself like a porcupine. An iron-spike projects from each wrist, one from each elbow, one from the nape of the neck, and each heel wears a fearful spur; and from the back, where the most formidable attacks are made, projects another, secured by a leather belt around the waist. (1836: 242–43)

This armor created a defensive perimeter around the warrior analogous to the sharp stakes set into the trenches that often surrounded stockaded towns; the spikes turned the warrior's very body into a counteroffensive weapon against seizure by the "cunning adversary" in the bush.

Not all armor, however, was visible: "big persons" in the region have long been known for their capacity to render their bodies impervious to weapons. In the mid-nineteenth-century narrative of Korombo discussed in the previous chapter, Korombo the slave-dealing warrior had powers of impenetrability: "they were not able to kill him; they chopped him, (but) the cutlass did not enter (his body); they shot at him with a gun, (but) the balls did not hit him; and he was able to fly" (Schlenker 1861: 5). Korombo's body was Closed; his impenetrability, moreover, was linked to his capacity for violent penetration and to his extrahuman extension through powers of flight.

Ordinary people, in the meantime, used a range of strategies and ritual techniques to defend their own bodies against such predators as Korombo. When slave raiding escalated during the eighteenth and nineteenth centuries, travel was potentially a journey into death or disappearance, roads and rivers being channels along which those who raided for slaves might be moving. Ijagbemi tells us that during the nineteenth century,

> To travel from Yonibana to Petfu, or from Ronietta to Bathbana—distances of about five miles each—in those days, one might find it necessary to sleep on the way; because one could not travel along straightforward roads, for fear of falling into the hands of warrior parties. . . . Sometimes it would be necessary

to offer sacrifice before undertaking such journeys. If one was unlucky and fell into the hands of war parties on the way, one would be captured and sold into slavery. . . . Farmers and traders moved in groups, and carried arms and protective shebes (charms) with them. (1973: 40)[7]

The "shebes" *(ɛ-sɛbɛ)* that Ijagbemi mentions were protective amulets similar to those I describe at the beginning of this chapter. Some of these conferred the defensive containment of Closure, while others produced invisibility. Thus for those who needed to leave their town, traveling unarmed, unaccompanied, and on the open road—especially through areas of bush that could conceal a raiding party—was unthinkable: the best they could do was to enclose and conceal themselves. Like a carefully camouflaged stockaded town, the body was protected not only by ritual Closure but also by medicines producing the cloak of visual chaos called "Darkness" (aŋ-sum).[8]

As with techniques of Closure, techniques of Darkness were both "weapons of the weak" used by ordinary people to evade the predatory gaze of slave-raiders and warriors, and techniques of power and display used by the latter against the former. "Darkness medicine" (Temne *ka-woso*) does not cause its users to disappear into thin air, like the Invisible Man without his bandages, but prevents them from being seen by producing a veil of visual confusion around them. This is just one application of the multilayered concept of Darkness that denotes a range of contexts of concealment such as verbal secrecy, the hidden knowledge of ritual specialists, and the trance-like states these specialists sometimes enter (Shaw 1991).[9]

The Temne Poro cult, with its important historical role in the training of warriors and the organization and regulation of warfare and peace, is especially renowned for its control over states of Darkness through its medicines and its practices of verbal and ritual secrecy. The medicines enable Poro adepts to enter "crossed" *(pɔŋk)* states in which the distinction between this world *(nɔ-ru)* and the spirits' world *(ro-sɔki)* is collapsed, giving them miraculous capacities such as being unharmed when cut by weapons (an ability that they demonstrate in public performances by cutting themselves with knives). The color black is often used on ritual objects to denote Darkness, as Pa Sese, a diviner and Poro official I knew in Makeni in 1978 described to me:

Black (bi) *is a hiding place* (aŋ-maŋkanɛ)—*black or Darkness. If you have this kind of knowledge, others want to destroy you. This black can hide you from your enemies. The other meaning is "there the knowledge is." It is a secret* (aŋ-gbundu). *I can cut my arm, go into the hiding place, and when I come back there's no blood.*

These linked meanings of Darkness as powerful secret knowledge and as a hiding place from enemy attack are fitting, conveying nicely the duality of concealment as both a means of protection and a dangerous source of power wielded by cult officials.

In the late-twentieth-century landscape I knew before the spread of Sierra Leone's rebel war, the warfare of the nineteenth-century colonial period had been over for at least eighty years. During the intervening six decades of the Protectorate—Sierra Leone's second colonial period—circular stockaded towns had been prohibited by the British,[10] and had given way to ribbon development as towns moved and stretched in lines along the colonial roads and railway. In a striking parallel to the earlier construction of stockaded towns, however, diviners I knew from the 1970s to the early 1990s erected ritual defenses through techniques of ritual Closure that encircled bodies, houses, and farms with invisible defensive barriers. These defenses were (for the most part) not raised against human enemies but against incursion from spirits and witches. Yet the protection they afforded was sometimes likened, as we have already seen, to that of ancestors or warriors fighting to defend their town against enemy attack. Not only, then, did bush spirits take on the character of raiders, but they could also be kept at bay by ritual simulacra of the very defenses used against human raiders.

The protective Closure of the body against external penetration was a particular concern for many late-twentieth-century politicians, businessmen, and chiefs. These "big persons" and their kin often went to diviners and herbalists to "bulletproof" their bodies against attack from their political and commercial rivals. At that time it was not so much assassination attempts with ordinary guns or knives that were anticipated; the most insidious attacks were carried out invisibly with weapons known as "witch guns" (e-piŋkar a serɔŋ in Temne) that shoot tiny ritual missiles with deadly powers of penetration. To defend themselves, some big persons washed their bodies with medicine; some had steam baths over boiling infusions of herbs; some had an amulet (aŋ-sɛbɛ) made; and some commissioned short versions of a gown known as aŋ-roŋko, formerly worn only by chiefs and warriors. These gowns, as Opala (1982) has argued, appear to have their origin in Mande "war shirts" stamped with potent Arabic writing to render warriors impervious to weapons; in both Limba-speaking and Temne-speaking parts of Sierra Leone they are made by powerful diviners and blacksmiths, soaked in medicines, dyed reddish-brown with camwood, stamped with cryptic black symbols, and sewn with a pocket on the left-hand side containing dangerous medicines. The politicians' and businessmen's version of this shirt is a short vest concealed under the clothes to render the wearer's body impenetrable to both conventional and invisible weapons. Thus even in the absence of war, the Closure conferred by a war shirt and the idiom of shooting and bulletproofing were salient in relation to late-twentieth-century experiences of political and commercial rivalry.

Recently, in the rebel war that has been waged in Sierra Leone since 1991, techniques for the protection of the body have taken on a new and horrific relevance. Both Closure and Darkness are crucial techniques of defense for soldiers, rebels, civil militia fighters, and many civilians, who wear medicines that either repel bullets or produce a Darkness that enables wearers to see enemies before they themselves are seen. Such medicines take many forms: some wear a small horn filled with medicine sewn into their cap; some wear an amulet around their arm; some bite a special ring; some rub liquid medicine over their body; some simply repeat potent Islamic verses. Stories circulate about fighters who are suddenly obscured by visual chaos—strikingly similar to the "fog" Alvares describes nearly four centuries ago—as one or more people deploy their Darkness medicines. In 1992, my friend Michael related an account told to him by a soldier who had been on the war front: *"A Fula soldier from Guinea and a famous rebel leader were in combat, shooting at each other. The Fula grew tired of the shooting and used his medicine. Suddenly, everything became confused, and he disappeared."*

Pa Kaper Bana and the First World   So far, I have argued that the violence and terror of the centuries of slave raiding are remembered nondiscursively through meanings, images, and practices that shape the landscape into a memoryscape. The marauding attributes of bush spirits, the ominous nature of roads, techniques to protect human space through Closure and Darkness, and images of "short people" appearing out of the depths of the bush and attacking anyone they see during elections, can all be understood as mnemonic.

This does not mean, however, that they form a single, homogeneous body of ideas and practices that everyone shares in the same way. Most people I knew were Muslims or Christians (or both) who would talk about bush spirits as a reality; some, however, expressed skepticism about the existence of spirits; others acknowledged spirits' existence but emphasized that these beings should be kept at bay through prayer to God instead of through Closure medicines; and others again expressed both of these convictions in different contexts, and used Closure medicines anyway. Such "personal pluralism" was common. Most of those I knew owned some form of Closure medicine, but used a wide variety of techniques, objects, and substances. We should not, then, imagine social memory as a kind of unified Durkheimean *conscience collective* with powers of recall—a criticism to which Connerton's (1989) concept of social memory is vulnerable. At the same time, the fact that the meanings and practices that constitute social memories are diverse and often contested should not blind us to the fact that they are also shared, and that sharing does not imply uniformity (see Launay 1992). Unless this were so, meanings and practices could not be contested at all.

With these points in mind, I conclude with Pa Kaper Bana's narrative memory of the slave-trading past and its chronotopic materialization in the landscape. Here the violence of slave raiding is recalled discursively, and it is understood not only to have left traces in the present landscape but also to have brought about the physical destruction of an earlier world. Pa Kaper Bana combined his duties as ritual subchief of Bombali Sebora chiefdom with his own allegiance to Methodism, and his story has a somewhat Christian apocalyptic flavor: this is very much *his* narrative.

When I returned to Petbana in 1989, he began to talk to me about the town's past, often reciting lists of ancestors. He did not, however, recount any narratives. Then one evening, sitting with him on his veranda, I told a Temne story of the creation of the world that the missionary Schlenker had collected in mid-nineteenth-century Port Loko. Schlenker's text is as follows:

> Our fathers did not tell us much about the creation of the world, they only told us that when God made the world, he put it on the head of a giant, who was below (it). This person carries the world on the head. . . . He, on whose head the world was put before, has died, and another man carries this world again on the head. When they put the world on him, he was in a sitting posture, and turned towards the East. They told us that this person turns himself, but that he turns softly, so that people cannot know it; except that time when he turns towards the West, then men know it; because at that time there arises an earthquake, so that houses and trees fall down. At that time when this person falls down, and dies, the whole world is at an end, and every thing in this world will perish. (1861: 12–15)

Pa Kaper Bana immediately responded, *"It is true."* When I asked him if he knew the story, he said he did. He delayed telling me his version, however, until the very morning of my departure, and asked me to make a libation of palm wine to the ancestors first: the narrative was one that concerned them. This narration, then, was framed by what Bellman (1984) calls "the doing of secrecy," the creation of a separate context of meaning by bracketing a situation from everyday discourse.

Pa Kaper began to tell me of a different world and time, a distinct spatio-temporal universe that he called the "First World" *(a-daru da-tɔtɔkɔ or aŋ-yanama a-tɔtɔkɔ)*. Although Pa Kaper did not tell a creation story, he described an earlier world that—as in the story in Schlenker's collection—ultimately ended in annihilation. In depicting this First World, the dominant images Pa Kaper Bana used were those of a landscape marked by the constant terror and danger of slave raiding. The roads in particular were channels for the disappearance and commodification of the most defenseless of the First World's inhabitants:

> *If a child is born, and he follows this road, him alone, and meets a warrior, he* [the warror] *will seize him* [the child] *and sell him. He will say, "Pa Road, lend me this one." He will seize him, gbap! The one who bore him, if he/she approaches there, he will cut his/her head off. . . . The first world in the old days, it was an angry world* (a-daru ra-baŋ).

Popular African images of the road as a bringer of death and an insatiable consumer of human lives are, as several scholars have documented (Auslander 1993; Bastian 1992; Masquelier 1992; Weiss 1996: 179–201; White 1993 and 2000), potent metaphors for an "immoral economy" of colonial and postcolonial commerce and transport. Pa Kaper Bana's account suggests that, in Sierra Leone, at least, such images have even deeper historical roots, drawing upon a slave-raiding past in which associations between death, "bad" forms of commerce, and the terrors of "Pa Road"—a personalized, malevolent entity in his account—were all too clear.

The First World was the setting for encounters between Europeans and Bay Bureh, the hero of the Hut Tax War that followed the imposition of the British Protectorate:

> *When Bay Bureh was sitting down* [was in power], *he took the white people and made them scare the birds!* [Laughs] *An angry world.*

Bird scaring is the children's task when the rice is growing: Bay Bureh's power, then, was such that he was able to force even the British to perform demeaning farm work—an image that generated laughter. Yet the premise for this comic image was a morally irreparable world of persistent violence: an *"angry world."*

Children, who were so vulnerable to warriors on the road, could only survive under the protection of their own town's warriors, as well as by containment and concealment within the town. Pa Kaper Bana continued:

> In that world, small children like this [indicates a child], when they are in the town, if day breaks, you won't see them. You won't see a child like this, unless a warrior is behind that child. The warrior will hold the cutlass, because he is able to defend the [child's] life.

Human life in this *"angry world"* was lived in precarious spaces that were in constant need of defence. Not only social space but also social time was at issue, moreover, for the succession of generations was rendered insecure by the dangers to which children growing up in this environment were subject.

The First World, according to Pa Kaper Bana, was separated from the one in which he lived by a cataclysm from God (K-uru), who turned the earth over and destroyed its "angry" inhabitants:

> RS: How did this first world end?
>
> PKB: It was taken and turned over (lafthɛ). The first things, all the bad ones, they were pressed underneath. He [K-uru] started again, a new world. The people of the older days were short, short, short, short, short! They were the ones who disappeared, yɛn! The first people, those short people, they came and troubled the world. That was why K-uru turned them over. He made a new world again.

Motifs of the destruction of an earlier world by earthquake or fire recur in other parts of West Africa (see, e.g., Arazu 1978: 177) and may be part of a regional set of cosmological images. The nineteenth-century narrative from Schlenker's collection that I told Pa Kaper Bana, in which an earlier world was destroyed by earthquake when the earth turned toward the west instead of the east (1861: 13), shares with Pa Kaper's account the image of a reversal and inversion of the land itself.

At the same time, Pa Kaper's images also draw upon biblical themes of apocalypse, divine punishment, and new creation.[11] He did not feel that his Methodist Christianity was at odds with his office as the chiefdom's ritual subchief, and he often juxtaposed and synthesized Christian and Temne ideas and practices. Earlier, for instance, he had told me that the First World had ended in flood—a version that retains the image of destruction by covering the land. In addition, one of the two terms he used for the First World, aŋ-yanama a-tɔtɔkɔ, incorporates the Mande/Arabic loan word for Hell *(aŋ-*

yanama) used by both Muslims and Christians, combining very effectively both the moral dread and the present subterranean location of that *"angry world."* Both the Christian and West African imagery thereby convey a spatialized "horizontal" break in the flow of time from past to present.

This break in continuity was also vividly conveyed by Pa Kaper Bana's images of the fierce inhabitants of the First World—people who were physically different from human beings today. No-one who committed the acts against other people that characterized the First World, the implication seems to be, could have had an ordinary human form. As in the magical flight and physical impenetrability of Korombo the slave-dealer, such actions are registered in the body itself, which takes on animal qualities appropriate to the bush:

> RS: *Those people of the First World, were they different from us?*
> PKB: *They were like chimpanzees. If you look around, the ones you see of that First World, they were people who had hair on their skin, like the chimpanzee. They were not of the same height as us. The first people were short, short, short, short. But you could not confront them. That is why K-uru covered their world.*

Pa Kaper Bana went on to tell me that Bay Farma Tami (the sixteenth-century Mane leader), Bay Bureh (the leader of the nineteenth-century Hut Tax War), and Bay Simbo Keti (his own ancestor, the founder of Petbana Masimbo), all shared these strange, nonhuman features: *"Bay Bureh, when you look at his beard, it is thick like a forest, not so? Even the hair in his ears, it was long—isn't that how you see him?"* And *"Bay Farma Tami, if you see him, he looks like ka-rushi* [a species of monkey]. *Like the hair of ka-rushi."* "Like chimpanzees," furthermore, these First World people were *"short, short, short, short."* This characteristic suggests a connection to the short, fierce people from the deep bush who were sometimes described to me as emerging during elections to attack people. In this image, the pursuit of political power by postcolonial "big persons" *(aŋ-fəm a bana)* draws out the latent presence of beings from the depths of the bush whose own "angry" world is evoked by the potential for violence in this one.

But there is nevertheless ancestral continuity between that world and this one. Bay Simbo Keti and those others who founded Petbana by clearing the bush, cultivating the land, and fighting to defend it from enemy incursion, are the ancestors *(aŋ-bɛmba)* of the dominant lineages *(ɛ-bɔŋsɔ)* in the town today:

> *If we are able to see this world today, we bless our people. These are the people that I have told you about. Pa Gbay Rok. Pa Me Yanke. Pa Theren. Pa Gbenki. Pa Kaferi. Pa Mansa*

Kelonko. They fought the war in this land. Because of that, we are able to live. . . . They made the land. When they finished, we remain. Their layer (aŋ-dɛk) *has passed.*

The term *aŋ-dɛk*—a loan word from the English "deck"—is normally used for the floors of two-story houses, as well as for the seven levels of heaven and of the underworld in Islamic cosmology. Its use in Pa Kaper Bana's narrative implies, as did God's turning over the earth, a sense of the past as a sedimented spatial layer qualitatively different from the present, of a "horizontal" break between that world and Pa Kaper's own. Yet his ending also emphasizes continuity and resilience through the "vertical" connections that linked Petbana to the ancestors he named. Earlier, Pa Kaper had invoked their names when he instructed me to pour them a libation of palm wine before he began the story, and his conclusion now completed his framing of the narrative of the First World within their ancestral presence.

Pa Kaper's narrative memory tells us that traces of the turbulent, slave-raiding past persist—but only as dead, buried remnants of old pots and other artifacts that are sometimes unearthed when building a house or digging a well. Instead of the raiding spirits or the "short people" who attack during elections—both of whom actively "presence" the animate qualities of enemies and warriors in a living part of the landscape—Pa Kaper's narrative places a spatiotemporal break between the First World *"pressed underneath"* and the present world above. Given the power of verbally discursive memory to connect us to that which we remember—and therefore potentially to draw the First World to us—it is not surprising that Pa Kaper delayed before telling me this narrative or that he ritually framed it with the ancestors' presence. By invoking the ancestors, he effectively performed a verbal Closure, containing the angry inhabitants of the First World through the power of the very people who had fought them in their own time and place.

Conclusion   The dislocation and terror of the Atlantic and legitimate trades are, I argue, embodied in the memoryscape I knew in various ways. They are remembered through their incorporation into existing cosmological forms; yet in the process, those forms seem to have changed beyond recognition. The transformations of the slave trade are registered in a transformation of the landscape from one inhabited by spirits who were neighbors to one pervaded by spirits who were raiders. And alongside the permanent presence of marauding spirits, there is also the intermittent presence of short, ferocious people from the deep bush who emerge during elections, when the threat of violence has been all too imminent.

The violence of the past is also remembered through ritual practices of Darkness and Closure—techniques similar to others in many areas of Africa, but forming part of a habitus that "produces history on the basis of history" (Bourdieu 1990: 56) in particular regions. In this part of the upper Guinea coast during the centuries of the Atlantic trade and legitimate trade, the necessity for concealment and impenetrability—living with the rumors and realities of raids, inhabiting stockaded and hidden settlements, farming areas of bush that might conceal slave-raiding enemies, traveling along hidden and difficult paths, and avoiding direct roads and rivers upon which agents of death might be moving—gave understandings of Darkness and Closure a historical and regional specificity, shaping the landscape into a mnemonic space of disappearance and the body into a hidden fortress.

Finally, through his more discursive narrative memory, Pa Kaper Bana, the Methodist ritual subchief, depicted a different transformation. Instead of the negative changes undergone by spirits of the land during the course of the slave trade, Pa Kaper tells of an apocalypse that brought an end to the "angry" world created by the slave trade. For Pa Kaper, the era of slave-raiding was remembered in a semi-biblical form, in images of divine judgment, of past apocalypse, of the earth's upheaval, and of a discontinuous past that is literally buried underground. These late-twentieth-century images and ritual forms were more than anachronistic "survivals" of a past landscape. Through them, the past was embodied as an active presence in practices and perceptions of the landscape—"internalized as a second nature and so forgotten as history" (Bourdieu 1990: 56)—that shape the present.

Postscript   Since Pa Kaper's death in 1991, the rebel war that began in that year meant that violence and terror became much more than memories. The landscape—especially the roads and the bush—again became one of disappearance and death, where many have been slaughtered and mutilated, and teenagers and children have been abducted into new forms of slavery as fighters or sex slaves. The raiders emerging from the bush to burn and loot villages and towns were not spirits or short bush people, but rebels and other fighters. Enclosure in fortified towns was no longer an option when some of these marauders were armed with automatic weapons and rocket-propelled grenades. Instead, massive numbers of Sierra Leoneans have had to leave their communities for enclosure in displacement camps within the country and in refugee camps in neighboring Guinea. Pa Kaper Bana's First World returned in an even "angrier" form than before, turning his images of a past apocalypse into a nightmarish reality.

In many parts of the world, postcolonial violence and terror are experienced through images of apocalypse in which a dis-membered present is torn from a harmonious memory environment of the past (De Boeck 1998). Yet, as Pa Kaper's narrative and the practical memories I have explored bear witness, experiences of death, disjunction, and even annihilation also form part of both nondiscursive and specialized discursive memories of Sierra Leone's past. Terrible as it has been, the rebel war is just the most recent (although undoubtedly the worst) of a series of "apocalypses."

In noting this, however, we also need to pay attention to the ways in which, to quote Cole once more, people "have developed mechanisms through which they are able to re-member themselves again and again" (1998: 628). Although those in the Temne-speaking communities I knew from the 1970s to the 1990s carried practical memories of invisible raiders from the bush, they had also succeeded in "re-membering" themselves as moral communities after the slave trade and colonialism, maintaining through discursive memory the sense of ancestral continuity that I found when I arrived in Matotoka and Petbana, and with which Pa Kaper ended his story of apocalypse. Perhaps, even after the literal dismemberments of bodies and families during the rebel war, people may be able to re-member themselves again.

Roads to Life, Roads to Death

Materializing Memory through Divination

Early in my fieldwork, other foreign scholars conducting research in Sierra Leone were occasionally puzzled by my interest in Temne divination. *"Those techniques of divination,"* one told me, *"they're not Temne, they're all Mande!"* Another remarked: *"The Temne don't really have a culture; they've borrowed it from other people."* Temne ritual specialists did not, however, share these views of cultural authenticity: *"it's ours because we borrowed it,"* they often replied when I asked if a particular cultural practice had originated from another group. Most anthropologists and historians today, steeped for nearly two decades in studies of hybridity and in critiques of reified concepts of ethnicity and primordialist ideas of culture, would probably agree with these ritual specialists' understandings of what makes a cultural practice "theirs." All the techniques of divination *(ka-thupǝs)* that are the subject of this chapter were originally brought by Mande migrants and are variants of the many forms of Muslim divination circulating in Africa and in other parts of the Muslim world. Yet as I wish to show, these transregional techniques are often made to recall a local past through their reworking by Temne diviners.

African divination systems have often been viewed as producing a construction of wholeness, harmony, and continuity through ritual processes that root the present in the time of the ancestors. But Temne divination practices invoke a less straightforward history—as the above remarks about their presumed cultural "inauthenticity" suggest. First and most obviously, the hybrid character of these divination techniques materializes a hegemonizing process through which Temne communities were Islamicized and "Mandeized" as Mande and Fula political power developed in the region.[1] Second and less obviously, moreover, these divination techniques often embody and rework images of the landscape shaped by the slave- raiding past that I examined in the previous chapter. If Temne divination constitutes a form of social memory, then, it is very different from that which De Boeck describes for divination in Congo, the latter conveying an "ideologically important vision of the unchanging continuity of the cultural order in the natural and social world" (1998: 43).[2]

Divination Practices   In this chapter, I am concerned with everyday techniques of divination. These include aŋ-bɛrɛ ("the river pebbles"), in which small river pebbles (and sometimes cowrie shells) are cast, built up into a pattern, and interpreted; aŋ-mɛmnɛ ("the looking glass"), in which the diviner communicates with spirits who appear in a hand mirror; ta-faŋt ("the cowrie shells"), in which cowries are thrown and the pattern of their fall interpreted;[3] aŋ-thasabiya ("the rosary"), in which the diviner counts off beads from a Muslim rosary and then looks up the meaning of the number obtained in an Arabic divination book; ka-sɔŋt ("the sand"), in which marks made in a small heap of sand are "read";[4] aŋ-ramɔli, in which the diviner makes, then interprets, patterns of dots on an Arabic slate (aŋ-walka); aŋ-sarafilo, in which a small woven mat weighted at the far end moves or stands still in answer to the diviner's questions;[5] aŋ-listikar, in which the answer to the client's problem is revealed in the diviner's dreams; and aŋ-yina Musa, in which the diviner (or an assistant) gazes into a mirror placed on top of an Arabic diagram and a bowl of medicine, enters a trance, and communicates with a spirit called "the Jinn of Musa." Most diviners (aŋ-thupɔs) I knew practiced between one and three of these methods.

These techniques are practiced in small, typically private sessions that normally take place in a side room of the diviner's house, behind closed doors. Most clients want to keep their problems (and often their identities) hidden: many, as we shall see in chapter 6, are married women who travel outside their husband's town to consult a diviner without the knowledge of those in their marital home. But it is not only because of their clients' needs for confidentiality that diviners hold their ritual consultations in private rooms: conducting divination outside, in space that is uncontained and unprotected by medicines of Closure, makes a diviner vulnerable to attack by dangerous spirits and witches. Most diviners I knew would not even discuss divination in open places: my conversations with diviners, consequently, usually took place in small, closed, airless rooms.

The hidden rituals of private divination contrast with less everyday forms of divination that are performed as a public spectacle in the open space of the town. These latter are rituals to identify witches, thieves, and adulterers, and are known by a separate term—*ma-thǝn*, "the splitting," as in the splitting open of a container to reveal the hidden contents within. They are the special preserve of diviners successful enough to have obtained a government license, and are the subject of chapter 7. One technique of divination—aŋ-yina Musa mediumship, which concludes my outline of divination techniques above— falls in between these two poles of hidden enclosure and public disclosure. An expensive and prestigious form of divination, it is normally carried out on behalf of relatively wealthy persons, such as chiefs and successful farmers and traders. Diviners usually conduct it in a house's central parlor, a semi-public place in which visitors are received and doors to the outside are usually left open. Yet unlike the public techniques of "splitting a divination," aŋ-yina Musa is not concerned with the ritual accusation of specific wrongdoers; along with the more everyday forms of divination outlined above, it is used to diagnose the underlying cause *(aŋ-sabu)* of individuals' problems and the prescription of remedial ritual and medicine. Accordingly, I include it in this chapter.

One of the most obvious ways in which the past is embedded in Temne divination techniques lies in their Mande and Islamic origins, as I shall discuss below. But what do we know of divination in this area before these Muslim Mande techniques became established?

"Fetish-Men who Throw Lots"   At the turn of the sixteenth century, before the ascendancy of Muslim ritual specialists, Temne-speaking diviners used techniques that Fernandes described as "throwing lots":

> In the case of sickness they have no medicine nor know its rules, and only if someone is sick they go to the fetish-men *(feyticeyros)* who throw lots to know why he is sick; they always find that it is the idols *(os ydolos)* who send the sickness, and order that to him should be sacrificed a dog, a goat, or a chicken, for these are the animals they are accustomed to sacrifice. (Fernandes 1951 [1506–10]: 86–89, trans. David Beach and Jeanne Penvenne).

We do not know, however, what kinds of "lots" were thrown by these "fetish men." Writing a century later, the Portuguese missionary Alvares is more specific in his account of a technique used by early-seventeenth-century diviners to diagnose illness and identify the human agent responsible:

> They have various . . . forms of divination, but we need not discuss them all. . . . When they take to their beds, the first thing they do is to consult *Accaron*.[6] Like Ocosias, they send messengers to the most famous sorcerers, who put a thousand lies into their heads. The sorcerer, this servant of hell, puts on the fire a small pan containing a little water. When the water begins to boil, he asks the devil if the sick man is going to die. If the boiling dies down, this is a sign he will live; or if the water cools down, he will die a natural death. But, should the boiling continue, in order to find out if anyone is giving him poison or is otherwise responsible for his death, the sorcerer names the man's relatives. If the water sinks back when one is named, he is not to blame; but if it boils over, they consider that the person named is the guilty one. (Alvares 1990 [c. 1615], 2, chap. 3: 4)

The technique Alvares describes of the pan and the water that boils with an intensity controlled by a spirit ("the devil") is, to my knowledge, no longer practiced, although in both divination and healing, heat and coolness have remained significant as materializations of sickness and health, danger and peace, anger and goodwill. And water, as we shall see, remains prominent in Temne divination today, as most diviners' tutelary spirits are river spirits.

This link between water and divination spirits is also evident in what Alvares tells us of a Christian convert called Cube who was formerly a diviner. Cube used to consult his tutelary spirit by throwing a pebble into water:

> This evil spirit gave Cube a pebble so that he could invoke him, and then the spirit hurried to him. . . . Cube threw the pebble into a container with water to perform the cursed invocation, and gain knowledge of anything he wanted to know. "If the pebble floats," said the devil, "do not be content; but if it sinks again, this is a sure sign that what you are seeking will come true." This form of consulting the future, see. The pebble is the chief devil. They have given to any *More* the faculty of being *bana*, and all have a pact with the devil, and see him in material form. They believe that the *Corofins* can obtain favours for them from God; they give them everything so that they can gain a share and learn to know the future. (Alvares 1990, 2, chap. 5: 4–5, note [c])

Again, this form of divination is—to my knowledge—no longer practiced.[7] But like Cube's spirit, diviners' tutelary spirits today are usually enshrined in a pebble (a river pebble, in fact), are associated with water, and are known by the same term for "spirits" (aŋ-kərfi) as that used by Alvares ("the *Corofins*").

Cube had apparently been a successful diviner and healer, because he had healed the powerful Mane king at that time, whose title (like that of the sixteenth-century Mane leader who first occupied this area) was Bay Farma:

> Farma sent for Cube in order to cure him, Cube was afraid. The evil angel tells him: "Fear not and go, for today you will achieve power over the king." So Cube went, and to the great amazement of all, cured the king within 4 days. While there he carried out various tricks in front of his hosts, through the skill of his devil. (ibid.)

Cube's capacity to heal the sick king derived from forces embodied in objects from the local landscape: he was guided by a tutelary spirit ("the evil angel"; "his devil") enshrined in a stone, and he healed with medicinal plants.

Alvares also writes that ritual specialists of a different kind—Muslim clerics and healers called *"bexeris"*—had developed special relationships with rulers on the coast further north:

> The Moors have brought the infernal sect of the infamous prophet, and these grandees are so spell-bound by the ministers of this false sect that the kings do nothing of importance without their counsel. When they go to war or despatch armies, apart from covering their shirts, shields and bows with large numbers of amulets, and encasing their arms with others and hanging some from their necks, (the *bexeris*) prepare for them certain medicines which, the *bexeris* say and the kings believe, if carried provide a royal assurance against loss of life. (The *bexeris*) affirm this, not because they believe it or think it true but, as they admit to some of the Portuguese, because it affords a means to keep in the good graces of these grandees, so that by attending in this way to what the grandees want to hear the *bexeris* obtain the best part of their lands. (Alvares 1990, 1, chap. 1: 9)

Although these Muslim specialists were not yet as influential in the Sierra Leone of Alvares's time, Mande Muslim clerics were well known in the latter region as "great wanderers, roaming everywhere" (Alvares 1990, 2, chap. 26: 24). One of them, a "wise *bexerim*" called Cimba Famore, paid a visit to Alvares in order to meet a fellow specialist in the knowledge of God (24 and op. cit., "Annual Report": 13–15). Alvares also tells us that another such specialist (whom he calls a *"moze"*) cured Bay Farma's son Sertua of smallpox, but incurred the latter's wrath when he took a shirt as his due for a ritual offering he had either prescribed or performed: "Sertua was scandalized," Alvares comments, "and believed that these clerics are self-seeking, as indeed they are" (Alvares 1990, 1, chap. 3: 7, note [a]). And finally we are told that the tutelary spirit of Cube the diviner—"the chief devil" according to Alvares's early-seventeenth-century Jesuit cosmology—has "given to any *More* the faculty of being *bana*." *ɔ-mɔre* is the Temne term for a Mande Muslim ritual specialist, which, with the addition of *-bana* ("big" or "great"), becomes "great Muslim cleric." Alvares's use of this term in connection with capacities conferred by the tutelary spirit in Cube's pebble could suggest that as early as the beginning of the seventeenth century, foreign Muslim specialists and their techniques were becoming integrated into the local ritual landscape. It was in the eighteenth and nineteenth centuries, however, that the Islamic ritual knowledge of specialists like Sertua's healer became hegemonic.

The Islamicization of Oracles   In Petbana Masimbo, my host during my 1978 fieldwork was Pa Alfa Koroma, a widely renowned Muslim diviner in the area. Pa Koroma was the great-grandson of a Muslim Mandinka cleric, Pa Alhayi (Alhaji) Koroma, *"the mɔrebana* [big mɔre], *who went to Mecca,"* as he is remembered. Pa Alhayi had come from Moria, a small Mande kingdom founded in the early eighteenth century and centered on the town of Furikaria, in the present-day Republic of Guinea (see Skinner 1989: 92–94; 1997a: 3–4). He originally settled in Petbana at the invitation of the Kalokohs, one of the ruling lineages in Bombali Sebora chiefdom. They wanted him to help them in their succession to the chieftaincy, which rotated among the ruling lineages: *"because the chieftaincy is a matter of spirits,"* Pa Moses Kalokoh told me, *"the mɔre and the chief had one mind: where the chief was, the mɔre was."* Pa Alhayi built his house at the edge of town, forming the nucleus for a new part of Petbana that was thereafter known as "Moria" as a reminder of the mɔrebana's distinguished external origins (plate 6).

Migrant Muslim ritual specialists like Pa Alhayi played an important part in the spread of Islam in the Sierra Leone hinterland (see Skinner 1978; Turay 1971: 65). Foreign Muslims have been coming to the Sierra Leone hinterland for centuries, mostly as ritual specialists and traders drawn by interregional commerce (Fyle 1979b; Howard 1997), including the slave trade (Jones 1983: 75–77) and subsequently trade with the Colony of Sierra Leone (Skinner 1997a). They came in especially large numbers in the eighteenth and nine-

teenth centuries, when Muslim Mande and Fula peoples founded new, powerful states to the north, most notably that established by Karamoko Alfa's jihad
in Futa Jallon in 1747–48. From these states, Muslim clerics called aŋ-mɔre
(if Mande-speaking) or aŋ-ləfa (if Fula) in Temne—clerics who taught the
Qur'an, divined, healed, made written amulets (ε-sεbε) and prepared liquid
Qur'anic medicine *(ma-nasi)*—came and settled in Temne-speaking towns
and villages. Temne chiefs sought to incorporate the foreign power of Islamic
knowledge by inviting these specialists to become their personal diviners and
healers: like the *"bexeris"* farther north up the coast whom Alvares castigated
in the early seventeenth century, these specialists became ritual advisers to
Temne rulers and made amulets and war medicines for them.[8] The considerable religious and political influence of these Muslim specialists is described
in this late-eighteenth-century account:

> In the villages of the tribes around them they erect schools, and teach their
> young gratis, to read and write Arabic; and their missionaries, by temporizing
> with the prevailing follies and foibles of the different nations they visit; by
> assuming to themselves the sanctity and authority of the servants of God; by
> abstaining from all strong liquors; and, above all, by pretending to have power
> over every species of witchcraft; and, by their trade in making charms, do so
> insinuate themselves into the confidence of the chiefs and principal people;
> that I have never visited a town in this part of Africa where I did not find a
> Mandingo man as prime minister, by the name of *bookman,* without whose
> advice nothing was transacted. (Matthews 1966 [1788]: 68–68)

Through the influence of these "bookmen" (and the potent political presence
of the states from which they had come), Islamic knowledge acquired an authority that came to supersede that of local diviners and healers.

The itinerant specialists whom Matthews and others describe were often
encouraged to settle through an offer of marriage with a woman from one of
the ruling lineages in a chiefdom. One of the most renowned of such "strangers" *(aŋ-tik)* was Mori Bundu, a Fula specialist who made amulets for Gumbu
Smart, a wealthy Loko trader and powerful political leader on the Rokel river
in late-eighteenth-century Temneland. Later, Mori Bundu married a daughter
of Naimbana, the Regent Chief of the western Temne chiefdom of Koya. After
settling in the Koya town of Foredugu, Bundu became one of the wealthiest
and most powerful men in the region: "As an outstanding Mori-man," Ijagbemi writes, "his personal prestige and influence was great over the sur-

rounding chiefs including Smart" (1968: 55). In addition to mediating for Temne chiefs the powerful Islamic knowledge of Mande and Fula elites, the literacy and mobility of Muslim specialists were often translated into forms of political mediation through letter-writing and ambassadorial roles (Skinner 1978: 44).

Some aŋ-mɔre actually became subchiefs. Pa Ansumana Fonike, for example, "a Mori-man from Sankara" (Ijagbemi 1968: 190) in the early nineteenth century, was given the position of Muslim subchief (u-ləmami) in the town of Rokel after he had made amulets for the ruler of the Temne chiefdom of Masimera at that time. Through their marriage to women from ruling houses, moreover, the children of these strangers acquired land and chiefly status via their mother's lineage (ma-kara; see Turay 1971: 63)—a link that is given considerable weight in Temne cognatic kinship practices.[9]

Thus incorporated into ruling elites, these foreign specialists did not try to erase the ritual practices they found when they settled in Temne towns: "The willingness to accept chieftaincy," as Turay writes, "also meant a willingness to accept traditional customs, the result being a large-scale adaptation of Islamic concepts to traditional Temne customs" (1971: 63–64; and see Skinner 1978). At the same time, however, Muslim hegemony developed through Mande and Fula ritual specialists' appropriation of divination, healing, and amulet-making. These specialists promoted their literate Islamic knowledge, with its esoteric books of divination and dream-interpretation, as a superior counterpart to the earlier forms of Temne divination and healing with which they were competing. Their medicine and amulets—ma-nasi, the liquid words of written Arabic verses washed off a wooden slate, and ɛ-sɛbɛ, Arabic diagrams inscribed on pieces of paper that are folded, sewn up, or encased in leather— were added to, and sometimes supplanted, Temne medicines made with plants and other local ritual substances (aŋ-tɔl and ma-fɔy).

Muslim techniques of divination—the Qur'anic slate, aŋ-walka; Muslim prayer beads, aŋ-thasabiya; the sand, ka-sǝŋt; "the jinn of Musa," aŋ-yina Musa, and many others—were introduced with claims of superior efficacy over non-Muslim forms. In most of these techniques, diviners employed objects from the material technology of Muslim prayer and Qur'anic learning— prayer beads, the wooden slate, the prayer mat, and written Arabic letters and words—as vehicles for communication with Allah and his intermediaries. In addition to being thereby imbued with the power of Muslim prayer and the prestige of transregional literate knowledge, the potency of these techniques was also underscored by the political and military might of the northern states from which they came, and by the wealth of the Mande and Fula traders who traveled and settled throughout the Sierra Leone hinterland. In order to compete with these foreign specialists, Temne-speaking diviners and herbalists adopted their techniques, their material culture of prayer, and (to varying degrees) their knowledge of written Arabic.

The literate Muslim diviners I knew continued to make claims of the superiority of Muslim ritual power over local forms. Such power entails the knowledge of esoteric secrets—even of *"all the secrets in the world,"* as Pa Santigi, a diviner and Muslim subchief explained during my 1989 stay in Petbana. He told me of the amazing power of a body of occult Muslim knowledge called *aŋ-lasərar*, whose name derives from *asrar*, the Arabic term for "secrets":

> It's a *"learning"* (ka-karaŋ). *You can't teach it to women, or they'll destroy their co-wives. All the secrets in the world will not be secrets* [if you learn it]: *you will know them. Those who learn it are aŋ-ləfa* [Muslim specialists]; *they can cause madness, and cure it, by making amulets* (ɛ-sɛbɛ) *and liquid Islamic medicine* (ma-nasi). *It's a book. You can use it to kill a part of a person's body, and to make an enemy move. You can make someone mute for ever, and can move a whole house from one place to another. With aŋ-bɛrɛ* [river pebble divination], *you learn some secrets, but not all the secrets in the world. Only with aŋ-lasərar can you learn all the secrets in the world.*
>
> *If you do this aŋ-Lasərar for someone, some do it in the town, some in the bush, some thigh-deep in water, for seven days. You use the long rosary beads* (aŋ-thasabiya). *You take four books. You draw a circle around yourself in the bush, with white rice flour* (ka-bo). *You can call wild animals to come and lie down in front of you. You can call bush spirits—you can even call them into the town.*
>
> *I've seen a Muslim specialist* (ɔ-ləfa) *use this. There was a crocodile catching people in the town, and they called ɔ-ləfa to catch it. He sat in a house and called the crocodile three days after he started an-Lasərar. In the morning, it came out of the river into the town, right up onto the veranda. He told the crocodile to open its mouth, and it did. He put an amulet inside. People wanted to kill the crocodile, but the man said "no." It went back to the river, and he told the people that they wouldn't see that crocodile again. The next day, they saw the crocodile by the side of the river, dead.*

Thus local ritual techniques such as aŋ-bɛrɛ divination are not rejected as incommensurable with aŋ-Lasərar, but are subsumed within the latter's totalizing frame in a relationship of part to whole. One who knows aŋ-Lasərar can overturn the foundations of the world we know—of that which holds a house in a particular place, and which makes the human body and mind work properly. The local landscape is encompassed by the specialist's control of the potent Muslim text: thus beings that embody power and danger—wild animals and bush spirits—are rendered powerless and domesticated, effectively erasing the difference between bush and town. Through accounts such as this one, knowledge of textual Muslim secrets is depicted as the key to omniscience and mastery.

These hegemonizing claims are highly gendered: Pa Santigi began by claiming: *"You can't teach* [aŋ-Lasərar] *to women, or they'll destroy their co-wives."* Throughout my fieldwork, I heard repeated claims from Muslim specialists and others that it was dangerous for women to know "too much" literate Muslim knowledge. Although women were encouraged to pray, and many girls were given a basic Qur'anic education alongside boys in the village schools I knew, Muslim claims about the dangers of Islamic ritual knowledge in the hands of women placed women at a disadvantage if they wished to learn Islamic divination techniques. The few female diviners I knew (with one notable exception, Ya Yebu, who will be introduced in chapter 4) used the techniques of "the river pebbles" (aŋ-bɛrɛ), "the looking glass" (aŋ-mɛmnɛ), and "the cowrie shells" (ta-faŋt), which are less directly associated with Arabic literacy and Muslim prayer than are techniques such as aŋ-listikar, aŋ-yina Musa, aŋ-walka, and aŋ-thasabiya. Thus while we know little or nothing about female diviners before the eighteenth century, it seems likely that this Islamic ritual transformation entailed the dissemination of a strongly gendered discourse about the maleness of esoteric Muslim knowledge.

Finally, although diviners—like their early-sixteenth-century counterparts whom Fernandes describes above—continued to prescribe remedial sacrifices, the kinds of offerings they made were transformed by Muslim Mande practices. Fernandes tells us at the turn of the sixteenth century, remember, that people gave "the idols" offerings of dogs, goats, and chickens, "for these are the animals they are accustomed to sacrifice." Chickens have remained perennially suitable, but dogs have ceased to be used, and goat sacrifices have come to be given a more negative moral significance as apotropaic defenses against witches. Instead, sheep have become the preferred—but often prohibitively costly—sacrificial animals for Muslims and non-Muslims alike.

Moreover, the Mande loan word s-athka (derived from the Arabic sadaqa), adopted into Temne to denote "sacrifice," also encompasses the Muslim notion of "charity." Diviners today often prescribe special gifts of food, kola nuts, cloth, and money to be given to others (especially children and beggars) as offerings whose ritual efficacy flows from the blessings *(baraka)* that their recipients request God (K-uru or Allah) to bestow upon the giver. At the same time, non-Muslim concepts of sacrifice coexist and compete with this understanding of "charity." When I returned to Petbana in 1989 and found that Pa Alfa Koroma had passed away six years earlier, I gave a sheep s-athka for him. When the sheep was slaughtered, Petbana's imam recited Muslim prayers, while Pa Kaper Bana, the ritual subchief of Bombali Sebora chiefdom, simultaneously invoked the names of Petbana's ancestors. Whereas Pa Kaper Bana told me afterwards that Pa Koroma had consumed the "life" *(aŋ-esəm)* of the sheep through its blood, Pa Santigi later insisted that *"Pa Koroma didn't eat any of that meat,"* arguing instead that the sacrifice had prompted God to send blessings to Pa Koroma. Thus for Pa Santigi the s-athka had been a Muslim "charity," while for Pa Kaper Bana it had been an ancestral sacrifice: differently situated actors invest acts of s-athka with heterogeneous and historically resonant meanings.

But the dominance accorded to Muslim forms of sacrifice and divination means that such ritual polyphony is not usually the juxtaposition of equal voices. The fact that most Mande loanwords in Temne relate to Islamic concepts and practices (Turay 1971: 65), that most Temne ritual offerings take the form of the Mande-derived s-athka, that most Temne diviners use techniques defined as "Muslim," that the casting of river pebbles (aŋ-bɛrɛ)—which is not so defined—is often accorded less prestige, and that every technique (including aŋ-bɛrɛ) has a Mande-derived name, may all be seen as witnesses to the era of the coming of the Muslim "strangers." As the silent argument between Pa Santigi's and Pa Kaper Bana's interpretations of sacrifice attests, however, the ritual hegemony of these strangers and their ritual practices has not gone unchallenged by those who define their own ritual forms as "Temne" rather than "Muslim."

Over the past twenty years, moreover, the argument between Muslim and "Temne" ritual forms has been superseded by another. For reasons that will be explored in the next chapter, the ritual practice of Muslim specialists who apply the esoteric Islamic sciences through divination, healing, and amulet-making has come to be condemned as "polytheism" *(shirk)* by (predominantly) urban Muslims who espouse a range of conservative Islamic ideas. Muslim diviners, accordingly, find their formerly hegemonic skills under attack.

These past and present struggles are, as we shall see, embodied both in divination techniques and in narratives of these techniques' origin. But the Islamicization of oracles and the recent decoupling of divination from ideas of "true" Islam are not the only aspects of the past to be thus materialized: the landscape of death and disappearance explored in the previous chapter is also made present, shaping Temne divination into a ritual memory of Atlantic as well as Islamic transformations. In the following section, I turn to ways in which these memories are made to converge and compete in three stories of the origin of divination.

The Story of the Cave   When I asked diviners about origin stories for divination, most replied *"I met divination when I was born,"* adding that they did not know how it began. Three diviners, however, each told me a different version of the narrative that is the subject of this section. Although this narrative is not widely known even among ritual specialists, it nevertheless tells us a great deal about the presence and contending nature of memory in Temne divination.

I first heard the story in 1978, from Pa Alfa Koroma in Petbana, who used it to tell of the origin and superiority of his own technique, aŋ-yina Musa divination. He began with an account of transmission, then turned to an account of persecution, concealment, disclosure, and penetration:

> aŋ-yina Musa started from the first Muslim scholars (aŋ-karmɔkɔ) who had four eyes and could see the spirits. aŋ-yina Musa is a Muslim spirit. He transferred his knowledge to the Qur'an. He showed his knowledge of divination to some of the Muslim people, and they wrote it down. So this knowledge is written in the Qur'an, and the Muslims read it. First there were unbelievers (aŋ-kafri). If these unbelievers came upon you and you were praying, they beat you down and stopped you praying. The Muslim people, now, were having these problems, so they went to the karmɔkɔ to "look" [divine] for them—how are they going to hide so that these unbelievers won't see them again? So when they went, the karmɔkɔ "looked" and told them to go up the hill and hide in a hole there. So, after the Muslims went into this hole, the spider, Pa ŋes ("Father Spider") wove his web over the entrance. When the unbelievers were looking for these Muslims, now, they were able to trace their footsteps to this place, but when they came to the entrance they saw the web and they said: "These people are not here. If they were here, the web would not be here." . . . So they themselves went to this karmɔkɔ to "look." The karmɔkɔ told the unbelievers to go up the hill and enter the hole, for the Muslims are there.

I was initially puzzled by this story. Pa Koroma's account did not seem to correspond to the history of Islam in the region; there had been, for instance, no persecution of Muslims that I knew of. Over time, however, I recognized Pa Koroma's narrative as a reworking of the well-known hadith of Muhammad and Abu Bakr's evasion of the the hostile Meccans in a cave during the hijra, their flight from Mecca to Medina.[10] In Pa Koroma's version, this important Muslim hadith has become a Temne narrative in certain interesting ways: the friendly spider who spins a web over the entrance of the hole to deceive the pursuers, for instance, is identified as Pa ŋes ("Father Spider"), a popular trickster figure in Temne stories. And like all powerful Temne ritual specialists, the first Muslim scholars who transmitted the knowledge of aŋ-yina Musa divination had four eyes *(ɛ-fɔr t-anlɛ)* denoting a supernatural vision shared by all who have extrahuman powers. These early Muslims are thus described as spiritually powerful in ways that are locally important. It was not until I heard a different version eleven years later, however, that I became aware of other local and regional memories that this story has been made to recall through its migration and residence in Sierra Leone.

This second version was told to me in 1989 by Pa Biyare Seri, a diviner in the town of Mafonke, near Makeni. Pa Biyare used aŋ-bɛrɛ, divination by river pebbles—a technique that is defined as "Temne" rather than "Muslim" and is ascribed connotations of both venerability and "backwardness." Earlier, during my first fieldwork in 1978, he had told me that aŋ-bɛrɛ was the oldest divination technique, and that it used to tell warriors where enemies were hiding. Then, in 1989, he expanded on this through a narrative in which he neatly reversed the message of the originally Muslim story, turning it into a claim that the powers of aŋ-bɛrɛ diviners *(aŋ-mɛn)* such as himself were superior to those of Muslim specialists:

> *When Konkomusa* [a diviner-ancestor] *brought aŋ-bɛrɛ, when the work came, some were big warriors* (aŋ-kurgba) *and some were big Muslim diviners* (aŋ-ləfa). *When the angel* (aŋ-maleka) *came, they came to find out—when these warriors went to war, they went everywhere looking for people to kill. The good angel came and covered the whole area. He hid in a hole. When he hid in a hole, they were looking everywhere for him. So the angel made a spider's web to cover the hole. . . . They brought the Muslim diviner* (ɔ-mɔre) *to find out what was in this hole. He couldn't find out. So the* [non-Muslim] *diviners* (aŋ-thupəs) *divined and found it was this place, where the spider's web is. The aŋ-bɛrɛ diviners* (aŋ-mɛn) *were able to find the place, but the Muslim diviners* (aŋ-mɔre) *could not.*

Pa Biyare was an old man when he told me this story, and his version is jumpier and more fragmented than Pa Koroma's: the *"he"* who *"hid in a hole"* is not identified, for instance, but seems to refer to someone other than the protecting angel who *"covered the whole area."*

What both Pa Koroma's and Pa Biyare's versions have in common, however, is a depiction of a landscape of terror in which the best available defence
consists in enclosing and concealing oneself from forces of violence and
death. But in Pa Biyare's version, the story has undergone a further reworking
from its hadith origins: the fugitive's attempt to hide from death at the hands
of warriors (ɛ-kurgba) who "went everywhere looking for people to kill" replaces the
Muslims' attempt to escape from persecution by unbelievers in Pa Koroma's
version. No longer a story specifically about the first Muslims, it is clearly
located in the history of warfare, raiding, and concealment on the upper
Guinea coast that I explore in the previous two chapters. In the nineteenth-
century Sierra Leone hinterland, as we have seen, the professionalization of
warfare did indeed result in the warriors of Pa Biyare's account roaming
around and taking advantage of whatever opportunities for raiding and pillag-
ing they found (Ijagbemi 1968; 1973). And long before this, as we have also
seen, the symbiotic relationship that developed between the Atlantic slave
trade, warfare, and the "invasion" of certain foreign groups had already created a landscape of terror in which the best defenses were indeed enclosure
and concealment from forces of violence and death.

Thus Pa Koroma's and Pa Biyare's versions are competing claims about the
ritual efficacy of aŋ-yina Musa and aŋ-bɛrɛ, "Muslim" and "Temne" divination, continuing a two-hundred-year-old "argument" over ritual practices and
meanings that began when Muslim Mande techniques gained ground over
local divination techniques. But in these two accounts a different memory is
also embedded: the originally foreign narrative of Muhammad and Abu Bakr
hiding from the Meccans in the enclosed, concealed space of the cave has
been reconfigured as a story of Sierra Leone's past, set in the landscape that
this Atlantic and colonial past created.

Finally, in the third version of the story we turn to a more recent argument
over the commensurability of divination and Islam among conservative Muslims. This version was told by the late Pa Yamba Nhoni Kamara, a diviner
living in Freetown who was a committed Muslim but had never learned
to write Arabic. His primary divination technique—the looking glass (aŋ-
mɛmnɛ)—was viewed as less explicitly "Islamic" than techniques that entailed Arabic writing. During my 1989 fieldwork, I found Pa Yamba struggling
with new conservative Muslim sensibilities that were especially pervasive in
Freetown at that time. Deeply concerned about increasingly dominant representations of divination as incompatible with "true" Islam, he protested that
his own ritual occupation was surely legitimate because, he insisted, "Divina-

tion is in the Qur'an." He substantiated this claim with his version of the narrative of the cave:

> *They will seek someone. A person will hide. People will try to find him, but they will not be able. When they use divination, they will reveal where he hides. Do you understand? There is a pit* (aŋ-biŋ); *a spider will entangle* (gbaŋkthanɛ) *it; this person that is hiding will be inside it. You understand? He will go to the diviner and he will tell him, "When you are walking, if you find a pit that is entangled with a spider's web, that person is inside it." Do you understand? Divination will reveal that, and it will be so. When he looks, he will know that this person is inside. It* [divination] *is not bad. It is* [only] *now that some people are saying it is bad, but it is not bad.*

Pa Yamba, then, created a counternarrative to conservative Islam by explicitly returning the story of the cave to its textual Islamic origins. In his version, divination is not only a powerful means of finding what is (literally) concealed beneath the surface, but also derives from the ultimate source of Islamic authority. Pa Yamba turned this story into a much more authoritative narrative than a hadith: by ascribing to it the status of a Qur'anic text, he attempted to validate divination with the very claims of scriptural origin that conservative leaders have used in order to eradicate divination from "proper" Islamic practice. (At the same time, however, he ignored the morally problematic aspect of this story, given that the diviners are helping the Meccans to find Muhammad's hiding place. See note 10.)

In these three versions of the origin story, different kinds of memory are involved. First, we see clear examples of memory as the politics of the past: all three diviners discursively reconfigure the originally foreign narrative to address ongoing struggles over successive ritual reformations in Sierra Leone's history. But a second, less discursive kind of memory is also embedded in the story. In Pa Biyare's version in particular, the story of the fugitives, the warriors seeking to kill them, and the disguised hiding place invokes a local history of terror from Sierra Leone's nineteenth-century colonial (and, before this, its Atlantic) past. While this memory is less discursive in the sense that it is less intentional, however, it cannot be described as a practical memory: it forms part of an explicit verbal statement about the past, and is therefore closer to the discursive rather than the practical end of the spectrum of memory discussed in the introduction. Instead, given that this memory is not the deliberate goal of the story, it corresponds to what Cole, following cognitive psychologists, calls "incidental memory":

To deliberately remember how to get to your friend's house means to make remembering the directions the deliberate goal of the action. If on the way you pass the house you lived in as a child, and remember your childhood, then that memory of your childhood is called incidental memory: it is incidental to the deliberate goal of getting to your friend's house. (2001: 133)

Thus Pa Biyare's intention was to tell a story about the past in order to substantiate his claim that diviners who use his own technique are more powerful than Muslim diviners. But in enacting this "politics of the past," Pa Biyare's narration of concealment and capture was filtered through Sierra Leone's slave-raiding past, which was incorporated into the story as an incidental memory.

In the remaining half of this chapter, I turn from an originally foreign narrative to three originally foreign divination techniques. I examine, respectively, aŋ-bɛrɛ, the casting of river pebbles; aŋ-mɛmnɛ, "the looking glass"; and aŋ-yina Musa, the mediumship of "the Jinn of Musa."[11] Like Pa Biyare's narrative image of warriors, these techniques embody a regional past through the imagery embodied in their material practices and inscriptions.

aŋ-bɛrɛ's Ancestries   Like the other techniques outlined in this chapter, aŋ-bɛrɛ divination, the casting of river pebbles (and sometimes of cowrie shells), was introduced by Mande specialists. Many diviners told me that this technique has come from the Kuranko, the Temne's Mande-speaking neighbors to the northeast, who arrived in the seventeenth century; its name, in fact, is derived from bɛrɛ, the Kuranko word for "stone" (Jackson 1989: 51–66).[12] Further signs of Mande influence endure in one of the names given to a collection of several larger stones that are sometimes placed in front of the pattern of pebbles: some diviners call these stones "the ancestors" (aŋ-baki), and others call them "Konkomusa," the name of the diviner-ancestor who first brought aŋ-bɛrɛ. This second name suggests a derivation from "Kankan Musa" (or Mansa Musa), the famous fifteenth-century pilgrim-king of the ancient Mali Empire that once dominated the Western Sudanic region to the northeast of Sierra Leone. The name of aŋ-bɛrɛ's ancestor, then, traces transregional historical connections.

But aŋ-bɛrɛ's foreign origins can be pursued far beyond the Mande diaspora of West Africa. The original forbear of this technique in North and Sub-Saharan Africa is Muslim sand divination (khatt ar-raml), which is associated with a thirteenth-century divination manual written in Morocco by al-Zanati, and is also the subject of a critique by Ibn Khaldun in fourteenth-century Tunisia (Brenner 2000: 11 and 13; see also el-Tom 1983: 241–45]). Khatt ar-raml involves building up tetragrams from a series of single and paired marks made in the sand in a divination tray, forming patterns that are virtually identical to those that I shall go on to describe for aŋ-bɛrɛ. This technique has circulated to Darfur, where el-Tom (1983: 203–55) describes in fine detail the complex applications of *ramul* divination, as it is called in Berti-speaking communities; to Moundang communities in Chad (Adler and Zemplini 1972: 50–70); to the Indian Ocean island of Mayotte, where it is used for the calculation of horoscopes by the casting of roasted seeds (Lambek 1993: 210); and to Southern Africa, where it has, according to van Binsbergen (1995, 1996), influenced Shona four-tablet divination. Brenner, in fact, traces the spread of divination techniques derived from khatt ar-raml to "virtually every region of Africa where Muslims have penetrated in the past" (2000: 13), including seventeenth-century Madagascar, the seventeenth-century Mutapa court in what is now Zimbabwe, the Mande zone of West Africa, and western Nigeria, where even the globally renowned technique of Yoruba Ifa divination seems, he argues, to be among khatt ar-raml's remote offspring (2000: 14–21). Beyond Africa, moreover, this technique has been described in Yemen, was popular during the fourteenth through seventeenth centuries in southern France, Italy, and Byzantium, and was even translated into Latin, Greek, and Provençal (Brenner 2000: 13–14).

Despite its far-flung Muslim connections, however, aŋ-bɛrɛ is usually regarded by Temne diviners and their clients as a pre-Islamic technique: "*aŋ-bɛrɛ is the kafri* [unbeliever] *form of divination*," as Pa Koroma put it. Although many diviners cast aŋ-bɛrɛ on a Muslim prayer mat and utter the Muslim prayer, "bismillahi rahmani rahim" (in the name of Allah, the Merciful, the Compassionate) when they begin a divination, most such diviners (including many of those who also told me that this technique originally came from the Kuranko) characterized aŋ-bɛrɛ as a very old and particularly "Temne" form of divination. Both the claim of its Kuranko derivation and of its locally established "Temne" status are, in fact, compatible with each other: as I observed at the beginning of this chapter, people often insisted that cultural borrowing *made* an originally foreign practice "theirs." aŋ-bɛrɛ's special status is also indicated by the name given uniquely to a specialist who uses this technique—*u-mɛn*—as distinct from the generic term "diviner" (u-thupɔs) given to those who use all other forms of divination.

It is interesting to contrast aŋ-bɛrɛ with two other techniques of Temne divination that also seem to derive from khatt ar-raml, and that (unlike aŋ-bɛrɛ) are regarded as unambiguously "Muslim." These are *ka-səŋt* ("the sand"), in which the diviner makes a pattern of dashes in a small heap of sand, and *aŋ-raməli* (whose name derives from *khatt ar-raml*), in which the diviner uses pen and ink to draw dashes that form two curved lines on an Arabic slate. None of the ka-səŋt or aŋ-raməli diviners I knew, however, built up the distinctive straight parallel lines of both raml and aŋ-bɛrɛ through repeated castings; instead they either interpreted the pattern they had made in the sand, or counted the dashes on the slate and looked up the resulting number in an Arabic divination manual.

With its Kuranko connections and the local ritual meanings it contains, aŋ-bɛrɛ may have been incorporated through a process separate from that through which ka-səŋt and aŋ-raməli were assimilated. Given that many Temne-speaking groups expanded eastward and acquired Kuranko chiefs in the seventeenth century, aŋ-bɛrɛ may have been the product of an earlier—and less specifically "Muslim"—process of Mande borrowing than that which took place when eighteenth- and nineteenth-century Mande specialists from further north introduced divination techniques that were strongly marked as "Muslim." Ka-səŋt and aŋ-raməli, with their stronger Islamic associations, could thus have superseded their forgotten relative, aŋ-bɛrɛ.

What of the local, vernacular significance of aŋ-bɛrɛ? Its river pebbles embody water spirits. Diviners collect pebbles that attract their attention along the banks of rivers and streams, often picking up stones that are shiny and translucent or that have a striking color or shape. These stones attract attention, several diviners told me, precisely because they are animated by the river spirits who dwell in them. These links among water, pebbles, and divination spirits resonate with those I noted earlier in this chapter, in Alvares's account of the early-seventeenth-century "stone and water" technique used by Cube, the Temne-speaking diviner who converted to Christianity (1990, 2, chap. 5: 4–5, note [c]). River pebbles are objects of the local landscape, materializing forces of the water highways that were crucial as routes of transport and trade on the upper Guinea coast for centuries. Some diviners, in addition, use cowrie shells (ta-faŋt) with (or instead of) the pebbles. While the diviners I knew were not aware of the Indian Ocean origins of cowrie shells, they knew that cowries come from the sea. Pa Fode Gbla, an aŋ-bɛrɛ diviner in a small village called Mayan a few miles from Matotoka, told me that he mixed river pebbles and cowries together because the pebbles and cowries *are all taken out of water*," adding that water *"is a meeting place for spirits."*[13]

So paradoxically, through the incorporation of a "foreign" form of divination from Kuranko-speakers, Temne-speaking diviners have retained the use of water and stones, a long-standing feature of local divinatory practice in this area. In aŋ-bɛrɛ, the technique that began as Islamic sand divination, with distant relatives dispersed over the whole of Muslim-influenced Africa and beyond, has thus become a "non-Muslim" ritual form. Pebbles gathered from the nearest river replace sand, and local water spirits replace the literate spiritual authority of al-Zanati's divination manual. Yet although aŋ-bɛrɛ's far-flung historical connections have been forgotten, the oracular patterns spelled out by its stones recall other translocal circulations, as I explore in the following section.

Casting aŋ-bɛrɛ: Roads to Life, Roads to Death   When diviners cast aŋ-bɛrɛ, they arrange the river pebbles (or cowrie shells) in ones and twos into a pattern of four lines determined by an emerging sequence of odd and even numbers (Shaw 1991). As Pa Yamba, the Freetown diviner whose version of the cave hadith we read above, explained, *"in aŋ-bɛrɛ, when I put all of them* [down], *they come out different, different. Line by line, line by line, in four lines."* I was taught the rudiments of the casting of aŋ-bɛrɛ in 1978 by Pa Biyare in Makeni, whose version of the cave story we also read above. He used to throw a handful of pebbles upward with his left hand and catch them in his right, then count off those he had caught in pairs until either one or two stones remained. He would place this remaining stone (or pair of stones) on the mat in front of him, and then cast the stones again, thereby building up the first row of pebbles from right to left, as in Arabic writing. After completing the first line of four single or double stones, he would construct the second, third, and fourth rows under it. When, after counting the stones from a casting, a single one remained, he set it down in the pattern; when two remained, however, he placed all that he had caught in pairs along the row until the latter was complete, and replaced the last two stones in the pile of pebbles that remained. Pa Biyare continued adding to the rows until he had built up a pattern of four parallel lines of single and paired stones, which he then examined in order to discern the answer to his client's question (Shaw 1991).

These four parallel lines of aŋ-bɛrɛ are called "Roads" *(ta-soŋ)*. Interestingly, "Road" is also the name given to one of the sixteen signs generated in khatt ar-raml divination (Brenner 2000: 14) as well as in Berti *ramul* divination (el-Tom 1983: 208), in both of which "Road" is denoted by a vertical line consisting entirely of single marks. In Arabic texts written by al-Buni and

Figure 2. The Roads of aŋ-bɛrɛ divination

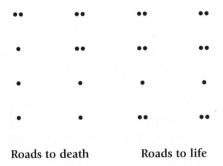

Roads to death   **Roads to life**

al-Adhami, the figure of the Road in khatt ar-raml stands for enemies and rivals (el-Tom 1983: 255), while in Berti ramul divination, it represents a personified character. According to el-Tom, "the Road *(tariq)* is depicted as a young man and because he is very active he normally acts as a messenger for the elders. Road, as is clear from the root meaning of the word, could also refer to a way out, to a journey as well as a mediator" (1983: 208–9). In neither of these forms of sand divination, however, is "Road" the generic term for the signs themselves, as it is in aŋ-bɛrɛ divination.

Roads, paths, and trails are, of course, recurring images in divination and other ritual forms with which we are familiar. They may, for instance, stand for divination itself as the trail blazed from the unknown to the known in Ndembu divination (Turner 1975), or for the path that the client follows from the "wilderness" of suffering to the "settled" condition of well-being in Giriama divination (Parkin 1991). But what concerns me here are the ways in which such cultural images are historically and locally constituted, for the meanings that roads are made to convey are neither timeless nor universal. During the Atlantic trade and the colonial legitimate trade in the Sierra Leone hinterland, remember, roads (as well as the "water highways" of rivers) were crucial for the flow of commerce and wealth, but were also hazardous channels of attack by slave-raiding enemies.

Some diviners I knew divided the Roads of aŋ-bɛrɛ into two "Roads to Life" *(ta-soŋ ta a-ŋesəm)* on the right and two "Roads to Death" *(ta-soŋ ta rə-fi)* on the left. These Roads formed a pattern that was, to use Werbner's term, microdramatic (1989: 21), iconically depicting people, events, encounters, and ritual actions and substances in a microcosm that resembles a larger whole. The Roads could represent a sequence of events set in motion by the hidden cause (aŋ-sabu) of the client's problem, or they could stand for the client's journey—sometimes a literal journey, and sometimes a transition in the client's life, often from illness to either health (on the Roads to Life) or deterioration (on the Roads to Death) (Shaw 1991). Individual stones (or pairs of stones) that were distinctive in some way, both through their position on a Road to Life or Death and through their shape or color, stood iconically for landmarks along clients' ritual paths. Several pairs of stones clustered together in the first two rows, for example, could be a crowd of people at a funeral;[14] a single white stone could be a sheep sacrifice that the client must make; a pair of red stones could be a destructive "swearing" medicine *(aŋ-sasa)* sent to attack a witch; or a pair of stones at the end of a Road could be a child's grave.

When he taught me, Pa Biyare selected only from among the stones on the Roads to Life for his interpretations. He gave no reason for doing so beyond telling me that this was the way he had learned to divine, but his focus on the Roads to Life may have maximized the auspiciousness of the divinatory outcome, or minimized the potential dangers of contact with malevolent spirits.

The Roads of aŋ-bɛrɛ also operate as communication routes between the diviner and the spirits, as well as with other extrahuman entities. Pa Yamba described these Roads as highways along which spirits and their messages travel during divination: *"Some* [Roads] come *from the spirits' world* (ro-sɔki),*"* he explained, *"and some from the shades* (aŋ-mɔmpəl) *of the dead. Some come from this world* (nɔ-ru). *Along these Roads, the messages come and meet me."* But because spirits are unpredictable, their movement can be either beneficial or problematic for the diviner. Accordingly, the Roads to Life and the Roads to Death respectively channel positive and negative mobility, as Pa Fode, the diviner from Mayan, explained to me. *"This work,"* he said, *"is always to help people for the better. But there are times, when you meet the spirits, that you meet them on a bad road. You won't always be favored when you ask for something. They're always working toward the good and the bad."* Pa Fode protected himself against attack from harmful entities that might come down the Roads to Death by placing a bottle of liquid Islamic medicine covered with amulets next to the left-hand Roads when he consulted aŋ-bɛrɛ. *"It's a block,"* he answered when I asked him why he had placed it there, adding *"all the bad things coming this way cannot pass by this bottle."* He had effectively created a spirit roadblock to control the movement of potentially troublesome forces down the highways of aŋ-bɛrɛ (plate 7).

While the mediatory but adversarial Road is a single figure in Arabic texts on khatt ar-raml in North Africa and the Sudan, then, Temne diviners have reshaped the Road into a much more encompassing trope. Through the pervasive imagery of roads in this technique, Temne diviners seem to have invoked but reworked the dangerous potency with which routes of transport have been endowed through the history of this region. The Roads of aŋ-bɛrɛ channel valuable messages from the spirits to the diviner, but they can by the same token draw attack by malevolent beings. This resonates both with the significance of the Road in khatt ar-raml, in which this figure stands for enemies and rivals (el-Tom 1983: 255), and with the ambivalence of routes of transport in the Sierra Leone hinterland. As we saw in the previous chapter, you never know who is traveling down the road toward you, or whether the road will lead you on a journey to life or death. By dividing the Roads to Life from the Roads to Death, Temne diviners have reconfigured the dangerously mixed potential of routes of transport from their region's past, separating out the latter's positive and negative qualities and thereby gaining ritual control over their potent but problematic ambiguities.

Through a Glass, Darkly

"Let me tell you," he said, producing a looking-glass and a calabash from his bag, "that without the discovery of the looking-glass which is the same as the water in the calabash, we would still be riding each other's backs instead of camels." Syl Cheney-Coker, *The Last Harmattan of Alusine Dunbar*

In the above excerpt, Alusine Dunbar, a diviner and visionary in Cheney-Coker's novel of Sierra Leonean history, praises the high-powered divinatory properties both of the looking glass and of another reflective surface it resembles — water in a container. Although I cannot give a date of origin for looking glasses in Sierra Leone, their use as divinatory devices may have spread with the influx of foreign Mande ritual specialists and the growing hegemony of Muslim divination techniques in the eighteenth and nineteenth centuries. Like khatt ar-raml, mirror- or water-gazing (hydromancy) is well established in North Africa and Muslim West Africa.

Diviners like the fictional Alusine Dunbar in Muslim West Africa often recount that an image of their own soul, or of a jinn, appears in their oracular mirrors (Prussin 1986: 75). Spirit optics such as these derive from techniques of vision and knowledge that contrast markedly with those of the visual technology of mirrors and lenses developed in Enlightenment Europe.[15] In Britain during the Enlightenment, as Comaroff and Comaroff discuss, the looking glass formed an important component of seventeenth and eighteenth century techniques of self and "rational" transparency (1991: 185–88). Missionaries who went to Africa drew upon these techniques to create Christian subjects, often giving hand-mirrors—"window[s] into a new way of seeing and being" (Comaroff and Comaroff 1991: 185)—as gifts. By enabling a detached, examinable self to be brought into focus, these "windows" formed part of an optical technology in which the ability to distinguish divine light from heathen darkness, to see rather than to be blind, were linked to the capacities of the reflective, inward-looking individual for self-scrutiny.[16]

But in Temne-speaking areas, where the influence of Muslim specialists has been much greater than that of Christian missionaries, diviners use their looking glasses to produce Darkness, not light. As we saw in chapter 2, the Temne term *aŋ-sum*, "Darkness"—an extension of the word for the darkness of night—encompasses meanings of secrecy, invisibility, and powerful hidden knowledge that effectively reverse European Enlightenment equations of darkness with ignorance. When diviners gaze into their mirrors, they enter the Darkness that ordinarily cloaks the spirit world (ro-sɔki), and are thereby able to see and communicate with spirits. Several of the divinatory looking glasses that I saw, in fact, had no reflective surface left; they were not, after all, ordinary optical devices.

What did diviners see in their looking glasses? Pa Yamba told me: "*The Darkness will come slowly, slowly. I'll see the light of what I'm looking for. . . . If you sit next to me, . . . I'll hear you, but it will sound as if you're in a hole.*" For Pa Yamba, then, the Darkness of the looking glass contained a special form of light and sight that removed him from ordinary states of perception and enabled him to see that which is normally veiled from human vision. Similarly, Pa Ibrahim Sankoh, a diviner in Wellington, just outside Freetown, told me: "*First the glass is clear, then Darkness comes out. Then you see many different people—the yina* [Muslim spirits]. *They ask what you've come for. You'll see the glass as empty if you don't have eyes.*" The "eyes" he refers to are the "four eyes" (ɛ-fɔr t-anlɛ) with which diviners and certain other ritual specialists are endowed, their two visible eyes supplemented by two invisible eyes that enable them to see spirits and witches. The vision of spirits that looking glasses make possible is just as much a property of the beholder's special senses as a property of the glass itself.

Some Temne diviners' looking glasses are intersected by two lines of crossed threads that are wound around the mirror in opposite directions, dividing the mirror's surface into four: these are "the Crossroads" *(ta-soŋ tə-*

pəŋkinɛ) (plate 8). Like the mirror's surface, which draws the viewer's eyes into another world beyond the glass, the Crossroads' converging lines lead the diviner into Darkness. The Temne term for "crossed" *(pəŋkinɛ)* roads is cognate with that for "mad" (peŋk), the latter term also standing for the "crossed" state that diviners attain when they enter Darkness and are neither in this world (nɔ-ru) nor in the spirits' world (ro-sɔki). But, as Pa Yamba went on to describe, the Crossroads of aŋ-mɛmnɛ divination also open up a landscape through which the diviner is able to tap into flows that traverse and circulate the invisible worlds of spirits and other beings:

> *The spirits come to the Crossroads. At the center of the Crossroads, you get all the messages you are looking for. However big a thing is, it is to the center that it has to come. All these roads, they have meanings. If something is hidden, the road will tell you in the center. . . . Messages will come from different directions. The spirits have roads between ro-sɔki and nɔ-ru; witches have roads between ro-serɔŋ (the land of witches) and nɔ-ru; the dead have roads between ro-kərfi (the land of the dead) and nɔ-ru. I see these roads when I do divination. I see different people when I travel along the road. There are Crossroads between nɔ-ru and ro-sɔki. One big road and many small ones. It's the same for the other [invisible] lands.*

Thus according to Pa Yamba, the Crossroads form an intersection in a network of roads connecting this world (nɔ-ru), the spirits' world (ro-sɔki), the land of the witches (ro-serɔŋ), and the realm of the dead (ro-kərfi). By entering this intersection, he gained access not only to routes of travel and transport between these invisible realms but also to nodes of communication through which all otherworldly messages have to pass.

Like roads, crossroads have a broad currency as ritual symbols (especially divinatory symbols) both in Africa and beyond. But as with roads, it is important to situate this recurring divinatory image in relation to the local meanings that crossroads have acquired in specific regional histories. If, as we have seen earlier, roads acquired a powerfully ambivalent potential in Temneland as channels of both trade and slave-raiding, wealth and disappearance, crossroads intensified both the positive and negative aspects of this potential by gathering several roads in one place. *"At a crossroads,"* Pa Moses in Petbana told me, *"people can come from different directions to harm you."* It is not only human enemies who make crossroads powerful and precarious places, however. Road junctions are ominous gathering points for bush spirits and witches, where deadly forces moving along different courses are focused in one place by converging routes of transport. Pa Ibrahim Sankoh described crossroads as dangerous sites of spiritual ambush: *"At night, people avoid them, because witches go there. It's a trapping place because everybody goes there."* Sacrifices to get rid of witches and harmful spirits, accordingly, are usually left at the crossroads because, as I was often told, *"everything goes there—spirits, people, the dead. It protects you from misfortune coming from everywhere."*

Through the Crossroads in aŋ-mɛmnɛ divination, diviners reconfigure the dangerous potency of a landscape in which both valuable messages and great danger may be approaching, as diviners often reiterated to me, *"from all directions," "from everywhere."* Here diviners seek to control the power of these converging Roads, using them to draw flows of concealed knowledge: when *"something is hidden,"* as Pa Yamba put it, *"the Road will tell you in the center."* In the Darkness at the Crossroads between invisible worlds, then, diviners receive the messages—and strive to avoid the dangers—that come "from all directions."

In exploring aŋ-bɛrɛ and aŋ-mɛmnɛ, my focus has shifted further along the spectrum from discursive to practical remembering, for the diviners I have discussed here invoked images of a past landscape through divination techniques without expressing these as explicit recollections of the past. These diviners, as we have seen, did not intend to recall a past landscape, but sought to navigate roads and crossroads of the spirits for the purposes of divination. In so doing, however, they used visual images of roads and crossroads that—like Pa Biyare's incidental memory of a landscape of concealment in the cave hadith—were historically mediated by knowledge of what roads and crossroads meant in this region prior to the twentieth century. Roads, as we have seen, meant the potential for both prosperity and death, and roadblocks meant control over this ambivalent potential. Crossroads, meanwhile, magnified both these positive and negative possibilities by channeling them from multiple directions, creating either *"a trapping-place"* or a central node of communication in which you can find *"all the messages you are looking for."* At the same time, these diviners turned the power and danger of roads and crossroads to their own ritual purposes, recasting these features of a remembered landscape as vehicles whose dangerous potency they could appropriate.

The Jinn of Musa   In aŋ-yina Musa divination, diviners multiply the optical properties of the looking glass threefold. This is a technique of spirit-mediumship in which either the diviner or an assistant gazes into a assemblage of three surfaces—a hand-mirror, a blackened square, circle, or cross at the center of an Arabic diagram, and a container of water turned black by ink washed off an Arabic inscription (ma-nasi). As in aŋ-mɛmnɛ divination, the diviners I knew usually described being drawn into Darkness through the special optical properties of these surfaces.

We have already seen that water-gazing is practiced in other parts of Islamic-influenced Africa. Doutté, writing nearly a century ago, mentions a form of divination in North Africa that could just as well have identified aŋ-yina Musa divination by Temne diviners in Sierra Leone: an assistant gazes into a reflective surface such as a mirror, or into ink in the central square or "house" of a symbolic diagram (1909: 391). aŋ-yina Musa's name, in fact, evokes translocal historical origins. aŋ-yina, a Temne loanword from the Mande term *jina* ("jinn"), indexes a specifically Muslim spirit, as distinct from the more generic Temne category of spirits, aŋ-kərfi. Like "Konkomusa," the ancestor of aŋ-bɛrɛ divination, "Musa" may, according to Trimingham (1959: 122), denote Mansa Musa, the fifteenth century ruler of the Mali Empire. Alternatively, given the circulation of stories about potent secret texts called the "Seven Books of Moses" among West African Muslim specialists, it is also possible that "Musa" might refer to the prophet Moses (Benjamin Soares, personal communication, November 1998). "aŋ-yina Musa," then, may have originally referred to the patron spirit behind the reign of Mansa Musa, or perhaps to the great king or to the prophet Musa himself, transfigured into a spirit after death.

None of the diviners I knew made any explicit reference to Musa as a prophet *(u-nabi)* or a king *(u-bay)*.[17] Nevertheless, the transregional origins of this spirit and his form of divination are remembered in these diviners' emphases on an-yina Musa's foreign Arab origins, his knowledge of potent literate Qur'anic "secrets" *(ɛ-gbundu)*, and his alien and fearsome appearance. Pa Ahmadu Fonah, a diviner in the small town of Rokirfi, a few miles from Petbana, drew on these attributes while explaining to me why aŋ-yina Musa divination is superior to all other techniques:

> aŋ-yina Musa divination is ahead of all other [kinds of] divination because it's from Arab people. It comes from this Arabic writing. There they [the diviners] picked it. They got it from the white [Arab] people. When they started, these black people learned from it. The white people learned from K-uru Masaba (God, the great king). For the writings (ma-gbal), it's aŋ-yina Musa who comes to show you himself; he's stronger than all other ɛ-yina. He stands and holds the rosary beads (aŋ-thasabiya) in his right hand and a book in his left hand. He is frightening to look at. He is white, just like you.

By "white people," Pa Fonah meant Arabs, whom he viewed as having acquired their literate knowledge directly from God. They, according to Pa Fonah, transmitted their knowledge to African Muslims (*"these black people"*).[18] But African diviners can also gain this knowledge directly from the spirit aŋ-yina Musa, whose foreign appearance—white, and holding a book and rosary beads—are marks of his Arab origins, his Qur'anic knowledge, and his spiritual power.

Concealment and Cinematic Vision   It was Pa Koroma in Petbana who first introduced me to the "jinn of Musa." A gentle, generous, and unassuming man, he built up a wide reputation as an accomplished aŋ-yina Musa diviner and healer before he died in 1983, and he was especially respected for his ability to cure insanity (which, like aŋ-yina Musa divination, requires exceptional spiritual power). What is distinctive about aŋ-yina Musa, Pa Koroma once told me, is his face: when you look at it all you can see are flames. Pa Koroma did not, however, look into this face himself; like many aŋ-yina Musa diviners, he consulted the fiery spirit through an assistant, whom he put into a trance (pəŋk). During my 1978 fieldwork, Mami Yeno, a friendly older woman who was his wife's brother's wife, usually traveled from a neighboring town in order to work with him as aŋ-yina Musa's medium.

For Pa Koroma to work through an assistant rather than acting as a medium himself was consistent with Temne constructions of power (aŋ-foso) and agency. To control a situation through indirect or hidden means, in which one is the underlying cause (aŋ-sabu) of another person's actions, is to have more power than someone whose actions are direct and obvious (Shaw 2000). In keeping with the understanding that the most powerful ritual specialists are those with the capacity to act *through* others, to subsume their agency, Pa Koroma put Mami Yeno into a trance and, through the power of his Islamic medicine (ma-nasi) and prayers, controlled her encounter with the spirit.

At the beginning of the first session of aŋ-yina Musa divination I attended in June 1978, Mami Yeno sat on a Muslim prayer mat in the central parlor of Pa Koroma's house. In front of her Pa Koroma placed a white bowl of water blackened with Qur'anic slate-water (ma-nasi), and dropped a gold ring into the bowl. On top of this bowl he rested a wooden slate (aŋ-walka) inscribed with an Arabic diagram (aŋ-gbal), and over the center of this slate he placed a small mirror. He dropped some slate-water into Mami Yeno's eyes, giving her the "four-eyed" spirit vision that would enable her to see an-yina Musa and the normally invisible spirits' town (ro-sɔki); then he rubbed the slate-water over her face, arms, and upper body. Covering her with a large white cloth, Pa Koroma stood with his hand on her head and recited prayers with his rosary beads (aŋ-thasabiya), which he held—like an-yina Musa himself—in his right hand. He called the ancestors (aŋ-baki) of Petbana and the spirits to come from their town: *"Let the dead* (aŋ-baki) *and the spirits* (aŋ-kərfi) *come. Let what is hidden come. Let a town appear, and let the people of that town tell us what we want to know."* As he said this, Mami Yeno trembled gently and began to announce the arrival of Petbana's ancestors, some of whom brought messages:

> *Pa Rok, who died long ago, has come. The father of Pa Kaper Bana has come. Pa Mende Mereke has come, who died long ago. Pa Wore has come. Ya Bom, mother of Alfa Moru, has come. Pa Sori has come. Pa Raka has come, but he says there is going to be a death in the town. Pa Yamba has come. Bomo Kalokoh has come.*

Suddenly Mami Yeno's shaking became violent, her voice rising to a shriek as she cried *"Alfa yina-Musa!"* Pa Koroma rubbed her head firmly, told her to look at the divination spirit without fear, and recited prayers with his rosary beads until her trembling became softer and her voice returned to normal. At this point, Pa Koroma indicated that the clients seated around the room could ask their questions. When they did so, Pa Koroma repeated the questions to Mami Yeno; she silently conveyed them to aŋ-yina Musa; the spirit silently replied; Mami Yeno repeated his answers to Pa Koroma; and Pa Koroma repeated them with some elaboration to the clients.

Mami Yeno did not, then, act as a medium whose body and voice were taken over by a spirit: this was spirit mediumship without spirit possession. Instead of embodying aŋ-yina Musa, her body and senses were controlled by Pa Koroma through his prayers and medicine. She conversed with aŋ-yina Musa in her own voice, becoming a link in a chain of communication between this divination spirit and Pa Koroma's human clients. If aŋ-yina Musa had "seized" Mami Yeno's body, Pa Koroma told me afterwards, she would have gone insane or even died: capture by a spirit was, in fact, his usual diagnosis for insanity. Later, Pa Koroma also explained to me that the Qur'anic medicine he had dropped in Mami Yeno's eyes gave her four-eyed vision, while the white cloth that covered her disguised her as a spirit: *"It makes the spirits think she's one of them. They think she's called them for a meeting."* Thus instead of either a possessing spirit temporarily inhabiting a human body in order to speak to humans, or a masked human controlled by a spirit for a human audience, here we have a "masked" human, controlled by another human, impersonating a spirit for a *spirit* audience.

Here, then, we do not find the various cultural logics of spirit embodiment that are recurring features of spirit possession—such as the "paradox of agency" in which mediums gain a voice by giving theirs up to a spirit (Jackson and Karp 1990); the embodied political metaphor of a spirit "mounting" a subordinate human (Matory 1994); or the "poetics of contrast" between men and women, invaders and invaded, possessing and possessed (Boddy 1989). Rather, in Pa Koroma's and Mami Yeno's practice of aŋ-yina Musa we find a logic of concealment, visual confusion, enclosure, and concern for the protection of the integrity of bodily space—logics and concerns that parallel those discussed in relation to spirits of the landscape in chapter 2.

After the divination, Mami Yeno told me that she remembered nothing of what she had experienced in her encounter with aŋ-yina Musa and the ancestors—an erasure that may reflect the gendered asymmetries of agency and voice in her division of divinatory labor with Pa Koroma. It was Pa Koroma who claimed control over Mami Yeno's encounter with this spirit: he wrote the inscriptions, prepared the Qur'anic medicine, induced (and brought to an end) Mami Yeno's "crossed" state of trance (pəŋk), invoked the ancestors' and aŋ-yina Musa's presence, and regulated the conversation between Mami Yeno and aŋ-yina Musa with his prayers, his questions, and his instructions. Mami Yeno's contact with aŋ-yina Musa was thus more tightly regulated by a human (and male) overseer than is a possessed medium's self-erasure in the spirit's presence: in a sense Mami Yeno had, ironically, less voice than a medium in a possession cult who becomes entirely subsumed by her spirit's agency. While it is common in spirit possession for a medium to retain no memory of what happens when a spirit speaks and acts through her—in accordance with the paradox through which such a medium gains agency and voice only if her actions and words are not "hers" (e.g., Jackson and Karp 1990)—Mami Yeno's forgetting of her encounters with aŋ-yina Musa may, instead, indicate Mami Yeno's renunciation of agency and voice in her oracular partnership with Pa Koroma.

In contrast to Mami Yeno, diviners who gazed into the assemblage of the mirror, diagram, and water themselves, without the mediating presence of an assistant, gave me vivid accounts of what they saw when they covered themselves with the white cloth and entered the Darkness (plate 9). Pa Fonah described being a relatively passive onlooker upon an unfolding scene, telling me: "*I see dead people* (aŋ-fəm a fi), *spirits* (aŋ-kərfi). *Angels* (aŋ-maleka) *come.*

I see my own [tutelary] *spirits* (ε-yina). *aŋ-yina Musa is on one side; the ancestors* (aŋ-baki) *are on the other."* Most other aŋ-yina Musa diviners I knew gave a similar sense of being a viewer of a scene peopled by ancestors, spirits, and other entities, often conveying this vividly by comparing their perceptions to the experience of viewing electronic media. *"A sort of screen is brought to me, which I see,"* a yina-Musa diviner called Pa Saidu in Rosengbe told me in 1978. *"I sit in this world* (nɔ-ru),*"* he continued, *"but the picture comes with the spirits. I see the spirit world* (ro-sɔki). *It comes to me like the cinema."* And Pa Koroma, laughing but clearly proud of the astonishing powers of the divination technique for which he was well known, once told me: *"Even the Europeans are imitating this aŋ-yina Musa. You go to the cinema and you see certain things there; it's the same with aŋ-yina Musa!"* Eleven years' later, when I returned in 1989 after the demise of centralized electric power and the rise of generator-powered video shows (see Richards 1996b: 102–4), the technology had changed but the analogy was the same: *"the white men have the video, but we have aŋ-yina Musa,"* I was teasingly informed by several diviners.

The cinematic quality of these diviners' visionary experience contrasts with the illusory image created for aŋ-yina Musa: the spirit is made to misidentify the person talking with him. And although diviners or mediums obtain verbal rather than visual information through their conversations with aŋ-yina Musa, this interaction is encompassed by the conditions of temporary visual advantage that the diviner creates by tricking the spirit. To see without being seen oneself, like those who become invisible through Darkness medicine, is to have power over others—even, in this case, over a fearsome spirit. Even if a diviner does not exercise the powerful "agency-at-a-remove" of those who draw oracular knowledge from the spirits through control of a medium, he (and the masculine pronoun is appropriate here) still has the capacity to extract verbal knowledge from aŋ-yina Musa through a visual illusion that conceals his true nature. He may not subsume a medium's actions within his own ritual agency, but he is able to view without being viewed, talking to the spirit while watching him on *"a sort of screen"* and remaining hidden from spirit scrutiny himself by the Darkness of the white sheet. Given that spirits themselves have penetrative vision that enables them to watch human beings without being detected, aŋ-yina Musa diviners are effectively appropriating spirit vision, turning its gaze back on the spirits themselves. Thus these diviners not only use techniques of Darkness as a means of defence against seizure in the ways that I discussed in the previous chapter; they also turn Darkness into a means of "spying" on the spirits.

The Writings   The Arabic inscriptions and magic squares that aŋ-yina Musa diviners use to make their Qur'anic medicine (mɑ-nɑsi) and to draw the gaze of the covered medium into Darkness are called "Writings" (mɑ-gbal) in Temne.[19] In North Africa and parts of Islamic West Africa, such Writings are known as khatim, the Arabic for "seal." Deriving from Sufi knowledge and practice, many are based on an esoteric science that assigns a numerical value to each letter of the alphabet, and thereby links the letters and words in a magic square to the structure and hierarchy of the cosmos. Such squares are commonly divided into nine cells or "houses," with the middle house (sometimes called a "mosque" in parts of West Africa) either inscribed with the name of Allah or left blank to represent God's power at the center of the cosmos (Prussin 1986: 75).

The diviners I knew had usually copied their teacher's Writings into a school exercise book. Each diviner had a different corpus of Writings; some were ultimately derived from North African or Egyptian manuals for divination and amulet-making, while others were revealed in dreams by tutelary spirits. Written in a mixture of Arabic and Temne, most defied straightforward reading by those literate in Arabic. Perhaps because of this impenetrability—and, even more importantly, because I did not know the oral prayers that must be used to activate the Writings—the aŋ-yina Musa diviners I knew were usually quite willing to show me their own handwritten texts, to allow me to copy a page or two, to copy pages for me themselves, to allow me to take photographs, and to tell me what was written. Although knowledge of these inscriptions is "a secret" (aŋ-gbundu) that is usually passed from teachers to students in exchange for several years of labor (see Bledsoe and Robey 1986; Soares 1997), this knowledge is incomplete unless the student is taught how to *use* the inscriptions. The purpose of the inscriptions is not to convey a transparent "meaning" to a reader: this is practical, effective knowledge.

Pa Koroma's aŋ-yina Musa Writing (plate 10) came, he told me, from a book he called *"Shamsu ma-rof"*—probably a Temne vernacularization of *Shams al-ma'rif*, a thirteenth-century North African manual for divination and amulet-making by al-Buni. *"In this book,"* Pa Koroma disclosed, *"are all the things that are happening in the world. It's a kind of map."* In this Writing, a central black square is surrounded by elongated and crossed Arabic letters; at the bottom are the letters "MD" (possibly signifying "Muhammad"), at the top are ambiguous letters that may spell *el-lail,* "the night" in Arabic (perhaps relating to the Darkness that the medium enters), while to the right and left are figures resembling keys that do not appear to be letters at all.[20] Inside the square formed by these crossed words and figures, just above and below the central black square, is written "ya Allah" ("Oh Allah"), followed by the hard letter "h" and by "n." When Pa Koroma explained this Writing to me, he said:

> *The whole thing is a house* (aŋ-seth), *a compartment for the spirits. The lines are sort of walls to prevent the spirits spreading about and hurting anybody. The Arabic words are tying the fence. I recite these when I use the rosary beads. The black part is what it between us and the spirits. It is the Darkness* (aŋ-sum) *between them and us, so that they do not harm us. Its power penetrates into the mirror and allows the covered person to see the other world. And it is the Darkness that makes a person tremble. S/he* (o) *is not in this world or in the other world.*

So through Pa Koroma's Writing, the spirits were enclosed in a "house" whose boundaries were "tied" with binding words in both oral and written forms. By creating a spirit house whose magical walls obstructed uncontrolled and harmful movement into the human space beyond, Pa Koroma effectively rec-reated—but at the same time reshaped—the ritual Closure *(kaŋtha)* with which diviners and others protect human houses and bodies from external spirit incursion. While humans ordinarily use such techniques to keep them-selves safely contained in a landscape of marauding spirits, Pa Koroma created a portion of space in which he could contain the normally unfettered move-ment of the spirits in a "compartment."

Pa Koroma positioned another kind of barrier at the center of his "house" of Writing: the black square in the Writing's interior protected humans by placing Darkness between them and the spirits. But this black square is also, as Pa Koroma said, *"that Darkness that makes a person tremble."* Through it, he put Mami Yeno into a state known as pəŋk—a term that (as we have already seen) also designates "madness," and one that is, moreover, cognate with the term for "crossroads" (ta-soŋ te-pəŋkine, "the crossed roads"). In this "crossed" state between this world (nɔ-ru) and the "other world" of the spirits (ro-sɔki), Mami Yeno was able to penetrate the spirits' world and trick aŋ-yina Musa into revealing secrets to Pa Koroma. Thus while, as we saw in chapter 2, medi-cines of Darkness have long been used to make travelers, fighters, and refugees on the upper Guinea coast invisible to those (both humans and spirits) who might seize or kill them, Pa Koroma turned the spirit optics of Darkness to his own purposes of disguise, illusion, penetration, and revelation.

Conclusion   The divination techniques explored in this chapter bear wit-ness to an Islamic transformation that occurred when Muslim migrants were given positions of ritual and political authority in the Sierra Leone hinterland

during the eighteenth and nineteenth centuries. Yet although earlier divination practices were replaced by the more prestigious Muslim Mande techniques that these migrants brought, this Islamicization of oracles was never
total or complete. Thus one Mande offspring of Muslim sand divination, aŋ-
bɛrɛ, had its Islamic past erased, becoming an oracle of local water spirits and
coming to carry, at least for certain diviners and their clients, positive values
of venerability and locality.

While some diviners recount discursive, intentional memories of these
techniques' pasts in reworked narratives of the cave hadith and in accounts of
the foreign power of "the Jinn of Musa," they also embody contrasting kinds
of memories in their practice of divination techniques and (more rarely) in
their narration of origin stories. As we have seen, these include what Cole
(2001) calls "incidental" memories, which encompass both Pa Biyare's narrative memory of predatory warriors in his version of the cave story, and practical memories of a past landscape in divination images that are not explicit
expressions of recall. These divination images—roads that lead to Life and
Death, crossroads that draw invisible powers *"from all directions,"* and houses
that are ritually Closed containers—are invested with meanings from the history of a landscape at the interface of local, Atlantic, and metropolitan worlds.

The ritual use of microcosm, in which the social or spiritual world is modeled and manipulated through material objects or inscriptions, is common in
techniques of divination (see, e.g, Turner 1975; Werbner 1989: 19–60; Shaw
1991). Pa Koroma, remember, described the book (*"Shamsu ma-rof"*) from
which his aŋ-yina Musa Writing had come as *"a kind of map"* that contained
"all the things that are happening in the world." But through the divination techniques described in this chapter, diviners map landscapes that are also times.
Through chronotopic ritual microcosms in which a landscape *is* a history, diviners appropriate the dangerous potency of hidden habitations, enclosed
towns, and hazardous but powerful roads and crossroads. Using their own
versions of the techniques of Darkness and Closure that gave people the capacities to live in such a landscape, they rework historically constituted sites
of power and danger. Diviners thus "remember" the landscape of the slave
trade nondiscursively when they create a microcosm and work with divinatory spirits who control its ritual space, thereby converting it into their own
ritual power.

Diviners' Knowledge, Diviners' Lives

To become a diviner is to gain divinatory knowledge and authority. But in the upper Guinea coast, different kinds of knowledge have been constituted through different historical processes: the Atlantic trade, the legitimate trade, the dissemination of Islam and Christianity, the imposition of European colonialism, and applications of Western education and technology have built up layers of disparate forms of knowledge that have been made to reverberate, to comment upon each other, and often to argue. As Lambek writes of Islamic expertise on the Comoro island of Mayotte, what appears today as a pluralistic multiplicity is in fact a historically produced sedimentation of layers of knowledge:

> When we examine "culture" in Mayotte we see a complex layering of multiple forms of knowledge. Without necessarily being able to construct the history of this formation one can nonetheless be "historical" simply by not taking what one observes as a single unified structure but instead recognizing its intrinsic heterogeneity. (1990: 35)

It is not only the diversity of heterogeneous forms of knowledge that makes them lived histories. It is also—and especially—in the operation of certain kinds of knowledge as hegemonic that histories of conquest and domination are often registered: successive impositions of authority generate authorized epistemologies that are presented as superseding prior ways of knowing (Taussig 1987). Partly as a result of these emerging hegemonies, representations of diviners and their knowledge as sinister have become commonplace in Sierra Leone. Diviners, as we shall see, have to negotiate these representations.

In exploring divinatory knowledge in this chapter, I try to trace its historical production and its arguments and convergences with competing forms of knowledge. I also examine how these processes are drawn upon and debated in diviners' lives. But first, my initial task is to establish that skills of divination and healing do not form an untouched "traditional" baseline on top of which all other forms of knowledge have been sedimented: they have been constituted and reconstituted in different historical contexts that have themselves become embedded within diviners' knowledge and experience. This presence of the past in divinatory knowledge can be seen in diviners' encounters with tutelary spirits.

Spirit Contracts   Most diviners claim to have "four eyes" (ε-fɔr t-anlε)— two ordinary eyes and two invisible eyes to penetrate the Darkness veiling the spirits from ordinary human sight. But diviners require more than this special four-eyed vision; they also need an ongoing relationship with a tutelary spirit (or sometimes with several such spirits) who mediates access to the knowledge of other spirits and thereby to the hidden, extrahuman realm on which divination and healing depend. Usually this is a river spirit, often a Muslim jinn (a-yina), and typically white in color and of opposite sex to the diviner. The tutelary spirit bestows knowledge in the form of specific "secrets" (ε-gbuŋdu) that include the capacity to use a particular divination technique and to realize the healing (and harmful) properties of medicinal plants. If the future diviner is pursuing an Arabic education, the spirit instructs him (such diviners are nearly always male) in knowledge of special written words. Pa Ahmadu Fonah, for instance, was studying with Pa Alfa Koroma in Petbana when his dream came:

> *I learned Arabic from Pa Abu in Magbitheno. I heard that Pa Koroma at Petbana was better, so I jumped to him. I was not married—I was a young man—and I learned from Pa Koroma for nine years. I dreamed they* [tutelary spirits] *gave me an Arabic slate* (aŋ-walka); *they told me to read it. They wrote on it and gave it to me to read. They were white spirits* (ε-yina), *sometimes two, sometimes three.*

In most cases, this spirit either appears to the novice in a dream or emerges by the riverside, offering to impart the knowledge of how to divine and heal in exchange for a sacrifice (s-athka), often that of a sheep. These initiatory encounters with spirits are usually both gendered and contractual.

Pa Abdul, a successful young diviner in Magburaka when I first knew him in 1977, told me how his own relationship with his tutelary spirit had begun:

RS: *How did you become a diviner?*

PA: *The gift (aŋ-boya) I have is a lineage gift. My great-grandfather was a great warrior. When he died, my grandfather, Pa Kaper Bongo, took over the warriorship. When he died, he left his gift with his son, who was a famous hunter. When my father died, he called me to him in a sacred forest near Makomp [Abdul's lineage home]. My eyes were tied with a white cloth, and I slept. I saw a fine white woman, who said that my father had asked her to transfer the gift to me, and asked me what kind of gift I would like: to be a famous warrior, hunter, chief or Muslim specialist (ɔ-mɔre)? I replied that I wanted to learn Arabic and to learn what is hidden. I said, "Whenever something is hidden, I want to know how to find it." After this, she stretched out her hand and we greeted each other as a sign of handing over the gift. Then she gave me a red cloth with perfume in it. Anyone who has this perfume and puts it in their eyes can see hidden things.*

The gift from the white woman aŋ-yina was for a certain period only—five, ten, or twenty years [Abdul did not want to divulge which]. After this, the power stops unless there is a review of the whole arrangement, and she will have to be given certain things, such as a sheep. . . .

I disappeared (dinɛ) when I went to sleep and spoke to the woman. I was gone for two days; the woman had taken me to ro-sɔki [the spirit world]. When she left me, and I came back, I was not myself. I was dizzy for seven days. When I returned, they made sacrifices. My family brought some rice flour, an egg, three cents, and some raw gold to the forest. They put these things in a bowl with a white cloth spread on top. They fired seven bullets and all turned their backs and returned to town. So I do not need to prepare any medicines: the gift is inside me.

Pa Abdul's spirit's gift of a spiritually charged red cloth and perfume, his offerings to her of a sheep, rice flour, and raw gold, and the contracted, temporally defined character of these reciprocities subsume both a patrilineal legacy and a contractual agreement. As a patrilineal legacy—a "lineage gift"—his father's endowment of the white spirit tied together different generations of fathers and sons with exceptional capacities. These capacities could be manifest through different kinds of knowledge and skill: warfare, hunting, ruling, or mastering the esoteric Arabic knowledge of ɔ-mɔre. The white spirit's lineage gift, however, had to be periodically renegotiated by striking a new bargain after an agreed number of years.

In many accounts I heard, diviners' initial encounters with their tutelary spirits had explicitly contractual qualities, taking the form of a bargain struck after a short discussion. Sometimes the divinatory skills that the spirit offered were represented as an attractive form of "work" *(ma-paŋth)* that would be exchanged for ritual payment. Ya Yebu, a female diviner we will meet again later in this chapter, described her first encounter with her tutelary spirit in these terms:

> *I saw a spirit* (ɔ-kərfi), *who came with a message from the Place of Spirits* (ro-sɔki). *I hadn't given birth to my first child then. I went to wash clothes at the river. The spirit said to me, "I have work that I want you to do with me." He said, if I like the work, I should pay three sheep. The first thing that he gave me was* aŋ-bɛrɛ [river pebble divination].

In other accounts, trade and commerce become the dominant images of such bargains. Pa Koroma in Petbana told me of his own negotiations:

> *I saw the spirit* (aŋ-yina)—*she was small—when I'd begun my Arabic education. She was a Muslim. She said, "You've seen me and I've seen you. What do you want me to do for you?" I said, "Since I'm learning the Qur'an, I'd like to discover certain things for people, so they'll pay me and I'll get money. I'd like you to give me that knowledge." The jinn agreed, and asked "If I do, what will you do for me?" I said I would give her a sheep.*

Pa Koroma and the female jinn thus agreed upon the exchange of a sheep for divinatory knowledge—a form of knowledge that would itself become, through divinatory practice, the basis for a form of "commerce" in which hidden knowledge is exchanged for money.

Diviners' relationships with their tutelary spirits of opposite sex are sometimes sexualized, and sometimes edged with rules concerning relationships with human spouses. In an extreme (and rare) instance of such rules, a spirit might tell the diviner not to marry at all. Pa Koroma's former student, Pa Fonah, was told by one of his female spirits, for instance, *"If you want to learn, don't marry."* *"I married,"* Pa Fonah told me, *"but she* [his wife] *died."* *"Did the*

DIVINERS' KNOWLEDGE, DIVINERS' LIVES / 107

spirit mind your marriage?" I asked, after expressing sympathy. *"I don't know,"* replied Pa Fonah, *"perhaps that's why she died. All of the women [spirits] help me. Sometimes one of them comes and visits me in a dream."*

Spirits, of course, make bargains and have sexualized relationships with humans—especially those who become ritual specialists—virtually every-where and at all times. I would like to suggest, though, that the *form* that such bargains have taken in the visionary experiences of Temne diviners crystallizes in intriguing ways a particular commercial relationship that developed during the Atlantic trade.

Landlords, Strangers, and Euro-Africans   In both their contractual and gen-dered character, and in their association with rivers, diviners' alliances with tutelary spirits recapitulate a long-established feature of the upper Guinea coast called the "landlord-stranger" relationship. Here the "stranger" (Temne *ɔ-tik*), a newcomer who wishes to settle and/or to have land to farm, brings a respect-offering *(aŋ-laŋbe)* to the "landlord," the chief or lineage head in a particular place, and an agreement is set up: often the stranger, for instance, helps to clear the landlord's farm, and gives the landlord a portion of his own harvest. Like Abdul's arrangement with his tutelary spirit, the agreement is both "inherited" by the descendants of those who made the original compact and subject to periodic renegotiation: "If both parties fulfil their obligations, the tenant will be allotted land year after year by his landlord, although theo-retically the arrangement is reviewed at the end of each farming season. Should either party to the agreement die, his successor, as family head, must renew the arrangement" (Dorjahn and Fyfe 1962: 392).

Diviners' relationships with tutelary spirits, though, have more in common with a rather different kind of landlord-stranger arrangement. In the era of the Atlantic trade European slave traders were especially advantageous as strangers, just as Muslim Mande and Fula migrants were in the eighteenth and nineteenth centuries. By the sixteenth century, European private traders—lançados—were dispersed in villages throughout the upper Guinea coast and the Senegambia (Rodney 1970: 77). Both at that time and later, most of these foreign traders lived by rivers or other bodies of water, settling "as individuals in towns and villages on islands or along the river-banks, under the protection of the king or chief who ruled there" (Dorjahn and Fyfe 1962: 392). Bringing otherwise unobtainable commodities, the lançados were accommodated and given pro-tection and brokerage by local rulers; in return they paid rent, gave their land-lords obligatory gifts, and sometimes paid commission on trade (394).

This kind of relationship developed from local practices of hospitality to guests, including African traders. In the early days of commerce with Europeans, Portuguese lançados were categorized, Rodney notes, as "guests" rather than "strangers":

> The Portuguese applied the term *estrangeiros* ("strangers") to all their rivals; and the Africans, coming first into contact with the Portuguese, adopted this word to designate whites other than Portuguese. On the other hand, the word used by the Portuguese to refer to both the African chief and the *lançado* was *hospede*, meaning either "host" or "guest," according to context; and for the sixteenth century it is important to consider the model of Afro-Portuguese relations as that of "host and guest" rather than the more impersonal "landlord and stranger." (Rodney 1970: 83)

African hosts' relations with Portuguese guests, according to Rodney, were characterized in the sixteenth century by the exchange of "gifts" that often, as time went on, became indistinguishable from profit-oriented barter. By the eighteenth century, when foreign "guests" had become "strangers" and local "hosts" had become "landlords," "this exchange of presents was a standardized procedure known as 'service,' and the African rulers clearly looked forward to a profit" (Rodney 1970: 85). Thus over time, relationships between chiefs and European traders came increasingly to resemble commercial contracts. Yet obligations toward each other—such as landlords' moral accountability for their strangers—meant that landlord-stranger relationships were (and still are) considerably more than business arrangements (85).

These obligations were often shaped through forms of marriage. We have already seen in chapter 3 that chiefs encouraged eighteenth- and nineteenth-century Muslim strangers to settle in a particular place by offering them a wife. In previous centuries too, offers of marriage were the means through which traders—both European and African—were brought into a relationship of affinity (and therefore obligation) to their hosts (MacCormack 1983a: 277). Alvares details certain aspects of this relationship that were repugnant to his early-seventeenth-century missionary sensibilities in his account of the "abominable custom of *cabondos*":

> Someone goes to one of their villages to deal in cola, rice, etc. He selects his host, who parades in front of the trader his whole household of women/wives and tells him to choose one. . . . If he wants a woman, he is given one, for all

purposes; and they are content to accept this, out of self-interest. For apart from the normal expenses, as long as the trade goes on with the woman's parents and relatives, and until he leaves, the poor "son-in-law" pays up—because he clothes the "father-in-law" and pays very steeply for these devilish arrangements. . . . And if after taking one he goes off with another of those he was shown, his own woman reports him. (Alvares 1990, 2, chap. 4: 4)

In addition to clothing his father-in-law, the trader also had to clothe both the woman herself and any children she bore from their relationship (Rodney 1970: 84). In addition, the European newcomer was usually denied land for cultivation and was therefore dependent on his African host for his food supply (Rodney 1970: 204; Brooks 1993: 189). Any lapses of fidelity on his part, moreover, could be punishable by the seizure of all his goods and sometimes even by his death (Rodney 1970: 83–84, 201).

These relationships between African women and European men were thus circumscribed by exacting rules that differed from those of other forms of marriage. While husbands who were not strangers had important obligations toward their wives and in-laws (as we shall see in the next chapter), they had their own lineage land to farm and were part of an alliance between two lineages that was valuable to both sides. In most marriages, then, the husband was not totally dependant on his wife's father for his food supply and for social support. And in eighteenth- and nineteenth-century marriages linking Mande and Fula strangers and Temne-speaking chiefs, as we have seen, these Muslim migrants were associated with the power of the states from which they had come, and they were sometimes given land to cultivate (Howard 1997: 37). Husbands in these instances were not bound by their in-laws to the same strict sanctions for infidelity to which European lançados were subject: although the lover's husband was entitled to retribution, the wife's father could not ordinarily punish his son-in-law by total confiscation of property or by death. Through these rule-bound and sexualized relationships, landlords created ties of affinity with wealth-bringing Europeans that the former exploited for commercial advantage (Brooks 1993: 189). The women who entered into these relationships, moreover, pursued their own objectives, acting as interpreters of language and culture, collaborators in trade, and crucial intermediaries between African and European commercial spheres (Brooks 1993: 137; MacCormack 1983a: 278).

If European private traders were in a relationship of dependency on their African hosts and wives, this was not true of their Euro-African children. Like their fathers, these children often identified themselves as white (Brooks 1993: 194; Rodney 1970: 203), but they were also incorporated into ruling cognatic descent groups through their mothers (MacCormack 1983a: 278). They became—like their mothers—important commercial and cultural inter- mediaries; some were able to acquire political positions through their mater- nal links (278), while others were involved in commerce full-time, acting as interpreters, commercial advisors, and river pilots, and buying goods for Euro- pean ships (Rodney 1970: 203–14). Some became dominant figures in the region: in 1728, for instance, Jose Lopez de Moura destroyed the slave factory at Bence Island on the Sierra Leone River when the Royal African Company's factor tried to cut out the role of Euro-African middlemen such as Lopez (Rod- ney 1970: 213–4). And, Rodney tells us, "as late as 1821, one of the villages on Port Loko was ruled over by Pa Antonio, described as having 'a brazen crucifix suspended from his neck,' and claiming descent from the Portuguese" (1970: 215).

Like diviners' tutelary spirits, then, both European traders and their Euro- African descendants lived on or near bodies of water, opened up powerful flows from "outside," entered into contractual exchanges that were mediated through a gendered, sexualized, and very rule-bound relationship, and were categorized as white.

Palimpsest Spirits

> The Krifis are said to reside in the wood or bush, and sometimes to make a noise before sun-rise, as if one were striking a tin-pan. Some, they say, look like White men, some like the Mori-men (Mohammedans), i.e. of a Mulatto complexion.   Schlenker, *A Collection of Temne Traditions, Fables and Proverbs*

The above resonances between white spirits and white traders should not, how- ever, lead us to conclude that relationships between diviners and their tutelary spirits are simple Durkheimean reflections of historical relationships with Eu- ropeans. In Sierra Leone, the whiteness of diviners' tutelary spirits is explicitly identified as the whiteness of Europeans (Temne *aŋ-potho*, from "the Portu- guese")—but this is a category, remember, that encompasses Euro-Africans and their descendants. Most male diviners I knew told me that their tutelary spirits looked "just like" me. Any doubts I had about how literally they meant this evaporated when, during my first period of fieldwork, I entered the house of Pa Abdul, the diviner whose visionary experience is recounted above, and saw a picture of a young man and woman who looked to me like the white Peace Corps volunteers who comprised some of the most visible and numerous "strangers" in Sierra Leone during the late 1970s. Neatly dressed in T-shirts and bell-bottoms, they strode down the road confidently. Their very European whiteness was clearly more specific than that of beings who are merely spiritually "other." And these, Abdul told me, were his tutelary spirits.

Yet despite their European appearance, tutelary spirits like Abdul's do not merely mirror the European side of landlord-stranger relationships. "Instead of seeing [such beings] as a mirror image of one thing or another," as Spyer writes in her analysis of the red-haired "sea wives" of Aruese pearl divers, "it is perhaps better to imagine an open-ended kaleidoscope that refracts, fragments, reassembles, and illuminates aspects of commercial, gendered, and interethnic exchanges" (1997: 531). By the same token, neither are diviners' spirit tutors straightforward instances of mimesis, in which one mimes that which is strange and powerful in order to master it (Stoller 1995). While these white spirits certainly seem to incorporate the power of landlord-stranger relationships, they do so as signifiers that refuse to be anchored to a single referent. For one thing, the spirits exercise considerable control over "their" diviners, whereas European traders hardly had comparable dominance over their African hosts and wives: it was the hosts and wives who seem to have had the upper hand. For another thing, the Europeans were male, while the white spirits are typically female, the usual exceptions being either when a diviner has several tutelary spirits, or when the diviner in question is female and her tutelary spirit is correspondingly male (as in Ya Yebu's account above).

And we must not forget another recurring characteristic of diviners' spirits. As the missionary Schlenker wrote of Temne-speakers' understandings of spirits in mid-nineteenth-century Port Loko, "some [spirits], they say, look like White men, some like the Mori-men (Mohammedans), i.e. of a Mulatto complexion" (1861: xi). Like those nineteenth-century spirits, the tutelary spirits of most late-twentieth-century diviners I knew combined the appearance of "White men" and "Mori-men." While some diviners—both non-Muslim and Muslim—describe their tutelary spirit as ɔ-kərfi, the generic Temne term for "spirit" (as Ya Yebu did in her account above), most diviners who use written Arabic in their techniques claim a relationship with a Muslim jinn, aŋ-yina. In certain other parts of the Muslim world, jinn are perceived as wild, "outside" forces of the bush in counterpoint to a civilized Muslim sphere. Instead of embodying a contrast to all things Islamic, Sierra Leonean ɛ-yina are spirits who *are* Muslim: they know the Qur'an, they write Arabic, and they impart the "secrets" of special written words and prayers. As we saw above, Pa Ahmadu Fonah, Pa Koroma's former student, was given such a lesson in his initiatory dream: *"I dreamed they gave me an Arabic slate* (aŋ-walka) *and told me to read it. They wrote on it and gave it to me to read. They were white ε-yina, sometimes two, sometimes three."* As diviners' spirits, ε-yina seem to intensify the power and skills of the eighteenth- and nineteenth-century Muslim migrants who settled in large numbers in Temne-speaking communities. If, as we saw in chapter 3, chiefs appropriated the foreign power of Islamic knowledge by inviting Muslim specialists to become their personal diviners and healers and by incorporating these migrants into alliance relationships through marriage, diviners incorporate this power through relationships with female ε-yina.

Thus, instead of being supernaturalized Europeans, Euro-Africans, or Muslim Mande migrants, diviners' spirits seem to detach and recombine powerful aspects of each of the different parties—both foreign and local—in landlord-stranger relationships. Many of these aspects, moreover, are drawn from different (although overlapping) historical periods and combined as chronologically heterogeneous palimpsests. These spirits take on the "whiteness" of Europeans, Euro-Africans, and (in the case of Pa Abdul's bell-bottomed and platform-heeled spirits) late-twentieth-century Americans, who channel powerful "outside" flows from another world. But these attributes are fused with the contractual muscle of dominant African hosts, the potent Islamic knowledge of the Muslim Mande "strangers" who were most numerous in the eighteenth and nineteenth centuries, and the heavily rule-bound relationships with powerful African wives through which Atlantic flows were tapped from the sixteenth through the eighteenth centuries. These "palimpsest spirits" thereby recapitulate but also reconfigure the most potent aspects of relations and practices from the "commercial, gendered, and interethnic exchanges" (Spyer 1997: 531) of Atlantic commerce, Muslim trade, and postcolonial encounters as they negotiate exchanges between one world and another.

"Atlantic" Seizure: Knowledge as Capture   Sometimes, though, bargains between diviners and spirits are reneged on. These arrangements may not, in fact, be willingly embraced in the first place: spirits sometimes capture those they want as their human mediators, releasing them only when satisfied that the reluctant diviner's ritual payment has been made (or will soon be forthcoming). The future diviner may, for instance, be sent an episode of sickness or insanity that, either in a dream or when taken to another diviner for diagnosis, is revealed as a sign that the patient had been "seized" *(wop)*. When, for example, a diamond digger in Koidu called Pa Ahmadu Conteh returned to his home town of Lunsar in 1974 for his grandfather's "Forty Days" funeral, his leg developed a topical ulcer that would not heal. *"I had a dream,"* Pa Ahmadu told me in 1978. *"I was told to take up divination and give a sheep, or I wouldn't get well. I had an operation. When I recovered, I went to a diviner, who told me I must take up divination."* Pa Ahmadu had been seized by the tutelary spirit of his grandfather, who had been a diviner. His grandfather began to teach him divination with aŋ-thasabiya, the rosary beads, in dreams, and Ahmadu offered the tutelary spirit rice flour, water, and a white kola nut. He was unable, however, to buy the sheep the spirit had demanded. Four years' later, in 1978, Pa Ahmadu combined his diamond digging with divination, but was still unable to "redeem" *(wura)* himself by completing his payment to the spirit: *"I am sick now, and will be sick until it gets what it asked for. I need to find a sheep for my grandfather's spirit. When I find a diamond, I'll get money and make the sacrifice."*

Sometimes, moreover, the initiatory dream itself takes the form of an abduction without any prior broken contract: spirits simply "see" *(nəŋk)* the people they want, "seize" them, and bind them. *"I didn't learn divination,"* Pa Conteh, a diviner in the village of Mabureh, near Petbana, told me, *"When I slept, I dreamt a spirit tied me up and said we should do this work. When I woke up the next morning, I could do it. I gave an egg."*

This spirit-seizure often entails forms of absence, displacement, and disappearance. Like children who vanish in the forest when a bush spirit captures them, some diviners vanish when taken by their tutelary spirits. Abdul, remember, "disappeared" when the white female jinn carried him off—*"I was gone for two days; the woman had taken me to ro-sɔki"* (the spirit world)—and for seven days afterwards he was "dizzy," "not himself." Although most diviners do not claim to disappear physically when their spirit seizes them, many become temporarily "crazy" (pəŋk), entering a "crossed" state in which they are neither properly located in the world of ordinary human beings (nɔ-ru) nor in the worlds of the dead (ro-kərfi) or of the spirits (ro-sɔki). In this psychically displaced condition, those seized by a spirit often become physically displaced as well, compelled to wander the roads in a state of madness until a relative finds them and brings them back.

This is where, I suggest, a further twist develops in the ritual reconfiguring of aspects of the Atlantic trade. As we have seen in chapter 1, the most common way of obtaining slaves was through the seizure of captives during raids.

Another frequent means was seizure and enslavement in lieu of outstanding debts (Rodney 1970: 102–6). Where the creditor was a European stranger, his landlord usually provided security for the credit his stranger extended to others and recovered the debts himself: "If debts were unpaid," according to Dorjahn and Fyfe, "the landlord paid them and recovered the loss by selling the debtor or his relatives" (1962: 394). The imagery of grabbing, catching, and seizing, and the association of debt with seizure and disappearance, thus acquired considerable prominence during both the Atlantic trade and the colonial legitimate trade that succeeded it.

Temne contains a number of Portuguese loanwords (carried over from the Luso-African trade language once spoken on the coast) that attest to the prominence of this imagery. According to the linguist Turay:

> "Grabbing" features prominently in the loanwords from Portuguese. . . . **bekar** (*aborcar,* monopolise, embrace, grab) Grab, fall on someone or something suddenly, **kamper** (*campar,* encircle, fence, camp) Encircle, ambush, **panya** (*apanhar*) Catch, seize are all possible clues as to how unwilling slaves were obtained. (1976: 34)

This Temne-Portuguese vocabulary of capture derives, as Turay suggests, from raiding for slaves, as well as from the practice of forcibly selling into slavery those who failed to repay a debt (see Rodney 1970: 102–6).

In arguing that contemporary diviners' experiences of spirit-seizure are historically mediated I am not, of course, suggesting that "seizure" had the same meanings during the Atlantic and legitimate trades as it did in the late twentieth century.[1] Nor am I claiming that the seizure of Temne diviners by their tutelary spirits has its origin solely in the history of trade with Europeans rather than in African ritual meanings and practices.[2] After all, while the capture *of* knowledge has long been a salient trope of learning in Western contexts—in keeping with Europe's travel-exploration-adventure-colonization proclivities—seizure *by* a being who bestows certain kinds of knowledge and capacity is common in parts of West Africa (e.g. Amadiume 1987; Jackson 1982). But presenting "African meanings" and "European trade" as mutually exclusive sources for diviners' experiences of seizure is itself problematic. It presumes the maintenance over several centuries of separate spheres of African ritual on the one hand and trade with Europeans on the other—Europeans who had since the late fifteenth century, remember, become integrated through marriage into villages scattered throughout the upper Guinea coast, participated in African rituals, and fathered lineages of Euro-African descendants. It also presumes that this trade with Europeans, which was so successfully appropriated by African land-lords and wives, was not invested with African meanings and did not, in turn, place its own stamp upon the historical development of those meanings.

Through their visionary experiences, I suggest, Temne diviners convert the dangers of Atlantic and nineteenth-century seizure and the terrible power ac-corded to debt in their region's past into transformative encounters with spir-its. Like metaphors of "mounting" in Yoruba spirit possession (Matory 1994) and like the figures of the unquiet preconquest dead in Columbian sorcery, "in which the history of the conquest itself acquires the role of the sorcerer" (Taussig 1987: 373, emphasis deleted), Temne diviners convey their experi-ences of seizure by spirits in images that carry considerable historical freight. Historical processes that made wealth appear, made people disappear, and recast the social world appear transmuted, through diviners' initiatory expe-riences, into extrahuman capacities to heal, to harm, and to find what is hidden.

Personal and Collective Memories   If diviners' visionary experiences of spirits are historically mediated, however, they do not constitute identical ver-sions of a single "collective" memory. This brings us to a recurring problem for scholarship on social memory: how do we conceive of "memory" beyond the boundary of the individual, but without creating a reified, homogenized notion of "collective memory"? Cole (2001) observes in this connection that in many classic works (notably Halbwachs 1992 and Nora 1989), notions of social memory are not only constituted through a dichotomy with personal memory but are also implicitly modeled on individual thought processes. This problem is especially pronounced when the focus is ritual, as in Conner-ton's depiction of commemorative ceremonies as shaping "communal mem-ory" (1989: 61) through an embodied performance of the past that is pre-sumed to be the same for all participants (1989: 71–72).

In order to avoid the dichotomy (as well as the implicit homology) be-tween personal and "collective" memory, Cole (2001) focuses on "memory techniques"—social and cultural practices by means of which people shape social memories, and through which social and individual memory articulate together. Similarly, Temne diviners' visionary relationships with spirits who capture them, make contracts with them, and bind them in quasi-marital rela-tionships are both ineluctably social and ineluctably diverse. Differently situ-ated diviners with disparate circumstances draw upon different aspects of enslavement and of landlord-stranger relationships from their region's past in their encounters with tutelary spirits. As Spyer puts it in her study of Aruese pearl divers and their undersea wives, diviners' spirits thereby "open up novel spaces for the construction of agencies" (1997: 517) in individual diviners' lives. In the rest of this chapter, I explore how they do so.

Ya Bay's Loads   I met Ya Bay Kolone in Freetown during the rainy season of 1992, when I attended a ritual performed for Pa Yamba, the diviner whose descriptions of the Roads of aŋ-bɛrɛ and the Crossroads of aŋ-mɛmnɛ we encountered in the previous chapter. At that time, Pa Yamba was preparing to undergo a (greatly feared) hernia operation in hospital, and he decided to offer a sacrifice to the spirits who had contributed to his ritual powers. He asked several ritual specialists he knew to officiate, one of whom was Ya Bay—a warm, vivacious older woman who, when she heard of my interest in diviners and divination, invited me to come and visit her (plate 11).

Ya Bay had an remarkable range of ritual specializations. As well as being a diviner and healer, she had senior titles in three cult associations: *Yaŋ Digba*, an official in the women's Bondo association; *Na Soko*, a female official linking the men's Poro and the women's Bondo associations; and *Ya Bay* ("Mother Chief"), the title given to a woman who controls the medicine of the deadly thunder swear *(aŋ-gbɔm).*[3] Like diviners' tutelary spirits, the spirits of these associations may "call" and "seize" people they wish to initiate as officials. In the two rooms on Blackhall Road at the edge of Freetown's East End in which Ya Bay lived with her husband, she told me of how these ritual specializations had been thrust upon her through spirit-seizure.

For most Temne women I knew, linear accounts of "my life as a narrative," unfolding from birth to the present along a straight timeline, were foreign forms of self-fashioning. Usually, I got fragmentary stories over the course of different visits that created a mosaic rather than a narrative flowing from a beginning to an end. Yet on my very first visit, Ya Bay's words came rushing out, unstoppable in spite of her husband's interruptions and my questions:

YB: *I don't know my age. When they gave birth to me, we were twins. My companion [twin] returned [died], and I was left behind. While my mother was breastfeeding me, my sisters were playing with me, and pushed me into the fire. I was hurt: my mouth was burned. Before morning came, there were worms coming out of my mouth, and there were also boils. I was about to die. They were trying to heal me, and they took me to my mother's home in Limba country. When I had been healed, my father swore* (seŋa), *and all those who knew about* [were responsible for] *my illness died. After the swearing, my father died—I was just like this child* [indicating a small child]. *He was a paramount chief. They brought me to Freetown. And when I was brought I stayed here for a long time. I got married. I gave birth to many children; some of them are grown now. I fell sick* (tuy): *it was a big illness.*

Her husband (interrupting): You went crazy (pəŋk)—*tell the truth!*

YB: I was moved everywhere [by the sickness]. *They searched for me, and I was in the bush. I spent three years in the bush with my child, and my child died in the bush.*

RS: *Sorry, Mother, sorry. How big was your child?*

YB: *My child was about to start walking, but had nothing to eat. I had no milk—my breasts were dry—and the child started crying like a cat. He was my third child. My hair became "dreads." They searched for me, and they found me in the bush. I was taken, then, to my own town* [where she was born] *to be healed. They succeeded in healing me, and I was brought to Freetown, and I was lost again and went to the bush. And God* (K-uru) *sent an angel* (ɔ-maleka).

Her husband (interrupting): Let's tell the truth: it was a spirit (ɔ-kərfi)!

YB: *The person* (ɔw-uni) *was short, a very short person. He took me to the road and he disappeared. I didn't see him any more. I sat there until about five o'clock, and a car came. It was white. The owner of the car was a white man, and he had black men in the back. When the white man saw me, he told the driver to stop the car. He came down and looked at my palms and my eyes. He told them to put me in the back. One of the black men told the white man that his mother knows about medicine, so he asked the white man to take me to his mother to be healed: I was a person, and if they took me to his mother, I would be healed. The white man agreed. We took the ferry and we entered that town* [Mange Bureh]. *They left me in the house of that woman, and money was left in the hands of the woman to take care of me. The white man went back, and he brought everything: clothes, food, and a bed. He returned and handed over all of these for me. I was healed. And when she divined for me, the woman said I had a "load"* (a-kothe) *on my head. I belonged in the association of the Ya Bay, so the spirits were drawing me, and I should take up the load* (gbasi a-kothe). *My people should prepare the load and give it to me. Because they had failed to do so* [earlier], *they* [the spirits] *had followed me in Freetown, and until I took up the load I would never be healed. I was healed, and they prepared the load and gave it to me.*

RS: *Why do you call it "a load?"*

YB: *It's a load because it's heavy for me. I have to heal, I have the thunder swear* (aŋ-

gbɔm), *the first load. I was also called for twins, and for Digba Sowei. I was called
to the Poro and was given the title of Na Soko. Not all ɛ-digba are called to be Na
Soko; I'm a link between the Digbas* [women's Bondo association officials]
and the Sokos [men's Poro association officials]. *I started divination. I used
the looking glass* (aŋ-mɛmnɛ) *to do it. I started getting better. But another medicine* (aŋ-tɔl) *called me, and that was the Sowei.*

RS: *What happened when the Sowei medicine called you?*

YB: *I went crazy again and shouted abuse at the Sokos and Digbas, so they took me to
a diviner. They divined for me and told me to become a Digba. I was taken back
to the bush. I built the ka-yaŋka* [the society house for Digba initiands]. *I
was sent to the Sowei. My children took care of me. They helped me in this. I was
in ka-yaŋka for six years before I was taken out, because there was no money. I
had nobody to help me, only my children. After I was taken out, they* [the spirits]
*pulled me back for another load. I was disturbed again, and I went back for an-
other load. I went to work for three years.*

RS: *What was the load you took up after that of the Digba?*

YB: *I was called back by the Ya Bay medicine, because I had abandoned it. I didn't
want to work with it any more. But K-uru* (God) *didn't agree. That's why I'm
quiet now. I have ta-bari* (twin medicine). *I am healing people. When a child
is sick, I heal it. Stomach aches and headaches, I can heal them.*

In this breathless narrative, Ya Bay recounted how she had been acted
upon by invisible beings since her birth. The daughter of a paramount chief
in Kambia District in the northwest, she was born a twin (ka-bari) but was
"left behind" in this world when her companion twin "returned" to the dead:
until she later established and made offerings to a twin shrine (aŋ-seth ŋa tə-
bari), her lonely companion kept trying to draw her from the world of the
living. She was, moreover, very nearly killed by other unseen agencies when
she was an infant: her mother's co-wives used witchcraft against her, causing
her to fall into a cooking fire and burn her face badly. Her face became so
seriously infected that she was soon near death, and was only healed when
her mother carried her to her own natal town for treatment, away from the
witchly jealousies of her father's home. But her father (and, she told me later,
her mother) died a few years' later, and Ya Bay—still a child—was brought to
Freetown to be brought up by relatives. Her adult life in Freetown, though,
was no less marked by the deaths or disappearance of especially close kin,
by periods of displacement and disorientation of extrahuman origin, and by
problematic relationships deriving from marriage. As she told her story, some

of the tensions of the most recent of these marital relationships—that with her second husband—manifested themselves in her husband's repeated interruptions and authoritative "corrections" of her story. Ya Bai, however, did her best to ignore these.

Tragically, her first episode of spirit-seizure and disappearance cost her the life of her young child, who followed her twin and her mother to the Place of the Dead. Ya Bay's connections to social personhood—her children, her marriage, her settled life in a town, and even her braided hair—were severed as she disappeared from her marital home, *"moved everywhere"* by invisible and unspecified forces that took her into the spirit-space of the bush and turned her hair into matted dreadlocks. She managed to survive, she later told me, only by eating vegetables and cassava planted in the farm clearings she came across, and by occasional gifts of food from people working and cooking at their remote farm huts. Eventually, however, she was reclaimed and relocated in human society when she was found, returned to her kin, and taken to her natal home for a cure. Thus while, at the beginning of her life, a move from the dangers of patrilineal space (and her mother's marital home) to the protected interior of her mother's natal home was necessary for the healing of her burned face, the wandering affliction that had caused her to disappear from her own marital home was healed (at least provisionally) by her return to the place that relocated her in the nucleus of her kin.

This cure was, however, only a temporary respite in a series of episodes of spirit-mediated displacements that were to punctuate her life. Carried away once more from settled human sociality, Ya Bay *"was lost again"* in a second episode of wandering in the bush until she was brought back by four guides. The identity of the first of these in her narrative was a point of contention between her and her husband:

YB: *And God* (K-uru) *sent an angel* (ɔ-maleka).
Her husband (interrupting): Let's tell the truth: it was a spirit (ɔ-kərfi)!
YB: *The person* (ɔw-uni) *was short, a very short person.*

When Ya Bay gave this guide a relatively elevated Islamic status as an "angel," her husband interjected that it had been a less distinguished being—a spirit. Adroitly sidestepping the issue, Ya Bay then adopted a third term—a "person," an inclusive category that can encompass humans, spirits, and angels alike. This person's "shortness" is reminiscent of that of the "short people" described as emerging from the deep bush during elections; but instead of seizing her, he opened a path from the spirit realm of the bush back to human sociality. He ended Ya Bay's disoriented wandering in the wilderness by conducting her out of the bush to a road—itself (like the bush) an unlocated place of passage, but one that engraves a clearly defined, linear route to human settlements. Her wait by the road moved her, in addition, from the less structured temporality of the bush to the curious precision of clock-time as a white man appeared in a white car *"at about five o'clock."* Although the white man was closer to ordinary human personhood than the spirit or angel "person" who had guided Ya Bay out of the bush, he was associated with transport routes, automotive technology, and rapid, clock-timed mobility rather than with any particular location: we do not know where his journey began or where it would end. But this man's Sierra Leonean companion provided both a destination—a named town, Mange Bureh—and his closest kin connection—his own mother—through whose healing capacities Ya Bay's social personhood could be restored (*"I was a person, and if they took me to his mother, I would be healed"*).

Given direction (both literally and figuratively) by this man and his mother, the white man provided Ya Bay with the material means to establish a temporary home and regain her personhood: clothes, food, a bed, and some money. Finally, Ya Bay's new host and healer divined the hidden agency of the spirits behind Ya Bay's dissociation and prescribed the means to heal her: she had to take up the ritual "load" of the thunder-swear medicine (aŋ-gbɔm). Although it was Ya Bay who had to carry this load, it was "her people" who had to prepare it for her: thus the load not only tied her to the spirits who had called her but also reattached her to her own human kin and husband, whose failure to take appropriate action at her earlier "seizure" by the spirits had been the cause of Ya Bay's displacement.

It was through this "load" that Ya Bay became a member of an association of ritually powerful women, all of whom bear the title of Ya Bay ("Mother Chief"). Like other members of the Ya Bay association, she gained the capacity to control the thunder swear, a collection of ritual materials that, when activated through ritual swearing, becomes an instrument of deadly justice by striking wrongdoers. Then, following her healing induction into this association, she was "called" and "pulled" for years by a succession of spirits who insisted that she should carry *their* loads too. Ya Bay thereby became an adept in virtually every Temne cult association and ritual specialization available to women. She was *"called for twins,"* compelled to stabilize the unbalanced presence of her dead twin—who was trying to draw her into the Place of the Dead—by establishing a shrine called "the house of twins" (aŋ-seth ŋa tə-bari). Remarkably, she was also called to become both a Digba (or, using the better-known Mende term, Sowei), an official in the upper echelon of the women's Bondo cult association, and Na Soko ("Mother Poro"), a female official in the men's Poro association—a position that made her *a link between the Digbas and the Sokos* [Poro officials]. And finally, like many Digbas and Poro officials, divination (in her case, with the looking glass [uŋ-mɛmnɛ]) formed another of the ritual loads she carried.

Just how heavy the "loads" were for Ya Bay is conveyed by the extraordinary length of her six-year ritual seclusion for her initiation as a Digba-Sowei. Neither Ya Bay's husband nor her kin were helping her any longer, and her dependance on the meager resources of her children meant that she had to "redeem" *(wura)* herself from her initiators by working for them for several years in her state of ritual separation. But when her six years of labor were finally at an end, she made the mistake of trying to put down her oldest ritual burden—the thunder medicine of the Ya Bay association. As a result, she had to endure yet another ritual marathon: three more years of "work" as she took up that load again. Finally, in the rainy season of 1992, her loads were balanced, although inordinately heavy.

Ya Bay experienced her relationship with the spirits and medicines that seized her in terms of their demand for her labor. During her second induction with the Ya Bay medicine, she *"went to work* (ma-paŋth) *for three years"*: while that work was actual physical labor for the human officials who initiated her, she also spoke of her ritual duties for cult association spirits and medicines in terms of work. Her selection of the term "load," which she used repeatedly to describe her obligation to spiritual forces, is significant:

YB:　I was healed, and they prepared the load and gave it to me.
RS:　Why is it called "a load?"
YB:　It's a load because it's heavy for me. I have to heal, I have the thunder swear, the
　　　first load.

Carrying headloads is women's work. It is women who carry pots, buckets, and bowls of water for the household, who tote heavy baskets of produce to sell at the market, and mainly they who hawk small trade items (oranges, bananas, mangoes, cakes, groundnuts, fish) around towns and motor parks on enamel trays balanced on their heads. What she owed the spirits who abducted her, then, was female labor: without performing this work the spirits would once again seize her and take her from her settled, urban, home into their own alien territory.

Through Ya Bay's gendered imagery of "work," of carrying "loads," we learn that her spirit-seizures inaugurated a life of forced labor that is highly suggestive of the enslavement of women during the Atlantic and legitimate trades. Because higher prices were paid in the New World for male slaves, and because female slaves were in higher demand in the internal slave trade, remember, the slave trade developed a bifurcated form, in which most enslaved men were exported across the Atlantic, while most enslaved women were sold as domestic slaves and wives in the internal slave trade. This gender bifurcation, historians argue, had a demographic impact on the ratio of men to women in those parts of Africa that were integrated into the slave trade. And this imbalance, combined with the availability of female slaves, facilitated polygynous marriage, enabling rulers and wealthy merchants in particular to marry large numbers of wives (Manning 1990: 131–32; Thornton 1996: 42). At the same time, the skewed gender ratio is believed to have increased women's agricultural workloads (Thornton 1996: 41)—especially in such areas as the upper Guinea coast, where land is relatively plentiful but shortages of labor (especially during bush-clearing and at harvest time) are problematic (Richards 1986). While some argue that women were purchased as slaves for their reproductive capacities, most historians maintain that female slaves seem to have been primarily valued as productive laborers (MacCormack 1983a: 272; Robertson and Klein 1983; Thornton 1996).

Slaves who became wives were in a much more vulnerable position than wives who were not slaves: they were subject to abuse from their husband and his kin because they were stripped of their own kin's support (Thornton 1996: 42–43, 44). Because Temne men's marriages with properly connected women were valuable alliances that were drawn upon for political support and labor recruitment, the active presence of a woman's kin backed her room to maneuver within her marriage. Wives who were slaves, on the other hand, lacked this leverage. They could neither refuse nor leave their marriages except by running away—and many would have been deterred by knowing that their husbands had medicine that would afflict them with sickness if they tried to escape. In their kinless, unprotected state, moreover, they were likely to end up with another owner even if they did run away (see Robertson and Klein 1983: 11–12). And although slaves who were wives were not altogether without room to maneuver in marriage, their strategies were severely curtailed without the presence of kin to back them.

Like a wife who was a slave, Ya Bay's (ritual) labor was coerced, and her relationship with her main tutelary spirit was a form of marriage. When I asked her about her spirits, she began by mentioning that she had inherited the personal spirit behind her father's chieftaincy—a white female spirit who had never "seized" her. She then went on to describe a marital relationship with a male spirit who became her husband:

YB: From my father, I got a white woman spirit. She helped my father get the para-mount chieftaincy: he was ɔ-kaŋde (the paramount chief).

RS: Do you also have a male spirit?

YB: Yes, he comes and has sex with me. He is fighting my husband; he is jealous. My [human] husband took me from my spirit (ɔk-ərfi) husband, and my spirit hus-band was providing the means to feed me [through her healing], so is it not right that my husband should pay? My spirit husband had told my husband he should make a sheep sacrifice. He refuses. He can't afford it. So the spirit makes him sick.

Ya Bay had, on many occasions, complained that her second husband (who was also a diviner) did not work and had no money. When she got sick, she often complained, he could not pay for a cure for her. And like any husband whose wife went to another man, her spirit husband—who, as Ya Bay pointed out, provided her livelihood by bestowing the capacity to heal—had the right to be properly compensated by the new, human husband (in this case, with the ritual payment of a sheep).

Ya Bay's relationship with her spirit husband seemed to have begun, in fact, during her difficult marriage to her first husband:

RS: Did you have problems with your first husband?

YB: Yes. My spirit was angry because my husband wouldn't cure me when I was sick.

RS: Did you have co-wives?

YB: Yes. I found them and married them to my husband! There were four of us. But they didn't like me; they were jealous. I had children and they didn't. My husband treated me badly, so that my co-wives would not bewitch my children. He only gave me rice to eat and feed my children with—nothing else. My spirit was angry with my husband for this, and wanted to take me away, so he sent the sickness— not to kill me, but just so that I would take up the load. My husband was afraid when I got sick; he didn't want me to stay in the house.

The jealousies between co-wives that had caused Ya Bay's suffering as a young child, then, were repeated in her first marriage. When her first husband failed to provide adequately for her and her children he justified this, according to Ya Bay, as a way of preventing witchly attacks upon her children that might be generated by her co-wives' jealousies. Yet this neglect is *not* appropriate behavior by a husband toward his wife—especially his senior wife—as Ya Bay conveyed in her tone of complaint when she described this to me. Had her mother—and more especially her father, the chief—been alive, her husband would surely have behaved differently (and if he did not, her relatives in Freetown would probably have felt compelled to put pressure on him). But as things were, with inadequate support from her remaining kin, there was very little that Ya Bay could do about her husband's bad treatment. In this respect, at least, she was like a slave wife stripped of kin and without the usual means of redress for her husband's behavior.[4]

Instead of arousing the ire of Ya Bay's kin, this conjugal neglect sparked the action of her tutelary spirit, who abducted her to his own realm of the bush in order to compel her to *"take up the load"* of their ritual relationship. In one way, her displacement from her marital home by this spirit traced a well-trodden route followed by women in unsatisfactory marriages who take a lover and ultimately seek to end their first marriage and marry him. Even slave wives sometimes ran away to a new husband and owner. Ya Bay *did* leave her first husband because of a new lover who subsequently became her husband—but he happened to be a spirit. And although he enabled her to leave a marriage in which she was like a slave-wife in her lack of recourse against her husband's neglect, he then imposed upon her a spirit marriage that effectively made her a slave-wife in several other ways: he abducted her from her home, forced a life of unremitting labor upon her, and prevented her from *"putting down the load"* and leaving him.

Although her spirit husband's presence gave Ya Bay some leverage over her second human husband, she remained subject to the spirit's authority indefinitely: unlike a human marriage, she could not leave this marriage to the spirit. And although on one occasion she acknowledged that her spirit husband provided—as a husband should—the basis for an income through the healing powers he gave her, more often she described herself as unable to put down the "load" she had to carry for him. *"I cannot leave this work,"* she once told me, *"or I shall die."* She had to continue to carry her ritual burdens, however heavy they were.[5]

The images through which Ya Bay experienced her induction into her ritual specializations themselves carry a load—a heavy mnemonic freight. They also offer a gendered contrast both to male diviners' contractual, landlord-stranger transactions with their spirits and to male diviners' experiences of seizure alone, without the hard labor of load-carrying for a spouse afterwards. Through her visionary experience of capture, unrelenting labor, and a spirit marriage she could not dissolve, Ya Bay recapitulated historical experiences of enslavement that were noticeably gendered. At the same time, she also made them speak to her own experience as a woman in a near-kinless marriage. Her visionary encounters were in many ways unwanted, painful, and almost as dislocating as the seizure of captives in Sierra Leone's slave-trading past. Yet through them she drew on the power of that past and of her own personal past, turning their terror and oppression into her capacity to heal.

Ya Yebu: "Knowing Too Much Arabic"   The acquisition of divinatory knowledge involves forms of memory that are gendered in another way. When Muslin Mande divination techniques were adopted in the eighteenth and nineteenth centuries, as we saw in chapter 3, the specialists who introduced them also brought the widespread Muslim notion that such techniques are for men only. This hegemonizing process is reproduced today through ideas that esoteric Islamic knowledge is inappropriate for women. Thus the few women engaged in divination either practice less explicitly "Muslim" forms of divination (like Ya Bay), or act as medium-assistants to male aŋ-yina Musa diviners (like Mami Yeno, who worked with Pa Koroma). In this section, however, I discuss a female diviner called Ya Yebu, who flouts this division of divinatory labor by using one of the most powerful literate Muslim techniques of divination: aŋ-yina Musa.

Because of the gender conventions associated with esoteric Islamic knowledge, women have been at a disadvantage if they wished to learn literate techniques of Islamic divination. As we have seen, most Temne diviners I knew understood their techniques to be Islamic, but not all such diviners are entitled to call themselves aŋ-mɔre or aŋ-lɔfa, the Mande and Fula loanwords in Temne for literate Muslim ritual specialists. Only those who have attended an Arabic school and have pursued further learning in Islamic divination with an established u-mɔre or u-lɔfa can legitimately use these titles, and those who do so have almost invariably been men.

Students who wish to acquire this privileged knowledge apprentice themselves to a teacher who gradually instructs them in the "secrets" (ɛ-gbuŋdu) of Islamic divination, amulet-making, and healing. Over a number of years the teacher allows them to copy his written formulae and diagrams from Arabic divination books, teaching them the hidden oral prayers that enable these powerful written forms to be used without danger, while the students perform farm and domestic work in their teacher's household. As Bledsoe and Robey (1986) observe, writing about Islamic knowledge in Mendeland, the teacher thereby converts his "wealth in knowledge" into "wealth in people":

> In effect, the longer he can delay giving up secrets, the more he benefits. Although he does impart some important secrets, he may withhold completely what he regards as his most powerful ones to maintain a competitive advantage over former students. Students can never be certain what knowledge is being withheld or how much is left to gain. (1986: 216)

When students leave their teacher they usually give him gifts of fine clothes and sometimes money: Pa Koroma, for instance, told me that he had given his teacher a cow, "forty pounds" (eighty leones, which was indeed forty pounds sterling before 1978), a pair of shoes, a shirt, a cap, and a gown for the teacher's wife. A ceremonial meal is held for such "graduations"—a sheep or cow is sacrificed, rice is cooked—and forms the occasion for the teacher to give the student his formal blessing *(aŋ-ruba)*, without which all the student's knowledge will be ineffective.

At some point in their training in Islamic divinatory knowledge, apprentice aŋ-more commonly have a contractual encounter with a tutelary spirit of the kind I described earlier in this chapter. Typically, this spirit is a Muslim jinn (aŋ-yina) who offers to reveal "secrets"—often Arabic words and medicinal herbs—as part of an agreed exchange. Pa Koroma, remember, made his bargain with his tutelary spirit at this time:

> I saw the jinn—she was small—when I'd begun my Arabic education. She was a Muslim. She said, "You've seen me and I've seen you. What do you want me to do for you?" I said, "Since I'm learning the Qur'an, I'd like to discover certain things for people, so they'll pay me and I'll get money. I'd like you to give me that knowledge." The jinn agreed, and asked "If I do, what will you do for me?" I said I would give her a sheep.

Training by a human Qur'anic teacher, then, is usually complemented by a Muslim spirit's contracted tutelage.

Very few women, however, have access to the "secrets" of Islamic divination. In Petbana, Ya Aramata, who was married to the Muslim subchief and diviner Pa Santigi told me: *"They don't want girls to go too far in Qur'anic learning* (karaŋ)," when I asked her during my 1989 stay if she had ever wanted to be a diviner herself. Although it is good, I was often told, for women to have some Qur'anic education—and girls as well as boys attended the more elementary classes in village Qur'anic schools—they were usually discouraged from learning "too much." This pattern was established during the time of heavy Muslim migration to Sierra Leone in the eighteenth and nineteenth centuries, when "for those who were lucky . . . girls were sometimes allowed a few years of primary Islamic education, only to be removed after they had learned the mechanism of prayer and a few *suras*" (Ojukutu-Macauley 1997: 93).

In and around Petbana, the reason most people gave for this was not that women lacked intelligence. It was rather, as Ya Aramata continued, because *"if they know too much, they'll harm their co-wives."* Most male Muslim diviners I knew echoed the views of Pa Fonah, Pa Koroma's former student in Rokirfi, who emphasized that if a woman were to pursue the study of the Qur'an and Islamic divination with him, he would teach her *some* secrets, but not as many as a male student. Like Ya Aramatu, he explained that *"when they learn too much Arabic, they can use it to harm their co-wives"*: Qur'anic knowledge is understood as putting an even more dangerous edge upon a perceived tendency of co-wives to use witchcraft against each other. The "male" character of Islamic divinatory knowledge, then, is explicitly grounded in the structural position of women as wives in polygynous, virilocal marriage.

Married women's vulnerabilities to others' suspicions of witchcraft also meant that most female diviners I knew (with the exception of women like Ya Bay, who started divining as the outcome of the diagnosis of a severe affliction) took up divination when they were widows, or when they had adult children. They were thereby less subject to the tensions between co-wives that characterize the earlier stages of women's married lives.

Because of these obstacles in the paths of female diviners in general and female Muslim diviners in particular, I was intrigued when, during my 1989 stay in Petbana, Pa Moses Kalokoh told me that I should meet a remarkable diviner from his family: Ya Yebu Kane, his mother's brother's daughter. She was remarkable, he said, not only because she was a skilled diviner who *"sees the truth,"* but also because of her knowledge of Arabic and her use of the "wonderful" Islamic divination technique, aŋ-yina Musa, in addition to the more usual techniques of the looking glass (aŋ-mɛmnɛ) and river pebbles (aŋ-bɛrɛ). So guided by Pa Moses' son, Frances, I waded through a rice swamp to Malal, a village a few miles from Makeni, where Ya Yebu was harvesting rice and living in a small farm hut with a young girl she was healing. Later she came on a visit to Petbana (plate 12), and told me of the harsh conditions she had endured during her Qur'anic education, when she worked in her teacher's household:

YY: *My parents told me I had to learn. I was very small. . . . When I was with my teacher* [at the Arabic school], *I fetched wood, brought water, helped to do the cooking. But when they served the rice, it was only the leftovers that they gave to me.*

RS: *How did you learn divination?*

YY: *When I started divination I was young, married, and pregnant with my first child. I didn't learn this from anyone.*

RS: *Where were you living?*

YY: *At that time, I lived at Masori. I was born there. My husband came from Roboli.*

RS: *How did you start?*

YY: *I used my* [four] *eyes.*

RS: *Did you learn from a dream?*

YY: *No, I didn't. I saw a spirit* (ɔ-kərfi) *who came with a message from ro-sɔki* [the Place of Spirits]. *I hadn't given birth to my first child then. I went to wash clothes at the river. The kərfi said to me, "I have work that I want you to do with me." He said, if I liked the work, I should pay three sheep. The first thing that he gave me was* aŋ-bɛrɛ.

RS: *What about the looking glass* (aŋ-mɛmnɛ)?

YY: *The same spirit showed me.*

RS: *What about* aŋ-yina Musa?

YY: *Because I learned some Arabic* (I karaŋ), *for* aŋ-yina Musa *if you know a little Arabic and if you have* [four] *eyes, it won't take you long* [to learn]. *I learned it from my husband before he died. He learned Arabic—he was* ɔ-karmɔkɔ [a Qur'anic teacher]*—he taught people and used* aŋ-yina Musa *alone. The spirit is still helping me now; he's still with me. He's a man.*

Unlike most other female diviners, then, Ya Yebu was a young wife when she first encountered her tutelary spirit; indeed, it was her work as a young wife—washing clothes at the river—that brought her into contact with the spirit. Unlike most diviners' wives, moreover, she was able to use her marriage to develop her own divinatory capacities, learning the prestigious aŋ-yina Musa technique from her husband.

There were, however, subtle differences between Ya Yebu and male aŋ-mɔre. Firstly, while the synthesis of Islamic and Temne forms is a standard feature of the practice of Temne Islamic diviners, Ya Yebu's repeated use of the Temne term ɔ-kərfi for her tutelary spirit suggests a relationship with a more indigenous being than does the Manding loanword aŋ-yina ("jinn"), the term preferred by other aŋ-more I knew. Ya Yebu's own name, secondly, is a Temne name: unlike every male u-more I knew, she did not use a name that signals a specifically "Muslim" status—for a woman, a name such as Khadiatu, Zainab, Adama, Mariama, or Hawa. And third, the first divination technique her tutelary spirit taught her—one that she maintained all her life—was aŋ-bɛrɛ, the technique usually accorded a "Temne," non-Muslim status. None of this, of course, meant that Ya Yebu's Islam was "superficial," this being the usual accusation made of those who engage in religious synthesis and pluralism by those with Western religious sensibilities attuned to either-or notions of allegiance (see Shaw and Stewart 1994). On the contrary, Ya Yebu's commitment to Islam was abundantly clear to all—especially when, one day during her visit to Petbana in 1989, she harangued members of the town about their poor mosque attendance. *"The Christians are winning from the Muslims"*; she exclaimed, *"[only] nine people in the mosque* [for the Friday prayer]!"

As what Tsing calls an "eccentric subject," Ya Yebu reworks "the very matrix of power that gives [her] the ability to act," and thereby "demonstrates the limits of dominant categories" (1993: 232). Her career as a diviner challenges and collapses the distinctions between "Muslim" and "Temne" that recapitulate local Islamic history—a history that effectively relegates the few female diviners to forms of divination that have acquired connotations of an earlier, "backward" ritual layer.

Ya Yebu's practice and experience of aŋ-yina Musa divination also differed from that of the male diviners I knew. While, for example, Pa Koroma's aŋ-yina Musa divinations with his assistant, Mami Yeno, were closely controlled encounters in which humans were protected by their firm separation from spirits, Ya Yebu blurred this separation and relinquished this control. For Pa Koroma, as we saw in chapter 3, cloaking Mami Yeno with the white cloth was a crucial defense against her seizure by spirits. According to him, Mami Yeno was able to penetrate the Darkness that concealed spirits from humans, while the white cloth produced a form of Darkness that disguises a human as a spirit, giving the medium a visual advantage over those she sees in the spirit "town." When Ya Yebu practiced aŋ-yina Musa divination, however, she repeatedly threw off the white cloth that covered her, complaining that it was too hot. In this uncovered condition she continued with the session, sometimes shaking, sometimes not, sometimes with her eyes closed, and sometimes with them open—thereby making the distinction between being in a "crossed" state and an ordinary state less obvious (to me, at least).

For Ya Yebu, being cloaked from the spirits by the white cloth was an empty form of defense in any case: aŋ-yina Musa divination, she claimed, *entailed* seizure by spirits. *"When I hold the beads and call the spirits* (aŋ-kərfi) *and the ancestors,"* she told me, *"they seize* (wop) *me, and I throw the beads down. When you are calling the kərfi and the ancestors, they come in the mirror. I see them with my* [four] *eyes."* She thus experienced herself as being seized by the spirits *and* at the same time as being able to observe them in the looking glass. Unlike other aŋ-yina Musa diviners I knew, then, Ya Yebu did not use Darkness as a means of defense against spirit seizure or as a means of tricking aŋ-yina Musa. While these other diviners sought to control the dangers of the spirit landscape with techniques of Darkness that maintained the separateness of spirits, she discarded these precautions. Eschewing disguise, she used the spirits and ancestors to make her both a viewer of *and* an active, intentional participant in the spirit world through the looking glass.

Ya Yebu's use of the written Arabic diagrams called "Writings" (ma-gbal) again reveals a contrast with that of male aŋ-yina Musa diviners. In her Writing for aŋ-yina Musa divination (plate 13), a circle is quartered by one horizontal and one vertical line—"crossed roads" (ta-soŋ tə-pəŋkinɛ), Ya Yebu explained—with the point of their intersection marked by a black dot. Inside the quarters of the circle are clusters of smaller black dots—two dots in one quarter, three in the next two, four in the last—for which Ya Yebu had no explanation. A small arch, in addition, sits upon the horizontal line in the upper left quarter. From the midpoint of each quarter at the circle's perimeter four lines radiate outward, each ending in figures that resemble Arabic letters but that do not correspond to particular letters in any obvious way. In between these radiating figures, at each end of the crossed roads immediately above, below, to the right, and to the left of the circle, the prayer "ya Allah" (Oh Allah) is written four times. The letters that form these words begin in disconnected fragments, but they become fuller and clearer as one reads clockwise, starting at the top. Ya Yebu described these four parts of the diagram as "towns" *(ta-pet)*, each of which have prayers as names. They are, she said, *minka yeri*, "the town below" *(ka-pet do-pil); sadidan*, "the town of the right" *(ka-pet kə-diyɔ); salamu alekum*, "the town above" *(ka-pet do-kɔm);* and *alhamdulillahi ka-shiran*, "the town of the left" *(ka-pet kə-mɛrɔ)*. Finally, while these towns of prayer at each end of the intersecting Roads are oriented to the four cardinal directions, the diagram as a whole is oriented to one direction by two further prayers at the top and bottom of the Writing: "bismillahi rahmani rahim" (in the name of Allah, the Merciful, the Compassionate) at the top, and "bismillahi rahmani Allah" (in the name of Allah, the Merciful Allah) at the bottom.

Ya Yebu depicted the spirit of divination, an-yina Musa, as being seated at the center of this Writing: *"When I am covered, the spirit (ɔ-kərfi) sits in the middle,"* she told me when I asked about the central cross. These intersecting lines form Crossroads, she said, that take her in between this world and the world of spirits: *"This Writing is the Writing that makes Darkness, and I am in between* (do-thɔŋ). *The crossed roads—when you are going straight, you meet the scattered roads* (ta-soŋ tə sakanɛ). *The crossed roads resemble* (balanɛ) *what it is to be both in this world* (nɔ-ru) *and in the world of spirits* (ro-sɔki)." Again, Ya Yebu's depiction of the Writing's transformative capacities departed in intriguing ways from that of Pa Koroma. Whereas Pa Koroma, remember, constructed a "house" of writing that safely contained an-yina Musa behind Closed walls, Ya Yebu placed an-yina Musa at the junction of the Crossroads, replacing an image of the spirit's enclosure with one of his latent mobility. And instead of either engaging in a passive "cinematic" surveillance of the spirits and the landscape, or (like Ya Bay) being involuntarily displaced by spirit abductors, Ya Yebu placed herself on one of the roads in this landscape, moving toward the crossroads that form the spirit's seat: *"when you are going straight, you meet the scattered roads."*

Thus whereas the most prestigious (and male) aŋ-yina Musa diviners work through a medium and use both a disguise and a cinematic, visionary gaze, Ya Yebu's ritual agency was based on a more intimate encounter with spirits. Her excursion into Darkness entailed seizure by spirits, travel along the roads of the other world, and a close connection with an uncontained an-yina Musa himself. If this made her a less distinguished diviner at one level, it also made her more powerful at another, for she did not seem to need the protective walls of Closure or the disguise and the remote viewing applications of Darkness. She was neither killed nor (like Ya Bay) rendered insane by spirit seizure; instead, she turned the dangerous potential for capture and displacement into her own intentional participation in the other world, and thereby into her ritual capacity as a diviner.

Diviners and Islamic Modernity   At the time that I encountered Ya Yebu in 1989, Muslim ritual specialists found themselves cast as embodiments of degenerate "backwardness" as the influence of modernist forms of Islam grew in Sierra Leone. It is worth remembering that historically, on the upper Guinea coast (as in many parts of West Africa), Muslim ritual specialists have usually been fluid enough to adapt their practices to—and synthesize them with—local ritual practices and ideas, such as divination. But during my 1989 and 1992 stays, I found that although most diviners regarded themselves as Muslims, they were themselves the objects of much critical scrutiny in attempts to define "true" Islam in Sierra Leone. Since the mid-1970s, transnational flows of aid from and educational scholarships to the Gulf states and Egypt, as well as increased travel opportunities for the hajj to Mecca (for those with resources), created a new political and moral economy of Islam (Bangura 1997; Skinner 1997b: 147–52). Increasingly, as in other parts of Africa, Islamic authorities have sought to bring local ritual practice into line with modernist and scripturalist definitions of Islam as a unitary, cosmopolitan orthodoxy (see Bernal 1994; Ferme 1994; Watts 1996). Many Sierra Leonean imams, especially in urban mosques, told their congregations during the Friday prayer that consulting a diviner is *shirk*, "polytheism," and that the fires of Hell (Temne *ro-yanama*) would engulf those who do so.

Especially exacting have been the demands of a new Islamic movement, the Bashariyya, founded in Freetown in 1979 by a charismatic Temne Muslim leader, Imam Bashar. Upon his return from a period of higher Islamic education in Saudi Arabia, Imam Bashar started preaching a conservative and populist form of Islam, denouncing corruption and excessive consumption among politicians, top civil servants, and religious leaders, and painting vivid pictures of the punishments awaiting them in Hell. His popular standing grew in proportion to widespread despair with the collapsing postcolonial state, and his message of morality was underscored by the relatively modest bungalow he inhabited in a poor area of Freetown's East End.

Like many other Islamic reformers, Imam Bashar combined public political criticism with the castigation of local forms of Islamic practice that he "did not see in Arabia" (cf. Ferme 1994), including divination. While the Imam's concern was with Islamic orthodoxy, his dual condemnation of diviners and politicians resonated with popular political critiques in Sierra Leone. As we shall see in chapter 9, unscrupulous politicians are often rumored to have acquired their power through the use of ritual murder allegedly prescribed by diviners as a way of obtaining human body parts for ingredients of medicines that make them "shine" (Ferme 1999; Richards 1996a: 143–45). Among the Bashariyya, divination was an object of such censure that members were required to sign a form declaring that they would not practice this form of "unbelief"; only then were they given their membership cards.

In addition, as such bureaucratic emblems as forms and membership cards suggest, the Bashariyya—like many other modernist Muslim movements—developed an organizational apparatus that enabled it to act as "an alternative political and economic platform to the state" (Watts 1996: 284). With money raised by its members, it provided clinics, schools, and welfare funds; it bought land and used the labor of its young men's organization to farm this land for food and cash-crops; and it supported the building of mosques that formed the nodes of a network spread across the country. Its disciplined organization and successfully materialized moral economy stood as a rebuke to the national "politics of decline" (Zack-Williams 1989) in Sierra Leone, and made its denunciation of diviners and divination compelling.

By denouncing diviners, neither Imam Bashar nor other Muslim leaders said anything particularly new or unique in Sierra Leone. Diviners have long been morally ambivalent figures, sometimes implicated in "human leopard" scares during the colonial eras (as we shall see in chapter 8); this ambivalence, moreover, was further fed by rhetoric on the evils of diviners and divination in various kinds of Christian as well as Muslim discourse. Those who respected and revered Imam Bashar did not necessarily agree with him, however, often saying *"I met diviners and divination when I was born, so I will continue to use them."* But even outside the Bashariyya's formal membership, large numbers of Muslims in Freetown attended the Friday prayer at Imam Bashar's mosque and took his graphic images of hellfire engulfing diviners and their clients very seriously.

Diviners—including those in rural villages—also heard this message, and sometimes gave up divination as they grew old and prepared for death. In Petbana, the Muslim subchief and diviner Pa Santigi told me that he would like to give up divination soon. He was under considerable pressure from his brother-in-law, a somewhat conservative imam of the main mosque in the provincial capital of Makeni nearby, who was outspoken about the evils of divination. Even while he practiced divination, Pa Santigi's ambivalence about it was manifest in his unusually frequent use of the pious but unhelpfully vague diagnosis that his clients' problems were *"just from God."* This etiology was often unsatisfying to his clients, many of whom had their own readings of their predicaments in terms of witchcraft or spirit attack, and seemed to have resulted in a dwindling clientele at the time of my 1989 visit.

Pa Santigi's ambivalence might be seen as an internal debate over forms of knowledge that are not only heterogeneous but also construed as incompatible. As Lambek writes of heterogeneous knowledge in Mayotte,

> To the degree that the various disciplines or discourses present in Mayotte are incommensurable, they can be articulated only through a local hermeneutic in which each constructs an interpretation of the other. Thus we see a kind of

ongoing conversation between and within persons, where positions and contradictions are sometimes rationalized but sometimes staked out tacitly, *lived out.* (1990: 33)

I saw many such "conversations" among the diviners I knew. The longest one I witnessed was lived out in the ritual career of Pa Yamba.

Pa Yamba: From Playing to Praying   In 1978, the year that Imam Bashar formed his movement, I met Pa Yamba (plate 14). That rainy season, when I was trying to get to know diviners in Freetown, I was directed to Pa Yamba's two rooms in Lucas Street in the city's crowded East End, not far from where Imam Bashar would later build his Bombay Street mosque. Outside, a painted sign announced: *"Yamba Nhoni Again. This man can cure all problems."* He was pleased about my interest in his skills, telling me that, in addition to being a diviner and healer, he was an adept in the Poro society ("Pa Yamba" being the name of a senior Poro official). He was, he said, especially famous for his performances (which he called his "play," *wol*) in public Poro displays at Christmas: he handled poisonous snakes, cut himself with knives, and allowed himself to be buried alive, emerging unharmed to demonstrate his powers over death. As I visited him over the next few weeks, I learned that he was originally from Yonibana, in southern Temneland, where his father and grandfather had also been diviners. I asked him why he had become a diviner himself:

> When I was young, I saw big people come to my father. My father got a lot of respect, so I wanted that life. My father didn't go to school, but because he was a diviner and a herbalist, he had money and respect. Also, a woman died when she was about to give birth. My father said he was going to deliver the child, and he did. I was there, and my interest grew.

Pa Yamba's father practiced river pebble divination (aŋ-bɛrɛ), and taught this to his sons.

Pa Yamba had no education in Arabic or the Qur'an—a lack that he felt keenly later on in life. He built on the knowledge he had learned from his father by traveling all over the country, attaching himself to ritual specialists whose knowledge he wished to acquire. A diviner in Kono, the diamond district in the east, put liquid medicine in his eyes that allowed him to see witches clearly. From a diviner in Segbuema, in the south, he learned how to apply the "pot" ordeal *(aŋ-gbɔt)* to find witches, thieves, and adulterers. And in Pendembu, also in the south, a Kissy diviner taught him the cowrie shells (ta-faŋt) and the looking glass (aŋ-mɛmnɛ) techniques—two divination methods that, as we have seen, have been accorded a more Islamic identity than the river pebbles of aŋ-bɛrɛ. When I knew him, he used the cowries and looking glass rather than the river pebbles, whispering the Muslim prayer Bismillahi Rahmani Rahim ("In the name of God, the Merciful, the Compassionate") as he began.

Pa Yamba's switch from river pebbles to cowries and mirrors, and his incorporation of the Bismillah prayer, signaled a shift to a more Islamic ritual affiliation—a shift that recapitulated in his own life the earlier Islamic transformations that Temne diviners made during the eighteenth and nineteenth centuries. He told me that he had made this change when he moved to Freetown: *"aŋ-bɛrɛ takes too long,"* he claimed, *"people in Freetown are busy."* Actually, aŋ-bɛrɛ as practiced by the diviners I knew takes no longer than the cowrie and mirror techniques. But Muslim allegiance is important to most Temne residents in this city (which is built on land that Temne consider to be theirs), establishing their difference from both the Christian Krio professional elite and the former British colonial rulers, while at the same time affirming a literate, monotheistic, globalized affiliation of equivalent prestige (see Banton 1957: 118). And at another level, the reason Pa Yamba gave suggests that a different kind of time operates in the city—a time of "busy schedules," work discipline, and regulated hours and minutes—in terms of which Muslim techniques appeared more compatible with Freetown's modernity than the casting of river pebbles.

When I returned to Freetown in 1989, I found that Pa Yamba had given up his Poro association "plays" in which he had felt such pride and was talking much more about "praying" (*sali*, a generic term for the practice of Islam) and about God (to whom, interestingly, he continued to refer by the Temne term "K-uru" rather than the Arabic "Allah"). But he still enjoyed talking about his expertise in the forms of ritual he had relinquished, and he gave me an account of a favorite strategy he had used to acquire some of it:

> *If I met a* [cult association] *house I would just enter, and sometimes I was told that "This is a Wunde* [a Mende male cult association] *house. You cannot leave. We will hold you. You will be here a long time. If you behave well* (bepi ŋ rusma finɔi), *you will get some leaves* [medicinal herbs]. *When you stay for a long time, and when your time is up and your mind turns to go back, and if we see that you are an upright person*

(w-uni tolɔŋ), *you will go." After that, the Kissi people in Segbuema another time—when I went there, I met a beating* [of drums] *in the house. The Kissi had brought a* [masked] *spirit; it is called "Landa." They came from Pendembu. They came to stay with the chief. Well, they gave them a whole house. When the moon was white at night, I heard people playing. I entered, and I met the spirit standing. . . . They rubbed white rice flour on my body. I sat near the spirit and became a karaŋde* [a student at a Qur'anic school] *to the spirit. Do you understand? Well, they held me for one year and five months. When they left me, they carried me to Pendembu. They washed me. I got their own leaves.*

In a remarkable reversal of agency, Pa Yamba used these cults' powers to seize and forcibly initiate intruders as a means of acquiring knowledge, turning his captors into his teachers through his eagerness to learn, his good behavior, and his already extensive knowledge of divination and medicines. Using a telling image, he described himself as having been a karaŋde—a Qur'anic student—to the spirit. He thereby redefined his position from that of a captive, subject to the agency of others, to that of a devoted Qur'anic school student whose perseverance would be rewarded by his teacher's blessing—as indeed it was when knowledge of the "leaves" of each association was conferred upon him. And through this image of himself as a karaŋde, disparate forms of ritual knowledge from successive historical processes were rendered equivalent to each other, filling a gap in Pa Yamba's personal history by redressing his lack of a Qur'anic education.

Yet now, he told me, he had left his participation in cult associations behind:

But how a person goes, when you look at it keenly, you will know that all these things are just small tastes (ɛ-thɑmsnɛ) *of the world. You should not wait until you are old before you leave all these things. You should know that K-uru owns you. You should fear him. What I was doing, if it was mistaken, I beg forgiveness. For tomorrow, for where I will go when you* [God] *take me back. I fear you; that is why I was doing this work. Do you hear? . . . If the eye comes out a little, or if the mouth bends a little, I can heal it. I will not say that when I am praying, I should not heal. I should heal, because if I heal, I will get a good "means"* (aŋ-sabu) *to K-uru* [a good way to gain God's blessing]. *It is a good name* [that you get when you heal]. *. . . I will put my hand into healing. Into the leaf that K-uru made. It is not a spirit's leaf. It is there that I will "play" with this work. But when I see that I too am getting old tomorrow-tomorrow* [in the future] *I will beg so that K-uru Masaba* [God, the great king] *will help me.*

Pa Yamba, by now an old man, was reconstructing himself in line with increasingly dominant Muslim images of the horrors of the afterlife for those who did not renounce such evils as the cult associations before it is too late. He saw all the ritual secrets he had acquired in his life as *"small tastes of the world"* that he now had to relinquish out of his fear of God—his "owner"—coming to claim his life. Yet Pa Yamba did not abandon the use of all his ritual knowledge. Medicinal plants, he claimed, were made by God (*"the leaf that K-uru made . . . is not a spirit's leaf"*) and he believed that his healing was a source of God's blessing to him. Unlike many of his other ritual activities, he felt healing to be compatible with his life as a Muslim: *"I will not say that when I am praying, I should not heal."*

On my last visit to Freetown in 1992, I found Pa Yamba as exuberant as ever, despite his advancing age and deteriorating health. His pride in his knowledge of medicines was irrepressible, but he was very careful to situate this knowledge in terms of a moral dualism in which he repudiated the use of ritual powers for evil purposes:

> *I am so wonderful with this leaf! I am so wonderful with this leaf! But I don't do witch-craft. I don't eat people. But if you ask me to help you, I will help you. If you say "come and kill this person for me," I will tell you "I won't kill them." If the person has harmed you, I will drive them far from you. I will help you: your power will cover [overcome] them!*

All too aware of popular (and conservative Muslim) representations of diviners that linked him implicitly to witchcraft and to ritual killing for political and economic purposes, Pa Yamba sought to distance himself from these by describing the moral line he drew in his work. His great skill with "leaves" was not to be confused with the witch's invisible consumption of people, while his ritual assistance, he stressed, empowered his clients without killing their enemies.

A few days' later he told me—for the first time in the fourteen years we had known each other—about the tutelary spirit behind his capacity to divine and heal, a female water spirit called Yombo who had appeared to him on the riverbank when he was a boy. He showed me a small, round basket neatly covered with red cloth, hung with tiny bells, and sewn with radiating lines of cowrie shells: this housed the river pebble that embodied Yombo. Her pebble inside, he told me, was a small one, red and white, that came from the river-bank where he had first encountered her:

PY: *I saw her. She held me. I wasn't myself. I trembled. It took less than half an hour. I saw the spirit. She said, "I like you!" I was afraid—I wanted to run! She gripped me. I began to tremble. She asked me to find a white fowl, that first time. Then she asked me for a sheep. She asked me for money: five cents. She asked me for a white cloth, as if it were the bridewealth for marriage. She told me she would help me with divination.*

RS: *Had you joined the Poro by then?*

PY: *No. I was small, but I had sense; I wasn't a small child. That time, when I slept, I went into the bush, I saw many people [spirits]: they danced, they played. This is a good spirit. She helps me divine and heal. She doesn't kill people.*

RS: *Does Yombo object to your wives?*

PY: *No; she doesn't deny me, but I don't ask her. If I say "I want this woman; help me," I'll get sick and die! She's jealous! I see her when I dream.*

So by the river, Pa Yamba was seized by Yombo ("*she held me*"), experienced the dislocation of spirit-capture ("*I wasn't myself*"), and was told the terms of a contractual relationship between them: in return for ritual payments that Pa Yamba perceived as akin to bridewealth, Yombo would make him a diviner. As with several other diviners' accounts I heard, the relationship between Pa Yamba and Yombo had a sexual quality, dictated primarily by Yombo ("*I like you!*") and negotiated with caution by Pa Yamba ("*I don't ask her. . . . I'll get sick and die! She's jealous!*"). And just as in 1989 he had stressed that his knowledge of medicinal plants was on the positive side of a moral divide, he now made the same claim about Yombo: "*This is a good spirit. She helps me divine and heal. She doesn't kill people.*"

Remembering the debate Pa Yamba had had with himself over the religious propriety of healing three years' before, I asked him if he thought K-uru would mind about Yombo. He replied:

Well you see, this Yombo, if this had been a bad stone [used for harming people], it's the fire [of Hell]—K-uru doesn't want that! But this one, it's her who wanted me, not me who wanted her. And I heal with her, so she's not a bad thing. But K-uru says, "however fine it is, I don't want anyone to keep a stone."

This time Pa Yamba was much more ambivalent. Yombo was a good spirit, the source of his powers to heal—powers that he had stressed, in our 1989 conversation, were compatible with "praying." These positive qualities did not, however, make her acceptable to God: "*K-uru says, 'however fine it is, I don't want anyone to keep a stone.'"* Yet as it was she who "caught" Pa Yamba; how much choice did he have in the matter? He felt that his seizure by Yombo placed his relationship with her outside the sphere of choice, although both she and the divinatory capacities she conferred were demonic in the eyes of the new Islamic authorities that Pa Yamba respected.

Such issues were easier in relation to participation in the cult associations, which involved a clear choice between "playing" and "praying":

> *When I was "playing" in the Poro, if I "played," I didn't pray. If I didn't "play," I prayed. The soko [Poro] people were so angry when I gave up "playing"! They asked why I had given up the Poro? I said, "Tomorrow, I will die. When I die, K-uru will send people to me,* [to find out] *everything I've done, if I've prayed or if I haven't prayed. Because to pray is the proper thing.*

Determining what is *"the proper thing"* was problematic for Pa Yamba when many Islamic leaders had moved from an older encompassment of local ritual knowledge to its outright rejection, rendering their authoritative forms of Islamic modernity incommensurable with divination and other forms of local ritual practice.

Yet such incommensurabilities did not always move Pa Yamba's life in a straight, unidirectional line from "playing" to "praying." During my 1992 visit to Freetown, Pa Yamba was very concerned about a hernia operation he needed. Before undergoing it, he was anxious to offer a sacrifice to the spirits and ancestors he had cultivated when he was actively "playing" in the cult associations he had joined. So one morning in July he called me to his home, where a few officials of the Poro society sat around Pa Yamba's small parlor, drunkenly grumbling about the inadequate amount of rum they had been given. A small group of Ya Bay women from the aŋ-gbɔm association (including Ya Bay Kolone, whom I met there for the first time) sang, beat tortoise shells, and danced in ritual shirts made of red and white strips. Both the Poro men and the Ya Bay women took three white chickens into Pa Yamba's bedroom, announcing to invisible presences in the room that they had come to give a small thing for the health of Pa Yamba. They passed the chickens out of the door to be slaughtered and cooked by Pa Yamba's daughter, expelled one of the grumbling Poro men from the room for taking more than his share of the rum, resumed their beating and dancing, and rebuked the greedy Poro man by singing: *"If K-uru gives you something, you should give to others."*

While this went on, Pa Yamba sat outside in his parlor on a chair on the other side of the bedroom door, beaming: *"In all the societies, all the societies, I am the chief,"* he declared. I asked, rather tactlessly, why in that case he sat outside. *"If they make a mistake, I will go inside,"* he replied without missing a beat. Throughout, Pa Yamba managed to combine a dignified pleasure in being the focus of this event, an air of authoritative supervision over the proceedings, and a marked detachment from the ritual actions themselves. This combination effectively enabled him to maintain both a "Muslim" aloofness from transactions with spirits that the Islamic sensibilities of his life now demanded and the agency-at-a-distance that acknowledged his earlier mastery of ritual forces. If, in his self-fashioning as both a diviner and a Muslim, and in his difficult choices between "playing" and "praying," the trajectory of a regional history of Islam was recapitulated in one person's life, both the past and present from this history were now reconciled—at least temporarily—in this ritual through which Pa Yamba prepared for his operation.

"Modern" Knowledge and Occult Powers in an Era of State Collapse In urban Sierra Leone in the early 1990s, even before the rebel war overran most of the country, the spheres of "modern" education and employment had become unhinged from those of money and commodities. This tearing apart of spheres that had previously been cast, according to what Ferguson calls the "myth of modernization" (1999), as connected stages along a trajectory of "progress," had a profound effect on those who viewed themselves as pursuing modern lives. For some, it demanded a rethinking of the relevance of "occult" practices such as divination that had long been viewed as constituting the very antithesis of a "modern" life.

Since the nineteenth century, diviners and divination have been integral to a discourse of "backwardness" and moral danger in Sierra Leone. As we know from the work of Taussig (1987) and others, epistemologies of conquest include claims of moral ascendancy that equate the ritual knowledge of subordinates with the demonic and the uncivilized (e.g., Ginsberg 1983; Meyer 1999; Stewart 1991). The Bashariyya movement has not been the only religious institution to condemn diviners and divination from the pulpit; in a wide range of Sierra Leone's Christian denominations too, the evils of diviners and divination form a frequent topic of sermons in rural and urban church settings alike.

Yet by damning the ritual knowledge of diviners and deeming it "backward," Muslim and Christian authorities endow this knowledge with an ominous and subversive potency in a process that Taussig describes as "that fold-ing of the underworld of the conquering society into the culture of the conquered . . . as a chamber of mirrors reflecting each stream's perception of the other" (1987: 218). Thus Western-educated Sierra Leoneans often attribute a superior potency to "herbalists," "fortune tellers," and "native doctors," as diviners are sometimes called. Some describe diviners and their esoteric skills as participating in an African "science" that may be more effective than Western medical techniques, and view divinatory knowledge as standing for a powerful realm of concealed African modernity that lies beneath the more tangible signs of Sierra Leone's "Third World" status. But at the same time, such ideas about diviners' knowledge are linked to a literate, Western-educated discourse of class- and race-based Otherness, and derive from colonial, Christian, and modernist Islamic ideas about the demonic and "backward" nature of diviners.

How did diviners become "backward" in Sierra Leone? Historically, European terminologies of "fetish-men," "juju-men," and "witch-doctors" suggest that diviners have been made to embody a diabolic African alterity for several centuries. Yet these terminologies conceal the fact that from the fifteenth to the nineteenth century, as we have seen, many European lançados on the upper Guinea coast were themselves active participants in local ritual practices—including divination, sacrifice, and medicine. Later, however, these lançados' nineteenth-century successors, the British in the Crown Colony of Sierra Leone, were not in a comparable relationship of dependency on African hosts: indeed, they exercised considerable military force against the Temne-speaking communities around them. Both the colonial officials and the missionaries who followed them, moreover, brought nineteenth-century European ideas of race, civilization, and "paganism" with them. African divination and local medicine came to stand for the antithesis of everything European, not only in colonial and missionary discourses but also in certain Temne representations that had incorporated these discourses.

A Temne myth of God's division of Africans from Europeans collected in the mid-nineteenth century by the missionary Schlenker in the town of Port Loko provides a striking example of how, at that time, divination and other local ritual practices were made the basis of a stark contrast between Africans and Europeans:

God said: "Go and separate them; carry the white ones to the water side; as to the black ones locate them in the country." The servant came, and separated them, he did as God sent him (to do); and went and told God: "I have done as thou hast said." God took out all sorts of implements, and gave them to his servant, and said: "Go." For those in the country he gave (to the servant), that he might carry to them all sorts of agricultural implements; as to those close the water side, he went and gave them all sorts of shipping implements. To the white people he gave artisans, and taylors, and clerks. As to those in the country he gave them blacksmiths. The artisans made houses for the white people, and ships [Temne *tra-bil tra-potho,* "European canoes"] for to walk on the sea; that they might get money, and that they might be gentlemen; and he put them close to the water side. The black children he put in the country, and on hills, and in forests; he taught them to make grass-houses and mud-houses, and to make farms, and he made them to do all laborious work; but white people have not to do this work, they have not to make country medicines, they do not practise divination; as regards all these things, he put them only on the black people. (Schlenker 1861: 21–23)

In this narrative the former integration of Europeans into African social and ritual practice, and their dependency on powerful African landlords, is erased from discursive memory, replaced by a "poetics of contrast" (Comaroff and Comaroff 1987) based on ideas of culture and race in which Europeans are everything that Africans are not. Also erased are the signs of modernity in divination itself—the white spirits, with their renewable contracts, and (as we shall see in chapter 7) the intimate connection between public divination and the slave trade itself. The world is simply divided into "European" money, water, transport, writing, bureaucracy, and "gentlemanly" prestige on the one hand, and "African" land, cultivation, physical labor, "country medicines," and divination on the other. In this narrative (collected in the context of a European mission that was itself, we can probably assume, responsible for disseminating the idea that "European" writing and "African" divination form a binary opposition), we can thus see the beginnings of a discourse in which divination and "country medicines" are made into the obverse of all those things—money, writing, transport—that characterize modernity.

These ideas about Western knowledge and practice in the nineteenth century were underscored not only by the association of Europeans with money and writing but also by the military force and political power of the British colony in Freetown.[6] They were further reinforced by the imposition of the Protectorate at the end of the nineteenth century and by the extension of the colonial administrative apparatus over the Sierra Leone "hinterland." Memories of British colonial power remained pivotal in shaping attitudes to European knowledge in postcolonial Sierra Leone. Bledsoe and Robey, discussing

Mende attitudes to European *(pumoi)* knowledge in the 1970s and early 1980s, write: "The Mende say European outsiders were able to dominate Africans during colonialism because of their powerful knowledge of Western civilisation, especially its technology. A Mende who desires a pumoi standard of living today must learn this special knowledge. The essential key of access is English literacy" (1986: 217).[7]

Western education has not, however, been viewed as an unalloyed boon among Sierra Leone's rural majority. Precisely because its special potency has been seen as allowing those who wield it to accomplish much with a minimum of effort, Western education also "implies an easy life without hard work" (Bledsoe and Robey 1986: 217). As in the nineteenth-century Temne narrative above, European knowledge and literacy have long been perceived as incompatible with "laborious work." "This . . . system of education," Ojukutu-Macauley observes, "left its graduates despising manual work as being menial and fit only for illiterates" (1997: 105). Thus while a literate Western education has been regarded as an avenue to wealth and success, it has also been viewed as morally problematic. Ya Yebu once expressed this nicely when (speaking in 1989) she compared the education of *"children of nowadays"* to the much more serious process of her own Qur'anic schooling *"in those days"*:

> In those days, when they told you to learn, you had to learn. But children of nowadays, they don't learn. They only say, "Go to school." And when they send them to school, they don't learn the English book or the Arabic book, but they learn prostitution. And they wear those "Lady Diana" shoes!

Not only, then, did Ya Yebu see a Western education "of nowadays" as failing to instil proper literate learning of either "the English book" or "the Arabic book"; she also saw it as failing to instil moral knowledge. Instead of acquiring a moral and academic training, "children of nowadays" (especially young women) assimilated tastes for such foreign commodities as "Lady Diana shoes" that evoke desires for a world of unlimited spending power, and they learned wrongful ways of securing this spending power by selling their own bodies.

But in the early 1990s, it was clear that Western education had turned out to be anything but a "key of access" to "a [Western] standard of living" or "an easy life without hard work." The country's precipitous economic fall since the 1970s, leading to the collapse of the state and the escalating rebel war, was accompanied by a widespread loss of faith in Western education's promise to deliver a "modern" and "civilized" future. Not only did state schools virtually cease to function, as schoolteachers went unpaid for months at a time, but it also became clear that most students had either unemployment or a job pay-ing less than survival wages to look forward to at the end of their difficult journey through a collapsing education system (see Richards 1996b: 28–29, 36, 125–27). By the time of my 1992 fieldwork, soon after a military coup had displaced the hated All Peoples' Congress regime, the wish to become a soldier had replaced the desire to become an educated professional among the sons of several of my friends in Freetown. Thus "in a nation built up for two hundred years or more around systems of schooling in which Western models have been held out as the ideal" (Richards 1996b: 36), the progress narrative of Western education as the key to modernity's benefits was seen by many Sierra Leonean youth as an empty illusion.

At the same time, forms of ritual knowledge long deemed "backward" ac-quired a new importance by the early 1990s—both in Freetown, where the struggle to make a living as a trader, to run a business, or to find employment generated a steady clientele for diviners, and upcountry, where the war (which had not yet spread to Freetown) created urgent imperatives for the ritual pro-tection of the body. In the following section, I trace these processes through the story of Ibrahim.

Ibrahim's Education   When I met Ibrahim Sankoh, a Muslim diviner in his forties in 1992, he described himself as an electrician. But after a conversation about divination his manner toward me warmed noticeably; he told me that he too was a diviner, and he invited me to visit him in his house in Welling-ton, a suburb on the main road out of the city (plate 15). It turned out that he saw himself (as well as me) as engaged in the awkward task of making a living by applying disparate forms of knowledge—Islamic and Western, ritual and technological—that, he felt, were only partially compatible with each other.

Much of Ibrahim's divinatory knowledge was conferred in his dreams by Muslim tutelary spirits (ε-yina):

RS: *How did you become a diviner?*

IS: *I started through a dream. I dreamed different kinds of people [spirits], some white, some black. They came to visit me. Some took me to the bush and showed me leaves—I dreamed them every night. I didn't tell anyone: some dreams you have, you shouldn't tell anyone or you'll die. They showed me different words; they told me the names of things [spirits] I should call when I wake. When I call them, they appear in the looking glass. An aŋ-yina comes and explains to me. They told me how to call that aŋ-yina. That first time, I had two ε-yina, a woman and a man.*

Ibrahim thus had several tutelary spirits, *"some white, some black,"* male as well as female, suggesting the composition of diverse powers and capacities in the knowledge he was given. This dream-knowledge that the spirits imparted was grounded both in the local terrain (the identification of specific medicinal plants in the bush) and in the transregional circulation of esoteric Islamic learning (the memorizing of potent words and names with which Ibrahim invokes the spirits' presence in his looking glass). Although Ibrahim was not reluctant to tell me his dreams, his initial understanding of his initiatory dreams as best left unspoken to others was itself part of the mores of this learning of potent, esoteric Qur'anic "secrets" (aŋ-lasərar; see Bravmann 1983: 30–45).

With the coming of this dream-knowledge, though, Ibrahim felt that he had to make a choice. *"At that time,"* he told me, *"I knew Arabic. But first I was Christian; I was called Jacob. I became a Muslim after the dream—it's Muslim work."* Ibrahim moved, then, between contrasting forms of knowledge that he saw as requiring him to adopt different names and religious affiliations. Such transitions in religious identity are common in Sierra Leone, as Muslim children fostered in Christian households or attending Christian mission schools have tended to become Christian (and vice versa), and women from Christian households who marry a Muslim husband have usually become Muslim (or vice versa). These conversions are usually not huge personal transformations but rather constitute what I call "personal pluralism," in which a person has one official religious affiliation while maintaining another in less formal settings. The Krio proverb *"uman no gɛ wan rilijɔn"* ("a woman has no [one] religion") nicely conveys the personal pluralism of married women, for example, who practice both the religion of their husband and that of their natal family.

Because, for Ibrahim, divination was "Muslim work," his principal affiliation had to be Muslim:

RS: *Wouldn't you have been able to do this work if you'd stayed a Christian?*

IS: *Maybe some people could, but I couldn't. Although the Bible has some of the same words. And they have Adejobi* [an independent church from Nigeria, renowned for healing and prophecy], *and the Seven Books of Moses are the same as aŋ-lasərar* [a corpus of secret Islamic knowledge].

While, then, he felt that certain esoteric forms of biblical knowledge were compatible with (and even *"the same as"*) the knowledge required for the "Muslim work" of divination, his own schooling had not included these powerful "secrets" of Christian learning.

Ibrahim's family came from Kambia, in the northwest, but he was born in Freetown. Long before the initiatory dream that prompted his return to his Muslim affiliation, he attended an Ahmadiyya school at Freetown's Ferry Junction, run by the Sierra Leone Muslim Brotherhood. But later, his educational trajectory changed:

"I used to attend a Muslim school—an Ahmadiyya school. But in Form One, when I was 14 years old, I was baptized a Christian. After that, I went to secondary school in Kolenten, near Kambia. I became a Christian to get a scholarship to go to Kolenten— a Catholic school—for five years." The Ahmadiyya movement, which is considered to be heretical by orthodox Muslims, was founded in nineteenth-century India. Its missionary organization was pledged to spreading a British curriculum within an Islamic context, and its schools combine a Western curriculum in English with Qur'anic learning in Arabic. Given the realities of a world shaped by European colonial power and by the progress narrative of Western science and technology, Muslim children should not, it was felt, get "left behind" by their Western-educated peers. The first Ahmadiyya school in Sierra Leone opened in 1937 (Skinner 1997b: 142). For Ibrahim, however, the opportunities offered by a scholarship at a Catholic school were perceived as better still: thus Ibrahim left the Ahmadiyya system and became Jacob, a promising Catholic student, in order to have access to the advancement that a Western mission education was expected to give him.

But for Jacob, the "special knowledge" of a Western education did not turn out to be a "key of access" to a Western standard of living—"an easy life without hard work." It became clear that in Sierra Leone's steep economic decline since the 1970s, neither a Catholic secondary education nor the various forms of Western technical education that Jacob acquired afterwards would secure the kind of work he anticipated:

I became an Agricultural Extension worker at the Ministry of Agriculture—the IDA [International Development Agency]—*in Port Loko. But the work was too hard, so I left it. I learned electrician's work in Lunsar for three years, at St. Joseph's Vocational School. But I couldn't find work, so I returned to Freetown and became a tailor. Then I had the dream, and did divination as well as tailoring.*

So after he turned from being an agricultural extension worker in Port Loko (where *"the work was too hard"*) to an electrician in Lunsar (where he found no work at all—not surprisingly given that the country's electricity supply had all but vanished from many provincial towns), and finally to a tailor in Freetown (work that required no formal Western training), his dream instruction by tute-lary Muslim spirits opened up a diverging path of knowledge with a different set of opportunities as a Muslim ritual specialist. Jacob became Ibrahim again.

Building on the knowledge of his dream, Ibrahim studied a body of ad-vanced esoteric knowledge, aŋ-lasərar, with a Fula Arabic teacher (ɔ-karmɔkɔ): "*I gave him a cap, clothes, trousers, and shoes,*" Ibrahim told me, "*not money, or I wouldn't get a blessing. I learned it in two weeks. I performed a retreat* (aŋ-kalawa). *I didn't eat rice, I just prayed.*" He acquired a reputation as a skillful diviner and, with the precarious economic conditions in which Freetown's inhabitants lived in 1992, he had no shortage of clients hiring him to help with their businesses, their prospects as traders, their search for jobs, and their court cases, as well as their sickness and marital problems. His clients were not wealthy, and Ibrahim was still struggling financially, but at least divination provided him with a steady income.

Once more, Ibrahim's change of trajectory did not entail a wholescale transformation: he continued tailoring alongside his work as a diviner, and he still hoped to find a job as an electrician someday. While he was proud of his Islamic knowledge and did not regard his spirit-mediated divinatory skills as "backward," he nevertheless evaluated the "modern," urban, English-literate sphere of Western technological knowledge he had been trained for as more prestigious and desirable. Yet he was also conscious of the fact that, unlike his Western schooling and technical training, the diviner's education that he gained from his tutelary spirits and his Fula teacher gave him a fairly viable means of livelihood at a time when Sierra Leone was moving beyond eco-nomic decline into state collapse. Given the disappearance of opportunities for Ibrahim to use his "modern" skills in the early 1990s, the Seven Books of Moses might well have been a more useful form of Christian knowledge for him than the missionary education and vocational training he had received.

Conclusion The heterogeneity of diviners' knowledge, I have suggested, is composed of diverse layers of palimpsest memories. Visionary relationships with tutelary spirits seem to combine and recombine aspects of the cosmopol-itan processes and relationships through which the flows of Atlantic, legiti-mate, and translocal African trades were channeled. These practical memories condensed in diviners' spirits, moreover, intersect with more discursive mem-ories of contested historical processes. Thus female diviners and healers were assigned by a growing Islamic hegemony in the eighteenth and nineteenth centuries to an earlier, un-Islamic layer of ritual knowledge in a discourse that assimilated gender difference to temporal difference. But in turn, male Muslim diviners of the late twentieth century found themselves deemed "backward" and morally degenerate by the dominance of modernist Islamic discourse. Likewise, with the growing hegemony of Western literacy and technical skills during nineteenth- and twentieth-century colonialism, diviners' knowledge (whether Muslim or not) was reduced to the "non-modern." But the failure of the state and the spreading rebel war rendered the progress narratives of Western education, Christianity, and modernist Islamic movements largely irrelevant to many young people in the early 1990s. The most effective forms of knowledge for Sierra Leone's youth became military skills, while the ritual knowledge of diviners found a renewed prominence.

In the choices, dialogues, struggles, twists, and turns of their lives, the diviners in this chapter assimilated, debated, negotiated, and experimented with diverse layers of knowledge from Sierra Leone's history. While the discursive and practical memories present in these layers of knowledge are certainly shared, they are not thereby homogenized and "collective." Ya Bay, Ya Yebu, Pa Yamba, and Pa Ibrahim drew upon these social memories differently, generating new possibilities for personal and ritual capacities as they dealt with their own circumstances and contradictions.

Postscript   Pa Yamba recovered from his hernia operation. He lived through the terrible nine months of AFRC and RUF rule in Freetown from 1997 to 1998, but died soon after. When I returned to Sierra Leone in the summer of 2001, I was unable to trace Ya Bay and Pa Ibrahim. Ya Yebu died a few years ago. But Pa Santigi still practices divination in Petbana.

I also found that young people's attitudes to education were very different from those I describe above from my 1992 visit. With processes of demobilization and rebuilding underway, and with a UN- and NGO-driven boom in Freetown, the relative status of education and military skills have now reversed. Teachers' salaries, however, still remain unpaid for months at a time.

1   Ruins of Bunce Island House.
Bunce Island, September 1989.

2 Views of Sierra Leone in the late seventeenth century. From A. and J. Churchill, *A Collection of Voyages and Travels* (London, 1732). This illustration previously appeared in Christopher Fyfe, ed., *Sierra Leone Inheritance* (London: Oxford University Press, 1964), 31.

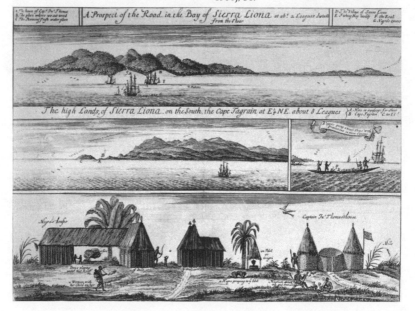

3   ɛ-kaŋtha hanging inside the doorway of Pa Yamba Nhoni Kamara's room. Freetown, August 1989.

4   S-athka of seven miniature axes embedded in a block of wood. Petbana Masimbo, June 1981.

5 Stockades around a fortified town (Pen-
dembu?) in the late nineteenth century. From
T. J. Alldridge, *A Transformed Colony: Sierra
Leone as it was, and as it is. Its Progress,
Peoples, Native Customs and Undeveloped
Wealth* (London: Seeley and Co., Ltd., 1910),
174.

6 Children returning from school to "Moria." Petbana Masimbo, May 1978.

7 Pa Fode Gbla casting aŋ-bɛrɛ. The back
door is open to provide light for the photograph. Mayan, December 1977.

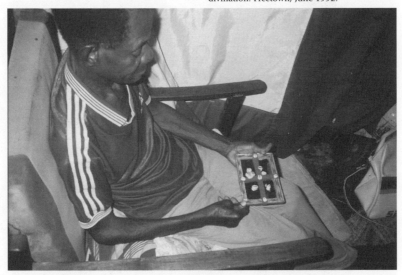

8   Pa Yamba Nhoni Kamara using a mirror quartered by the Crossroads in aŋ-mɛmnɛ divination. Freetown, June 1992.

9   Pa Ahmadu Fonah prepares for a session of aŋ-yina Musa divination. He covers himself with the white cloth. Petbana Masimbo, September 1989.

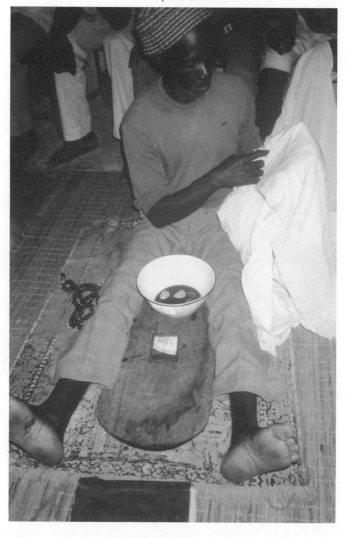

10 Pa Alfa Koroma's Writing for aŋ-yina
Musa divination. Petbana Masimbo, June
1978.

11   Ya Bay Kolone. Freetown, July 1992.

12   Ya Yebu Kane. Petbana Masimbo,
October 1989.

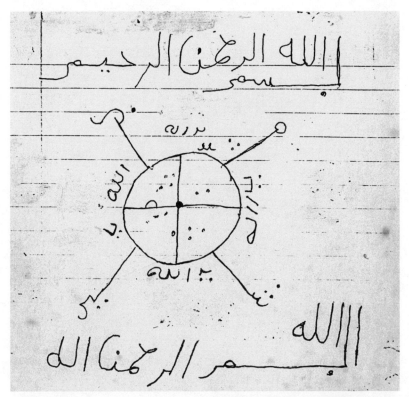

13 Author's hand copy of Ya Yebu
Kane's Writing for aŋ-yina Musa divination.
Petbana Masimbo, October 1989.

14   Pa Yamba Nhoni Kamara and his sister.
Freetown, July 1978.

15 Pa Ibrahim Sankoh preparing an amulet (aŋ-sɛbɛ). Wellington, August 1992.

16   Pa Santigi's wives cooking for his cooperative harvesting group. Petbana Masimbo,
October 1989.

17   Red Water ordeal for witchcraft in the
early nineteenth century. Engraving by G. R.
Nylander, from "West-Africa Superstitions:
Trial by Red-Water, Among the Bulloms," *The
Missionary Register* (1819): 496–99.

18 "Sengbe Pieh and ECOMOG" by Degool (Amadu Tarawalie), Jones Star Youths Organization, Jones Street, Freetown. Photograph by Tim Waites, in Joseph Opala, *Ecstatic Renovation* (Freetown: Sierra Leone Adult Education Association, 1994).

19 Cartoon, *New Shaft* (Freetown), July 28–August 3, 1992.

A Thing under the Water

If you know a woman, you know a thing under the water.   Temne proverb

During my first period of fieldwork, several months went by before I realized that most diviners' clients were women, who often visited diviners secretly. Their covert consultations of diviners were framed by meanings of women's treachery and betrayal in their marital homes that, I later found, refashion a historical paradigm from the warfare and raiding of the Atlantic and legitimate trades. In order to understand how practical memory is involved in women's and men's consultations of diviners, it is first necessary to examine how the gendered character of warfare and raiding has been remembered in rural marital relationships.

As I do, however, I must also point out that I describe relationships as they were before the spread of the war to the Makeni area, and before Makeni became a rebel stronghold. While marriage goes on, children are born, and crops are grown, I no longer know *how* these processes take place, and how they intersect. While I do not wish to give the impression of complete socio-cultural rupture by putting everything in the past tense, neither do I wish to write in a timeless ethnographic present that fails to acknowledge the massive dislocations of the conflict. Accordingly, when I use the past tense, I do so in order to locate my observations about women and marriage during my three

149

periods of fieldwork in 1977–78, 1989, and 1992. But first, let us go back to another war more than a century ago.

The War and the Woman's Dream   In the hinterland of late-nineteenth-century Sierra Leone, a Kpa Mende woman who had married into the Yoni Temne town of Ronietta dreamed that enemies attacked the town. When she told her dream openly, she was ritually killed (Ijagbemi 1968: 269; 1973: 13). Why should a woman's dream have provoked such a response?

This event took place at the height of the wars of the colonial legitimate trade that, as we have seen, made life precarious in Sierra Leone's hinterland during the last quarter of the nineteenth century. It was also set in a part of southern Temneland that had no direct access to the major rivers and their tidewater trading centers that channeled the legitimate trade to and from the Colony in Freetown. Denied passage to these centers on the Rokel River to the north and, later, through Kpa Mende country to the river ports in the Bumpe and Ribi regions to the southwest, the Yoni Temne fought many wars against the peoples of these areas to secure access for Yoni traders (Ijagbemi 1968: chap. 6). It was precisely at the point when tensions were growing between the Kpa Mende woman's countrymen and the Yoni Temne into whom she had married that she announced her dream of attack and incursion.

According to Ijagbemi, the woman was killed because she "was indiscreet enough to relate that dream openly in direct contravention of the custom of the land which forbade women from relating such dreams openly" (1973: 13). This "custom of the land" draws upon four interconnected elements—dreams, women, incursion, and inappropriate disclosure. Dreaming, first of all, involves hidden activity that many diviners I knew located in a separate place called "the place of dreams" *(ro-mɜre)*, sometimes described as *"a big town dreamers go to"* (see Shaw 1992). Just as the hard edges of distinct shapes melt in the darkness of night, humans can, these diviners told me, mingle freely with spirits, witches, and ancestors in the dream-town. Dream encounters with spirits and witches, though, are dangerous and can signal an incursion of these alien forces. Certain of these dreams can, in fact, constitute "real" experiences of incursion. Among such incursion dreams are women's dreams of bush spirits—forces of the outside that are drawn into villages and houses by sexual attraction to sleeping women, inducing sexual dreams that make the dreaming women barren in waking life. These spirit seducers often "bring the face of the brother" of the woman they want (Littlejohn 1960b: 70)—a telling statement, given the cultural and historical meanings of marriage and affinity to be examined shortly. Certain other dreams of incursion or destruction have to be reported to the chief—for example, any dream in which the town is on fire, because this signifies a plot against the chief (Littlejohn 1978: 13). In this case, the "right to know" claimed by the chief entails obligations of both appropriate secrecy and appropriate disclosure on the part of the dreamer. Both sets of obligations, however, are represented in Temne gender ideology as problematic for women.

The Kpa Mende woman's dream, like women's sexual dreams of bush spirits, involved an incursion of harmful alien forces into a protected, Closed human space. And like the brother's face in women's bush-spirit dreams, the context of incipient conflict with the Kpa Mende is more than likely to have suggested a connection between the woman and the agents of attack. Finally, the woman's disclosure of her dream without (presumably) first reporting it to the chief violated imperatives both for his control over knowledge and for the verbal containment of the dream's dangerous potential.

In fact, it was the town's violent response to this infraction that eventually contributed to the translation of the woman's dream into the world of waking reality. Her son, Gbanka, left Ronietta after being forced to perform "humiliating ceremonies" connected with his mother's dream and ritual death (Ijagbemi 1973: 13). Gbanka subsequently became one of the most famous professional warriors of the nineteenth century. After a falling out with the elders of Yoni, he allied himself with the Kpa Mende—his mother's people and the enemies of Yoni—and fought devastating campaigns against his father's people and their allies in several Temne chiefdoms. He and his Kpa Mende followers sacked Ronietta in 1887 (Ijagbemi 1973: 20).

Gender as Memory   Like ritual practice, relationships between women and men may sometimes constitute a form of memory. In her interpretation of the women's zar cult in the northern Sudanese village of Hofriyat, Boddy suggests that Hofriyati constructions of gender are informed by past and present relations of external domination, such that marriage is made to represent "a rhetorical prototype for relationships between villagers and non-Hofriyati others" (1989: 192). Following the Comaroffs' (1987) exploration of how a consciousness of history is often constituted through a series of distinctions—cattle and cash, work and wage labor, rural and urban—that build up a discourse of contrast between two different eras, Boddy (1989: 192–93, 269–70, 301) argues that gender forms the basis of an analogous "poetics of contrast" in Hofriyat.

Temne understandings of gender and marriage can likewise be seen as re-figuring historical paradigms. This is not only because distinctions between men and women are "good to think with" as models of contrast, but also because the events and processes of Temneland's past have had important consequences for marriage and for representations of women. In contexts of raiding and warfare before the twentieth century, exogamous marriage created and maintained important alliances between groups, entailing considerable movement of women between different communities. But as these alliances often changed to enmities with the frequent shifts in power, resources, and interests that characterized both the Atlantic and legitimate trades, married women were also regarded as potentially suspect strangers, and they could (like Gbanka's mother) find themselves in a compromised position in their husbands' homes. This strangerhood was probably even more marked for female slaves taken as wives: most would have been seized during warfare and raiding, their dangerously unknowable kinship ties a potential source of future retaliation. Understandings of gender and marriage constituted by these predicaments can be viewed as social memories that articulate a historically prefigured model of relationships with strangers. But whereas for the endogamous Hofriyati, male domination of women is a metaphor for alien domination, Temne exogamy reverses this: it is wives, not husbands, who embody alien strangers in dominant gender discourse. Temne practices of exogamy and virilocality mean, in fact, that married women are not only metaphors for alien strangers in their husbands' communities: very often, as with Gbanka's mother, they *are* alien strangers.

Narratives of Incursive Marriage   The story of Gbanka's mother and her dream employs a repeated motif in Temne oral traditions: that of the married woman who assists in an attack by "her people" upon her husband or his town, either by deliberately revealing a secret or by covertly consulting a diviner in order to neutralize her husband's—or his house's, or his town's—defenses. In these narratives, as with that of Gbanka's mother, it is through the inappropriate treatment of dangerous knowledge that married women, "outsiders within" in contexts of shifting alliances and enmities, become mediators of alien incursion. From the perspective of the husband's group, this is treachery, but for "her people," of course, it is an act of loyalty: the treacherous wife is also the faithful sister.

We are given this latter standpoint of the "sister as heroine" in an account of a conquest by another prominent warrior, Gumbu Smart, who lived a hundred years before Gbanka. Smart was a remarkable figure in late-eighteenth-century Temneland: the son of a Loko chief, he was captured by slave traders and taken to Bance Island, but he so impressed his captors with his "smart-ness" that they renamed him accordingly and employed him as an agent to acquire slaves for them (Ijagbemi 1968: 46–51). Quickly becoming wealthy through his work as a slave-trading agent, he subverted the purposes of his employers by buying Loko slaves and training them as members of his own private army, thereby becoming able to intimidate his former English masters and regain his autonomy from them.

Eventually he sought land in Masimera chiefdom in southern Temneland on which he and his followers could settle in order to tap the trade of the Rokel River. The Regent of Masimera offered him land, requesting in return that Smart help recover sacred objects of the Masimera chieftaincy that had been seized by the neighboring Ro-Mendi Temne during a dispute. Smart agreed, and as part of his preparations for his attack on Ro-Mendi, he traveled to Melakuri in present-day Guinea, both to buy arms and to consult the divin-ers for which Guinea is still famed today. He would be helped, these diviners told him, by a woman of Loko origin (and therefore his compatriot) living in Ro-Mendi:

> Smart went to Melakuri and invited some Morimen [Muslim diviners] to Masi-mera, these Morimen were very light in complexion. After these Morimen had completed their work they told Smart to gather his war men, and assured him that he would succeed. . . . Then the Morimen said to Smart that during the fighting his war men would come across a young woman, yellow in complex-ion, and carrying a calabash of water. This young woman should not be harmed, for she was the one who would show them where the sacred things were. At Ro Lankono the warriors found this young woman, and she showed them where the two boxes containing the sacred things had been hidden— under a bamboo tree. (Ahmadu Smart Kanu, in Ijagbemi 1968: 321)

This recurring gendered motif of the female stranger who mediates the pene-tration of the community in which she lives by men from her natal home directs us to further intersections of marriage with domination and conceal-ment in Temne history.

An important context for such intersections is that of the historical rela-tionships between Mande-speaking migrants and the Temne communities they lived in (and sometimes ruled). As these powerful strangers were drawn into Temne communities, typically through the offer of marriage, they were drawn in relationships of obligation to their Temne wife-givers. Thus when, as we have seen in chapter 1, Port Loko was seized by the Susu in the second half of the eighteenth century, "the Timanees, who were then unable to resist, submitted, gave them wives, and placed many of the children of the principal men under them to learn the Koran."[1] But the matrilateral links thereby created were the eventual undoing of the Susu rulers, for in 1815 Moriba Kindo used his aunt's marriage to a Susu Alimami to obtain the Muslim political title of Alikali, and—with this prestigious new Susu Muslim status—organized resistance and seized back Port Loko for the Temne.

Some used their married daughters and sisters to turn the tables on dominant in-laws in other ways. In chapter 1, we gained a sense of the terror engendered by the violence and moral transgressions of the slave trade through the nineteenth-century narrative of Korombo's depredations. That narrative continues, however, with a description of Korombo's ritual entrapment through his wives' and affines' use of diviners:

> As to Korombo, because he conquered all people, therefore they acted deceitfully against him in order to kill him. They gave him many women, and told these women (that) when they were plaiting his hair, they might bring his hair. As for the pillow, whereon he was putting his head, when he lay down (they told them), that when they were going to wash (it), the water which they wring out, they should put that water into a bottle and carry it to the Mori-men. When he cut the nails, he said to the women: "Go and throw them away for me." And they took (them), and carried them to the people who sought his life. (Schlenker 1861: 9–11)

Like this strategy through which Korombo's apparently defeated in-laws penetrated his defenses through his wives, like the Loko woman among the Ro-Mendi Temne who revealed the whereabouts of buried chiefdom secrets to Gumbu Smart, and like Gbanka's mother's fatal dream narrative, the historical motif of women's dangerous secrecy or inappropriate disclosure in their marital home has a strong resonance in contemporary Temne marriage.

The ambivalent position of married women who can never be fully "in" their husbands' households has been well documented in the upper Guinea coast (e.g., Bledsoe 1980; Jackson 1989: 88–101; Ferme 1992). But this ambivalence is not only the product of the regional history of the upper Guinea coast; it is also a broader structural feature of exogamous, virilocal marriage and patrilineal descent. What we are concerned with here, then, is the intersection of a widely dispersed form of social organization with specific historical processes in a particular region.

Sundiata's Sister Set in the savannah to the northeast of the upper Guinea coast, the Mande epic of Sundiata, founder of the Mali Empire, tells of how the hero's sister, Nana Triban, was also the wife of his enemy, the Susu king Soumaoro. Sundiata's triumph over his enemy was made possible by his sister who, through seduction and deceit, persuaded her husband to reveal to her the secret of his magical invulnerability (Niane 1965: 56–58). The woman who is a loyal sister, a treacherous wife, and a conduit for dangerous secrets, then, is a salient image in other regions and other histories in which alliances forged through exogamous marriage often shifted and reversed themselves.

But the savannah region in present-day Mali (in the Mande "heartland") is also a region whose history intersects with that of the upper Guinea coast (in the Mande "periphery"). The same theme of wifely betrayal and sisterly (or daughterly) loyalty is repeated in narratives told in Mande-speaking Kuranko communities in northeastern Sierra Leone. In one such story, a daughter saves her father from being killed in a death-dealing stranger's guessing-game by seducing the stranger and obtaining the answers beforehand; in another, a bush-cow seeks to avenge a hunter's killing of her animal kin by turning into a beautiful woman, becoming the hunter's wife, and stealing his magical eyes (Jackson 1982: 209–13).

In Kuranko marriage—as in Temne marriage—a wife links her father's lineage to her husband's lineage, and is herself linked to both groups by different, and often conflicting, ties:

> Virilocal residence means that women from outside the compound (and in some cases from outside the village) come as relative strangers into a group whose cohesion depends upon a clear disjunction between insiders and outsiders. Although the in-marrying woman relinquishes all jural rights in her natal group, she retains sentimental links with it; in particular her active influence over her brother contrasts markedly with her ideally passive role as wife. (Jackson 1977: 90)

Yet unlike a Kuranko woman, a Temne woman never relinquishes her formal rights in her natal group; her natal group, accordingly, never loses their rights in her and her children. Each person belongs to two lineages: the father's lineage *(ma-kas)*, the dominant line through which land, residence, and clan name are passed; and the mother's lineage *(ma-kara)*, through which a daughter's or sister's rights in her natal home—to residence, land, or assistance with food (especially rice)—are extended to her children. Since, moreover, marriage between a man and his mother's brother's daughter is preferred, this means that membership of the *ma-kara* can extend over several generations.

In Kuranko marriage, to continue the comparison, the transfer of rights from a woman's patrilineage to that of her husband is regarded (in theory) as absolute and permanent, marked by the bride's agnates' declaration to the husband's group that "'She is your thief, your witch, your daughter, your everything. We have come to give her to you alive, but even when she is dead she remains your wife. You can flog her, abuse her, she is yours'" (Jackson 1977: 97). Temne men complain, in contrast, that "you always owe your wife's people" (see Littlejohn 1960b: 72). Temne marriage creates a permanent state of indebtedness, giving a man's wife's brother *(ɔ-nasin)* the right to enter his sister's husband's house and take any food and small possessions he finds there. Littlejohn writes, for example:

> One morning my interpreter was speechless with suppressed rage, when I asked him what was wrong he said a *nasin* had just come and taken away a new pair of trousers and a shirt. "You are always placating your nasin," he added, "they hold the marriage; they will take your wife away if you don't." (1960b: 73)

A man's obligations to his wife's brother can even outlast the marriage, as long as his wife had borne him children. Several years after his divorce, a friend of mine in Freetown was still regularly greeted by his ex-wife's brother with the words: "Thank goodness my brother-in-law is here—I need some money!"

This difference of emphasis between the permanent rights of the husband in Kuranko marriage and the permanent indebtedness of the husband in Temne marriage appeared, during my time in Sierra Leone, to be no more than that—a difference of emphasis. The formal statement quoted above through which a Kuranko woman's lineage transfers absolute rights to her husband's lineage does not mean that in practice Kuranko women cannot leave their marriages, that they are habitually abused, or that they are renounced by their natal kin. In fact, Jackson makes it clear that Kuranko women exercise strong claims upon their brothers in particular, and that most divorces are initiated by a woman leaving her husband and returning to her natal home (1977: 97–101). Likewise, the absence of a formal "mother's lineage" among Kuranko does not prevent a woman's children from having substantial rights over their mother's brother and his lineage (Jackson 1977: 131–34). But the difference between the formal rights conferred or retained in Temne and Kuranko marriage could assume considerable significance when we remember the historical relationship between Temne communities and Mande-speaking elites. It was through intermarriage—between Temne women and elite non-Temne men—that politically dominant Mande rulers (such as Susu rulers in Port Loko and Kuranko rulers in southern Temneland), economically dominant Mandinka and Fula traders, and ritually prestigious Muslim clerics (aŋ-mɔre or aŋ-lɛfa) were incorporated into Temne communities. The asymmetry between Temne and Kuranko marriage in terms of the formal rights of wife-givers may be seen as linked to hierarchical asymmetries between Temne and Mande-speaking groups. By becoming a wife-taker, the "big man" who drew others into debt was himself drawn into relationships of indebtedness with demanding Temne in-laws who might at any time "invade" his home and help themselves to its consumable contents.

It was not only for those who wish to avenge acts of violence and appropriation—as in the story of Korombo, the slave-trading warrior—that wifegiving could be a potential form of retaliation; more subtle forms of domination were also answered by more subtle forms of incursion and entrapment. As Littlejohn observes, "from the point of view of adult men each wife brought in is, as well as a source of children, the point of irruption of plundering nasin into the house. (Plundering is the word the Temne use of *nasin*.)" (1960b: 73). Thus in Sierra Leone, Sundiata proved just as vulnerable to the sisters of his male subjects as Soumaoro was to Nana Triban.

The Woman is the "Means" of the Man   Although, from a husband's perspective, a wife might be the "point of irruption of plundering *nasin* into the house" (Littlejohn 1960b: 73), marriage at the time of my periods of fieldwork was nevertheless a source of substantial benefits to men as husbands—benefits that are usually characterized as "wealth-in-people" (Bledsoe 1980). Historically, the upper Guinea coast has long been a region in which land is relatively plentiful but labor problematic (Richards 1986). Although the dominant lineages in a particular area control access to land, gaining such access has not usually been a problem for others: successful cultivation of the staple crop—upland rice grown through shifting cultivation and, increasingly, swamp rice—depends, rather, upon the capacity of a farmer to control the labor of others. Without adequate male labor to clear the bush for cultivation at precisely the right time before the rains arrive, female labor to weed the growing rice, and both male and female labor to harvest the ripe rice before pests eat it, the crop is poor (Richards 1986). Access to this labor is a function of a person's "wealth-in-people," obtained by building up ties of dependency and indebtedness through kinship, marriage, parenthood, wardship, pawnship and, up to the early twentieth century, slavery (see Bledsoe 1980: 46–79 for Kpelle; Richards 1986, Ferme 1992, and Leach 1992 for Mende). Women have long been pivotal here, not only because men are dependent on the labor of their wives and children but also because men control other men *through* women. Very importantly, men have depended upon women to cook for the cooperative work groups that performed labor-intensive tasks such as bush clearing and harvesting (plate 16). And through the marriage of a daughter (often through his wife's mediation), a man has usually able to make substantial claims on the brideservice labor of his son-in-law.

As well, then, as being the means by which men reproduce their patrilineage through children, women have also been the means by which men—who hold the land—are able to farm it, and the means by which men incorporate (and, as we have seen, entrap) other men and women through diverse "wealth-in-people" ties. A Temne proverb states, in fact, that *"the woman is the 'means' of the man"* (ɔw-uni bom, kɔnɔ yi aŋ-sabu ka w-an duni): she mediates his capacity to act upon the world. Her mediation between different individuals, lineages, generations, and places is, moreover, central to her own agency.

A Woman has no Town   The mediatory positions that women occupy in patrilineal, virilocal, exogamous, and polygynous social contexts entail contradictions that Karp characterizes as a "patrilineal puzzle" paralleling the so-called "matrilineal puzzle" for men:

> Matrilineal societies probably do pose problems for men who have to choose between "father love" and "mother right," as Malinowski described it, but women are often torn between conflicting interests and loyalties as well. . . . Iteso women experience contradictions in the conditions of their existence that could be termed a *patrilineal puzzle*. Patrilineal societies are composed of groups and categories that are reproduced by aliens, non-members who have married into them. (1988: 42–43)

What is often an abrupt and difficult transition for women, who move from their natal home into the alien space of their marital home, is a different kind of problem for men, who are dependent on these aliens whom they subordinate through marriage to reproduce their lineages. This is an irony upon which, Karp argues, women among the Iteso of Kenya comment subversively through their uproarious laughter during the marriage ritual (1988: 48–50). Temne women have negotiated the contradictions of their own "patrilineal puzzle" through concealed ritual action, as we shall see later.

Some of these contradictions are captured in a telling proverb about the consequences of women's movements between their natal homes and their marital homes (as well as through a succession of marital homes upon divorce and remarriage): *"a woman has no town"* (ɔw-uni bom, ɔ ba yɛ kə-pet). Let us turn to the social and spatial movements that make this so.

During my periods of fieldwork, a woman's transferral from her natal home to her husband's household was often a difficult one, particularly when by doing so she become subordinate not only to her husband and (especially) his mother but also to a senior co-wife. If she gave birth to a child (and thereby provided descendants for her husband's lineage), however, her status in her marital home shifted from "wife" to "mother" and rose accordingly. At a wedding I attended during my 1989 stay in Petbana, a speech by a senior male kinsman of the bride, Zainab, conveyed a sense of these transformations in a woman's life-course by comparing a woman's marriage to the initial bitterness and subsequent sweetness of kola:

> If you take a kola nut and put it in your mouth and chew it, it is bitter. When you swallow, then you get the whole taste inside you. Then you feel the sweetness of it. And then the saliva becomes "equal," and your mind will not forget about the kola. It is like marriage. The first time she goes, it is hard for her. It is there she will be before sweetness comes.

Zainab's male kinsman thereby encouraged her to stay with her husband through the inevitably difficult first stages: most divorces occur in the early years of marriage.

Despite the difficulties of their transition to a subordinate position within an alien household (and often an alien village as well), women, for their part, needed to get married because of their dependence upon men's labor. Land, as we have seen, is held by male members of a patrilineage. I was sometimes told by men in Petbana that female members of the lineage could not hold land because women's mobility (entailed by virilocal residence) prevents them from being fully apprised of the particulars of land disputes, thereby undermining their knowledge of land boundaries: a woman holds no land because a woman has no town. Women's mediatory passage between different places constructed a looser sense of the demarcations between different places, contrasting with that of their more sedentarily centered fathers and brothers. Nevertheless, women as lineage members still had rights to lineage land and to crops grown on it; some married daughters returned at harvest-time to take a share of the rice from their father's farm, and it was relatively easy for a woman to obtain land to farm from her father or her brother.

It was not easy, though, for her to obtain the male labor required to clear the bush in order to make a rice farm. Some women who gained wealth through trade were able to hire men to clear farmland, but this was rare. So when women worked on their husband's farm, they took advantage of land that had been cleared already, using the same piece of land the following year; they also intercropped, growing cassava, groundnuts, and vegetables together with the rice in upland farms. If they grew enough, they could sell these crops: women in Petbana, for example, took their produce to the market in Makeni, about three miles away, but few women made enough money by doing so to gain more than a limited economic autonomy.[2]

As well as being dependent on their husbands, women were also dependent upon other wives in a polygynous household (although many men were unable to accumulate enough for more than one wife's bridewealth). Women as wives regarded polygyny with ambivalence: the term for co-wife *(ɔ-res)* also means "rival." Among the advantages for a woman in a polygynous marriage was the reduction in her workload when a co-wife was brought into her husband's household. An older woman in Petbana, Yan Safi, told me that it had been she who had found three other women for her husband to marry, commenting: *"If you say you don't want a co-wife, you will ruin yourself with work. That is why we look for wives for our husbands."* As well as having a reduced workload, a senior wife—as Yan Safi had been—also had status and authority over her husband's junior wives, especially if she was instrumental in bringing them into the household. Some senior wives were able to give up farming and focus entirely on trade, building up their resources. Ya Adama, Pa Koroma's senior wife, had helped him to marry three other wives, and she was able to keep a small shop while her co-wives worked on his farm. When her co-wives complained about the amount of work they had to do in comparison to her, Pa Koroma supported her, telling them: *"Adama is the one who brought you to this house, so you should give her a rest now."*

But the ideal in which the senior wife in a polygynous household gains prestige and a lighter workload was not necessarily realized in practice. Ya Bay in the previous chapter, remember, had had a first husband who used the jealousy that his junior wives harbored toward her as an excuse for neglecting her:

> I found [my co-wives] and married them to my husband! There were four of us. But they didn't like me; they were jealous. I had children and they didn't. My husband treated me badly, so that my co-wives would not bewitch my children. He only gave me rice to eat and feed my children with—nothing else.

Polygyny, then, could have distinct disadvantages, even for senior wives.

Polygynous marriage was also less advantageous for junior wives, unless a woman happened to be her husband's "favorite" wife (ɔ-bathɛ). In theory a husband was not supposed to show favoritism and was expected to distribute resources and attention equally among his wives, who were expected to take equal turns in sleeping with him and cooking for him. The ideal was for co-wives to live together harmoniously, and although many did forge warm relationships, they did so with little structural support, for they were likely to come from different lineages and often different villages. If the first wife was involved in bringing in the others, this provided a stronger basis for close links among co-wives, especially if she was able to use her own network of kin and friends to do so. But there was usually an uneasy balance between cooperation and competition, and, because co-wives often competed for influence over their husband and over decisions within the household, conflicts could arise easily. Historically, moreover, during the Atlantic and legitimate trades the availability of female slaves increased both the incidence of polygyny and the size of big men's polygynous households, thereby possibly exacerbating the structural tensions in polygynous households.

It was children who, more than anything else, anchored women in their marital homes. As well as ameliorating a woman's status in her husband's household, transforming her from "wife" to "mother," the children she bore—especially her sons—also gave her long-term security, as they were expected to take care of her after she became a widow. Mothers and children, therefore, were mutually dependent. They constituted each other: as a Temne proverb expresses it, "the child is the mother; the mother is the child." But women were never anchored to the extent of being trapped in their marriages. A wife could withdraw her cooperation and refuse to cook, to work on the farm, or to have sex with her husband; she could go back to her natal home and require her husband to beg formally for her return; she could take a lover and perhaps leave her husband for him; and ultimately she could divorce and remarry. Women's protests had force because men were dependent upon their wives, and most were reluctant to lose one.

Throughout their marital life-course, women retained their clan names and their identities as a daughter and sister in their natal home, to which they returned for visits (especially for weddings and funerals) and sometimes for prolonged stays. A woman as a lineage member had considerably more rights of ownership and expression than as a married woman in her husband's lineage: as a daughter or sister, in other words, she shared in patriarchal authority, while as a wife she was subject to the patriarchal authority of others. In addition to their rights as lineage members, married women also had important claims over their brothers, as the bridewealth received from a daughter's marriage was normally used to enable her brother to marry. In particular, a brother was obliged to provide for his sister if she left her husband and returned to her natal home —although in practice brothers were not always happy to see their sisters return, especially if the dissolution of the marriage was permanent and the bridewealth subsequently used for the brother's marriage would have to be refunded.

These movements of women out from their natal homes to their marital homes, back to their natal homes for visits or when leaving their husbands, out again upon remarriage, and sometimes out to a sister's or daughter's marital home if, upon widowhood, they are not inherited by their husband's brother and they have no adult sons, constructed a social geography that contrasts with that of men. Shirley Ardener characterizes this contrast in other patrilineal, virilocal communities in terms of gendered social maps: "Any map generated by a man living among his concentration of male relatives, who become more distantly related to him as they live further from him, would look very different from that of his wife whose significant same-sex kin are widely dispersed, and whose male patrikin are concentrated elsewhere from her" (1981: 27). In the fixed, single-centered "map" of male patrilineal space, the dispersal of multiple, shifting centers in a woman's social and physical landscape appears as a "lack": "*a woman has no town.*" In the space of the village, moreover, women's space appeared literally marginal, articulating meanings of "back" and "periphery" in relation to "front" and "center." The most public places in the town and the house were, respectively, the centrally located and open-sided discussion-house *(aŋ-bare)* and the front veranda *(aŋ-gbəŋthəŋ)* of the house. Both were sites of men's discussion, and, in the case of the discussion-house, of senior male jurisdiction over legal cases. Behind the house, the site of women's food processing, cooking, and discussion was the back yard *(ka-darəŋ)* facing the bush. And farther out, at the nearest river or stream, women collected water, laundered clothes, and sometimes fished with nets.

Yet, as Ferme observes for Mende women's space, "the location of women and children on boundaries at different levels signifies both their marginality to some of these domains and processes, *and* their valued roles in mediating the transitions and transformations that link them together" (1992: 41). The focal space of the town in the patrilineal "map" of the built settlement is replaced by an emphasis on mediations, transactions, and interconnections in the fluid, moving "maps" that women traced through their passages among different groups and places.

There is a further duality to women's mobility. Callaway argues that although Yoruba women's movements through spatial domains controlled by men suggest dependence and subordination, these movements are also the means by which women select men for marriage, initiate divorce, and develop economic autonomy (1981: 185). Similarly, a Temne woman's imperative to move from her natal home to her marital home was, on the one hand, the alienating outcome of her dependence within a predominantly patrilineal and virilocal system. Yet on the other hand her movement, through subsequent migrations and visits to the towns of her mother, father, brother, or lover, could be transformed into strategies that increased her agency in her marital home. Instead of signifying a "lack," her capacity to move was turned into a capacity to act: *"a woman has no town"* because a woman has more than one town from which to choose.

For husbands, of course, this duality assumed a different significance. Women's movements were valued in mediation between lineages and in men's "wealth-in-people" transactions—in contexts, in other words, in which these movements were subsumed by men's agency. Women's movements on their own behalf, however, were often seen in terms of a dangerous lack of male control and surveillance—especially if we bear in mind the historical context of shifting alliances and frequent raiding during the slave trade and trade wars. In their trysts with lovers (both those that were real and those that were imagined by suspicious husbands), in the invasive "plundering" of their brothers, and in (as we shall see in the next chapter) their secret consultations of diviners, women as wives were often perceived as potential conduits for incursive mediations that might threaten the contained patrilineal space of the town and household.

Gendered Wealth in Hidden Knowledge   The contrast between women's movements and mediations that were subsumed by the agency of their husbands and those that were not is central to the issue of "wealth-in-people" outlined above. Of crucial importance to husbands' attempts to control their wives' mediatory capacities—and wives' attempts to evade this control—were practices of disclosure and secrecy. Hierarchical relationships involve asymmetries of knowledge: the authority of chiefs over their subjects, of elders over juniors, of initiates over non-initiates, and of husbands over wives are all underscored by the rights of seniors to know more about those under them than the latter know about them. The chief (ɔ-bay), for instance, became a "stranger" (ɔ-tik; see Littlejohn 1973: 298) to those in his chiefdom after spending up to a year in ritual seclusion known as Closure (ka-kaŋtha), during which he was initiated into the "secrets" of the chiefdom. While his "strangerhood" upon his emergence from Closure meant that his subjects officially lost their capacity to know him, he acquired the right to know about them. He had the right, for instance, to be formally told of the timing of initiations by the cult associations, and his permission was required before anyone could use a "swearing" medicine (aŋ-sasa) or call a witchfinding ritual. His counselors and subchiefs (ɛ-kapər), called his "eyes and ears," were expected to keep him informed of whatever happened in his chiefdom. Wealth-in-people implies wealth-in-*knowledge*-about-people.

This could involve contradictions for women. On the one hand, women were often represented by men as being prone to *"pull secrets outside"* (wura ɛ-gbuŋdu do-kaŋ). They are, men often told me, liable to reveal confidential knowledge through gossip, as well as being unable to control secrets of their cult association, the Bondo, as strictly as men control secrets of their association, the Poro. Their capacity for moral personhood was perceived to be compromised by this weakness—as exemplified dramatically by the ritual killing of Gbanka's mother in the late nineteenth century for openly recounting her dream of war. Often, the real issue was that of a woman's failure (or refusal) to channel her speech in accordance with a man's "rights-in-knowledge" over her—as was likely to have been the case with Gbanka's mother. In a witchcraft case in 1978 in a Temne migrant household in Koidu, the capital of the diamond district to the east, for instance, a woman who started to make a witchcraft confession was immediately rebuked by her husband—not (initially, at least) for being a witch but because she had first confessed to her co-wife rather than to him.

On the other hand, women were also represented by men as being "too secretive." This again was seen as reducing women's capacity for personhood, as (from the husband's perspective) it undermined her capacity to be a good wife: either withholding or freely broadcasting information that a husband claims the right to control were equally subversive of his rights in knowledge. It was particularly important for a husband that his wife should not keep secrets from him that concern his "wealth-in-people" rights over her reproductive and productive capacities. The late Pa Kaper Bana, the ritual subchief in Petbana, saw these problems of the male control of knowledge as deriving largely from women's "strangerhood" in marriage:

> A man sees a woman and marries her. He does not know the behavior of the woman, whether it is good or bad. Men should have patience, because women are not people to trust. . . . All the problems in the world are caused by women. When K-uru created the world, he created life through women. Women bear children. But there are women who go in different directions and cause problems. A woman can live with her husband and commit adultery, then she brings misfortune, and if I farm the rice will not grow properly if she does not confess.

If a married woman had a lover and did not confess his name to her husband, then, she was understood (by her husband in particular) as blocking fertility in several areas. Her husband's ancestors would withdraw their blessing and protection. He would suffer misfortune. The rice crop would fail. The woman herself would have birth problems and her children would fall ill if she did not confess to her husband by "calling the name" of her lover.

But for a woman as a wife, to tell your husband or your co-wife too much was often seen as foolish. "If you tell your husband or your 'rival' (ɔ-res, 'co-wife') about your money," Yan Safi told me, "your husband will take it from you. If you don't agree, he will beat you and take it and share it between your rivals. And your rivals, if they know you have money, they will go to the diviner to destroy it. Or they will tell your husband." Men saw certain women's secrets—such as those of the women's Bondo society, birth, and menstruation—as legitimate. For women, however, there was not always such a clear divide between "legitimate" and "illegitimate" secrets. Ya Nandewa, an official of the Bondo society in Petbana with whom I was discussing secrecy during my 1989 stay, told me: "It's good to have secrets. Women give birth, and men don't, so that is a secret for men to go there. If you're married, and your husband has a girlfriend, he would hide it from you, so why shouldn't you do the same to him?"

But what kinds of "wealth" in production and reproduction were men and women contesting through these struggles over knowledge and secrecy? In a recent recasting of the wealth-in-people concept in relation to Equatorial Africa, Guyer (1995) argues that the model of accumulation—of the quantitative addition of producers and reproducers—at the concept's core might be more usefully replaced by a model of composition, of the building up of heterogeneous powers and capacities through a multiplicity of people who own or embody diverse forms of knowledge. Applying this model to marriage and polygyny would, she suggests, entail tracing out

> the different facets of power that each wife brought: links to a new territory or trade network; taps into the power of specialists amongst her kin and their personal qualities of strength or skill; control of a centrifugal home front (as in systems of preferential marriage) or pathways to the outside; access to agricultural and other productive and spiritual knowledge appropriate to different environments as groups migrated. And then there are the personal qualities of women themselves. (1995: 116)

The "compositional logic" of wealth-in-knowledge that Guyer explores is grounded in past movements and migrations of peoples through the Equatorial forest, requiring constant quests for sources of new forms of knowledge. In the upper Guinea coast, however, the "wealth-in-people" practices outlined above were partly—and very importantly—a function of the labor requirements of agriculture in this "forest frontier" region (Richards 1986). They were also rooted in the history of the region: during the eras of warfare and raiding during the Atlantic and legitimate trades, leaders used "wealth-in-people" strategies to build up followings of supporters, whose security in turn depended on the ability of these leaders to protect them from slave-raiding (Bledsoe 1980: 63; Denzer 1971; Dorjahn 1960b; Murphy 1980: 201).

But we should also recall that Temne communities responded to the presence of (and, often, domination by) Mande-speaking elites by transforming themselves through their acquisition of Mande cultural practices—in other words, by incorporating powerful, elite knowledge such as techniques of warfare and Arabic literacy. Migrant Mande strangers, as Skinner notes, "often possessed a combination of resources and skills, including trade goods and knowledge of trading techniques and routes, military organization, literacy in Arabic, and specialized religious knowledge which was deemed important by local populations" (1978: 33). During the Susu occupation of Port Loko in the eighteenth century, remember, "the Timanees, who were then unable to resist, submitted, gave them wives, and placed many of the children of the principal men under them to learn the Koran." These incorporative practices of, on the one hand, acquiring your invaders' knowledge and cultural practices and, on the other hand, marrying your daughters to them, were linked. It was through the marriage of his Temne aunt to a Susu Alimami that Moriba Kindo obtained his title of Adikali (as well as acquiring the Susu Islamic practices of turbaning that ritually conferred it), which he then employed to authorize his rebellion against the Susu and his return of Port Loko to Temne control. Through their marriages to Temne women, powerful Mande "strangers" such as the Susu in Port Loko, as well as itinerant Mande and Fula diviners and traders in other Temne communities, often acquired or legitimized (or, at least, sought to legitimize) local positions of political leadership (Turay 1971: 63; Skinner 1976: 501).

But for these Temne communities, intermarriage between Temne women and powerful male strangers accomplished the incorporation of specialist "foreign" knowledge through the incorporation of the foreign specialists themselves. This was the way in which Muslim Mande and Fula ritual specialists (with their powerful literate knowledge of Islamic divination techniques and amulet-construction) and traders (with their knowledge of extensive commercial networks) were assimilated into Temne towns and villages (Turay 1971: 63; Skinner 1976: 501; see Bledsoe and Robey 1986 for Mende). It was primarily by becoming wife-*givers*, then, rather than by the wife-acquiring strategies Guyer describes, that Temne lineages and communities obtained wealth-in-knowledge from Mande strangers. The "plundering" Temne nasin thus acquired more than just food, clothing, and money from his Mande affines.

The direction of this flow of knowledge from wife-receivers to wife-givers returns us, once again, to the motif of the married woman who passes secret knowledge from her husband to her own kin, becoming a conduit for incursion by "her people" and thereby threatening her marital home's containment.

A Thing under the Water   The motif of the wife who acts as a channel for outside incursion was reiterated in men's attitudes toward certain ritual relationships between women and river spirits. Not all such relationships were viewed as suspect, however. The upper Guinea coast is famed in scholarship on gender for its female cult associations, known in Temne as Bondo and in Mende and Kpelle as Sande (see, e.g., Bledsoe 1984; Boone 1986; Lamp 1985; MacCormack 1979; Phillips 1995), into which girls are placed in order to initiate them into womanhood as a prerequisite for marriage. The Bondo association is given a predominantly positive significance as the cult that transforms girls into women and controls techniques and medicines of midwifery, although Bondo officials are also renowned for their ownership of harmful medicines and poisons. These ambivalent capacities form part of a wider set of understandings about connections between women and river spirits.

The most visibly prominent spirit in Bondo is a river spirit, *aŋ-nawo*, whose masked embodiment is carried and danced by a Bondo official. *aŋ-nawo's* wooden mask is ornately carved in the form of a helmet, at the base of which are a series of rings that Bondo officials describe as the concentric ripples of water that appeared when she was drawn from the river (Lamp 1985). The carvings on the mask usually consist of complex representations of plaited hair and of a variety of objects in which snakes, crocodiles, twin figures, cooking pots, and hens figure prominently. Mothers who bear twins have high prestige as "mothers of multitudes"; snakes and crocodiles are forms commonly assumed by river spirits, while hens and cooking pots belong in the women's space of the backyard behind the house and can be used in ritual to "maintain the household" (Littlejohn 1960a: 76; Lamp 1985: 3). Plaited hair, which is essential to the construction of female beauty, has a range of associations that link plaiting to ordered creation and generative power (Littlejohn 1963: 2; Schlenker 1861: 12–15; Lamp 1983: 12). Two female domains, then—the backyard and the river—are brought together in the iconography of Bondo masks and linked with symbols of orderly growth and birth. This interpenetration of village and river is reiterated in the ritual sequence of Bondo initiation (Lamp 1985).

Less well known than the Bondo association, and far less conspicuous than its collective ritual, are women's personal relationships with river spirits. A woman who wanted children could initiate a secret relationship with a river spirit, searching for a pebble by the side of a river that attracted her: the pebble entices precisely because it is animated by a spirit. She would take the pebble home and keep it hidden in a small tin, offering it libations of gin or a sacrifice (s-athka) of an egg and promising it a larger sacrifice of a sheep or chicken if it helped her have a child. If it liked the woman, it could appear in her dreams, often in the form of a snake, and tell her its name. Men, though, almost always regarded women's hidden rituals at their tiny water-spirit "shrines" as highly sinister. They often represented women's introductions of these external spirits into their husband's household as incursions equivalent to witchcraft, liable to render men impotent, their co-wives barren, and their children sick. While incursions mediated by women outside male control have been a problem for men, though, it is the *lack* of such incursion that appears to have been a problem for women as wives. Women's capacities and choices depended upon their own movement between different domains, and upon the "penetration" of the place in which they have a subordinate "wifely" status by the authority of their male kin, among whom *they* had authority as sisters and daughters.

Women's associations with spirits of the river have been fitting, given that in rural Temneland women's work—carrying water, laundering, and fishing—brings them into constant contact with streams and rivers. But it goes further than this. As we have seen, rivers have been historically "the *autobahnen* of the Guinea Coast" (Rodney 1970: 17) that connected towns together and enabled trade but that thereby also brought war and raids. Women's associations with rivers have not been limited to their fishing and domestic work but were also related to these dangerously mixed blessings of mobility and linkage. Women, like rivers, connected communities together, enabling men (and, of course, enabling themselves) to develop alliances with other groups through marriage. Although in the eras of the Atlantic and legitimate trades, alliances forged through marriage provided support and protection, these links through women could also become avenues of attack from those in other communities who "know your secrets." And just as rivers flow by the margins of human settlement with a mobility and an opacity that renders them unknowable, women were characterized by men as (literally) unfathomable: *"If you know a woman,"* claims a proverb, *"you know a thing under the water"* (maŋ tara w-uni bom e, ŋ tara a-re i ro-m-aŋt ratha)—or, in another version, *"if you know a woman, you know a thing in Darkness"* (ŋ tara a-re i ka aŋ-sum e). This normative perception of women as submerged, unfathomable, and hidden in Darkness recapitulates the historical connection between women's mobility and women's mediation of "outside" (and therefore unknown) forces: you never know what will be coming down the river, or emerging from the darkness, next.

In the following chapter, I explore how gendered historical images of women as conduits of alien incursion have also been remembered and refigured in men's and women's consultations of diviners.

6

The Hidden Ritual Process

Just over a hundred years ago, the warfare of the legitimate trade ceased in Temneland with the British imposition of the Protectorate and their defeat of Bai Bureh in 1898. At the level of the household, however, ideas of invisible attack by spirits, witches, and harmful medicine—and suspicions of wifely mediation of such attack—remained. Over four centuries of slave trading and trade wars have, I suggest, interwoven the broader features of what Karp (1988: 42–43) calls the "patrilineal puzzle" with practical memories of the potential dangers of in-marrying women in the Sierra Leone hinterland. Dominant representations of women as a "fifth column" in their marital home, examined in the previous chapter, often take the form of specific suspicions that married women might be secretly visiting diviners in order to harm members of their marital household. These suspicions, once again, do not take the form of discursive statements about the past. Instead, discourses about diviners and their dangerous female clients incorporate historically mediated understandings—on the part of both men and women—of wives as channels for outside incursion.

The women and men who are the subject of this chapter formed the everyday clientele of diviners I knew from the late 1970s to the early 1990s. They were not the powerful (and almost always male) patrons, much sought after by diviners, who use divination to secure their success (as we shall see in the final chapter). They were predominantly women who, together with a smaller number of (mostly junior) men, provided diviners with a regular but not particularly lucrative income. Their consultations and cures did not enhance a diviner's reputation and hence power. On the contrary, their private (and often secret) consultation of diviners marked both them and the diviners they used as highly suspect. Once again, my use of the past tense in parts of this chapter is meant not to suggest that people have ceased to consult diviners but to locate my knowledge of the circumstances and concerns of their consultations in the time before the rebel war spread to the Makeni area.

Before turning to women's concerns as diviners' clients, let us examine the sinister images that their consultation of diviners evoked.

Divination and Dangerous Women   Although women formed the majority of diviners' clients, most women did not readily acknowledge using private divination at all. During my first period of fieldwork, when I told people that I was interested in diviners and divination, most women I knew tended either to respond with noncommittal remarks or to insist that they knew nothing whatsoever about divination. Many men, by contrast, responded with laughter and wry comments about the problems that women caused by consulting diviners. Men often told me that a woman who is angry with her husband or lover could ritually *"hand him over"* by giving his name or pieces of his hair to a diviner, who would then use bad medicine to harm him. *"Some* [women] *get your hairs and nails and take them to an-mɔre to harm you; even footprints, they take earth from them to harm you,"* a young man called Braima told me when I first arrived in Freetown, describing practices that could have come straight out of the account of the demise of Korombo the warrior described in the previous chapter.

One reason why women's use of private divination has been seen as threatening is that it subverts the normative association between knowledge and authority upon which hierarchies and processes of "wealth-in-people" rests. We have already seen that in all asymmetrical relationships, those in a senior position claim the right to know more about those in a junior position than the latter know about them; this is especially true of men as husbands, who often claim that women are "too secretive." So for a married woman, consulting a diviner in private reverses the relationship of power and knowledge that is supposed to obtain between her husband and herself and is regarded as an erosion of her husband's authority over her. We have also seen that private divination usually takes place in a side room of a diviner's house, a hidden and contained space not only because the door is usually shut but also because the room is ritually Closed (kaŋtha) by amulets and other medicines. For a woman to consult a diviner inside this closed space, in a ritual process involving knowledge that the diviner draws from the Darkness of the hidden world of spirits, has typically been seen by husbands as a secret negotiation of the most ominous kind.

Women's consultations of diviners were, then, subject to considerable suspicion. In addition to this, dominant ideas, discussed in the last chapter, about ominous alliances between women and personal river spirits were drawn upon when men consulted diviners. When I asked Pa Yamba about the problems male clients brought to him, he replied:

> *There are men who are impotent. Maybe he's been given to a spirit who has made him so. Women do this to men. The wife does this if the man is very "lively" with women, and she gets jealous. Or if a man has two wives, the less favored wife tells her spirit to take care of him.*

On a subsequent visit to Pa Yamba my research assistant, Michael, recognized a friend of his who held a chicken as he waited in the parlor of the house. Pa Yamba told us later that Michael's friend was being attacked by a spirit who was making him impotent. A woman, he said, had taken a stone (embodying a river spirit) and spoken to it to make the man impotent, so he had just performed a sacrifice to get rid of the spirit by persuading it to accept the chicken as a substitute for himself. Michael, laughing about this afterwards, commented that his friend had always been a womanizer.

Such ideas about their dangerous ritual powers, whether in diviners' diagnoses or in gossip, could be a double-edged sword for women. On the one hand, some men and women said that fear of women's ritual reprisals increased men's motivation to treat their wives (and lovers) well. On the other hand, ideas about secret ritual connections between women and river spirits also contributed to a pall of suspicion over women's private consultations with diviners—for when women consulted diviners, they once again placed themselves in the ritual realm of river spirits who, as diviners' tutelary spirits, were typically the unseen powers behind divination.

Women as Diviners' Clients   If men tended to see women's uses of divination in terms of sinister stereotypes, what were women's own motivations when they visited diviners? Women and men, in fact, used private divination for broadly similar reasons, bringing a wide range of problems for diagnosis and remedial action. Both men and women consulted diviners when sick, as well as when their children were sick or injured; in addition, men were held responsible for finding a diagnosis and cure for their wives' sicknesses when these were regarded as serious. And while women brought reproductive problems such as barrenness, miscarriage, and menstrual irregularities, men brought problems of impotence. Both women and men asked about forthcoming marriages and journeys, and (more rarely) about court cases they were involved in. If they were traders, both men and women sometimes sought help in attracting customers, and if they lived in or near a town, men (but rarely women) asked about employment.

Despite a clear overlap of concerns, however, these issues were strongly gendered. They related to women's and men's lives in often very different ways, and these differences were reflected in gendered contrasts in the frequency with which women and men consulted diviners. Notably, it was usually women rather than men who brought their sick children to diviners and who consulted diviners about reproductive problems. As we have seen in chapter 5, a woman's security and status in her marital home depended primarily upon the children she bore for her husband's lineage. Men were, of course, concerned about their children as well. They were also dependent upon them because their children provided labor on their farms and prestige within their lineage and village. But fathers' interconnections with their children's destinies were not perceived to be as close as those of mothers, for whom *"the child is the mother; the mother is the child."*

Another reason why the problems brought to diviners related differently to women's and men's lives lies in the potential for multiple readings of women's reproductive problems and of children's illnesses. There are a range of etiologies for such problems, but prominent among these (in women's perceptions as well as men's) are interpretations in which a woman is blamed for her own difficulties in conception, pregnancy, and childbirth, as well as for her children's and co-wives' children's ill-health. These etiologies draw, once again, upon images of married women as "outsiders within." A woman might be unable to conceive, for example, because she is a witch and has contributed her womb to a feast with her fellow-witches. Or she might have problems with the birth itself because she has committed adultery and will be unable to give birth until she confesses her lover's name. Her child may be sick because her adultery has caused the child's patrilineal ancestors to withdraw their blessing and protection, leaving their young descendants vulnerable to attack by witches and destructive spirits of the bush. Or she might be an *"inside witch"* who *"opens the door"* to other witches by neutralizing the protective medicines that ritually Close the house, allowing *"outside witches"* to enter and gradually consume the life of her own or her co-wife's child.

The presence of these gendered stereotypes indicates the political significance that illness and other misfortunes could take on in a woman's marital home. Women were, of course, aware of the heavy—and potentially disastrous—interpretive load that such conditions carry. Given this potential, women—especially young women in junior positions in their husbands' households—usually did not want those in their marital home to know about the problems they brought to diviners: if a woman had, for instance, difficulties in conceiving a child, knowledge of this put her in a vulnerable position with her husband or co-wives. It is not surprising, then, that women sought control over the interpretive process through private divination, and that women asking about reproductive problems and sick children formed the majority of diviners' clients.

Mothers often took their children to diviners when the children were initially sick, without their husband's knowledge. If a child become worse and the illness grew more visible, the father and his lineage were increasingly likely to become involved. The father then either sent his wife to a diviner of his choice, or consulted the diviner himself, accompanied by his wife. Even if a father took his child to a diviner, then, the mother was almost always present. The reasons why women sought initial control over the process of diagnosis and healing—and usually did so in secret from their husband and his household—are clear from the contrast between the two divination sessions I describe next. Both of these sessions were for sick children, but whereas in the first of these the child's mother was absent, in the second she was present and was supported by her own mother.

Mabinti's Absence, Sampa's Presence   The first of these divinations took place in Petbana in May 1978, during my first period of fieldwork. Here Pa Alfa Koroma divined a diagnosis and cure for a sick child whose mother was absent. The mother, Mabinti, had traveled to Freetown and was unaware that her infant daughter had suddenly become seriously—and, as it turned out, fatally—ill. In her absence, members of her husband's lineage brought the child from their village approximately five miles away to consult Pa Koroma. They had had no previous connection with Pa Koroma, but chose him because of his reputation in the area. As part of the process of obtaining a cure, however, they found themselves involved in a struggle with Pa Koroma over the meaning of the child's condition, to which they responded by trying to focus the blame upon Mabinti.

The little girl, Baby, was about three years old, and had started to shake. Her father Ibrahim and eight members of his family sat on benches and stools around Pa Koroma's parlor. All those who accompanied Ibrahim—his father, his mother, his two brothers, his sister, his sister's husband, his sister's husband's sister, and his own (Ibrahim's) second wife—were related through him. None of Mabinti's kin were present. Pa Koroma sat on his prayer mat on the floor, holding his rosary beads (aŋ-thasabiya). In front of him were his divination manuals: three large books and two school exercise books filled with handwritten Arabic diagrams and verses. He had placed a small mirror on top of them. He asked a series of questions, and Ibrahim's father (IF) answered on behalf of his son:

> PK: *Why is the child brought here?*
> IF: *The child is not well.*
> PK: *Are you the real father?*
> IF: *Ibrahim Turay is the real father.*
> PK: *Do you want to know the sabu* [the hidden cause] *of the illness?*
> IF: *Yes.*
> PK: *What is the name of the mother?*
> IF: *Mabinti.*

Pa Koroma dipped his hand into a jug of liquid Qur'anic medicine (ma-nasi). He flicked some of it into the child's face, then rubbed it over her body.

> PK: *Why didn't you bring the child earlier?*
> IF: *We didn't know the sickness was going to trouble the child so much.*

Pa Koroma rubbed the mirror, reciting under his breath as he looked into it to communicate with the tutelary spirit behind his capacity to divine. He drew a series of dots in the back of one of the exercise books, wrote the name of the child's father and mother in Arabic, asked for the name of the child, and wrote this too. "*Where is the money to consult?*" he asked, and was handed the standard consultation fee at that time: forty Sierra Leonean cents. He picked up his rosary beads, counting them two at a time and reciting prayers under his breath. He asked if anyone present had learned Arabic and knew what the child's "star," her destiny, was. The group was silent, so he continued to count off the beads until he reached the end of the rosary, then, looking in one of his manuals, he said that the child's star involved sickness and spending money. He began divination by aŋ-sarafilo, picking up a small woven mat weighted at one end and, after tapping it with the consultation fee and the rosary, held it by one corner: it swayed back and forth and finally stood still. Pa Koroma asked it questions and, through its movements, his tutelary spirit revealed the answers:

> If there's a sabu [a hidden cause] for the sickness, come to the left hand. If you're going to show us the sabu, come to the left. Now stand still. Is it a spirit? Is the sickness strong? You said the sickness is strong; can we cure it?

It answered "yes" by moving according to his instructions. Pa Koroma turned to the family and accused its members of a form of witchcraft in which the life of a child is given to a spirit in exchange for wealth or success in a particular enterprise:

> You take the child from a spirit and bring her to me. You have paid the child to a spirit. If you redeem the child from the spirit, she will be cured.

This time Ibrahim responded:

> I am the father in this case. It is only my wife who has the child. If I am included in this handing over of the child, let me be found out.

Ibrahim's elder brother pleaded with Pa Koroma:

> Let you find the person who handed over the child to the spirit. Let us know.

But Pa Koroma resisted both Ibrahim's attempt to implicate Mabinti and exonerate himself and Ibrahim's brother's attempt to accuse a specific individual. He replied:

> I'm not going to point at one person. You know it very well among yourselves and you want me to lie. I will not lie.

Ibrahim and his relatives, however, continued to urge Pa Koroma to reveal if it was his or Mabinti's side of the family, the child's father's lineage (the child's ma-kas) or the child's mother's lineage (the child's ma-kara), that had made the bargain with the spirit. All Pa Koroma would say was that both the father and the mother should be present, because they had all made the arrangement with the spirit. The family agreed to send for the mother immediately, and begged Pa Koroma to fight for the child's life, giving him another eighty cents to give their words more weight. He agreed, but emphasized that the mother must be there during his attempt to cure the child. To protect Baby from the spirit attacking her, he rubbed liquid Qur'anic medicine (ma-nasi) over her, surrounded her with medicinal leaves, and placed her in his own room, which was ritually Closed from harmful forces. Ibrahim's sister stayed to take care of her. But it was too late: Baby died that night. Pa Koroma gave the family one Leone (approximately $1 in 1978) as an expression of sympathy.

This divination raised many questions for me about my own involvement. I had wanted to take Baby to the hospital in Makeni, three miles away. Pa Koroma sometimes sent sick clients there himself if he felt unable to help them. Yet I was reluctant to challenge Pa Koroma's knowledge and judgment—especially given his trust in allowing me to attend his divination sessions—and to come rushing in with Western medicine. But unaware of the kind of illness Baby had and of how rapidly young children's illnesses can intensify, I was shocked by her sudden death and deeply regretted not having tried to persuade Pa Koroma and her father to take her to hospital.

The divination of Baby's illness was very different from divinations in which the client was a woman. In Mabinti's absence, she was not represented or defended by anyone from her own lineage, the child's ma-kara: the only voices responding to Pa Koroma's accusation of the family were male and were from Ibrahim's lineage, the child's ma-kas. But when women consulted diviners in secret from their husband and his household—for instance by avoiding the use of diviners in their husband's village, and sometimes by visiting a diviner at night or just before dawn so as not to be seen—they were much better able to shape the diagnostic process. A common tactic was to go on a visit to a member of their natal kin—especially their mother—and to consult a diviner there. This is what happened in the second divination.

In August 1992 Ya Ai, a widow living in a village a few miles from Petbana, called Ya Yebu (the female Muslim diviner we met in chapter 4), who was the widow of Ya Ai's late brother. Ya Ai wanted Ya Yebu to divine for her daughter Sampa, who was married in Koya chiefdom to the west, and who had come to visit Ya Ai. Sampa had come specifically for this divination: her first two children had died, and now her baby was sick. Ya Yebu used aŋ-bɛrɛ divination and diagnosed that witches in Sampa's husband's household were not only responsible for her baby's illness but had also caused the deaths of her first two children. Although Ya Yebu did not name specific individuals, Ya Ai and Sampa understood her to be referring to Sampa's co-wives. Sampa's husband did not know that she was consulting a diviner, and it was understood that Sampa would not discuss the divination or the diagnosis in her husband's household. Ya Yebu gave her medicine to protect the child and to cause the witches to confess their hidden actions spontaneously: by this means, Ya Yebu avoided the "sin" *(aŋ-hakɛ)* that accrues to those who make direct accusations of witchcraft.

Sampa's visit to her mother enabled her not only to see a diviner without her husband's knowledge but also to consult one who was likely to be sympathetic to her problems. The fact that Ya Yebu was herself a woman would not have automatically entailed such support: as we saw in chapter 4, her views of young women *"of today"* (and their *"Lady Diana shoes"*) were fairly harsh. But Ya Yebu and Ya Ai had had a long and positive relationship as sisters-in-law (both women emphasized to me that they regarded each other as sisters), and one, importantly, in which Ya Ai was senior to Ya Yebu as her late husband's sister.

Ya Yebu's diagnosis exonerated Sampa from blame for her baby's illness, an outcome that was not the product of active negotiation between diviner and clients during divination. The degree of overt contestation during Ibrahim's consultation with Pa Koroma above was unusual for private divination, which was normally characterized by minimal verbal input on the part of the clients. Where there was an established relationship between diviner and clients, as between Ya Yebu, Ya Ai, and Sampa, the diviner already knew a great deal about the clients' circumstances and was likely to be well-disposed toward them, making clients' contestations during the divinatory process largely unnecessary. Clients' negotiations, then, were usually accomplished *before* the divination session itself and consisted of their selection of the "right" diviner.

This issue of the choice of diviner was important because most diviners—including many of those who are women, like Ya Yebu—share the normative ideas about the treachery and danger of women that female clients wish to avoid in a diviner's diagnosis. Diviners often reiterated popular stereotypes of women as dangerous to their husbands and children during informal conversations with me. When Pa Biyare in Makeni (the diviner who told me the second origin story for divination in chapter 3) taught me aŋ-bɛrɛ divination, for example, he made up imaginary cases and told me how he would interpret particular patterns of pebbles if they appeared during such a case. Cases in which a child died because of its mother's adultery recurred several times in his demonstrations. As the columns of single and paired stones he cast developed into patterns, he read scenarios into them:

> Like this, if somebody is sick and you're divining and get this, it means the person has something to say. If it's a woman, and she slept with another man, if she has a child, it will be sick and they'll call you. When the woman talks about this, then you know this is what she's done. If it's a man who calls you and you get this pattern, his wife has to "call name" [boɳt: confess the name of her lover].

Yet when women used private divination in the way that Sampa did—in secret, away from their husband's village, and with a diviner selected through a trusted member of their natal kin (especially their mother) or a close friend—they were usually able to avoid the consequences of these normative etiologies and to have some control over disadvantageous readings of their problems.

The situation was rather different for junior men who wished to consult a diviner. Both women and junior men usually preferred to consult diviners in secret from those with authority over them, but whereas for married women this usually meant traveling outside their husband's village to their natal home, for junior men it meant getting away from senior men in their own lineage. The following was a case in point.

Abdulai's Injury   At the beginning of the upland rice harvest in Petbana in September 1989, Pa Kaper Bana's brother's son Abdulai injured his ankle and was unable to work effectively on his farm. His parents were dead and he had no brothers; his relationship with Pa Kaper Bana and Pa Kaper's son Pa Moses, moreover, was very tense. As he only had one wife and small children to harvest the rice with him, and lacked the resources to call a cooperative work group (aŋ-kɔɳp) to help him, his minor injury had major consequences: a large portion of his crop was lost to birds, grass cutters, and other farm pests. He was unsuccessful in persuading relatives and neighbors—all of whom had their own farms to harvest—to help him with his work. This was partly because of the history of Abdulai's bad relationship with Pa Kaper Bana, in the course of which he had acquired a reputation for being disrespectful and "not afraid of anybody." Abdulai often asked me for medicine, and when I gave him painkillers, emphasizing that they were not a cure but would just mask the pain for a while, he was visibly frustrated and angry.

He consulted Pa Santigi, the only diviner in Petbana at that time, Pa Koroma having passed away six years earlier. Pa Santigi gave his usual diagnosis, telling Abdulai that his hurt ankle was *"just from God"* and would heal by itself. Abdulai was unhappy with this explanation, both because his need for a rapid cure was so great and because he suspected that the malice of his relatives was involved. But Pa Santigi was not only a pious Muslim who regularly reiterated *"it is just from God"* in his diagnoses; he was also a subchief who had a good relationship with Pa Kaper Bana. He was therefore most unlikely to have given Abdulai a diagnosis that blamed the problem on either Pa Kaper Bana or Pa Moses. Abdulai's reduced mobility, moreover, made it difficult for him to escape his uncle's sphere of influence by consulting a diviner outside Petbana. Subsequently, these relationships deteriorated to such an extent that, by the time I returned to Petbana for a visit in 1992, Abdulai had left the village.

Although it was an advantage for Abdulai and other junior men to get out of the range of the senior men with authority over them when they consulted a diviner, this was usually less imperative than it was for a woman to consult a diviner without her husband's knowledge. Men who use private divination were not as closely associated with the stereotypes of danger and malevolence to which women as diviners' clients were subject: for a junior man to consult a diviner might have been suspicious, but not necessarily sinister. There was no historical resonance to junior men's consultations of outside diviners, no recurring narrative motif of junior men as mediators of external attack, as there are for women. A junior man might have been suspected of treachery as an individual embroiled in particular relationships, but he did not have to avoid disadvantageous diagnoses informed by stereotypes of junior men as treacherous in general.

Alternative Readings   We have already seen that diviners' clients were tactical in their choice of diviners and of the time and place of divination. Yet they often seemed acquiescent during private divination itself; they did not normally argue or negotiate when diviners gave their diagnoses and prescribed rituals and medicine. After the divination was over, though, these clients sometimes felt dissatisfied with the diagnosis and ritual prescriptions they were given, and they exercised considerable agency in choosing what to do with the diagnosis and the diviner's instructions. They could carry out the diviner's instructions to the letter; reject the diagnosis and seek an alternative explanation with another diviner; accept the diagnosis but put off performing the ritual or buying the medicine until they had more money; or accept the diagnosis but modify or reinterpret the prescribed ritual. Through these choices, modifications, and reconstruals, diviners' clients accommodated the diagnoses and prescriptions of ritual specialists to the circumstances of their own lives, their own understandings, and their own priorities.

When I was in Freetown during my first fieldwork, a woman called Fatmata came to consult Pa Yamba about her baby daughter, who was ill and had become very weak. Pa Yamba divined with his looking glass and asked if she remembered dreaming that people had come together to take her child, and that in this dream she had struggled with them as they tried to pull the child away from her. This is a fairly standard scenario for a witchcraft dream: dream narratives like this often originate during divination, from the diviner rather than the client. Diviners are specialists in dreams (Shaw 1992): they not only interpret dreams when their clients bring them but also *ascribe* dreams to clients as part of the diagnosis. Clients usually accepted the diviner's authority over their own experience during the session itself, assenting to the inscription of a dream narrative upon their memory as part of the process of diagnosis and cure.

Fatmata agreed that she had had the dream Pa Yamba described. He made a belt containing protective medicine for her to wear around her waist for defense against further attacks by witches in her dreams. As further protection, he gave her a bottle of palm oil mixed with herbal medicine to rub on her child's body. He also instructed her to make a sacrifice in which the foot, liver, lungs, and a little of the ordinary meat of a cow should be cooked and offered to the witches with the words, *"the witches that are coming after this child, leave this child. We are offering this meat to you."* A sacrifice of this kind would persuade the witches to consume the meat as a substitute for the child and thereafter to leave the child alone. It differs from most other Temne sacrifices in that the food is not consumed by people but thrown away, often at the crossroads, the sinister space where witches and dangerous spirits congregate. Pa Yamba offered to carry out this ritual for Fatmata. But the next day she returned, telling Pa Yamba that she had just had another dream in which she had made a soup out of the ingredients Pa Yamba had specified for the sacrifice and fed it to the child. When she woke up that morning, she said, her child was strong again and was feeding properly.

Through her dream narrative, Fatmata appropriated the ritual Pa Yamba prescribed, translating it into a form that restored her control. She reinterpreted the meat as medicinal food that worked directly on the child instead of as a sacrifice that worked indirectly by buying off witches. Thus an action

that derived from the knowledge and practice of a ritual specialist was transformed into an action that derived from the everyday knowledge and practice
of an ordinary woman: cooking food and feeding a child. Fatmata's dream
transferred ritual agency from Pa Yamba to herself as she moved from a passive consent to Pa Yamba's authority to an active reappropriation of her own
dreams. Pa Yamba nevertheless counted this as one of his successes, because
the ritual ingredients he prescribed had, after all, healed the child.

Even when clients did not modify the ritual practices diviners prescribed,
they sometimes, like Fatmata, had a strikingly different "take" on the ritual
and its significance from those of the interpretations diviners gave. One gloss
on these alternative construals of ritual might be that they were "misunderstandings." Yet this would be to suggest that a ritual can have only one reading,
to accept that ritual specialists are the sole authorities on that reading, and
to ignore the interpretive movement of the apparent "misunderstandings" in
directions that have their own logic for the standpoint and concerns of the
client herself. This was the case in a different woman's construal of a sacrifice
for her sick child.

Khadiatu, another young mother living in Freetown (and to whom we will
return later), visited Pa Yamba when her two-year-old son fell ill and started
trembling. Pa Yamba told Khadiatu that her son had "four eyes": with this
special vision the child had seen a spirit, and it was this spirit that was making
him ill. She should therefore buy a chicken, dedicate it to the spirit, and keep
it near her son; a goat would be better, but if Khadiatu did not have the
money, Pa Yamba said, a chicken would do. He also told her to make a sacrifice of "mixed" offerings *(aŋ-faŋkadama)* with kola nuts, mangoes, and sweets.
She bought the chicken and made the faŋkadama at her mother's house, giving the fruit, sweets, and kola nuts away to children and receiving God's blessings in return. Her child recovered.

Khadiatu's understanding of the chicken sacrifice differed, however, from
the standard rationale offered by diviners. The specialists' explanation was
that the chicken (or other animal) is dedicated to the spirit responsible for
the child's illness and must remain in the compound so that the spirit can see
it there as substituting for the child: the spirit will then "take" the fowl when
it wants to. But Khadiatu told me that what was important about the sacrifice
was that the *child* should constantly be able to see the chicken. Like Fatmata's
dream, Khadiatu's interpretation involved a shift from a specialists' spirit-
centered account to a mother's child-centered account. Her interpretation gave
her child's strange eyes a focus that anchored him in the world of ordinary

human beings; instead of looking at a denizen of the spirit world, his gaze could now be directed back to the world of ordinary people in which she wanted him to stay. In substituting the child's gaze for that of the spirit, her explanation did not so much contradict the conventional diviners' interpretation as add a new dimension to it: now, both spirit *and* child had something to look at apart from each other.

In their alternative readings, Fatmata and Khadiatu reoriented their focus toward the human objects of, rather than the spiritual or medicinal powers behind, the ritual processes prescribed by Pa Yamba. Diviners often have considerable interest in the cosmological ideas and ritual that their work entails. But Fatmata and Khadiatu "domesticated" diviners' cosmologies and ritual knowledge by adapting these to their own concerns. Like women's passages and peregrinations between different places during their life-course, and like the interpenetrations of village and river in women's rituals, Khadiatu's and Fatmata's readings undermined the containment that separates the domains of humans and spirits by affirming the priority of their own domain of knowledge and practice.

Pa Koroma's Diagnoses   Let us turn, now, to a male diviner's standpoint and ask how his relationship with particular clients might have informed his readings of their predicaments. In May and June of 1978, Pa Koroma conducted divinations for five women who came to Petbana to consult him.

The first of these clients was Mariama, who, like many of the women who consulted Pa Koroma, was a kinswoman of his: his brother's daughter. She was a young married woman who had walked three miles to see him from the town of Makeni, accompanied by her mother, Na Fatu, and without her husband's knowledge. She had had pains in her stomach for three months, a symptom often associated with women's reproductive problems. Pa Koroma diagnosed that the cause was the third wife whom Mariama's husband had married recently: she and Mariama, who was the second wife, had quarreled. She was jealous of Mariama and had gone to a diviner to make her ill. Pa Koroma treated Mariama with herbal medicine and told her to activate a "swearing" medicine (aŋ-sasa) in secret against the person who had made her ill, without telling her husband. The swear would seize the co-wife and make her sick until she returned to the diviner to remove the illness from Mariama.

This was a sympathetic diagnosis for Mariama, placing her in a positive, innocent position within a shared moral discourse; yet at the same time, it displaced the stereotype of the perfidious woman onto her co-wife. In his account of malevolent collusion between a jealous woman inside the home and a diviner whose invisible attack she instigates, Pa Koroma reproduced dominant ideologies about women as mediators of external attack even as he exonerated Mariama personally from the blame with which these ideologies would tend to associate her. And the remedial ritual Pa Koroma prescribed—secretly activating a swearing medicine—is very likely to have been viewed by Mariama's husband and co-wife (had they known about it) as hostile rather than restorative, as itself an instance of a co-wife treacherously using a diviner to activate dangerous medicine against the household. Ironically, then, in negotiating a moral path by selecting a sympathetic diviner, women may themselves be caught within the hegemonic gender discourses that make such negotiation necessary in the first place.

The second client was Isatu, another of Pa Koroma's brother's daughters, who again came from Makeni and consulted him without her husband's knowledge. When she arrived, Pa Koroma was carrying out aŋ-yina Musa divination, assisted by the medium with whom he always worked, Mami Yeno. Isatu asked them about problems in her marital home: she was concerned about serious quarrels she had been having with her husband and others in his household. Mami Yeno, repeating the words of the "jinn of Musa" she heard in the Darkness, gave the following diagnosis:

> *If the man were present, and if one asked "Do you have dreams in which you had sex with a woman?" he would say "Yes." His elder brother does not like the woman, and has a [personal] spirit. During the day, he pretends to be good, but at night he makes the spirit have sex with the husband [as a woman] and makes the spirit have sex with the woman as a man too. They should take care so that the woman does not have birth problems. It will be a difficult problem to drive the spirit away. In her husband's home, the woman has done nothing wrong.*

This spirit, Mami Yeno said, would have to be persuaded to leave by giving it a sacrifice—one that would have to be carried out in secret from those in Isatu's husband's home. Pa Koroma emphasized that Isatu should not let anyone in her marital home know about this divination and diagnosis.

This was not a conventional explanation for women's problems in their marital home: instead of the standard scenario of the wife bringing in her personal spirit from the riverbank and sending it to attack members of her husband's household, here the husband's brother is made the agent of this incursion. Mention of a man—as compared to a woman—with a personal spirit was relatively rare both in diviners' diagnoses and everyday discourse. Like women's spirits, men's personal spirits were almost always described as coming from the river, embodied in a stone discovered on its banks. But unlike the children that women's personal spirits bestowed, what men's personal spirits usually gave was *money*, evoking historical connections between rivers and capitalist commerce. Many men's river spirits were, in fact, often identified as *aŋ-Yaroŋ* or Mami Wata, the alluring but dangerous light-skinned mermaid associated throughout Africa with material wealth and Western commodities. Mami Wata ensnares men (and sometimes, in the form of a man, ensnares women) in sexual dream relationships, initially bringing them wealth but ultimately bringing ruin, insanity, or death. It was less usual, but not unheard of, for Mami Wata's human lovers to send her to attack others. Although Isatu's brother-in-law's spirit was not directly identified as Mami Wata, the spirit's sinister seductiveness (as well as her capacity to change sex) was evoked by the description of her attacks upon Isatu and her husband by having sex with them in both male or female form, thereby blighting their fertility and disrupting their marriage.

This diagnosis, like that which Mariama received, identified Isatu as a moral and wronged person. It also drew, once again, upon the motif of an internal mediator of an external spirit's attack. Yet it reversed the gender of the malefactor in this stereotypical theme, making a male "insider" rather than a female "outsider" the treacherous agent of external incursion into the household. Although women certainly shared in gender ideologies that malign women, it is nevertheless significant that the reversal this diagnosis represents was made by the female medium, Mami Yeno. The diagnosis suggests a female gendered ideology of the household in which the marital home is itself viewed as a dangerous locus of alien forces, a place in need of domestication in order for the women who marry into it and the children they bear to thrive. Mami Yeno thereby shifted the moral focus to a standpoint from below and from outside, to that of a wife rather than of a lineage member, in such a way that the counterhegemonic implications of this diagnosis—unlike Pa Koroma's diagnosis for Mariama—were not entangled in and subsumed by dominant gender discourses.

Pa Koroma's relationship to the next person whose problems required diagnosis was, once again, that of father's brother. But this time his brother's daughter was a child, not a married woman, this difference in generation significantly shifting the politics of divination. The child was a little girl called Namina, with a swollen and painful stomach; her mother, Salematu, had brought her from the small town of Makama a mile and a half away. Salematu was married to Pa Koroma's brother, and she emphasized when she spoke to me afterwards that because of this Pa Koroma was *"really a father"* to Namina. Pa Koroma diagnosed that Namina had "four eyes," the doubled vision in which her two ordinary eyes were counterpointed by two invisible eyes, enabling her to penetrate the Darkness that conceals spirits and witches from ordinary people. Because of her extrahuman vision, witches had been teaching her witchcraft by feeding her human meat in her dreams. An ordinary person's stomach would not digest human meat: witches internally transformed their bodies by growing a second stomach *(aŋ-kuŋtha)*. As Namina had not developed this second stomach, her human stomach was painfully swollen. Her body, however, still maintained the possibility of control by Pa Koroma, who treated her stomach with seeds he gathered from the bush, ground up into a paste and fed to her. He also used liquid Qur'anic medicine (mɑ-nɑsi) to "close" the invisible eyes that had given her the four-eyed vision to which the witches were attracted.

He did not, though, give Salematu medicine to bring the witches' deeds into the open, as he had instructed Mariama to do. The witches who were trying to make Namina one of them were generic, anonymous witches: Pa Koroma did not suggest their identities, and Salematu told me later that she did not know who they were. As they were not attacking Namina but trying to recruit her, there was not the same concern over their identities and their exposure as in diagnoses in which witches were said to be consuming a child. Unlike Pa Koroma's two previous diagnoses, then, this was a morally neutral explanation—one that would not cause strife in his brother's household. Namina's problem was attributed not to anyone in her father's home but to external agencies whose identities were unspecified: the witches could have been anybody from Makama or from other towns nearby.

Salematu's husband—Pa Koroma's brother—came later in the day to see how Namina was. Namina stayed with Pa Koroma over the next few days, accompanied by Salematu, while she recovered. This was a situation in which Namina's illness was visibly pronounced—too pronounced at that stage for Salematu to have been able to take her to a diviner without the knowledge of those in her marital home. Her husband was in overall control of her visit to the diviner: although it was Salematu who took Namina to Pa Koroma and who stayed with her during her treatment, it was her husband who selected Pa Koroma and who came to check on Namina's diagnosis and treatment later.

The fourth of Pa Koroma's diagnoses for female clients was also subject to the surveillance of one of his male relatives. Two married women friends, Zainab and Aminata, came together from Makama—the same town from which Salematu and Namina had come—to consult Pa Koroma about why they had not become pregnant. There was a remote kinship connection between Zainab and Pa Koroma, as her grandfather was in the same lineage (aŋ-bɔŋsɔ) as his; Aminata, however, was related affinally, as the wife of Pa Koroma's wife's brother. A man, remember, is always indebted to his wife's brother (ɔ-nasin), and is expected to let him have (within certain limits) any possessions he chooses and any favors he requires: Pa Koroma's primary obligation, therefore, was to Aminata's husband rather than to Aminata. Although I did not ask at whose instigation Aminata had come, it is most likely that her husband had suggested (or at least knew of) the visit: she would hardly have chosen Pa Koroma if she were consulting a diviner without her husband's knowledge.

Pa Koroma gave the same diagnosis to both women, telling them that they each had "bad water" in their stomachs because a bush spirit had had sex with them in their dreams: the spirit semen blocked the passage of human semen, making it impossible for the women to conceive children with their husbands. Pa Koroma gave them herbal medicine to clean out their stomachs, and they stayed at his house for a few days while undergoing this treatment. This diagnosis was, like the previous one, morally neutral. Bush spirits are amoral external powers who invade the home without assistance from those inside, attracted inside by sleeping women with whom they wish to have sex—an act that either makes women infertile or causes them to bear monstrous children. Because women who received these unwanted visits from "night husbands" (as they are called in Krio) were not usually held responsible, this diagnosis avoided placing blame on either Pa Koroma's kinswoman Zainab, her friend Aminata, or any member of their husband's households. As Aminata's husband's household consisted of the in-laws with whom Pa Koroma was in a relationship of respect and indebtedness, it would have been very awkward for him to have ascribed such blame.

Yet this diagnosis also suggests an indirect but intriguing reference to Pa Koroma's relationship with his wife's brother. As we saw in the last chapter, it was said that when a woman has a sexual dream about a bush spirit, this "night husband" often "brings the face of her brother." This image of the spirit from "outside" entering a man's home and, in the guise of his wife's brother, usurping the fertility of his wife, echoes the sanctioned (but resented) "plundering" of his home by the human brother-in-law exercising his right to enter his sister's husband's home and take small possessions (Littlejohn 1960b). Pa

Koroma's diagnosis thus suggested an oblique reference to the image of the "plundering" brother-in-law even as he complied with his obligation to assist and respect his own wife's brother.

In these divinations, the five women exercised different capacities as clients. Neither Salematu nor (most probably) Aminata were able to choose the diviner or to control information about the divination, diagnosis, and remedial action. Their agency in consulting Pa Koroma was subsumed by that of their husbands, as these were men to whom Pa Koroma had ties of obligation as a brother and as a sister's husband respectively. In contrast, Mariama and Isatu—Pa Koroma's brothers' adult daughters—were able to act without such direction and surveillance from their husbands, but only because of their strategies of secrecy. They had good reason to act in secret: because Isatu was not on good terms with her husband and Mariama was not on good terms with her co-wife, they would immediately have been suspected of hiring Pa Koroma to harm the person in their marital home with whom they had quarreled. For young married women, whether or not it is possible to act in secret and to consult a diviner either with the relatively autonomous agency of Mariama and Isatu or with the "subsumed" agency of Salematu and Aminata depends, in turn, upon such contingencies as the nature and stage of the problem. These contingencies affect how much a woman's husband knows and how likely he will be to initiate a divination himself.

Shifting the standpoint, Pa Koroma's own power and agency as a diviner was both a condition and an outcome of these contrasting capacities of his clients. His divinations for Mariama and Isatu were embedded within his ties to them as brothers' daughters in a vulnerable position in their husbands' households; his reading of their problems accordingly produced diagnoses that ascribed blame to a member of their marital home and that supported his nieces' strategy of secrecy. His divinations for Salematu and Aminata, on the other hand, were encompassed by his obligation toward their husbands— his brother and his wife's brother—and his reading of their problems produced diplomatic diagnoses in which no-one in their marital home was blamed. Pa Koroma's own capacity to make particular diagnoses and prescriptions, then, shifted according to his position within the social space into which his relationship to particular clients placed him.

Mothers and Daughters, Sisters and Wives   By consulting a diviner to whom they were kin and/or by seeking their mother's help in selecting and consulting a diviner, younger married women like Isatu and Mariama (and, earlier in this chapter, Sampa), drew upon their position as daughters in try-ing to ameliorate problems they had as wives. A further discussion of women's multiple identities as mothers, daughters, sisters, and wives is therefore in order here. As we have seen in the previous chapter, a woman as a lineage member had considerably more rights of ownership and expression than she had as a married woman in her husband's lineage: as a daughter or sister, in other words, she shared in patriarchal authority, while as a wife she was sub-ject to the patriarchal authority of others.

This contrast between sisters as "owners" and wives as subordinates rests, as Karen Sacks has demonstrated, upon differential access to the means of production in what she calls "kin corporate" modes of production: "Here sis-ters and wives are two different productive relationships. In patrilineal and patrilocal situations, the former are owners and not producers, and the latter are producers and not owners. Yet every woman embodies these two different relationships" (1979: 122). Sacks concludes from this that women's member-ship of corporate lineages that are "owners" of land or other means of produc-tion entails sexual egalitarianism for women as sisters (but not for women as wives). This conclusion has, however, been criticized for its assumption that women's status is simply a reflex of their location within the relations of pro-duction (see, e.g., Moore 1988: 35). As critical as women's economic power certainly is, ascribing it a deterministic, totalizing role discounts the significance of cultural discourses about women—discourses that are of considerable con-sequence in the very construction and reproduction of women's status. Cul-tural representations of women and men are not automatic "reflections" of a material reality but products of tactical use by gendered social actors. Through such use, these representations have material consequences: gender stereo-types, for example, may not reflect the reality of women's productive power, but they are nevertheless a very effective rhetorical means of excluding women from certain kinds of actions and decisions (Moore 1988: 38).

For Temne women, their power as daughters and sisters—in which they shared in their lineage's ownership of land and had rights over their brothers and brothers' children because of the bridewealth their marriage brought to the lineage—was countered by negative representations of women as wives. These dominant images of the treacherous wife, either as a witch, a diviner's vindictive client, or an irresponsible keeper of a river spirit's stone all repre-sent, as we have seen, an insider who brings inimical external powers into the household. These images, as we have also seen, were grounded upon the memory-enhanced ambiguity of the wife as an "outsider within" whose loyalty to her natal family could supersede that to her husband. Most of the time, in fact, it seemed to be precisely the rights, obligations, and loyalties empowering a woman as a sister and daughter that were drawn upon in discourses that undermined her as a wife.

When a woman visited her natal home, then, she was usually able to exercise her considerable rights as a sister or daughter, but she had few opportunities to translate these rights into power in her marital home, short of using the threat of leaving her husband and returning to her natal home. Her movement from daughter to wife when she married, from wife to daughter and sister when she went on visits to her natal home, then back again to wife when she returned to her marital home, led her through repeated contradictions in her life experience. But for Temne women, divination provided a way around some of these contradictions, through a hidden ritual process in which alternative readings of women's problems were given form and translated into ritual practice. As this hidden ritual process was often realized through women's use of kinship ties, divination was an important arena in which Temne women *could* draw upon their rights as daughters—albeit secretly—to try to improve their circumstances as wives.

It was usually as her mother's daughter rather than as her brother's sister, in fact, that a young married woman could make this translation, as it was likely to be her mother, more than any other kinsperson, who guided her to a particular diviner and who accompanied her for divination. This involvement of women's mothers directs us to the fact that clients' uses of divination were, of course, not only gendered but also related to different points in the life cycle. For older women with adult children, their earlier concerns over their own marriage, their fertility, and their children's survival had shifted to the next generation. This was especially true in relation to their grown children's marriages and their grandchildren, as when Ya Ai called Ya Yebu to divine for Sampa, and Na Fatu brought Mariama to Pa Koroma. By going to a diviner with her mother, a young woman learned to use divination, and her mother's guidance could be seen as an extension of the latter's own past consultations of diviners during an earlier phase of her marital and reproductive life-course.

Through the agency of her mother, a woman's consultations of diviners also played a part in mobilizing the support of her natal family in addressing problems in her marriage. Although private divination was not an appropriate means by which a woman could directly renegotiate problematic relationships in her *husband's* household, a favorable diagnosis could, however, in-form her *parents'* negotiations with her husband's family during a difficult point in her marriage. It was typically a woman's mother who could be counted on to support her over problems in her marital home and whose influence was important in gaining the support of others in her natal family. If she was vindicated by the diagnosis of a diviner, she consulted with her mother, and if she subsequently decided to leave her husband, her mother could try to smooth the path for her eventual return to her natal home. If she consulted a diviner who was a kinsperson, moreover, this diviner could also act as her advocate with other kin. This augmented a woman's leverage in the one area in which she *could* directly use her power as daughter or sister to ameliorate her position as a wife: the possibility of leaving her husband.

Women's concerns changed as they moved through their life-course: if an older woman had several children and was well-established as a mother in her husband's household, her center of social and emotional gravity usually shifted toward her marital home. As a grandmother and mother-in-law, she had considerable influence and authority in her husband's household. At this time, her own mother was likely to have died, and as there was often considerable tension between brothers and sisters, her brothers rarely provided the same degree of support: it is important not to overemphasize a woman's own lineage as a source of unambiguous solidarity and backing, given that lineages, of course, have conflicts of their own. Among more senior women, in fact, the brother-sister relationship sometimes replaced the husband-wife relationship as a problematic tie generating difficulties that demand remedial action through divination, as in the following situation.

Yan Safi and Her Brothers   The late Yan Safi was a widow in Petbana whose marriage to her first husband had been inherited by his brother Pa Santigi, the pious Muslim diviner. She had enjoyed her position as her late husband's senior wife, and she had been able to make some money during her marriage by weaving baskets and colorful raffia fans. After her husband's death she continued to live in his house across the street from Pa Santigi, keeping a small store on her veranda in which she sold vegetables and condiments. Her leg had been amputated several years before. She first told me about how this had happened during my 1989 visit, when I asked her to tell me her life history. She explained it in terms of her brothers' witchcraft:

I am the eldest sister; the eldest of all my brothers and sisters. I put the youngest one through Qur'anic school. After he'd finished, the three eldest said why should I educate

the least one and not them? Because the younger brother—Lamin—had more wealth
than they did. Pa Santigi helped me; both of us paid the school fees. The other three were
jealous. Lamin was very clever at school. I tried to keep it a secret that I paid the fees,
but Lamin told the brothers when they asked him who was paying his fees. Then they
fought against me with witchcraft, and made my leg swell.

Four days later, we talked again. I asked her if she had ever asked her husband,
Pa Santigi, to divine for her; she replied that he had "looked" for her when
her leg had been infected and swollen. His explanation had been different
from hers, and, as we talked, her recollection of his diagnosis displaced the
account she had given me a few days earlier:

> YS: *He "looked" for the illness of my leg, before it was cut. When I get sick, I go to Pa*
> *Santigi and he gives me the s-athka* (sacrifice) *for it.*
> RS: *What was the aŋ-sabu* (hidden cause) *Pa Santigi saw for the illness of your leg?*
> YS: *He said let my lineage* (aŋ-bɔŋsɔ) *just cure it. It was an illness from God. He*
> *said I'm not going to die, just suffer.*
> RS: *When we talked before, you thought the witchcraft of your brothers was the cause.*
> YS: *Yes. When someone is sick, they're not going to have one mind. They will think of*
> *one thing, of another, and of another.*
> RS: *Which do you think was the true cause?*
> YS: *Pa Santigi was right, because God did not kill me.*

By asking Yan Safi about Pa Santigi's divination specifically and asking her to
choose between his diagnosis *(just from God)* and hers, I changed the discursive space of our conversation to include her husband the diviner and un-
thinkingly invoked his authority. She responded accordingly, giving his version of events priority over her own—although with far less convincing detail
than in our previous talk.

However ambivalent Yan Safi was about Pa Santigi's diagnosis, it is significant that she turned to him for help in divining the cause of her suffering. He
is not only a respected Muslim subchief *(u-saŋthki)* with a small Qur'anic
school of his own, but he had been in Yan Safi's estimation a generous and
considerate husband since his brother's death—her strongest source of support, together with her brother Lamin. He had, for example, helped her pay
Lamin's school fees. While his diagnosis did not confirm her sense of her other
brothers' malevolence, it also did not blame her for her own suffering. The
point that I wish to bring out here is that as a senior woman well established

as a mother and grandmother within Pa Santigi's lineage, Yan Safi was able to consult her husband as a diviner during a life-threatening crisis that involved problems with her natal family. This reverses the predicament of a younger wife in a more tenuous position in her husband's household who uses kin ties to consult a diviner over problems in her marital home.

Dispersed Affiliations and Matrilineal Paths   Women's uses of divination, then, involved them in movement and mediation between their multiple affiliations at different locations in social space and time (as wives, mothers, daughters, sisters, grandmothers, paternal aunts, maternal aunts). The prominence of mother-daughter links in these movements gave women's consultations with diviners a somewhat matrilineal quality (cf. Boddy 1989). Here, instead of being the vehicles for men's agency in building up "wealth-in-people" connections, women implemented their own connections actively, covertly, and for themselves. They acted, rather than being acted through, and they protected their capacity to act through secrecy—especially secrecy in relation to those in their marital lineage. And they tied together their own spatially and temporally dispersed affiliations through their consultations of diviners—as daughters of their mothers and their *ma-kara*, as daughters of their fathers and their *ma-kas*, as sisters of their brothers, as wives of their husbands, and as mothers and grandmothers of their own children.

These movements and mediations of female clients were traced through travel between different physical locales. Sometimes this entailed a young woman returning to her natal village and lineage home, and, because a woman's mother was often involved in her adult daughter's selection and consultation of a diviner, it could also entail the exploitation of matrilateral connections outside her natal home—her mother's marital home. In private divination, then, as in other aspects of her life, "A woman has no town" *(w-uni bom o ba ye ke-pet)*.

Conclusions: Gender as Memory, Memory as Gendered   In the previous chapter I argued that, as with ritual, marriage can be understood in terms of social memory. As we have seen, in the raiding and warfare associated with the Atlantic and legitimate trades, marriage was an important source of alliances; yet as these alliances shifted, women as wives also became a latent source of incursion from affines who had become enemies. Late-twentieth-century understandings of married women as potentially dangerous strangers in their husbands' homes may, I have suggested, be seen as social memories that recapitulate a historical paradigm of alliances and enmities among differ-ent communities.

From the perspective of men as husbands, women undermined spatial containment in certain important—and potentially threatening—ways. Etio-logies of women's reproductive problems as caused by women's dreams of sex with bush spirits, which not only come from an uncontrolled external space but which also often assume the form of their plundering brothers, were one expression of this. Ideas about women as "inside witches," opening the door of their marital home to witches outside and allowing them to come inside to consume the household's children, were another. Rumors about women who *"have a stone"* embodying a river spirit hidden in a small tin in their marital home were another. And in the present chapter, I hope to have dem-onstrated that men's fears about wives making clandestine visits to diviners outside their marital town and bringing dangerous medicines and spiritual forces back into their husband's household were yet another.

These representations reversed the gendered embodiment of historical conquests that Boddy describes for the women's zar cult in Hofriyat, in which "the apparently powerless and subordinate gender represents the apparent powerlessness and subordination of the community in wider perspective" (1989: 269). For Temne husbands, in contrast, the apparently powerless and subordinate gender did not represent the vulnerable community but instead potentially concealed the latent powers of both spirit and human invaders who threatened that community. Whereas, accordingly, Hofriyati men re-sponded to foreign incursion by the enclosure of women (Boddy 1989: 34, 192), Temne men responded by Closing themselves and their households—complaining as they did so that this Closure was subverted both by the impos-sibility of women's containment and by the Darkness that rendered women unknowable.

Yet if gender can be understood as memory—in this case, a practical mem-ory of the dangers and ambiguities through which marital relationships were constituted in the eras of the slave trade and trade wars—memory itself is gendered. Like Hofriyati women, Temne women "engage[d] the shifting bor-der with the outside world in the act of constructing themselves" (Boddy 1989: 301). Temne women used their imperative to move, to go out, to slip away, to mediate between different points in their social geography and mul-tiple identities, as the basis for their ritual action. Men, firmly centered in the genealogical space of their lineage town, wanted their wives to be more stable—more like them. They often expressed frustration with their wives' mobility and secrecy, which they recognized to be as impossible to contain as the rivers whose spirits they feared their wives used. The river spirits to which women turned—through their consultation of private diviners, through their covert offerings dropped on river pebbles hidden in small tins, and through their collective "secrets" of the Bondo cult—rendered their husbands impotent in more ways than one.

From Temne women's perspectives, incursions from their own centers of social and ritual allegiance external to their marital home were sometimes necessary for their own security and fertility within the latter. Their husband's household, which was often outside their natal village and away from their kin, was a somewhat alien space for *them*, especially in the early stages of marriage. Thus what may be "remembered" in terms of incursion and attack on the part of a husband (and co-wives) may have been, rather, a wife's attempt to "domesticate" her husband's household, making it a place in which she could bear and rear children, and build up her own resources through farming and trade. Seeking the children who would transform her husband's place into a secure home with a good future, women turned to river spirits—forces of the flowing highways that had long been crucial on the upper Guinea coast in building connections between people and places.

Postscript: Freetown, July–August 1992   Even before the rebel war spread beyond the south of the country, state collapse and the growing militarization of Sierra Leone had serious consequences for women. By 1992, the country had been moving along a trajectory of steep economic decline for three decades: the unit of currency, the Leone, had fallen from Le2 to the pound sterling when I first arrived in 1977 to Le1,000 to the pound during my 1992 visit. By 1992, it had become such a struggle for most people in Freetown to buy food that most traders in the market were unable to make more than a very small profit. Even women who used to be involved in lucrative international trade could no longer afford to do so. Under these circumstances, the best opportunity for wealth available for most women in Freetown was to become the wife or mistress of a man with resources. Women in Freetown, then, like women in Petbana and other rural areas, were dependent on their husbands and were in competition with co-wives and lovers for men's resources. They were not, however, dependent on their co-wives, as they were in rural areas, for sharing the work on their husband's farm. This meant that in Freetown women as wives retained their basis for rivalry but lost their basis for cooperation.

At the end of April 1992, a military coup by Valentine Strasser brought about a change of government in Sierra Leone. When I arrived in Freetown in June, soldiers—especially young soldiers—enjoyed almost celebrity status as *"our young boys,"* the heroes who had rid the country of the corrupt APC regime. Joining the army was, moreover, seen as a young man's only chance of a decent livelihood in the absence of any hope either of succeeding in business in Sierra Leone's depressed economy at that time or of finding an adequately paid job through educational qualifications. That August there were protest marches against the army in Freetown—not by opponents of military rule, but by young men who had been turned down when they tried to enlist as soldiers. And for young women the power, prestige, and relative financial security that soldiers enjoyed amidst the surrounding poverty also made the army a source of hope for them, in that soldiers became especially sought-after as husbands or lovers. A newspaper cartoon I saw in Freetown in August 1992 that commented on this situation depicted a wheelbarrow race. The competitors were naked women. Both the spectators enjoying the contest and the "prizes" for which the women were competing were soldiers. The caption read: *"Winner take soja* [soldier]." The naked wheelbarrow race was an apt image for a gender politics in which women, in this environment of armed and salaried heroes, had indeed been "stripped" of their capacity to do much more than to compete against each other.

I conclude this chapter with some of the consequences of these processes of economic decline and state militarization for the life of a young woman, Khadiatu, and with the ritual and social resources she drew upon to renegotiate these consequences. When I last saw Khadiatu at the end of August 1992, she was living in the East End of Freetown with her husband Ibrahim, who was a soldier, and with her two young sons and Ibrahim's parents. She was a trader who sold fish in the market nearby, going every morning to the wharf near her parents' house to buy her supply. At that time, Khadiatu was in the middle of a series of consultations with Pa Yamba about a woman in the same compound who was having an affair with Ibrahim. She told me the background to her consultations:

> She [Ibrahim's lover] *threatens me. She tells me I will not be in the house for long; my husband will get rid of me. She tells me she is enjoying my husband's money. Any time my husband goes out, he takes her and she comes back and tells me about it. At one time, she and I quarreled, and we were fined by the man in charge of the house. Then just after I went out, my husband paid the girl back her fine.*

Ibrahim's mother intervened on Khadiatu's behalf, but Ibrahim continued undeterred. His mother then cursed the girl, who took no notice. Khadiatu's mother tried to talk to Ibrahim, but her attempts were equally futile. Khadiatu's only recourse was to go to Pa Yamba, who gave her three kinds of medicine to drive the woman away and to restore her husband's good behavior: one kind to bury in the ground, another kind to put down the toilet, and another kind to wash with. Khadiatu thought that these had worked for a while, as for a short time Ibrahim seemed to have lost interest in the woman, but this apparent change did not last long.

Khadiatu's situation deteriorated again. During a quarrel, her husband told her that he would return her to her parents. Then the two women quarreled again, after which they were again fined by the head of the compound. Khadiatu recounted what happened afterwards:

> I went to the market to sell. My husband took money and gave the fine back to the girl. The wife of the head of the compound told me. The girl went to her and boasted. The girl is saying, "I'm not going out under the sun to get money!" . . . Later, my husband came back and told me I should give him back the Le10,000 he gave me for my business. I gave it to him.

The Le10,000 that Ibrahim took back from Khadiatu was equivalent to $20 in 1992, and it had been the initial investment for her purchase of fish. With it, she made approximately one dollar a day in the market if she was lucky. She wept when she told me about having to return it, and she said that she no longer wanted to stay with Ibrahim. "Could you live by yourself, without your husband?" I asked. She said that she wanted to be on her own, with her mother. She could manage, she thought, because a friend gave her fish to sell on credit every day. Her father was unsupportive, though, and was against her leaving Ibrahim and returning home. Awed by his son-in-law's position as a soldier, he refused, despite his wife's persuasion, to believe Khadiatu's account of her husband's behavior. The new military hegemony from which her husband's power derived had effectively blocked Khadiatu's "matrilineal path" to a rectification of—or an escape from—an intolerable situation in her marriage.

A week later, Khadiatu was happier:

> At a child's birthday party in this compound, the girl was dancing and singing. She sang: "This is my man; I will not leave him until I die." My husband helped me this time; he encouraged me to fight her. He held my jacket so that I could fight. I fought her and threw her in a ditch. People are now saying that he should publicly announce that he does not like the girl any more, but he won't.

But when I last saw Khadiatu just before I left Freetown at the end of August 1992, she had received another blow:

A woman came here who had just given birth to twins. My husband is the father. She did not greet me. I will complain to the sabu [the mediator for her marriage to Ibrahim]. *I didn't know about it before. My husband should have introduced her to me. He introduced her to his mother.*

As she felt that Pa Yamba's medicine was no longer effective, Khadiatu took the advice of her mother and consulted her mother's brother, who was also a diviner. He told her that the woman in her compound had consulted a diviner herself:

The girl upstairs went to a mɔre to drive me out, or to make me sick. I went to my uncle, a ləfa; he told me this. I went there yesterday. He told me that I should not just sit down [and do nothing], *because this girl is trying to scatter the marriage. He told me to make a faŋkadama* [sacrifice of "mixed" offerings] *with an egg. I will go to my mother's place and do this. The girl wants to fight. I want to fight back. . . . The girl's sister took ashes from another place and put them in my fireplace. I don't know why she did it, but I'm afraid. I'm not cooking in that place now. My husband's father's brother saw it and told me.*

Khadiatu's young children would have been even more vulnerable than she was to bad medicine ingested through food prepared on top of the corrupted ashes. By attacking the fireplace, the sister was attacking the household itself.

In October 1992 I received a letter from Khadiatu, written for her by a friend, telling me that there had been a confrontation between her parents, her husband, and his girlfriend. Her mother's ankle, she said, had been broken when the encounter turned violent. Given that a husband's relationship to his wife's mother should be one of formality and marked respect, this physical injury—whether inflicted by Ibrahim or his girlfriend—represented a very serious transgression. Not surprisingly, Khadiatu referred to Ibrahim in the letter as *"my former husband."*

I once asked Khadiatu whether she thought she was in a better or worse situation than a woman "upcountry," in a polygynous household. She said she would prefer a second wife to be brought in officially, because then the woman would understand the problems of the household instead of pursuing her own interests alone. Dependent on her husband despite her trading, and competing with other women for her security, Khadiatu was right when she said that she was in a worse position than a woman in a rural polygynous household. Instead of being the senior wife, having a reduced workload (ideally), and being able to draw upon the norms of good marital behavior that her husband could be pressured into at least appearing to follow, she had no effective leverage. Her husband did not have the same reluctance to lose a wife as he would had he been a farmer with large labor requirements, and he was indifferent to the fact that his behavior might cause her to leave him and return to her parents. He was also impervious to pressure from her mother and from his own parents, and was effectively making up his own rules. The only remaining sanction against him in these circumstances was, in fact, Khadiatu's use of divination and medicine. This was not one that she could make public, however.

The context of war and militarization brings us back—not full circle, but at a different twist of the spiral—to the warfare associated with the slave trade and with nineteenth-century colonialism in Sierra Leone's history. Not only did the terror of those eras become embodied through practices of containment and concealment, but, I have argued, it also shaped Temne gender dynamics and constructions of women, making wives potential conduits for external attack and giving a gendered dimension to understandings of Darkness and Closure. But in 1992, for Temne migrants in Freetown, women like Khadiatu were "contained" quite effectively by their economic dependency on men. Men like Ibrahim with resources and prestige, meanwhile, were so much in demand that they no longer needed to "contain" women in any case— although they might still have preferred to curtail women's consultations of diviners.

Ibrahim's injurious treatment of Khadiatu and his mother-in-law presaged far worse violations of women by soldiers and other fighters that were yet to come. While the amputation of civilians' limbs has become well known as a trademark tactic of the Revolutionary United Front rebels, less attention has been paid to these and other fighters' abductions of young women and girls for use as sexual slaves. According to Marc Sommers, who consulted in Sierra Leone in 1997 for the Women's Commission for Refugee Women and Children,

> male combatants who managed to escape from RUF base camps in April 1997 reported that young captive women constitute the majority of the base camp community they had left. Indeed, the example of the RUF fighters' well-known use of large numbers of young women as commodities (apparently, the higher

the rank of an RUF fighter, the more women they are allowed to keep) may be serving as a model for some military and civilian men. (1997: 13)

While most captured boys have been made into fighters and diamond diggers, those captured girls have become the modern equivalent of slave wives.

Such abuses are clearly of a different order from Ibrahim's ill-treatment of Khadiatu and her mother. But while in 1992 the privileging of young soldiers in a context of economic desperation allowed Ibrahim to place himself outside the norms of kinship and affinity, in subsequent years this empowering of militarized masculinity was to reach its logical conclusion in widespread rape, enslavement, and mutilation.

The Production of Witchcraft/Witchcraft as Production

Historical forms of power became not merely the means of coercion and subjection but (more interestingly) the conditions for creating particular potentialities—individual, social, and cultural. Talal Asad, *Genealogies of Religion*

If African witchcraft has long been an emblem of primordial irrationality in Western inventions of Africa (Mudimbe 1988), recent studies have instead established it as fundamentally implicated in processes of postcolonial modernity (e.g., Auslander 1993; Bastian 1993; Ciekawy and Geschiere 1998; Comaroff and Comaroff 1993 and 1999; Geschiere 1997; Meyer 1998b). In this chapter, I wish to extend this perspective by arguing not only that Temne witchcraft is modern but also that the modernity of witchcraft in this part of Africa is very old. Temne ideas of witchcraft, as we shall see, were shaped by intimate connections among witchfinding rituals, the Atlantic slave trade, and the modern forms of wealth and power that this trade entailed. These connections, in turn, are remembered in contemporary discourses about witchcraft that establish modernity as part of the historical imagination.

The Invisible City   In discussions of witchcraft *(ra-ser)* among many of the people I knew in Temne-speaking communities in Sierra Leone, I often heard references to an invisible region of space called "the Place of Witches" *(ro-seroŋ)*. This region, depicted as all around us, yet hidden from us, connects Temne towns and villages to a limitless urban world of wealth and rapid global mobility. Together with "the Place of Spirits" (ro-sɔki) and "the Place of the Dead" (ro-kərfi), it is one of three invisible regions of space in Temne cosmology that intersects with the visible world of ordinary human beings (nɔ-ru; see Littlejohn 1960b and 1963). No-one I asked gave the Place of the Dead or the Place of the Spirits much specific description, but it was a different matter with the Place of Witches: people I asked about witchcraft— whether rural farmers or members of the urban middle class, Muslims or Christians, men or women—usually drew vivid and remarkably consistent images. They often described a prosperous city where skyscrapers adjoin houses of gold and diamonds; Mercedes-Benzes are driven down fine roads; street vendors roast "beefsticks" (kebabs) of human meat; boutiques sell stylish "witch-gowns" that transform their wearers into animal predators in the human world (nɔ-ru); electronics stores sell tape recorders and televisions (and, more recently, VCRs and computers); and witch airports despatch witch planes—planes so fast, I was once told, that "they can fly to London and back within an hour"—to destinations all around the globe.

What are we to make of these images of affluent modernity, ultra-rapid international travel, high-tech media, and costly imported commodities—but also of animal predators and cannibalistic consumption? The evocation of a modern globalized topography—of time-space compression in "a multidimensional global space with unbounded, often discontinuous and interpenetrating sub-spaces" (Kearney 1995: 549)—is startling. Yet this unbounded and alluring global space is not one that ordinary human beings can inhabit. Although its presence may be recognized everywhere, its incompatibility with moral personhood and community is registered both in its intangibility and in its tropes of perverted and predatory consumption: the agency of the witch is necessary for the realization of one's desires within it. As in many other postcolonies, in Sierra Leone such tropes make a powerful moral commentary on a "politics of the belly" (Bayart 1993; Mbembe 1992)—a commentary that is especially salient in the context of a succession of "kleptocratic" regimes, a "shadow state" (Reno 1995) whose real workings take place "offstage," precipitous economic decline, and, since 1991, a devastating rebel war (Richards 1996b). It is common knowledge that over the past few decades the nation's mineral wealth has hemorrhaged into the overseas bank accounts of politicians and of local and foreign business tycoons, who have indeed built houses in foreign cities out of Sierra Leone's diamonds. And the juxtaposition of images of mobility, luxury, consumption, and predation on the witch city's streets speaks eloquently of the interconnections between two striking statistics: even before the rebel war, Sierra Leone had both one of the highest rates of infant mortality and one of the highest percentages of per capita ownership of Mercedes-Benz cars in the world. But these images also, I suggest, have a far deeper ancestry, drawing on representations that became pervasive as part of a much older globalizing process.

Witchcraft, Modernity, History   Witchcraft has received a lot of attention recently. In the 1990s, thirty years after structural-functionalism waned and witchcraft ceased to be "interesting" to anthropologists, Africanist scholars exploring the ethnography of modernity began to locate witchcraft in contexts with which, it had long been assumed, it could not be coeval. These include the postcolonial state (e.g., Ciekawy 1992 and 1998; Comaroff and Comaroff 1999; Fisiy 1998; Geschiere 1997; Geschiere with Fisiy 1994; Niehaus 1998; Rowlands and Warnier 1988); literate, Westernized, urban worlds (e.g., Bastian 1993; Meyer 1995 and 1998b; White 2000); capitalist enterprise and new forms of labor and migration (e.g., Apter 1993; Auslander 1993; Geschiere and Nyamnjoh 1998; Matory 1994; Weiss 1996). As embodiments of predation and of the "cannibalistic" consumption of human productive and reproductive potential, ideas of witchcraft often crystallize perceptions of the alienation of labor under (post)colonial capitalism, the social consequences of a cash economy, the contradictions of urban and international migration, the disparities generated by cash-cropping, and the dislocations of boom-and-bust cycles to which communities and regions are subject through integration into global markets.

As a critique of these analyses develops, however (Englund 1996; Englund and Leach 2000; Green 1997; Rutherford 1999), it is appropriate to clarify what I both do and do not mean by the modernity of witchcraft. First it is important to distinguish between modernity as content and as context. By modernity as content I mean the substantive issues addressed by ideas and practices concerning witchcraft: thus witchcraft may be identified as, for example, the nefarious, extractive means by which new elites accumulate their wealth, just as it may also be the means by which jealous relatives and neighbors invisibly attack elites, development projects, and the state (e.g., Bastian 1993; Comaroff and Comaroff 1999; Fisiy and Geschiere 1996; Geschiere 1997). Further, discourses of witchcraft and techniques of witchfinding may invoke objects and technologies that are understood as emblems of modernity: rubber stamps, X-rays, thermometers, televisions, airplanes (e.g., Auslander 1993; Comaroff and Comaroff 1999: 287; Piot 1999: 176), and the skyscrapers and Mercedes-Benzes of the invisible witch city I describe above. But this does not mean that at the level of content witchcraft is all modernity, all the time (Englund 1996: 259; Sanders 2000). As Green (1997) observes, practices of witchfinding are part of political processes, and their form may just as easily involve ideas of "tradition" as those of "modernity" (see also Rutherford 1997; Sanders 2000).[1] But as a *critique* of studies of the modernity of witchcraft, Green's argument is something of a red herring given that no-one (to my knowledge) has claimed that instances of witchcraft are addressed *only* to issues of modernity.

By modernity as context, on the other hand, I mean the workings of witchfinding and discourses of witchcraft as part of modern mechanisms and processes (such as the postcolonial state, or the Atlantic slave trade—the topic of this chapter), or, more broadly, of plural African modernities (e.g., Fisiy 1998; Geschiere 1997; Comaroff and Comaroff 1999). Here, the modernity of witchcraft inheres in its institutional and historical position, irrespective of the substantive content of specific instances of witchcraft. To tie this to the previous point, there may or may not be a congruence between modernity as context and modernity as content. This issue of congruence is the source of another red herring: Englund (1996) claims that "if the contemporary African lived-in worlds are all versions of modernity, it is little more than a tautology to assert that witches 'personify the conflicts of modernity'" (1996: 259). But given that his conditional clause implies the location of witchcraft in an encompassing context of African modernity, and main clause concerns particular understandings of modernity realized in such forms as the image of the witch, there is no tautology. Nor do specific assertions about modernity-as-content in ideas and images of witchcraft "reduce" the force of modernity-as-context arguments about multiple modernities, as Englund further claims (1996: 273). Most oppositional discourses *about* modernity themselves exist *within* modernity, and this is just as true of Temne images of the witch city (for example) as it is of the work of William Blake.

Englund's primary challenge, however, is to those who interpret witchcraft as a critique of morally problematic features of accumulation. He counters this interpretation through a discussion of witchcraft discourse among southern Dedza villagers in central Malawi, who, he points out, have lived with commoditization and a market economy since at least the late nineteenth century, when they supplied slaves for the Atlantic trade (1996: 262). Through their history of engagement with successive waves of foreign entrepreneurs, he argues, commodity production, market transactions, and accumulation have become "natural" features of their world. Those who accumulate material wealth are, however, subject to witchcraft accusation, but they can avoid such accusation if they constitute themselves as moral persons through gift-giving, patronage, and feasting (1996: 260). These ideas, England concludes, do not identify accumulation itself as problematic; instead, "witchcraft represents an argument about *how* that prosperity is to be achieved" (1996: 262).

It is clear from Englund's account that Dedza witchcraft is centrally concerned with ideas of proper personhood, but the argument that witchcraft is not also concerned with the propriety of accumulation is less than convincing. What Englund describes could also be characterized as the "laundering" of accumulated wealth (cf. Geschiere 1997) by distributing it according to local moral imperatives. According to England's depiction, accumulation does not appear, as he claims, to be morally neutral, but rather to be "guilty" until proved "innocent": unless wealth is socialized through acts of moral personhood, it is assumed to be morally negative, such that those who accumulate it risk being accused of witchcraft. If yet-to-be-socialized wealth were merely neutral, something else would be required to imbue it with negative valence, suggesting that accumulation is indeed morally problematic—or, at the very least, ambivalent.

While I do not agree with Englund's critique of studies of the modernity of witchcraft, however, I appreciate his insistence on locating discourses and practices concerning witchcraft in particular histories, and I share his view that "witchcraft provides a standpoint to reflect on *historicities*" (1996: 274). Until very recently, little attention has been paid to the historical production of witchcraft in Africa. Contemporary forms of witchcraft are usually linked either to postcolonial predicaments or to colonial processes that go back to the first half of the twentieth century. The point of releasing witchcraft from its ethnographic atemporality is lost if its "modern" character were read as standing in opposition to a supposedly primordial category of "precolonial" witchcraft: "probably less is known," as Comaroff and Comaroff comment, "about [witchcraft's] 'traditional' workings than anthropologists often suppose" (1993: xxviii).

Austen (1993) suggests, specifically, that some of its apparently "traditional" workings may in fact be products of the slave trade. And if, as Englund argues, the slave trade was merely one of several successive entrepreneurial encounters that served to naturalize capitalist accumulation for southern Dedza villagers, in certain other parts of Africa this accumulation is given a distinctly "unnatural" cast through memories realized in witchcraft discourses:

> The conception of witchcraft as an ambiguous attribute of power within Africa is often presented in ahistorical terms, as a timeless reflection of the tension between communal values and selfish individualism and anxieties about natural threats to subsistence. Our data on witch beliefs, however, are all relatively recent; with little exception they are drawn from societies that had long been involved with either the Islamic or European outside world. It is striking that several West Central African cosmologies link witchcraft with the deployment of victims in a nocturnal and/or distant "second universe," echoing, in more or less explicit terms, the experience of the Atlantic slave trade. (Austen 1993: 92)

Such echoes are especially clear in MacGaffey's work on BaKongo religion and history. MacGaffey tells us, for example, that here "the historical slave trade was assimilated to beliefs in contemporary witchcraft, both regarded as illicit traffic for profit in the souls of persons killed and transported by occult means" (1986: 62). Even more intriguingly, he later writes:

> Having stolen a soul, a witch may use it to pay his debts to other witches, or he may imprison it in a container . . . and force it to work for its master. . . . A person in this kind of captivity is called the "soldier" *(soldat)* of his witch master. His soul may be enclosed in a charm so that his anger at the way he has been treated may be turned against his master's victims. Or he may be sold to another master or even shipped to America to be put to work in factories making textiles and automobiles. (1986: 162)

Given this imagery of the capture, transatlantic passage, and forced labor of the soul, the experience of the slave trade seems not only to have become assimilated to preexisting understandings of witchcraft. It also appears to have shaped ideas of witchcraft themselves, and to have provided a model for their incorporation of more contemporary (and hardly naturalized) processes of extraction under industrial capitalism.

Another striking echo is present in a new form of sorcery called *ekong* in Duala, that part of the Cameroon coast that was first transformed by the Atlantic trade (Austen 1999; Geschiere 1997: 151–58). Those ensorcelled by ekong turn into zombies and are forced to work in invisible plantations on a magical mountain sixty miles from the coast; warning of such an attack may, moreover, be received "when someone dreams that he is taken away with his hands tied toward the river or the ocean while he cannot see the face of his captors" (De Rosny 1981: 93, quoted in Geschiere 1997: 152). Ideas about ekong thus pull in memories of the slave trade and superimpose them on experiences of colonial plantation labor in a palimpsest that relates to "the art of getting rich" in the modern state (Geschiere 1997: 137–68).

Like the invisible plantations of ekong and the American factories of Ba-Kongo witchcraft cosmology, Temne representations of the invisible witch city depict a different universe in which plundered value from ordinary human inhabitants of the visible world (nɔ-ru) is deployed by witches. Let us now examine Temne witchcraft in more detail.

Varieties of Temne Witchcraft When talking about witchcraft (ra-ser),[2] people usually describe the hidden acts of a witch (u-ser) whose spirit (aŋ-yina) or "shadow" (aŋ-mɔŋpəl) leaves his or (more usually) her body during dreams to go on invisible, nocturnal predations (Shaw 1992). Witches typically attack their victims by sucking the blood that holds a person's life (aŋ-ŋesəm) and by removing the heart (ka-buth), the inner center (aŋ-ŋesmər) of that life and the seat of thoughts and intentions, feelings and memories (Shaw 2000). The blood and heart is stored in the Place of Witches for later consumption and, until the heart is eaten, the victim will live—albeit as an empty shell. *"The baby may appear healthy in the morning,"* I was told by a young man during my first few months of fieldwork, *"but it will only be its flesh* (aŋ-der) *running about."* Victims are collectively consumed at meetings of witches' rotating credit associations (ɛ-susu)[3] in the Place of Witches, each member in turn contributing a victim for the group's regular feasts. Members of these "witch credit associations" sometimes recruit others—often children or other kin—by giving them meat in their dreams: parents, accordingly, instruct children to reject such offerings, explaining that any meat cooked or consumed in dreams is human (Shaw 1992). Witches develop a second stomach (aŋ-kuŋtha) for the digestion of human flesh that an ordinary human stomach cannot process: an ordinary human body, by implication, is a moral entity incapable of reducing other people to meat. Witches also, as we have seen, have "four eyes" (ɛ-fɔr t-aŋlɛ): two ordinary, visible eyes complemented by two invisible eyes that impart a special, penetrative vision. With their four eyes and two stomachs, witches could be said to grow a partial second body—a body of predatory gaze, perverted consumption, and no heart—that removes them from a shared bodily empathy with their victims.

The victims of witches' invisible "eating" are usually children (including those still in the womb, not forgetting the womb itself [aŋ-pɔru] as the source of future children) or sometimes elderly people. Most witches are popularly represented (by women as well as men) as women, especially as wives in po-lygynous households who contribute their co-wives' children or their own children for consumption at the secret feasts of their witch credit association. Healthy adults, who are too strong to be susceptible to invisible vampirism and cannibalism, can be attacked through other types of ra-ser. Witches may also shape-shift *(lafthɛ or folnɛ)* into dangerous wild animals of the bush—leopards, snakes, chimpanzees, elephants, and crocodiles—and attack their victims in these forms (1989: 102–18). Or they can beat their victims with sticks and whips that may be felt but not seen, rendering the victims weak or paralysed. Alternatively, they can invisibly steal growing rice through a prac-tice called *ka-thɔfi*, which usually involves placing the substance of a crop on an invisible mat and transferring it either from one farm to another or from the human world to the Place of Witches, thereby contributing to the latter's plenty. This causes poor yields of rice, the crop that is not only the mainstay of a rural household's subsistence but is also symbolically equivalent to people themselves in many contexts (see, e.g., Littlejohn 1960a; Richards 1986). Through another version of *ka-thɔfi*, which English-speaking Temne translate as "economic witchcraft," witches invisibly transfer money from other peoples' pockets to their own, or accumulate it in the witch city. Rumor has it that this is widely practiced by wealthy traders—especially Lebanese traders, who achieved rapid prosperity in both small- and large-scale commerce in Sierra Leone from the end of the nineteenth century onward. It was also described as endemic in the diamond-digging district in Kono, in eastern Sierra Leone (before the rebel war, at least, when the diamond district's civilian population was displaced by rebels, soldiers, and other combatants).

The most effective and deadly form of ra-ser, however, is the use of the witch-gun *(aŋ-piŋkar a seroŋ)*, a weapon constructed out of such materials as a piece of papaya stalk (or other tube-like object), a grain of sand (or other potential missile), and an explosive powder to activate it. A witch can take these objects and transform them into a piece of lethal artillery that may be used to shoot victims from considerable distances. This kind of witchcraft is depicted as practiced particularly by powerful, affluent "big persons" *(aŋ-fəm a bana)*—usually men, and precisely those depicted as owning the houses of diamonds and the Mercedes-Benzes in the witch city.

These guns, wielded by the most powerful witches, nevertheless form only part of the technology of the Place of Witches: the invisible city is described as the origin of all technological innovations in our own visible world. This claim entails a moral ambivalence about the powers and products of Western technology—an attitude that was conveyed in many of the witchcraft stories circulating during my stays in Sierra Leone. In the town of Magburaka in the 1970s, for instance, rumors spread about the disconcerting skills of a Temne-Lebanese teenager. A former schoolmate described him in these terms:

> An Englishman wanted to take him to England but his parents didn't agree. So he read books on his own and made radios and built lanterns.[4] He earned money by building radios. He could make a lantern with wonderful electronics—there could be movement inside it. He could make "robot" lanterns. So he has four eyes; he is a witch. He made a wooden aeroplane and a little engine, and it could fly. His mother was angry and broke it; she was frightened in case he was a witch.

The narrator claimed that the boy had "four eyes." All witches, as we have seen, have four eyes, and although not all those with this special vision prey on others, they all have the capacity to activate this predatory potential if they wish.

For the boy's mother, apparently, her son's identity as a witch was a frightening possibility that might still be arrested by her actions. That she was described as having destroyed a miniature working model of a plane is significant, as witches are said to be able to take miniature objects (usually groundnut shells) and transform them into full-sized planes and boats. The Englishman's offer was also rejected. From a European (and a middle-class Sierra Leonean) perspective, the Englishman would have been understood as having wanted to give this brilliant child educational opportunities abroad. But if we bear in mind the image of the invisible witch city, a more disturbing interpretation is possible: the Englishman's interest might also have been seen as a wish to take the boy to a place where he would be able to develop his strange witch capacities further. Like the Place of Witches, European and North American cities represented inaccessible urban landscapes of wealth, power, commodities, technology, mobility—and witchcraft.

These links among Europeans, Western technology, and witchcraft were often made explicit in commentaries on imported high-tech consumer goods. Michael, my first research assistant, remembered the reaction of his aunt several years earlier, on a visit from her home in a provincial town, to the new television in his family's parlor in Freetown:

> My aunt came from Magburaka. She saw our television in Freetown, and asked me if that person was inside the television. I said no; in Freetown there is a big camera with

which they are "snapping" the person you see in this television. And this camera sends
out the picture. So if you have a television you get the picture and you will be able to see.
She said, "Allah! The white men are witches! (aŋ-potho a-ser!) *The white men take*
their witchcraft out into the world so everybody sees it!"

European witches are represented as making their products public and visible, of having harnessed their powers of witchcraft to achieve material success and technological dominance in the world. African witches, in contrast, are represented as keeping their "wonderful" (Temne *ninis,* a term conveying both marvel and horror) inventions hidden and failing to make them available to their communities, thereby blocking Africa's material development. This connection with economic and technological development was often drawn in discussions of witchcraft, as it was at the end of my 1978 fieldwork, when a man was arrested in Freetown for having hired a diviner to kill his brother with a witch-gun. A journalist reporting the arrest lamented the use of such "scientific knowledge" for purposes of destruction:

> *What is this witch-gun? Does it possess a butt, barrell* [sic], *stock, safety catch and trigger, like any other gun? Exactly what goes to make its bullets? If we could put such scientific knowledge to good use, what a great continent Africa would have been!* ("Look Gron," *We Yone,* November 22, 1978, 4 and 10)

This is not a sarcastic expression of skepticism; the journalist's final sentence echoes assertions that I heard in many discussions of witchcraft. Such understandings represent "progress" and "development" as requiring, in a sense, *more* witchcraft—more accessible witchcraft, benefiting a greater number of people—rather than less.

Yet as the account of the inventive teenager and his mother indicates, these yearnings for the benefits of development do not mean that Western science and technology are always viewed with untrammelled admiration. Their categorization as witchcraft indicates, in fact, their ambivalent moral status, as well as that of the Europeans who produce them. European witches might *"take their witchcraft out into the world so everybody sees it,"* but Europeans are not represented as *sharing* much of it, or in fact much of anything, with others. Indeed, the Temne word for "Europeanness" or "Western ways" *(ma-potho)* designates a range of antisocial behavior—living a secluded life, exchanging abrupt greetings, not stopping to talk, not visiting others, eating large quantities of meat, and eating alone without inviting others—all of which are defining features

THE PRODUCTION OF WITCHCRAFT / 211

of Europeans in Temne experience (Turay 1971: 338). Such qualities of seclusion, selfishness, and greed are also precisely those that characterize witches.

In this sense, then, witchcraft may be seen as a form of "failed science," although not in the sense imagined by nineteenth- and early-twentieth-century European intellectuals writing about "primitive thought": the failure here is one of morality, not rationality. Like BaKongo representations of stolen souls laboring for witch masters in American car and textile factories, the gleaming but troubling images of the invisible witch city provide a commentary on problematic forms of wealth, power, technology, and mobility. Both sets of images evoke a vision of "a totalizing moral economy . . . in which the acquisition of money and power links parochial means for producing and destroying human value to potent foreign sources of wealth" (Comaroff and Comaroff 1993: xxv). Let us turn to the historical beginnings of this link between potent foreign wealth and the consumption of human productive value in this part of Africa.

The Production of Witchcraft   While contemporary Temne representations of witchcraft link the "cannibalistic" consumption of persons to wealth, imports, and technological power, for more than three centuries people had, in fact, been reduced to consumable entities and exchanged for foreign wealth during the Atlantic trade. The written sources for these centuries do not tell us much about representations of witchcraft, but they do describe in some detail the practices of public divination by which persons were transformed into slaves through their conviction as witches.

Our earliest detailed account of Sierra Leone, remember, was written by Valentim Fernandes at the beginning of the sixteenth century, probably on the basis of information from Alvaro Velho, who lived in Sierra Leone for eight years. In his fairly detailed account of shrines, images ("idols"), spirits, ancestors, sacrifices, burial practices, divination, and healing (Fernandes 1951 [1506–10]: 80–93; Fyfe 1964: 27–28), Fernandes makes no mention of witchcraft or techniques of witch-finding. His descriptions of divination for sickness, remedial sacrifice, and burial practices are worth quoting for the contrast they provide to later accounts that I shall examine below:

> In the case of sickness they have no medicine nor know its rules, and only if someone is sick they go to the fetish-men *(feyticeyros)* who throw lots to know why he is sick; they always find that it is the idols *(os ydolos)* who send the sickness, and order that to him should be sacrificed a dog, a goat, or a chicken,

for these are the animals they are accustomed to sacrifice. . . . Here is how they conduct their burials, and when a noble dies, or an honored man, they open his side and take out all the entrails; they wash them very well, and fill him with herbs like mint that smell very nice, and throw inside him rice-flour and rub him with palm oil, and make him a platform of 5 or 6 steps high, decorated with the best cloths there are in the area, like red or cotton cloths. Then they seat the dead man in a chair wearing the best clothes he has. . . . The day of the burial all the people gather in the place where the dead man is on the platform, and silence is ordered. And all give jewels according to their means to whoever they wish, with a declaration; if it is to the dead man they are buried with him, if it is to the dead man's relations each takes away what he has been given. (Fernandes 1951: 86–91, trans. David Beach and Jeanne Penvenne)

Additionally, if the deceased was a man who had killed many people in battle, the mourners would assemble armed, "play the drums as if for war" and "parade as they would do if going off to war" (Fernandes 1951: 90–91, trans. Beach and Penvenne). Fernandes also tells us that "the justice of the Teminis is that according to custom thus murder and all other wrongs and offenses are compensated for by money and no one is killed" (1951: 96–97, trans. Beach and Penvenne). It would be wrong, of course, to conclude from this that witchcraft, witchfinding, and the execution of wrongdoers did not exist in Temne-speaking communities at the turn of the sixteenth century. Yet it is interesting that, in contrast to their absence from Fernandes's sketch of these early days of the slave trade, later writers represent the ritual identification of witches, followed by their sale or execution, as a routine and highly visible part of practices of divination, healing, and burial. As Walter Rodney put it, "customary law in Upper Guinea [functioned] in a radically different way during the slave trade era than it did before and afterwards" (1970: 106).

Writing a hundred years after Fernandes, the Jesuit missionary Manuel Alvares provides a view of Sierra Leone during the time of Mane domination. In the intervening century, remember, the Mane had waged war and imposed their form of kingship upon local peoples such as the Temne. Initially, as we have seen, they sold captives to European slavers as a byproduct of their warfare (Brooks 1993: 293–94), but by Alvares's time they had become intermediaries in the Atlantic trade, the consequences of which were an acceleration in the flow of slaves and an escalation of warfare (Rodney 1970: 102). Warfare was not, however, the only source of the slaves the Mane sold.

According to Alvares, dominant etiologies at the time he wrote attributed

illness and death to a process of invisible consumption by enemies: "They enter-
tain a malevolent and false belief about their illnesses and physical ailments,
for they say, and they sincerely believe this, that God does not send death to
them, rather it is their enemies and rivals who are eating them up" (1990
[c.1615], 2, chap. 3: 4). Diviners ("sorcerers") gave similar readings of sickness
and death—readings that differed from those of "the fetish-men who throw
lots" a century earlier, during the time of Fernandes and Velho. Instead of "always find[ing] that it is the idols who have sent the sickness," malevolent human
agency was now sought among those close to the patient. In a passage on
divination techniques that we have already seen in chapter 3, Alvares writes:

> They have various other forms of divination, but we need not discuss them
> all. . . . When they take to their beds, the first thing they do is to consult *Ac-*
> *caron.* Like Ocosias, they send messengers to the most famous sorcerers, who
> put a thousand lies into their heads. The sorcerer, this servant of hell, puts on
> the fire a small pan containing a little water. . . . In order to find out if anyone
> is giving him poison or is otherwise responsible for his death, the sorcerer
> names the man's relatives. If the water sinks back when one is named, he is not
> to blame; but if it boils over, they consider that the person named is the guilty
> one. . . . If it does this, they fall on the poor man, and on the orders of the king
> kill him or enslave him. (Alvares 1990, 2, chap. 3: 4)

No longer solely a process of ritual mediation between "the idols" and the
human community amidst which they dwelled,[5] divination and the understandings of affliction it enacted and reproduced were now—under the aus-
pices of the new Mane rulers—integrated into the European slave trade.

This integration of divination into the Atlantic system receives more explicit comment in Alvares's account of other coastal peoples further to the
north—the "Banhus," the "Biafars," and the "Sonequei" (Soninke)—in what
is now Guinea-Bissau and Senegal. In detailing the injustices of slaving, "'the
most substantial trade' of Guinea," he complains that "the heathen . . . enslave
large numbers on the grounds that they are witches, an offense which they
can only prove by diabolic arts" (1990, 1, chap. 5: 3), such as the ordeals of
"red water" poison and of red-hot iron (1990, 1, chap. 7: 8–9). Among the
Banhus, the placing of a corpse on a platform—a mobile version of that described in Sierra Leone by Fernandes a century earlier as a means of honoring
the deceased—was now part of the material apparatus of witch-detection
and enslavement:[6]

When a sick man dies, they straight away ask him not to flee away but to reveal who ate him. . . . Four of the heathen then carry the dead man on a wooden grating like a bier, and sometimes they add the cloth the man wore when he died. They quickly make their way around the village, from one side to the other and through the open places. And whenever the ministers of the devil stop, it is said and falsely believed that the people in that spot "ate" the dead man. . . . The wretch whom the bier accused (by stopping) has to pay. His house is attacked and a host of his children are enslaved. (Alvares 1990, 1, chap. 7: 13)[7]

Alvares goes on to lament the fact that Portugal's Atlantic enterprises were indirectly responsible for these practices, emphasizing his church's condemnation of particular methods of acquiring slaves (while, nevertheless, it condoned others), yet placing more direct blame upon the "spite" of the "heathen":

Spite is (thus) one of the heads under which those who are sent to our Spanish lands [i.e., the Indies] are acquired, although this has been so strongly condemned in the bull promulgated by His Holiness in the year —— on the subject of the purchase of Brasilians. (ibid.; cf. chap. 5: 2–3)

The witchfinding divinations Alvares describes both entail and reproduce particular understandings of social relationships. If someone falls sick, on the one hand, "the sorcerer names the man's relatives" (chap. 3: 5) and looks for witchcraft among the victim's kin; if the victim dies, on the other hand, and the ritually interrogated corpse stops in front of another person, "a host of his children are enslaved." The ties that connect victims to witches, then, as well as witches to other witches, are those of kinship: witches both consume their kin and reproduce themselves through their kin. Alvares also tells us that when those accused belonged to families with means, they stood a much better chance of being exonerated in an ordeal. At that time, he writes, the most common trial by divination was the poison ordeal known as the "red water":

They boil the bark of *macone*, then seat the accused in a public place and give him the poisoned drink, which kills only those who have no-one to help them. As I have stated elsewhere, immediately after the person has drunk a calabash of red-water they give him a calabash of plain water to drink. If the accused expels the *macone* in one vomit, they consider him innocent. But if otherwise, he dies lamentably. The relatives of those who have to submit to the ordeal help them to prepare for it. Most of the accused vomit the poison before it can do them any harm, as a consequence of their taking antidotes beforehand, antidotes such as gold dust, the most commonly employed, or oil. They consult beforehand a sorcerer, to find out the right moment to take the poison, and sometimes they try it out on slaves or hens. So those who have the means thus escape the effects of the ordeal. (Alvares 1990, 2, chap. 3: 5)

Distinctions of power between those with and without "means," then, were translated into the distinction between those convicted and those absolved—a distinction that also determined whether the kin of the accused would also be sold into slavery. This intersection of inter- and intralineage politics (in the accusation of the victim's kin, and in the disparities among accusations of members of elite and non-elite lineages) with the economics of the Atlantic trade (in which the sale of whole families generated more wealth than the sale of single individuals) was to become even clearer as the slave trade gathered further momentum.

In the eighteenth century, the Atlantic trade reached its peak. By this time, English merchants had replaced Portuguese traders in their domination of the slave trade, and the Mane rulers had long been absorbed through intermarriage with their Temne-speaking subjects. These Temne speakers had meanwhile expanded and absorbed other groups, and were organized into several centralized chiefdoms; like their former Mane overlords, moreover, they had become intermediaries in the slave trade (Sayers 1927: 14). As in the era of Mane "invasion" and rule, the main sources of slaves were warfare and raiding, the divinatory conviction of witches and other wrongdoers, the pawning of dependents, and the seizure of debtors.[8] In the late eighteenth century John Matthews, an agent for an English slave-trading firm, wrote: "The best information I have been able to collect is, that great numbers [of slaves] are prisoners taken in war, and are brought down, fifty or a hundred together, by the black slave merchants; that many are sold for witchcraft, and other real, or imputed, crimes; and are purchased in the country with European goods and salt" (1961 [1788]: 146).[9] While Matthews was aware of a connection between witchcraft and the slave trade, he sought to justify the latter by arguing that it was both the strength of witchcraft beliefs and what he described as an "addiction" to witchfinding techniques in Sierra Leone that drove the sale of slaves—thereby reversing the main direction of their interrelationship. He wrote:

Though most unenlightened nations believe in charms and witchcraft, yet the inhabitants of this country are so much addicted to it that they imagine every thing is under its influence, and every occurrence of life they attribute to that

cause. . . . If an alligator destroys any body when washing or swimming, or a
leopard commits depredations on their flocks or poultry; if any person is taken
suddenly ill, or dies suddenly, or is seized with any disaster they are not accustomed to, it is immediately attributed to witchcraft: and it rarely happens that
some person or other is not pointed out by their conjurors, whom they consult
on these occasions, as the witch and sold. (1961 [1788]: 130–32)

Despite Matthews's self-serving misattribution of witchfinding to a Sierra Leonean "addiction," his description of practices of witch detection are of considerable interest. The "conjurors" he mentions would point out "some person or other" through ritual interrogations of the corpse similar to those
Alvares had written about, in a different language, nearly two hundred years
earlier.[10] Six bearers, according to Matthews, carried a bier on which was
placed either the deceased or the latter's clothes; the ritual power of the corpse
or the clothes controlled the bearers' movements. At the gravesite, a friend or
kinsperson stood before the bier, held up a reed, and addressed the funeral
litter: "and then he asks him what made him die—whether he knew of his
own death, or whether it was caused by witchcraft or poison"—to which the
deceased answered either "yes" by propelling the bearers forward involuntarily, or "no" through "a rolling motion" (Matthews 1961: 122–23). Such
burial divinations were "constantly practised" (129). Afterwards, distinctions
of position and privilege determined the scope of the consequences for the
kin of the accused: "the culprit is then seized, and if a witch sold without
further ceremony: and it frequently happens if the deceased were a great man,
and the accused poor, not only he himself but his whole family are sold together" (124). Those accused of poisoning were, however, usually permitted
the chance—apparently slim, in contrast to what obtained in Alvares's time—
to exonerate themselves by taking the "red water" poison ordeal. The accused
would be confined "in such a manner as he can release himself" (125) and
would then "escape" to the next town, declaring to its headman that he
wished to prove his innocence by drinking the red water. If the poison killed
him, he was declared guilty; if he vomited it up, he was provisionally declared
innocent—but if he then defecated within a day he was described as having
"spoiled the red water" and was accordingly sold (126). It was not only those
accused by corpses who had to undergo this ordeal: Matthews was told that
in the interior, "suffering the people to drink red water upon every trifling
occasion, was attended with such fatal consequences as would in time depop-
ulate the country" (129).

Writing fifteen years later, at the beginning of the nineteenth century, the traveler Thomas Winterbottom similarly states that explanations in terms of witchcraft were almost universally given for death (1969 [1803], 1: 260) and describes the divinatory interrogation of the corpse as a standard part of burial practices (236). The social disparities observed by Matthews are also noted by Winterbottom as producing divergent etiologies of witchcraft according to the power and status of the deceased. There were two possibilities: the deceased either identified the witch responsible, or acknowledged having been a witch who was finally killed by the agency of the personal spirit or countermedicine of an intended victim. "It is most usual," Winterbottom writes, "to assign the former cause for the sickness and death of chiefs, and other people of conse- quence and their connections; and the latter for those of any of the lower class" (236). When the first explanation was revealed by the movements of the corpse's bearers, the deceased identified the witch or witches responsible by selecting from among a series of names. The fate of those accused then rested upon their connections to power: "these," Winterbottom continues, "if they have friends to plead for them, are allowed the privilege of appealing to the red water ordeal in proof of their innocence; but if not, they are sold" (238; plate 17). The importance of having a "big person" "behind" you as a patron is underscored by these disparate outcomes. Such patrons would usu- ally have been members of the ruling lineages of a town or chiefdom—those who traced descent from ancestors who had cleared the bush to form the original settlement—and who could provide their supporters with protection from warfare and raiding in exchange for labor (Bledsoe 1980). During the slave trade, when every death and every serious illness seem to have entailed divinatory accusation as part of routine procedures of healing and burial, such important attachments were likely to have been essential in providing people with "friends to plead for them."

Four years after the publication of Winterbottom's account, the Anti-Slave- Trade Act of 1807 was passed by the British Parliament. This did not mean the end of the Atlantic slave trade, since other European nations continued it, but the Act represented the beginning of a process of eradication over the next several decades (Fyfe 1964: 155–65). It also represented the gradual decou- pling of witchcraft and public divination from the Atlantic system. One con- temporary observer, the English traveler Alexander Gordon Laing, commented on what he saw as a consequence of this decoupling in his journey through a part of Temneland close to the British Colony of Sierra Leone in Freetown:

> While I was at Ma Bung, a young girl died rather suddenly; and previous to her interment the following practices were observed. . . . A few hours after the

death of the girl, the Elders and the Greegree men of the town assembled in the palaver-hall, and held a long consultation or inquest as to the probable cause of the death. It was inquired whether any one had threatened her during her life-time, and it was long surmised that she might have been killed by witchcraft. Had the slave trade existed, some unfortunate individual might have been accused and sold into captivity; but its suppression in this country from vicinity to Sierra Leone, permitted the Magi, after a tedious consultation of three days, to decide that the death had been caused by the agency of the Devil. (1825: 85–86)

Laing's account is suggestive of a transition in the political economy of ritual knowledge—at least in areas near the Colony at that time. It suggests that toward the end of the Atlantic trade, as the divinatory accusation of witches ceased to be a means of transforming people into trade goods, etiologies of spirit-attack ("the agency of the Devil") acquired increased salience. These etiologies are not unlike those described by Fernandes when he reported that "it is the idols *(os ydolos)* who send the sickness" in the early days of the slave trade more than three hundred years before.

Witchfinding and the State

> The regulated mechanism of an ordeal [is] a physical challenge that must define the truth. . . . The search for truth . . . was also the battle . . . that "produced" truth according to a ritual. Foucault, *Discipline and Punish*

When British colonial authorities imposed a Protectorate over the Sierra Leone hinterland at the end of the nineteenth century, they imposed their own techniques of truth in the legal apparatus of the colonial state. Their opinion of oracular truth and of the divinatory techniques that produced it in the hinterland is clear in the following excerpt from the Chalmers Report of 1899. Here the Secretary for Native Affairs, J. C. E. Parkes, responds to questions about the system of justice administered by the hinterland chiefs:

1086. Is it your experience that the Chiefs in their own courts . . . take trouble to find out the very truth?—Much depends on the Chief: in some cases they do; in several others I am afraid they do not. . . .

1088. Would they require as stringent a proof in cases of murder as would be required in our courts?—In Mohammedan courts they would: in pagan courts not always.

1089. What would be the nature of the shortcoming in pagan courts?—In pagan courts the whole thing might degenerate into a trial by ordeal.

1090. What is the nature of the ordeal?—To drink a decoction of sass-wood, which is a poison, or by putting the hand in hot oil.

1091. Then how would the ordeal by sass-wood decoction operate? —In case the party drinking it throws it up he is innocent: in case he dies he is guilty.

1092. In cases of theft what kinds of evidence would be deemed suffi-cient?—Witnesses and evidence as in our own courts: both in Mohammedan and pagan courts. . . .

1095. In witchcraft?—Trial by ordeal.

1096. Always?—Yes. It is the same kind of ordeal as in the other cases.[11]

This written record of questions and answers, set down in a serially numbered sequence as "oral evidence," is itself part of the regulated practices of legal truth with which the colonial government sought to replace the judgments of oracles and ordeals. It was only through such practices, the questions im-plied—practices that produce "stringent proof" through "witnesses and evi-dence"—that "the very truth" could be discovered. "Mohammedan courts" in Muslim chiefdoms represented the closest approximation to "our courts" in this respect, while in contrast the techniques of truth employed in "pagan courts" had the tendency to "degenerate" into ordeals.[12] Moreover such "de-generation," Parkes affirmed, was always a feature of witchcraft cases.

Yet while they rejected the divinatory practices through which individuals were identified as witches, the colonial authorities nevertheless accepted local definitions of witchcraft as a crime and proceeded to try witchcraft cases in their District Commissioners' Courts (Fyle 1988: 83, 95; PRO, CO 269: 5, 1892–99). In these colonial witch trials, however, witchcraft was redefined in accordance with rationalist British conceptions of "proof": instead of the invisible "eating" of victims that had been so prominent in witchcraft convic-tions during the slave trade, emphasis was now placed on "physical evidence" in the form of the accused's possession of harmful ritual substances (see Fyle 1988: 95–96). Making this the defining feature of "the truth" meant that the range of actions that constituted witchcraft in the District Commissioner's Court was reduced to one side of an axis corresponding to the Western dichot-omy between "matter" and "spirit," "fact" and "imagination." And whereas, as Asad points out, oracles and ordeals are strictly "not evidence for reaching a legal judgment but the definition of a judgment itself" (1993: 91), they were now rejected as something they had never been: sources of "evidence."

Ironically, one consequence of these witch trials in colonial courts was to authorize the legal apparatus of the state—the court system, the police, procedures of arrest, fines, and imprisonment—as a proper arena for witchcraft cases. It retained that authority after independence, although such cases were now heard in Paramount Chiefs' Courts, thereby officially returning control over convictions of witchcraft to local rulers. Moreover, the colonial emphasis on the "physical evidence" of witchcraft now yielded to Temne understandings of witchcraft as invisible consumption; accordingly, the public divination techniques that alone have the capacity to discern the hidden "truth" of such consumption were accordingly integrated into these courts.[13] All diviners, especially those who perform public divinations, were now required to get a license from the police.[14] Thus authorized, these licensed diviners worked with the police, and their oracular findings were presented as evidence in court.

Witchfinding divination has ceased to be a requisite part of healing and burial in contemporary Temne ritual practice. I do not know how it has operated during the rebel war, but up to the early 1990s witchfinding was performed when there were a series of deaths (or when single deaths were construed as unusual) in a household or town (Shaw 1985; 1991). Only household heads were able to arrange such a divination, and only after seeking permission from—and paying a fee to—the Paramount Chief. Since few could afford these expenses (in addition to the Chief's fee, diviners often charged the equivalent of $20 or more for a public divination), this meant that chiefs and relatively affluent senior men still monopolized these techniques of truth. Conviction as a witch, however, no longer led to social death as a slave in the Atlantic system. Instead, it usually resulted in a beating, a fine levied in the Paramount Chief's Court, and the application of medicine to the eyes to extinguish the witch's supernaturally doubled vision. Instead of being integrated, via local elites, into the Atlantic slave trade, public divination was now integrated—again via local elites—into the state.

Witchcraft as Production   What potentialities were created by the imperative to find witches during the slave trade? Many of the subjectivities subsumed by Temne understandings of rα-ser—readings of illness and death as products of invisible consumption, dreams of eating meat, and dispositions toward particular suspicions and accusations—may, I suggest, be seen as such productions. I am not suggesting that understandings of witchcraft were absent before the slave trade, but that as techniques of witch-detection became part of routine healing and funeral practices through the impetus of the slave trade, these understandings were driven into particular forms. Temne knowledge of witchcraft, then, was at least partly a product of witnessing witchcraft divinations as they unfolded again and again. Repeated experiences of a funeral litter carried by bearers, of a man standing in front of a grave, holding up a reed, of questions he addressed to the deceased ("And then he asks him what made him die—whether he knew of his own death, or whether it was caused by witchcraft or poison"), of the bearers lurching forward as the deceased answered "yes," of the rolling motion of the funeral litter to indicate "no"—such procedures were "read with the whole body" (Bourdieu 1990: 76), assimilating understandings of witchcraft as an inevitable and ubiquitous part of the lived world.

Included within these understandings were implicit theories of social relationships—ideas of where loyalty and treachery lay, of the location of trust and mistrust, and of axes of conflict and solidarity. As we have seen, accusations and convictions of witchcraft were advanced in particular directions—inward, toward kin, and downward, away from members of ruling lineages and other big persons. In the literature on witchcraft in Africa, considerable attention has been paid to how witchcraft accusations are generated by tensions within structures of kinship, patterns of authority, and forms of hierarchy (e.g., Evans-Pritchard 1937; Geschiere with Fisiy 1994; Gluckman 1956; Turner 1957); this is in fact one of the sources of the supposedly "traditional" character of African witchcraft. Yet what if witchcraft—driven by such transregional processes as the Atlantic trade—had a more recursive relationship with these fault lines of conflict, being not merely their product but also the means of their exacerbation and intensification?

It was not only kinship but also growing distinctions of class that constituted the relations of power permeating witchcraft accusations. In the early seventeenth century, it is worth remembering, Alvares tells us that "they boil the bark of *macone*, then seat the accused in a public place and give him the poisoned drink, which kills only those who have no-one to help them . . . [while] those who have the means . . . escape the effects of the ordeal" (1990, 2, chap. 3: 5). Being "without means" meant being without either material resources or important links of kinship and marriage—especially connections, we may suppose, to the ruling Mane elite at that time. Nearly two hundred years later, in the late eighteenth century, contrasting trajectories of witchcraft conviction for the well connected and for those lacking such resources were also manifest in terms of distinct etiologies of witchcraft. Recall that according to Winterbottom, "for the sickness and death of chiefs, and other people of consequence and their connections," the divinatory interrogation of the corpse usually produced a particular person as the witch responsible for the deceased's death (1969: 236). But "for those of any of the lower class" the deceased usually acknowledged, through the same divinatory interrogation, having *been* a witch who was killed by a counterattack of the personal spirit or medicine protecting a "big person" the deceased had tried to harm. Dead witches could not be sold, but their living kin could be and often were.[15]

This last point raises a question about the popular images of the invisible witch city with which I began. If understandings of witchcraft were produced and reproduced through practices of witch detection in which, under the direction of rulers, big men, and members of elite lineages, those accused and convicted have usually been those with less power and wealth, why are big men, with their luxurious properties, sleek vehicles, and high-tech consumer goods, so prominent in representations of the Place of Witches today? Although big men were—and still are—rarely formally convicted in witchfinding divinations, they are often rumored to be sinister, witch-gun-toting figures whose power derives from the absorption of medicines made through ritual murder (Ferme 1999; MacCormack 1983b; Richards 2000)—a form of ritual "cannibalism" that I shall examine in the next two chapters. And although most convicted witches, I was sometimes told, might appear weak and unimportant in this world (nɔ-ru), they are "big persons" in the invisible city. Although powerful, wealthy persons, then, direct witchcraft convictions toward those most unlike them, it is upon them, together with the European world they mediate, that images of the true and hidden form of the witch are modeled.

For in addition to driving the production of witches and understandings of witchcraft in particular directions through witchfinding divinations, the slave trade itself provided apt metaphors of wrongful "eating" that were deployed in rumors about those who were its most visible agents. Phantasmagoric images of Europeans and of African elites as consumers of human life were reported throughout the centuries of the slave trade, as I shall discuss in the next chapter. While the sixteenth-century Mane "invaders" imposed their rule on local peoples and profited from the sale of the latter to European slave traders, they were themselves the subjects of rumors of grotesque forms of cannibalism (Alvares 1990, 2, chap.11: 1–2; Donelha 1977: 101; Rodney 1970: 56). And when, two centuries later, English merchants replaced Portuguese traders in their domination of the slave trade, they too—appropriately enough—became the objects of widespread cannibalism rumors that survive to this day (Matthews 1961: 152; Rankin 1836: 104). Inverting the relationship between accusers and accused described in the previous section, these rumors provided an apt idiom for Mane and European "consumption" of human "commodities" (cf. Miller 1976 and 1988).

The development of witchfinding as the ritual production of slaves for the Atlantic trade and as the source of particular kinds of knowledge and subjectivity about witchcraft is, then, only part of this story of witchcraft and the slave trade. Like Taussig's powerful account of Putumayo torture stories as a "*colonial mirror* that reflects back onto the colonists the barbarity of their own social relations" (1992: 164), the very imagery of witchcraft as the wrongful "eating" of people provided counterrepresentations through which those who profited from the ritual conviction of witches were implicitly recognized as the biggest witches of all. Although power may produce knowledge, it does not necessarily determine consciousness.

Making History: Memory and Modernity   I have argued that in the visions of global modernity materialized by the witch city, a political economy is "remembered" that once linked divinatory ritual, social relationships, and cosmological representations in Sierra Leonean towns and villages to a commercial system spanning three continents. During the slave-trade centuries, witchcraft and divination in much of the upper Guinea coast were part of an expanding Atlantic world in which inflows of European wealth and commodities were tied to the largest process of forced migration in world history. Witchfinding divinations developed as constitutive and persuasive practices that created a reality, like other rituals in other contexts, by "actively refigur[ing] meanings in line with changing perceptions of the universe" (Comaroff and Comaroff 1993: xxi). These forms of divination, then, were more than "ways of knowing" the world (Peek 1991); they actively contributed to its constitution.

By authorizing one of the principal ways in which persons were transformed into slaves, those who controlled witchfinding divinations accused those convicted of an invisible "eating" of others analogous to that in which they were themselves engaged. Yet at the same time, their own participation in an "eating" in which the appearance and accumulation of new wealth was engendered by the disappearance of people into oblivion was itself the object of commentary in the form of popular images, stories, and rumors that reversed the direction of formal divinatory accusation. I hope to have shown that we, in turn, may "divine" memories of these processes in representations of the invisible witch city and in the long-standing rumors of European and elite African cannibalism that they reiterate.

What can we learn about globalization and modernity from the witch city? One reminder that this ubiquitous but invisible city gives us is that an unbounded global space exists mainly as a function of specific kinds of power and capacity; that "there are continuous paths that lead from the local to the global, from the circumstantial to the universal, . . . only so long as the branch lines are paid for" (Latour 1993: 117). We learn that this global city is in many ways an eminently desirable space for those whose "branch lines are paid for": they need not hunger for meat or money; they have special capacities for rapid mobility; the most irresistible commodities may be theirs. But we also receive clear instruction as to what constitutes payment for this privileged access—the lives and wealth of others, misappropriated from an everyday African world. For all its allure, the witch city counters the poetics of optimism present in much writing on globalization with a "poetics of predation" (Comaroff and Comaroff 1993: xxvi) that equates global flows with the flow of blood. Built in the Temne historical imagination through an extended experience that tied transregional commercial flows and foreign commodities to a traffic in human lives, the witch city is a Sierra Leonean "cosmology of capitalism" (Sahlins 1988) that "remembers" this experience in its construction as a startling commentary on global modernity.

8

Cannibal Transformations

Experiencing Colonialism in the Sierra Leone Hinterland

Last month I went as usual to trade in Freetown. Ere I return Chief Bey Simerah and people concocted together and arrange to put an end to my life by charging your poor servant with Cannibalism, they have got as much ill disposed persons to prove me, and bring me under the crime of being an Alligator. A Charge that your petitioner is quite innocent of. Testimony of Kiyelleh, 1892, in Milan Kalous, *Cannibals and Tongo Players of Sierra Leone*

Historicizing Cannibalism   During the last quarter of the nineteenth century and the Protectorate era of the twentieth, accounts of ritual murder multiplied in the Sierra Leone hinterland. The above excerpt comes from a series of accusations and confessions concerning the "cannibalism" of deadly were-animals—"human alligators," "human leopards," and (later) "human chimpanzees"—who were described as capturing and ritually slaughtering people in order to make wealth-producing medicines from their victims' vital organs. Accounts of cannibalism such as these, as White (2000) demonstrates in her remarkable analysis of vampire stories in East and Central Africa, mark a way in which relationships entailed by colonial rule could be debated, evaluated, and commented upon. In many parts of Africa, moreover, such stories may be retold and recast in postcolonial contexts, in discussions of such con-

225

cerns as AIDS, political violence, and the sudden widening of economic disparities, thereby connecting colonial memories to postcolonial predicaments
(see, e.g., Geschiere 1997; Weiss 1996: 202–19; White 2000: 126, 130, 141).

In this chapter, I want to move in the other direction: experiences of colonialism were themselves mediated, I argue, by memories of earlier transregional processes. Specifically, I wish to suggest that the human crocodile and
leopard scare in colonial Sierra Leone reworked memories of still earlier rumors of European cannibals—rumors that spoke to morally deleterious forms
of power and commerce in Sierra Leone's Atlantic history. But tracing stories
of cannibalism historically and exploring them as forms of social memory
grates against a long-standing axiom that we cannot "explain" a story in terms
of its origins. Thus White (2000: 15–16), for example, takes issue with an
attempt to trace vampire stories in the Congo to stories of European cannibals
during the slave trade (Ceyssens 1975), arguing that by so doing the capacity
of vampires to convey heterogeneous local and regional concerns is subordinated to the issue of mere origins.

To explore cannibalism stories as memories, however, is not to reduce
them to generic, unchanging images disconnected from specific sociohistorical concerns; nor is it to make them impersonal agents that determine their
own passage down the years through passive human vectors. Instead, it is to
focus on a process of historical sedimentation similar to that which Ferme
describes for the practice of elections in late-twentieth-century southeastern
Sierra Leone, in which "political actors inherit cultural forms that shape their
practices and visions of a moral community, even when these are aimed specifically at subverting a particular legacy . . . or when this legacy is relatively
unconscious and emergent" (1999: 162). Rumors and accusations of cannibalism have long been (and still are) a dynamic part of these cultural forms
that configure visions of moral community. Accordingly, in this chapter I wish
to outline a history of Sierra Leone through the lens of cannibalism stories.
These are, of course, different stories, told in different ways, at different times,
and in different sociohistorical contexts. Yet I suggest that successive stories
about human consumption in a particular locality do not simply arise sui
generis, born again and again in different circumstances, disconnected from
memories of earlier stories. The current privileging of rupture in anthropology
can occlude the fact that the experience of rupture may not merely be a feature
of the postcolonial or colonial condition but a recurring historical predicament that may itself involve continuities. Through such continuities, people
tie moral perceptions of new sociohistorical rupture to memories of earlier

experiences even as they reconfigure those memories. Let me begin, then, to trace the cannibal stories through which this work of memory has proceeded.

Cannibalism and Conquest   "And even when they kill their enemies in battle they cut pieces of them and dry and smoke them and cook them with rice and eat it," wrote Valentim Fernandes of the inhabitants of Sierra Leone at the turn of the sixteenth century (1951 [1506–10]: 94–95; trans Alice Clemente). We do not know if Fernandes was outlining a practice his informant Alvaro Velho had seen (unlikely, in view of the sparse details he gave of a practice that would presumably have been startling to him), or if he was reporting a rumor, or giving a literal interpretation to the image of "eating" as a metaphor for defeat. All we can be sure of in this reference from five centuries ago is that there existed local ideas of cannibalism that were linked in some way with defeat and capture in war.

Earlier in Fernandes's account, we find another reference to cannibalistic consumption—and this time, man-eating is attributed to European slave traders. Fernandes tells of a group of Portuguese further north, on the Gambia River, who were met by a fleet of canoes whose occupants shot arrows at them. When the Portuguese managed to find a group of their assailants who would speak to them through an interpreter, the Portuguese explained that they had come not to make war but to trade, as they did already with the people of the *Canaga,* and had brought a gift for their king on behalf of the king of Portugal. Their adversaries were not impressed:

> They replied that they knew well how we had dealt with people in the *Canaga,* and that the Christians ate human meat and that all the slaves that they bought were carried away to be eaten. And because of that they did not want our friendship but they wanted to kill us all and to make a gift of them to their king who lived three days' from there. And they shot them with arrows. (Fernandes 1951: 34–35; trans. Alice Clemente)

In this story of the cannibalism of European traders we can, I suggest, catch a glimpse of the early incorporation of the Atlantic trade into local (and perhaps regional) meanings of "eating." Although we know next to nothing of these meanings in the time and place about which Fernandes wrote, it is clear that for this belligerent group on the Gambia at the turn of the sixteenth century, rumors of the European consumption of slaves identified trade with "Christians" as a form of predation. In an area that had been incorporated into long-distance trade flows well before the coming of Europeans (Brooks 1993), this was hardly a reaction of "isolated" Africans to sudden commercial contact with the outside world: from what Fernandes tells us, it was specifically the *kind* of trade—a trade that fed the "Christian" appetite for the consumption of humans—that was viewed as problematic.

We have a somewhat better (although still sketchy) idea of the sociohistorical context of a later set of cannibalism stories in Sierra Leone: those told about the Mane conquerors in the sixteenth and early seventeenth centuries. When Mane raiders arrived on the coast of Sierra Leone in the second half of the sixteenth century and subsequently imposed their form of kingship upon peoples of the area, Portuguese and other foreign contemporaries reported recurring stories that the Mane practiced cannibalism (Brooks 1993: 305). Andre Donelha, a Cape Verdean who traveled in upper Guinea between 1574 and 1585, writes of the Mane, for example: "They eat human flesh at any time and while at war, even that which belongs to (one of) their own nation. When they make war, the conquerors eat the conquered" (1977 [1625]: 101). A more detailed and grisly portrait of the Mane as the consumers of those they defeated is drawn by Manuel Alvares. The following is an excerpt from a less graphic part of his description:

> The Manes bear the cruel and hateful name of Sumbas, which means "eater of human flesh." If this name given to the soldiers, while they are such, is a fitting one it is not because they eat human flesh in their native lands. . . . But this practice is a military regulation, and they are most careful to observe it. In my view, it was their most powerful weapon of war, which spread terror and made their victory easier. . . . The malice of these savages reached such a height that if they happened to take any of the women who had been captured for themselves, when the fancy struck them they would send them to bath and on their return kill them and have them cooked. One must add that all this was a long time ago, and much has happened since. (1990, 2, chap. 11: 1–2)

Walter Rodney observes that Mane warriors were sometimes described as eating their captives "for courage and ferocity" (1970: 56) as well as to intimidate those they wished to conquer, and he argues that this suggests a militarized ritual function. But the words of Alvares in the last line of the above excerpt suggest that, rather than describing current Mane practices, he was repeating some of the stories that circulated about Mane domination among their local subjects. In his account, captive concubines are slaughtered and cooked; captives are made to eat each other; a baby is seized from its mother, stuffed with rice, and roasted on the fire; a father-in-law is fed (unbeknown) his own daughter at a banquet in his honor; a child is fed the meat of his slaughtered compatriots; and a local, non-Mane governor who criticizes the king is invited by the latter to a banquet in which he is to be the intended meal (Alvares 1990, 2, chap. 11: 1–4). Some of these stories recapitulate the association between reports of cannibalism and defeat and capture in warfare that were present in Fernandes's account a century earlier. Others concern violations that erase and invert bonds of concubinage, companionship, affinity, kinship, and political office. If we bear in mind that Alvares wrote when local peoples were subsumed within Mane political structures and were assimilating Mane military and cultural practices, while at the same time they were also incorporating their Mane conquerors through marriage (Brooks 1993: 303–5), these stories would seem to highlight the contradictions experienced in these processes of mutual absorption across marked disparities of power. The descriptions of meals and cooking depict acts of commensality that (we can probably assume) ordinarily created and maintained relationships but that are here turned around to attack the very basis of moral connection among people. Thus, instead of incorporating the Mane into local patterns of sociality, local peoples are forced to enact the Manes' violations of that sociality: "Not only do we consume you," the Mane are made to say in these stories, "but we also make you consume each other."

There was a further context for these stories: the symbiotic relationship that developed between Mane warfare and the Atlantic slave trade (Brooks 1993: 293–94). The Mane ruler Tora, Alvares tells us, "loved the Portuguese much" (1990, 2, chap. 11: 4). Rodney (1970: 102) argues that while supplying the traders with captives was initially a profitable byproduct of Mane conflicts with the local peoples they subjected, the seizure and sale of slaves came to be a primary motivation for such conflicts. Although it was the Portuguese and other Europeans who bought the slaves and carried them away, it was with the Mane intermediaries that local peoples had their most direct and violent experiences of Atlantic enslavement.[1] Thus the warfare that was frequently associated with stories of Mane cannibalism—stories that may, moreover, have played off earlier stories of the "eating" of war captives—was itself the means by which local African bodies were "consumed" by the slave trade. If the stories about cannibalistic cooking and meals and gruesomely inverted commensality expressed concerns about incorporating the Mane conquerors into local communities through affinal ties, these concerns would seem an appropriate response to the dangerous paradox of forging moral relationships with foreign overlords who have sold large numbers of people from your locality. Whether or not Mane cannibalism stories also drew upon earlier stories of the cannibalism of the Atlantic trade, the "eating" of humans is a powerful image for the articulation of Mane warfare and state-building with a form of commerce in which "consumable" bodies were captured and sold before disappearing forever.

Atlantic Cannibals   Other stories, circulating not just in Sierra Leone but along the length of Africa's Atlantic coast, were focused not on African intermediaries such as the Mane but on the Europeans who carried people away in the Atlantic trade. Although most of these stories were reported in the eighteenth and nineteenth centuries, they reiterate the claim in the early-sixteenth-century excerpt from Fernandes that "all the slaves that [the Christians] bought were carried away to be eaten." As in this accusation, most of these stories of Atlantic cannibalism do not seem to have contained much accompanying detail. In contrast to the gruesome particulars in reports of Mane cannibalism, nameless and faceless Europeans are simply described as eating African slaves, either on the slave ships themselves or at their distant destinations: there are no specifics of food preparation, cooking, banquets, or captives forced to eat their own kin and companions. If accounts of Mane cannibalism convey the difficulties of building affinal and other relationships with people who have conquered you and made your relatives and neighbors disappear into slave ships, the spare depictions of European cannibalism on those ships or across the ocean convey the idea of predatory foreigners with whom there is little or no direct relationship.

These stories of white cannibalism were focused not on the European traders who had settled on the coast but on unsettled Europeans who carried captives away in ships, and on those who received them at distant destinations. It was thus Europeans in conjunction with the forms of transatlantic mobility and transport they controlled who were important in these stories. For people living along the Atlantic coast or in the hinterland, the prospect of travel toward the coast, or the presence of the sea, of a ship, or of Europeans could elicit images of cannibalism.[2] In his famous *Narrative,* for instance, Equiano describes his terror at being brought to the slave ship and, upon seeing his European captors, he asks fellow Africans "if we were not to be eaten by those white men with horrible looks, red faces, and loose hair" (1969 [1789], 1: 72). And later, in 1835–40, a former slave in Freetown named Joseph Wright described his feelings when he and his companions were trans-

ported from Lagos to a slave ship: "when we saw the waves of the salt water
... it discouraged us the more, for we had heard that the Portuguese were
going to eat us when we got to their country" (Curtin 1967: 331). Here were
foreigners and vessels whose transatlantic passage reconfigured the ocean as
a space of deadly transformation, materializing the conversion of human bodies into money and foreign commodities as they moved back and forth across
the water.[3] Although these vessels wove connections between particular African places and the country of Europeans through the foreign goods they
brought, these connections did not reduce the experiential separation between "there" and "here" because the people carried away did not come back.[4]
Moreover, the opaqueness of these exchanges was itself embodied in the
opaqueness of the hulls of the ships that facilitated them; inside these hulls,
the experience of the Middle Passage was hardly less nightmarish than the
imagined scenario of African bodies being broken down into food.[5]

Most of these stories about European cannibalism seem to have been un-
elaborated but persistent and transregional, circulating in the West African
interior, on the coast, on slave ships, and even in the New World itself (Palmie
1995): these were Atlantic stories. Within their usually sparse details, however,
we can sometimes discern particular local meanings. Stories of Atlantic consumption in the kingdom of Kongo, for instance, detail how, instead of being
eaten, slaves' bodies were turned into the gunpowder and oil that the Portuguese carried to Africa—the very ammunition and commodities with which
the slave trade was pursued (Ceyssens 1975: 528–29).

We can also, I suggest, glimpse specific local meanings in an intriguing
reference to Atlantic cannibalism in John Matthews's late-eighteenth-century
account of Sierra Leone. According to Matthews, understandings of Atlantic
cannibalism in the Sierra Leone hinterland extended beyond those of simple
eating: an African captive sold to a European, he claims, "imagines the white
man buys him either to offer him as a sacrifice to his God, or to devour him
as food; and I have seen some of these poor wretched beings so terrified with
apprehensions of their expected fate, as to remain in a state of torpid insensibility for some time" (1966 [1788]: 152). The presence of ideas of sacrifice—
of the *ritual* consumption of a victim—in these rumors of European cannibalism in the region of Sierra Leone distinguish the stories from more generic
accounts of Atlantic consumption. Let us explore this further.

Ideas of Europeans who kill and consume captives as part of a sacrifice
carry a different—although no less grotesque—set of meanings from those of
Europeans devouring people for food alone.[6] While I do not know the specific
forms and meanings of sacrifices in the Sierra Leone hinterland two hundred

years ago, animal sacrifices (both in contemporary Sierra Leone and else-where) commonly engender beneficial and enabling transformations through the exchange of the victim's life for blessings and benefits (or, in the case of apotropaic sacrifice, for freedom from harm) from an extrahuman force to whom this life is offered. The rumors that Matthews reported depict a reversal of the position of Africans within that exchange, turning them from ritual participants into offerings. Instead of being those who benefit from a sacri-fice's generative circulations, African captives become the victims whose ritual slaughter benefits European others—a prospect so appalling as to throw many captives into "a state of torpid insensibility," Matthews tells us. What sort of boon the white man was viewed as receiving from "his God" for such a sacri-fice remains undisclosed. But whatever it was, these stories made it part of a European ritual process that integrated the transport of African bodies across the Atlantic into a further set of transactions with the Europeans' God—a pro-cess that ultimately channeled a return flow of foreign commodities and money back to the rulers and big traders on the coast and rivers of Sierra Leone.

Scholars who focus on the economic history of Sierra Leone have some-times argued that the Atlantic trade was less significant—because of its lower volume—than the internal trade in non-human commodities (Howard 1997: 27; Jones 1983: 87–88). Yet if we turn from purely economic criteria, the fact that people do not seem to have associated those other forms of trade with cannibalism indicates that the Atlantic trade had a significance that the inter-nal trade did not—a significance that extended beyond questions of volume. Matthews's statement tells us that in the Sierra Leone hinterland, many cap-tives (and, we can probably assume, many of those in the communities from which they were taken) experienced the Atlantic trade through ideas of an inverted ritual process in which the usually beneficial flows of sacrifice were turned into a means of cannibalistic extraction.

The conviction that slaves carried away in the Atlantic trade were eaten by Europeans persists in Sierra Leone to this day, although it is not linked to the idea of sacrifice. That linkage among cannibalism, sacrifice, and predatory trade does, however, resonate in intriguing ways with ideas of the ritual canni-balism of human leopards and crocodiles that circulated in the Sierra Leone hinterland a century after Matthews's account.

Colonial Power and "Cannibal Crimes"   These cannibalism stories of the late nineteenth century erupted during the first colonial era, nearly seventy years after the Crown Colony of Sierra Leone in Freetown had replaced the

Atlantic slave trade with the legitimate trade. The stories entered the colonial record as rumors and reports of suspicious killings, as part of the correspondence between hinterland chiefs and colonial authorities, and as accusations and confessions in colonial court cases. The accounts were not specific to any particular ethnic group—indeed, as Ijagbemi (1968) has documented, the notion of an "ethnic group" or "tribe" in the Sierra Leone hinterland was itself one of the outcomes of colonial intervention in the trade wars of this very era.[7] Instead, reports of these killings were common "in those parts of the forest zone most thoroughly transformed by commercial contacts" (Richards 2000: 89), especially in communities along the coastal Sherbro area in the southwest and along the major trade routes inland. In most of these accounts, the human victims' blood and organs were used either to create or to "enliven" powerful medicines, while the killings themselves often simulated attack by leopards, crocodiles ("alligators"), and chimpanzees ("baboons"). Human leopards, for example, were accused of ritually slaughtering their victims with a five-pronged "leopard knife" in order to imitate the signs of a leopard attack. Human crocodiles were described as using a medicine containing a tiny model canoe (Kalous 1974: 83, 76) that empowered humans to enter and animate either a crocodile skin or a "submarine canoe" that resembled a crocodile in the water.

Murder by shape-shifting into leopards and crocodiles, termed "the witchcraft of the leopard" *(ra-ser ɔ-sip)* and of the crocodile *(aŋ-kuy)* in Temne, was a well-known form of witchcraft long before the late 1800s.[8] Returning to Matthews's account a century earlier, we learn that: "If an alligator destroys any body when washing or swimming, or a leopard commits depredations on their flocks or poultry; if any person is taken suddenly ill, or dies suddenly, or is seized with any disaster they are not accustomed to, it is immediately attributed to witchcraft" (1961: 130–32). At the time that Matthews wrote, such attribution was (as I discuss in chapter 7) part of a ritual process in which convicted witches were sold into the slave trade by chiefs and big men. But during the nineteenth century, after the Atlantic slave trade was abolished, the colonial government made treaties with hinterland chiefs (Wylie 1977: 73–74) in which the internal sale of slaves was prohibited. Thus severed from the process of the commodification of persons, witchfinding divinations that had for several centuries turned people into slaves by convicting them as witches eventually tapered off.[9] But in the human leopard scare in the last quarter of that century, a different form of accusation developed in which established ideas of the shape-shifter's witchcraft were synthesized with ideas of harmful ritual action by malefactors in the more concrete form of human leopards. And this time, as we shall see, these stories were leveled *against* chiefs more often than by them.

For the colonial authorities who recorded and acted upon these accounts, the stories seemed readily appropriable into European conceptions of "cannibalism"[10] and "Fetish Custom" (Kalous 1974: 269), confirmations of "the extraordinary ignorance and superstition of the Aborigines" (32) and of the lowly position of these "Aborigines" on an evolutionary ladder beneath both the Irish and (much higher) the English (65). As Abraham (1976) points out, such conceptions were used as justifications for colonial rule. The Protectorate Ordinance of 1896, for example, was represented as a means of dealing "a death blow to [the natives'] barbarous customs and institutions," notably "native wars, plundering, slave trading, cannibalism, woman palaver and domestic slavery" (Kalous 1974: 9). But in the early years of the Protectorate, human leopard scares seem, if anything, to have increased rather than declined. They became, moreover, a recurring focus of colonial debates and decisions about the application of military force and the imposition of colonial rule (Kalous 1974: 279, 291, 304, 306). Colonial discussions of "cannibal crimes" thus had practical consequences that went beyond the realm of discourse in very concrete ways.[11]

Ironically, the accounts of cannibalism that were used to authorize the imposition of colonial force were stories that spoke directly to the consequences of the colonial political economy.[12] Let me begin, then, to outline these consequences.

Cannibalism and Colonial Commerce Throughout the nineteenth century (especially toward its end), the Colony's authorities advanced their penetration of the hinterland, signing treaties, inserting themselves (where possible) into processes of chiefly succession, intervening in the "trade wars," sending punitive military expeditions, and forcibly annexing territory (Ijagbemi 1968; Jones 1983: 131–61; Wylie 1977: 91–189).[13] Many of the struggles between the chiefs and the colonial government were over control of the legitimate trade: chiefs considered it their right to regulate commerce, levy tribute on trade goods, and assert their authority over traders by blocking the roads, much to the disapproval of the Colony (Wylie 1977: 74–75, 91–128). We have already seen, moreover, that chiefs had a long history of collaboration with (and control of) traders, drawing in such strangers as (earlier) Portuguese lançados and (later) Muslim traders and ritual specialists through intermarriage. While such collaboration between chiefs and traders remained strong during the legitimate trade (Richards 2000), chiefs were also aware that the wealth derived from this commerce gave traders the opportunity to pay their own professional warriors and thereby challenge the chiefs (Ijagbemi 1968; Wylie 1977: 178; Jones 1983: 128–30). When chiefs tried to assert their authority over both trade and traders, however, the colonial government often stepped in to restrain them.[14]

These struggles among chiefs, wealthy traders, and the Colony were intensified in the 1870s, when the demand for palm kernels increased rapidly (Mitchell 1962: 205), and the rivers that were essential for the transport of palm products became the focii of violent commercial rivalries. At that time domestic slavery, slave-raiding, and warfare formed the nuclei of massive contradictions in the workings of the legitimate trade. Domestic slaves, obtained by raiding weaker neighbors, were critical both for the production and porterage of cash crops for the trade and for the cultivation of food crops to provision the chief's body of warriors (Ijagbemi 1968; Lenga-Kroma 1978; Wylie 1977). Chiefs and big men established small hamlets called ta-fakay (in Temne) away from the towns, and settled them with slaves (Abraham 1975: 135; Wylie 1977: 77), concealing them from raiders from other chiefdoms who sought to seize both people and crops (Dorjahn 1960b: 115 and 121, n. 3). Chiefs then sold the cash crops and forest products from these fakay in the legitimate trade, thereby enabling them to keep their warriors armed with the weapons that would maintain the flow of captured slaves (Wylie 1977: 85). At the same time, chiefs' capacities to defend their chiefdoms from the raids of others depended on their warriors' capacities for warfare and raiding, and therefore on the chiefs' capacities to arm their warriors through the legitimate trade and to feed them by acquiring and controlling domestic slaves (Ijagbemi 1968: 181–213; Lenga-Kroma 1978, 1: 76–78, 153; Wylie 1977: 85). The British, for their part, sought to eliminate all of these interconnected processes—warfare, raiding, and internal slavery—that the legitimate trade had helped engender, and on which it depended.[15] Thus ironically, as Wylie notes, "the very wars and raids which [the British] wanted to end provided . . . the only capital which many of the smaller societies . . . could generate in order to make the system of exchange function; that capital was slaves" (1977: 86).

If these conditions meant a crisis of power and authority for the chiefs, they meant terror for the chiefs' subjects. It was at this time of intensifying contradictions and accelerating violence in the last two decades of the nineteenth century that accounts of killings by human leopards and crocodiles multiplied. The globalizing connections forged in pursuit of the legitimate commerce—linking together chiefs and Colony, warfare and enslavement, rural production and river transport, slave settlements and the global market— were experienced in terms of the violent disconnection of vital parts of the human body.

After the imposition of the Protectorate in 1896 and the suppression of the ensuing Hut Tax War in 1898, the contradictions of the legitimate trade took a different form: the Colony continued to promote the trade, but it forbade chiefs and big men from engaging in warfare, raiding, and the internal trade in slaves. Although trade in slaves was prohibited, however, slavery itself was allowed to continue until 1929. Pragmatism forced the Colony to compromise with the chiefs and big men over internal slavery, given that the Colony still needed the trade with the Protectorate for its own economic survival and "lacked the money and the manpower necessary . . . to economically exploit and to administer the colony without aid of the rural elite" (Rashid 1999: 215). The chiefs' access to labor was nevertheless considerably eroded by the prohibition on raiding and internal slave-trading, prompting them to seek alternative sources of labor and wealth.

Many Protectorate chiefs found these sources in their capacity, through their new position as agents of government, to "eat their chiefdom" (Dorjahn 1960b: 111). In relation to the government itself their powers had been curtailed: they were told, for instance, that "his Majesty must be regarded by them as . . . the Paramount Chief over all Paramount Chiefs" (Probyn, in Kalous 1974: 280). But at the same time the checks and balances that had formerly curbed abuses of chiefly power over their subjects were gone. For southern Temne chiefs—sacred figures who should not be allowed to die a natural death—the most important constraint had lain in the powers of their counselors and subchiefs *(ɛ-kapər)*, who were empowered to kill the chief when he fell ill. In practice this had meant, as Dorjahn points out, that minor illnesses were overlooked in a popular chief, while "a wicked man was dispatched after the slightest decline in health or well-being" (1960b: 114). This important sanction against a despotic chief was eliminated by the establishment of the Protectorate, while other powers of the kapər subchiefs were eroded, thereby removing the major checks on the chief's ability to "eat his chiefdom."

For many Temne chiefs in the Protectorate era, the "eating" of their own chiefdoms effectively replaced their warriors' slave raids on other chiefdoms in the previous century. This "eating" now took the form of monetized levies on their subjects that supplanted the tribute in food normally given (for ex-

ample) after the harvest, of extortionate court fees and fines, extrajudicial fin-
ing, and the attachment of their own additions to the colonial tax (Dorjahn
1960b: 130–35). It also took the form of labor levies for the cultivation of
cash crops on the chief's farm—a farm that tended to grow larger and larger
through land obtained in pledge or through seizure following dubious rulings
in the chief's own court (134).[16] Additional labor could likewise be obtained
through the court, as the chief would lend people money for the court's ex-
orbitant fees if the plaintiffs were willing to pawn a son as security for the
debt—an arrangement that became permanent when the court case was lost
(135).

Given these opportunities to make money from the chieftaincy and given
the lost powers of Temne kapər subchiefs to cut short an unpopular chief's
reign, there was an ever-increasing number of candidates for chiefly office in
southern Temne chiefdoms (129–30). This intensifying rivalry, in turn, undermined the system of succession through rotation among royal lineages and
through the established practice of the chief naming his successor: these were
replaced with "the election of the chief" by a colonially appointed Tribal Authority that consisted of the subchiefs and village representatives (116, 129).
Members of royal lineages, according to Dorjahn, characterized these elections as "fighting for the chieftaincy" and complained that "the candidate who
could pass out the biggest bribes to the Tribal Authority, the Assessor Chiefs,
and, formerly, to the Court Messengers present would secure the chieftaincy" (129–30).[17]

In the Protectorate era, then, trade with the Colony no longer relied upon
a system of exchange that functioned through war, raiding, capture, and enslavement. Instead it now involved chiefs "eating" the land, pawned youths,
and forced labor of their own subjects—subjects whose experiences of their
powerful patrons, I suggest, found expression in the continued salience of
human leopard, crocodile, and chimpanzee scares in the Protectorate era.[18]
And while the British sought to build a loyal rural elite, establishing the Bo
Government School for the sons of Protectorate chiefs, this special education
seems to have had the effect of amplifying perceptions of the new elite's predatory capacities: "Since the 1940s," Abraham writes, "an appreciable number
of those accused [of being human leopards] had been educated at the Bo
School" (1976: 128).

The Leopards of the Legitimate Trade   Instead of the anonymous and generalized European cannibals of the Atlantic trade, accounts of human leopard,
crocodile, and chimpanzee killings identified *known* individuals: substantial

numbers of chiefs and headmen were accused of being alien were-animals outside the bounds of moral human existence.[19] Certain of their accusers claimed that the killings had been committed to "make [the chief] powerful to govern the whole country" (Kalous 1974: 107), "to increase [the chiefs'] influence and continue the chieftaincy in their line" (94), and "to make the people [who did not obey the chief] of one mind in the country" (166). Chiefs, in turn, claimed that such accusations against them were the fabrications of discontented subjects ("All the evidence against me is false. My countrymen do not like me as a Chief" [277, also 132–33]). Some chiefs (and, more rarely, subchiefs) leveled accusations against their rivals—other chiefs, contenders for chiefly office, and wealthy subjects (137, 195, 217, 225, 236). Several traders in the legitimate commerce were also accused, either as collaborators with (Richards 2000) or rivals of the chief, including "a trader in palm kernels" at Moyamba in 1901 (Kalous 1974: 98), "a trader in a fairly large way at Bonthe" in 1913 (303), and "a Merchant and paramount chief of Poro" in Galinhas Chiefdom in 1914 (85). Another such trader was Kiyelleh in the southern Temne-speaking town of Rokon, with whose testimony the present chapter began. Accused in 1892 "of being an Alligator" by "Chief Bey Simerah and people" after having gone "as usual to trade in Freetown," he explained that "your poor servant is blessed in cattle and many things sufficient to be regarded as a rich man . . . on which account the surrounding Neighbours and Friends in the country grow envious" (217). Like Kiyelleh, and in important contrast to those accused of witchcraft during the Atlantic trade, those identified as human leopards or alligators were often wealthy: "Poor people are not accused of being human leopards," stated a witness, "It is only rich people with property" (196; also 194, 204, 219).

Often, chiefs' and big men's ritual advisors were included in this indictment. In human leopard accusations, the textual potency of "mori-men's" ritual knowledge was perceived as having been turned to their patrons' sinister purposes; their divination techniques ("Bundu proposed that Abdulai should be employed to look country fashion to find the woman" [Kalous 1974: 137]), their sacrificial skills ("The prisoner was a 'medicine man', and murdered the child" [111]), their written amulets ("The man who has [this writing] must get money, and it will make him a Chief" [107]), and their liquid Qur'anic medicine ("Nessi is a medicine made by the Murri men and is used by the human leopard society" [161]) were all viewed as carrying the potential for extractive, "cannibalistic" rituals of individual empowerment and enrichment.[20] Thus the very success of "mori-men" as diviners, healers, amulet-makers, and ambassadors to chiefs in the eighteenth and nineteenth centuries implicated them, along with their wealthy patrons, in the sinister exchanges of the legitimate trade.

Significantly, those who accused chiefs, traders, and diviners of human leopard, crocodile, and chimpanzee killings often located those they denounced within the problematic transactions of trade with the Colony. Witnesses made repeated connections between cannibalism, human sacrifices, and the production of wealth, often invoking the white man and trade with the Colony as the source of that wealth. A few also claimed that the ritual substances and practices in question deflected colonial surveillance (Abraham 1976; Jackson 1989). Charles Parkes, a government spy sent to Imperri, reported in 1894 that the words addressed to the notorious Bofima medicine while "feeding" it with blood were: "Do not let any trouble come to us. Let us get plenty of slaves. Do not let the Government know how to free them. Let us be rich" (Kalous 1974: 112). "It is good for trade," a prisoner in Moyamba said of the Bofima medicine in 1905 (116); it "was to be made in order to get riches," another prisoner in Moyamba claimed in 1908 (104); "to make men rich," echoed another (125). In a big case in Tindale chiefdom (in the southwest) in 1909, a witness stated that "the people . . . wanted to offer another sacrifice so that if they should do anything bad the white man should not find out about it, and they should get plenty of money from the white man" (172; see also 170 and 91). When questioned about "the object of the [Baboon] Society" in 1915, witnesses replied that this was "to be wealthy and influential," and "to be rich and to gain a big name and respect over every other person" (93–94).

Human leopards, crocodiles, and chimpanzees, moreover, were accused of catching and ritually consuming their prey in sites of rural production and along routes of transport for the legitimate trade. Instead of the European cannibals of the Atlantic trade, who sacrificed and devoured their human victims in an alien place—the enclosed interiors of slave ships, or the cannibal country of Europeans—the local cannibals of the legitimate trade operated in the bush near isolated farms and hamlets (fakay). Farms, Richards (2000) observes, are always somewhat hazardous places for children during busy times of year, when chimpanzees may snatch unsupervised babies left at the edge of the bush, and "mug" children running an errand between farm and village; but during the Atlantic trade and the legitimate trade, he suggests, these hazards of agrarian life took on a far more sinister significance (2000: 85). Indeed, the accounts gathered by Kalous confirm that it was the remote fakay in which slaves and other dependents cultivated cash crops for their patrons that became particular sites of disappearance from which women and children—especially slaves' children—would vanish under suspicious circumstances ("I came to the town and you made me go back to the farm: look how people have now caught my son" [Kalous 1974: 127; see also 43, 97, 121, 141, 224, 271]). Collecting palm kernels—the principal crop of the legitimate trade at that time—became a task of particular dread ("No one can be enter into the bush or field under the palm trees for the purpose of getting the Kernels" [34; see also 40]). Likewise, the routes of transport along which these and other products were carried to the Colony became conduits for stalking human leopards and deadly "alligator canoes" ("the brooks and high ways are inaccessible unless under guard with guns and cutlasses" [218; see also 69, 70, 189–90]).

The bush, the roads, and the navigable rivers, as we saw in chapter 2, had long been part of a landscape of death and disappearance during the Atlantic trade. But now this threat was transformed, as the spatial separation between disappearance "here" and acts of cannibalism in a European "there" had collapsed; now, in addition to catching their prey, the "cannibals" carried out their wealth-producing disassemblage of the human body "here." Instead of Atlantic conversions of human bodies into foreign wealth across the ocean, the legitimate trade's transactions between Colony and hinterland involved comparable conversions "at home," turning familiar places into sites of visceral extraction. Cannibals no longer abducted their prey to another world; now they walked among ordinary humans, transforming the known world—just as they themselves had become transformed—through processes of grotesque production and consumption.

The animal predators that the cannibals became—leopards, crocodiles, and chimpanzees—are, Richards (1996a; 2000) points out, the only animals in the upper Guinea forests that will stalk and eat or mutilate humans. Richards also suggests that peoples' experiences of these predators were changed by the legitimate commerce, given that the expansion in trade in forest products and the swelling river traffic led to increased human encroachment upon these animals' respective habitats. There are further reasons why these animals were prominent in the occult imagination during the political-economic transformations of the legitimate trade. In Temne chiefdoms, for instance, leopards are "royal" animals to whom the chief is sometimes compared (in coronations, for example), and hunters are obliged to give the skin, teeth, and claws of a leopard they kill to the chief of the chiefdom in which it is caught. In a sense, then, the chief is already a "human leopard"—but one whose power and stealth is supposed to protect and benefit his subjects. The transformative leopardskin clothing described for human leopards ("the leopard skin . . . covered his whole face and was tied down at the back"; "a cap and jacket of leopard skin"; "a leopard skin . . . from his neck to about his knees" [Kalous 1974: 55, 58, and 62]) would thus seem to suggest the presence of chiefly power turned rogue.

As for crocodiles, Richards (2000) presents the intriguing argument that they may index the relationship between traders and chiefs. He was told (in a Mende-speaking locality) that the smaller broad-nosed crocodile in upland forest streams is "mother's brother" to the more dangerous Nile crocodile of the larger rivers toward the coast—a kinship terminology that, he argues, suggests the historical relationship established through marriage between the chief and Mande merchants involved in the slave trade (2000: 94). I would add that this image of a kinship connection between coastal and upriver predators may also recall the intermarriages between chiefs' families and their European "strangers"—with the latter, remember, typically settled by the rivers and plying the waterways upstream for slaves to deliver to the coast during the Atlantic trade. While these kin ties might have "domesticated" the strangers, they also integrated the chiefs into predatory commercial flows down the waterways.

Chimpanzees, for their part, are known both by rural Sierra Leoneans and by primatologists, according to Richards (2000), for their occasional but serious attacks on young, vulnerable humans—"mugging" children, snatching babies, and sometimes biting victims on or near the genitals. Such behavior, Richards suggests, is disturbingly reminiscent of that of the raiders who, for several centuries, kidnapped young people in the Sierra Leone hinterland and sold them into slavery:[21] "It is not surprising," he writes, "that when an unsupervised child running an errand on a lonely forest path is 'mugged' by a chimpanzee the event evokes a strong folk memory of the process through which farm children disappeared into slavery" (2000: 85). In chapter 2, remember, Pa Kaper Bana made an intriguingly similar connection, describing the fighting, "angry" people of the First World who had seized children and sold them:

RS: *Those people of the First World, were they different from us?*

PKB: *They were like chimpanzees. If you look around, the ones you see of that First World, they were people who had hair on their skin, like the chimpanzee. They were not of the same height as us. The first people were short, short, short, short. But you could not confront them. That is why K-uru covered their world.*

Thus not only do chimpanzee attacks trigger incidental memories of fighters who emerge from the bush to carry off children, but the memory of those fighters has also been reworked in the image of the chimpanzee. And just as the *"short, short, short, short"* people described by Pa Kaper Bana are known for their violent emergence from the bush during elections, so too are human chimpanzees, according to a recent story in the Freetown newspaper *Concord Times* cited by Richards (2000: 101, n. 25). In these contemporary images of bush-dwelling "short people" and human chimpanzees, the violence of postcolonial politics and the memory of human commodification by chiefs and big traders are woven together.

Divining Leopards   In several cases, human leopard, crocodile, and (later) chimpanzee accusations were made in the context of rivalries between chiefs and wealthy traders: the trader Kiyelleh, remember, claimed that Bay Simera had had him accused of being an "alligator" because this chief envied Kiyelle's wealth. To control the process of conviction, certain chiefs now called divinations to find human leopards and crocodiles among their subjects in a new variant of the witchfinding divinations that chiefs had long controlled during the Atlantic trade (Kalous 1974: 77, 194, 196–97, 204, 218–19, 221).[22] Given that the export slave trade was no longer viable, these chiefs did not enslave and sell those identified by the diviners but instead seized the accused's property and slaves, fined their kin "according to [the accused's] rank and fortune" (214), and in some cases had those convicted burned to death (the latter finally causing the colonial authorities to intervene).[23] These chiefs thereby not only increased their wealth but also eliminated their rivals.

Yet as we have seen, chiefs were themselves accused at least as much as they accused others—and their accusers were not only their wealthy rivals. Many dependents became witnesses against their powerful patrons in the colonial courts, thereby using the colonial government for their own purposes— turning it, perhaps, into a kind of colonial diviner they could use to make visible the predatory acts of chiefs and big men. "People are ready to come forward with these charges on the slightest provocation," wrote a District Commissioner in 1931 (Kalous 1974: 66). While the colonial authorities placed emphasis on their own benign intervention in these cases, we also need to recognize the agency of those who enabled (and often initiated) this intervention by recounting to colonial agents their narratives of human leopards and crocodiles, cannibalism and wealth, human sacrifice and bad medicines. Many slaves denounced their owners (225): an Assistant District Commissioner in Moyamba complained that "the only people who were prepared to come forward and give evidence were Mendi slaves" (16).[24] In some cases slaves accused their masters of having compelled them to give up their children to pay a "debt" ("If we have any child, it belongs to you and I cannot refuse you" [139]; "As you are my slave I will take it by force" [120]). Nor were slaves the only dependents who testified about predatory patrons (although it should be remembered that domestic slavery was often subsumed within the idiom of kinship): a witness claimed that the "uncle" on whose farm he worked gave him the choice of either providing his stepson or being slaughtered himself (122). In so doing, dependents sometimes risked being arrested themselves, but even then they were able to make graphic confessions that subsumed their own actions within the malevolent agency of their patrons ("Pa Neng . . . came back to own that he was guilty . . . that it was Bai Sherbro who had always sent him to practice the catching of people in the shape of an alligator" [80]).

The Localizing of Cannibals   In these accusations and confessions, wealthy patrons (or their lackeys) are situated within a moral discourse of witchcraft. Some of these accounts—especially in Temne-speaking areas—are explicit depictions of acts of witchcraft that take place beyond ordinary human embodiment ("it [the victim] was there in the form of a spirit"; "Pa Lamina's spirit was inside the leopard" [Kalous 1974: 89, 231]), and by implication in dreams (see chapter 7 and Shaw 1992).[25] More usually, however, these accounts suggest concrete translations of these ideas of witchcraft: acts ordinarily understood as taking place in dreams and "in spirit" are fully materialized in the waking actions of malefactors in the visible human world. Thus instead of (or as well as) shape-shifting into a leopard, human leopards don leopard skins and wield "leopard knives." Instead of invisibly consuming their victims' blood and internal organs in dreams, these "cannibals" take blood and internal organs in fully enfleshed form to create or "feed" wealth-producing medicines. And instead of belonging to a witches' association in which each member incurs an obligation (a "debt") to provide a victim in turn for a nocturnal feast in the other world (failing which the member will be killed and consumed instead), the malefic ritual actions of human leopards are located within a secret "leopard society" with an identical "debt" arrangement, and whose nocturnal feasts are held in this world.

Accounts of materialized witchcraft, of apparently visible, tangible, and this-worldly acts of cannibalism, effectively translated witchcraft into a "language of the concrete" that was more closely commensurable with the language of "physical evidence" in the colonial courts. Yet this concrete language in human leopard accounts seems never to have been fully matched by concrete objects and events in the material world, much to the puzzlement of colonial officials who were confronted with corpses but were never able to find the paraphernalia of leopard, crocodile, and chimpanzee disguises. These objects had been described again and again in accusations and confessions and were sometimes even constructed as models: "No District Commissioner has ever been able to get hold of the Leopard dress, or knives," wrote the Acting Attorney General, "altho' models have been made from descriptions given by the accomplices" (Kalous 1974: 289; and see 58). The material reality of the submarine "alligator canoe" was equally mysterious. Accounts of this vessel in the 1950s depict a fabulous but deadly vehicle with mysterious powers of mobility and a simultaneously animal and machine-like appearance. Covered with animal skins (85) and fitted with a hinged glass front "like the glass windows of a car" (82, 72–73), it moved without paddles, and its occupants inside were able to "travel all night" under the water (84). "How air is supplied, or how the hinged door can be open or closed when the canoe is under water, I cannot attempt to explain," mused one official (73). And an Acting District Commissioner investigating a human chimpanzee killing in the town of Mange found nothing when he "searched the abode of the spirit (Krifi) which was supposed to keep [the chimpanzee skin]" (88): presumably he searched an area of bush in the belief that he was looking for an ordinary animal pelt, unaware that he should probably have been searching a more other-worldly "abode of the spirit," either the invisible Place of Spirits (ro-sɔki) or the Place of Witches (ro-seroŋ). The "language of the concrete" thus proved extremely effective in mobilizing the literal-minded colonial "diviner."

But one important aspect of human leopard accounts does not fit this picture of cannibalism as a form of witchcraft. The killings that activate "bad" medicines are often identified as sacrifices, a ritual form that does not, to my knowledge, ordinarily figure in understandings of witches' invisible activities. Ordinarily, animal sacrifices (as-athka) such as those I attended in Temne-speaking communities from the late 1970s to the early 1990s are open, transparent, daytime events that—ideally, if not always in practice—connect kin and affines together when participants eat the cooked meat of the sacrificed chicken or sheep. The life (aŋ-ŋesəm) of the victim, embodied in the blood, heart, and liver, is released and consumed by the appropriate spirits and ancestors, as well as by God (K-uru), engendering the beneficial flow of (for example) abundant rice and healthy children to promote the continuity and collective prosperity of the lineage or town.

In contrast, the accounts of sacrifice that form part of human leopard accusations describe the ritual offering of humans by those who are, in a sense, "animals." In hidden and nocturnal cabals in the bush, these ritual participants rob households, lineages, and settlements (sometimes their own) of their younger members—a theft that has especially serious consequences for upland rice-farming communities whose subsistence depends upon the coordination of labor. Richards points out: "By stealing young people kidnappers undermine community capacity for labour sharing. Parents are left to scratch their plots unaided. The social order based on subsistence agriculture comes under threat" (2000: 84). Thus instead of promoting the growth of healthy rice and children in the community, sacrifice by human leopards robs the victim's family and community of their capacity to feed, perpetuate, and renew themselves. Severed from the living body, the life concentrated in the sacrificial victim's blood, heart, and liver—life that would have sustained the growth of the child into a productive (and reproductive) adult—now produces a flow of power and money for chiefs and big men. Meanwhile, severed from its young member, the victim's family is left with a diminished capacity to produce and reproduce its future.

If this aspect of human leopards' noxious ritual actions represents a departure from ideas of witchcraft, however, it also represents a convergence with earlier stories of the Atlantic trade in which "the white man" buys a captive "either to offer him as a sacrifice to his God, or to devour him as food" (Matthews 1966: 152). Thus while accounts of human leopards play off understandings of witchcraft, they also, I suggest, play off ideas of wealth-producing but perverted forms of sacrifice from a prior "cannibalistic" trade. But in contrast to the indeterminate, almost abstracted Atlantic sacrifices by generic white men, the sacrificial transactions of the legitimate trade are given detailed depiction. Specific offerings are enumerated ("the Murri men had told them to pull some 'salaka.' . . . a black cow, a black fowl and a crazy person" [Kalous 1974: 163]); particular body parts ("the genitals are cut away and used in preparation of fetish" [66]) are used to prepare specific medicines ("they had a fetish . . . the Bofima and it was customary to make human sacrifices to it" [112]); and named ritual specialists prescribe the sacrifice and prepare the medicines ("Abdulai said to him: 'You want a strong mind to get that and the only way to get it is to kill your daughter or your sister and get the blood'" [137]).

Thus just as the invisible cannibalism of witches was made tangible in accounts of the fully embodied cannibalism of human leopards, crocodiles, and chimpanzees, the remote human sacrifices enacted by Europeans left their Atlantic locations and were incorporated, in human leopard accusations, into a local corpus of clandestine ritual practice controlled by chiefs, big men, and diviners. The Atlantic trade's replacement by the legitimate trade resulted, then, not in the disappearance of "cannibals" but in their becoming more *locally* embedded.

Conclusion: The Past as Prism   In studies of memory, an overwhelming focus on the past's mutability and appropriability has tended to obscure the mutability of the present—the ways in which memories form a prism for the configuring of present experience. Thus in certain parts of Africa, Atlantic memories may be sedimented within colonial encounters. I have argued that in the Sierra Leone hinterland, Atlantic stories that Europeans devoured slaves and sacrificed them to their God were reconfigured during the legitimate trade through accusations that chiefs and traders devoured, sacrificed, and made their dependents into medicines. The fact that people told stories connecting both of these forms of commerce to the ritual consumption of human life is not, however, to imply that accounts of human leopards and crocodiles were "but modern versions of eighteenth-century slaves' beliefs that they were being transported to the New World to be eaten" (White 2000: 15). But, turning around White's characterization of the colonial refashioning of witchcraft elsewhere in Africa (21), I would argue that while ideas about the "cannibalistic" nature of both trades were not constant, they had continuity. Human leopards and crocodiles were, I suggest, just as much about the past as about their colonial present—about the cannibalism of the Atlantic trade (memories of which, remember, live on to this day) that formed a lens through which the predatory and extractive relationships of the legitimate trade could be evaluated. Images and accusations of colonial-era cannibalism that were shaped through this prism of memory, moreover, contributed just as surely to the making of a transformed world as did colonial imperatives for the production and transport of goods and as did the world markets in which these goods circulated. Human leopards, crocodiles, and chimpanzees did not merely clothe colonial transformations in figurative cultural images; these images of entrepreneurial were-animals helped form the colonial world itself.

9

The Politician and the Diviner

As he went deeper into the city, passing the new houses and the sky-scrapers and the grand highways of Independence, I knew the price he felt of containing and unleashing such powers, saturating the air with such demonic insurgencies. Ben Okri, "Night of the Political Magicians," in *Songs of Enchantment*

Colonel Akongo decided to drive to the coast to clear his mind of all doubts about the justice of his decision, and to feed on the contempt that he felt for the ruling class. He laughed when he recalled that incongruously with their three-piece woollen suits and the Sunday charade of going to church, they were the biggest practitioners of sorcery. Syl Cheney-Coker, *The Last Harmattan of Alusine Dunbar*

These excerpts from Okri's and Cheney-Coker's visionary novels refer to popular ideas about politicians, "sorcery," and "magicians" that form the subject of this chapter. In Okri's *Songs of Enchantment* (1993: 144–70), the "political magician," a blind master sorcerer who covers the city streets with dead butterflies, generates earthquakes, and causes collective hallucinations, unleashes his powers of "demonic insurgency" on behalf of the Party of the Rich. Okri's imagery is drawn from a widespread idiom in contemporary West Africa in

247

which impoverishment, corruption, and political domination are represented as forms of terrible enchantment. In popular Sierra Leonean political critiques, this idiom of enchantment usually takes the form of rumors about malignant ritual arrangements between diviners and politicians or other "big persons" —arrangements which, as Cheney-Coker has one of his characters express it in the excerpt above, make members of "the ruling class . . . the biggest practitioners of sorcery" (1990: xv).

At one level, as many scholars have pointed out for other parts of Africa, contemporary images of elite sorcerers, political magicians, and such creatures as zombies, witches, vampires, and cannibals speak to the contradictions of modernity and its occult politics and economies (Auslander 1993; Bastian 1992: 148–208; Ciekawy and Geschiere 1998; Comaroff and Comaroff 1999; Geschiere 1997; Masquelier 2000; Meyer 1998b; Weiss 1996). Such images are usually located in a postcolonial age of violence, disjuncture, corrosion, decay, and grotesque excess. At another level, however, these ruptures and dissolutions also reinscribe colonial ruptures and sustain their memory. As Dirks observes, "the sedimented effects and legacies of colonial power [live] on in postcolonial societies and psyches" (1992a: 7; see also Cole 1998; De Boeck 1998; Ranger 1996; Stoller 1995; Werbner 1998). But as I argue in the previous chapter, we might also ask how in certain parts of Africa, experiences of colonialism were themselves configured by "the sedimented effects and legacies" of the Atlantic slave trade.

While in chapter 8 I explored how rumors of the Atlantic cannibalism of Europeans were reconfigured in later accounts and images of human leopards, in this chapter I trace the reworking of human leopard accounts as colonial memories in the Sierra Leone of the early 1990s. Experiences of postcoloniality are simply the most recent of the contradictions of modernity to be commented on through images of cannibalism that have been continually refashioned, creating stories that—like modernity itself—are both "new" and "old." Mnemonic images of cannibalism were not, however, the only form of remembering that had salience in the early years of the last decade of the twentieth century.

Ecstatic Renovation: Remembering the *Amistad*

But the president had turned the country into a joke, plundered it and shared the loot with his friends. . . . Now, the postal stamps and monetary bills, the ones with the head of the president, the ones that no one wanted to buy but had to buy, were infested with the stench of the garbage that the country had become. . . . He consulted a fortune teller who told him: "Look at the country. It is experiencing a plague worse than the one that happened thirty years ago, when the crippled soldiers came home from the British campaign in Burma." Syl Cheney-Coker, *The Last Harmattan of Alusine Dunbar*

Hands-In-Motion,
Minds-At-Work,
Rise-Oh-You-Kindred-For
EXTATIC RENOVATION!   DUS (Isah Kabbia), rap lyric[1]

On April 29, 1992, a coup ended the reign of the All People's Congress (APC), the ruling party that had presided over twenty-four years of Sierra Leone's economic and political decline. While the economy had deteriorated during those years of the APC, going into a steep downward spiral when the government hosted the Organization of African Unity Conference (OAU) at immense cost in 1980,[2] the state's apparatus of control had been fortified by building up the army and paramilitary and by consolidating a one-party system (see, e.g., Zack-Williams 1989). A decade after the OAU Conference, however, the national coffers were empty; even the military was starved of funds. The real workings of Sierra Leone, meanwhile, were concealed behind the facade of the state in a politics of shadows (Reno 1995) that ultimately became an impossible illusion to sustain. When, in 1991, the rebel war broke out in the southern and eastern parts of the country, Sierra Leonean soldiers often found themselves having to fight without equipment, salary, or rations. A year later, a group of young army officers returned to Freetown, seized power from the APC, and established the National Provisional Ruling Council (NPRC).

As we saw at the end of the postscript to chapter 6, this coup, the rebel war that catalyzed it, and the reign of the new regime that it inaugurated had tragic and chilling consequences. And later, when it became clear that this regime was not only unable to end the rebel war but was also guilty of corruption and crime itself, disillusion was registered in such readings of the NPRC acronym as *Na Pikin Rule Contri* ("children are running the country") and *Natin Pass Repeated Corruption* ("nothing beyond repeated corruption"). But in the honeymoon period of popular (but guarded) optimism following the regime change of April 1992, hope was focused upon the youthfulness of the army officers who formed the new National Provisional Ruling Council and in particular upon its chairman, Captain Valentine Strasser. At twenty-seven,

Strasser was the world's youngest head of state. Strasser's NPRC proclaimed a "revolution" to weed out the corruption of the past, creating two Commissions of Inquiry to investigate the origins of the property and personal fortunes amassed by politicians and senior civil servants in the old APC regime. This process of purging and renewal wsa also concretely realized in the urban landscape of Freetown and other cities through the repainting of public buildings, the repair of neglected roads, the introduction of a monthly street-cleaning day for civilians and, five months later, the restoration of a regular electricity supply to Freetown and other major urban centers that had until then suffered a virtually continuous blackout for several years.

At the end of 1992, however, the new government discovered an attempted countercoup involving members of the old regime, and it executed seventeen alleged conspirators on December 29. The prospect of the return of the APC government was so dreaded, at this point, that support for the NPRC increased. Shortly afterwards, nationalist wall paintings, roadside sculptures, and other forms of street art—part of an informal urban renewal dubbed "Extatic Renovation" by DUS, a rap artist whose lyrics open the beginning of this section—started to appear in different parts of Freetown, created mostly by working-class youth:

> During the emotionally charged period at the beginning of the new year, when the NPRC was perceived as under threat, working class youths in Freetown suddenly took to the streets to support the revolution. They formed themselves into neighbourhood "youth organizations," and set about patching streets, cleaning gutters, making planters, and painting curbs and median strips on a massive scale throughout the city. . . . Soon afterwards, they expanded their efforts into patriotic art celebrating the revolution—wall paintings, cement sculptures, public monuments, and road-side decorations in the shape of military weapons painted in army camouflage. (Opala 1994: 4)

As part of their "ecstatic renovation," these youth organizations took up the story of the *Amistad* revolt. Wall paintings and cement statues of Sengbe Pieh, the Mende captive who led the uprising, proliferated in Freetown; young artists copied Nathaniel Jocelyn's 1839 portrait of Pieh, often transforming the generic, toga-like dress in which he was painted into a Sierra Leonean war shirt, country cloth, or a chief's formal gown (Opala 1994: 11, 21, 24, 31) (plate 18). Just a few years earlier, however, the story of Sengbe Pieh and the *Amistad* events of 1839–42 had been virtually unknown in Sierra Leone. While the *Amistad* has been the topic of numerous books in the U.S., it was neither included in Sierra Leone's official history, nor in school curricula, nor in oral histories (Osagie 1997: 66). Its celebration as public memory in 1992–93 was the outcome of the dovetailing of several developments.

First an American anthropologist, Joseph Opala, introduced Sengbe Pieh into the popular domain in a 1986 article for a Freetown newspaper as part of a series on key figures in Sierra Leone's history (Opala 1994: 8–9, 36, n. 9). He also included Sengbe Pieh—and, importantly, Nathaniel Jocelyn's portrait—in a book he fostered, *Sierra Leone Heroes* (1987), and he highlighted the *Amistad* story in a course he taught from 1986 to 1991 at the University of Sierra Leone's Fourah Bay College, entitled "Art, Anthropology, and National Consciousness." Second, the playwright and theater director Charlie Haffner was a student in this class in 1986; inspired by Opala's lectures on the *Amistad* revolt, Haffner wrote a play about it, *Amistad Katakata*, and for five years he traveled around Sierra Leone performing it with his theater group, the Freetong Players. Third, just as the NPRC coup unfolded in April 1992, a symposium on the *Amistad* happened to be taking place at Freetown's City Hall, with a twenty-foot model of the ship sitting on the city hall steps: youths celebrating the regime change took this model ship and "paraded it through the streets, chanting praises to the soldiers and Sengbe Pieh" (Opala 1994: 10). And fourth, Strasser, the new head of state, was in the U.S. for medical treatment in September 1992, and by coincidence he was able to attend the unveiling of a new statue of Sengbe Pieh in Hartford, Connecticut, amidst much publicity (Opala 1994: 9–10; Osagie 1997: 75–80).

Thus one-hundred-fifty years after the *Amistad* captives returned, their forgotten story was (through a remarkable series of events and coincidences) given compelling significance as an emblem of the nation's emergence from the long night of APC rule. This was a classic instance of the politics of the past in the present: as Osagie writes, "Pieh's ascendancy to national recognition and identification has rebounded to memory because of its present usefulness in the new political environment" (1997: 80). But in contrast to this movement from forgetting to discursive public remembering—a remembering in which the captives' Middle Passage experience was inscribed with the concerns of the present—other, less discursive memories of the slave-trading past mediated the meanings and experience of the NPRC coup.

Demonic Insurgency   The tropes of renewal, cleansing, and generational succession of "ecstatic renovation" were accompanied by images of what Okri calls "demonic insurgency." Following the failed countercoup and the executions of December 1992, Lt. Karefu Kargbo announced in a statement on a

BBC World Service broadcast that part of the evidence for the countercoup attempt was a *"written agreement"* between the conspirators and an *"illiterate herbalist"* (BBC "Focus on Africa," Jan. 4, 1993). This written agreement was placed in paradoxical counterpoint to the "illiteracy" of the "herbalist"—a term that usually designates a specialist who divines, heals, and makes medicines based upon knowledge of local plants and relationships with local spirits. The use of the term "herbalist" reveals that the ritual agent in question was not a Muslim specialist using techniques of divination and medicine based upon Arabic writing and literate Islamic knowledge, but one who has often been regarded (especially in Freetown) as "backward." The reference to the *"illiterate herbalist"* thus suggests that not only did the alleged plotters place themselves (and had planned to place the country) in the domain of sinister ritual forces, but also that these were forces of regression and degeneration. Likewise, when a powerful civil servant from the APC regime was investigated by the Commission of Inquiry, rumors flew that those who searched his property had found a huge black snake—an embodiment of an evil medicine or spirit behind his power—and that this snake had been fed with human beings. His capacity to "prey upon" others in his former position was, through these rumors, given a powerful double meaning.

Such accounts of "demonic" supernatural consumption by or on behalf of those in power provide forceful images of the perversion of political morality and of dislocations in the moral economy (Auslander 1993; Barber 1982; Bastian 1992: 148–208; Comaroff and Comaroff 1999; Geschiere 1997; Marshall 1995; Masquelier 2000; Meyer 1995 and 1998b; White 2000). As Marshall observes of similar discourses in Nigeria, postcolonial political consciousness is constructed through understandings of power in which the supernatural is an extremely important idiom. "To align oneself with the wrong sort of supernatural and material powers," she writes, "and to regulate one's conduct according to the wrong set of precepts opens up the space in which the 'failure of the nation' is manifested" (1995: 247).

While "illiterate," non-Muslim diviners receive particular opprobrium, *all* diviners—including Muslim ritual specialists—are subject to public disdain as "backward." Ideas about the "backwardness" of divination (ideas that, as we have seen, developed during nineteenth century colonization and missionization) form the flip side of a discourse that constitutes national politics as part of a modern, rational, "enlightened" public sphere incommensurable with occult practices. Politicians who consult diviners and hire them to gain office, then, are deemed not only corrupt but also debased, perverting the proper operations of government with degenerate acts of "fetishism." Yet these representations of politicians and their sinister diviners are, I will argue, much more than internalizations of colonial images of "backward" African superstitions.

In popular critiques of the corrupt wealth and dominance of those in the old APC regime, the latter's wealth and power were often perceived to be linked to evil medicines prepared by "bad" diviners or to compacts with malefic spirits. These critiques recapitulated colonial-era accounts of extractive chiefs in league with demonic diviners, preying on their dependents as human leopards. Those few who, by enriching themselves through dubious means, had greatest access to the products and privileges of modernity in the form of Western consumer goods and high-tech international mobility, were thereby associated with images that have come to carry both meanings of "backwardness" and memories of the malignant spiritual powers behind rapacious leaders.

As the Commissions of Inquiry set up by Sierra Leone's new NPRC government continued to probe into the means of enrichment of many of those formerly in power, the *Globe* newspaper in Freetown for the week of August 22, 1992, carried the front-page banner headline "JUJU FOR COMMISSION." In the article beneath it, the author described how two women—one a bank employee—had been seen as they stood at the edge of Government Wharf, chanting *"unknown words"* and throwing a small packet of folded papers into the sea. Afterwards a boy retrieved the papers from the water, finding sheets of letterheaded business notepaper filled with magic squares of Arabic words and numerals, tied together with white thread and *"perfumed with a strange smelling scent."* Such diagrams, as we have seen, are constructed by Muslim specialists (known as mori-men, alfa-men, or marabu in Sierra Leone Krio) in order to resolve the problems and fulfil the desires of their clients, and they are activated by ritual words and actions that these specialists prescribe. When such actions include the throwing of ritual materials into water—especially the sea—this often embodies the intention for something to remain hidden, to be lost in the depths of a vast and impenetrable medium. The author of the *Globe* article interpreted the ritual on the wharf as an attempt to use a ritual prescribed by a diviner to conceal illicit enrichment from the Commissions of Inquiry, and he went on to assert a further link between the power and affluence of the former regime and invidious forms of ritual practice:

> As the commission gets underway with cases of corruption being exposed everyday, business people, politicians and government officials have been doing all they can to cover

up their nefarious activities. This has not stopped some from seeking the aid of juju men, Marabouls [sic] and Medicinemen so as to save their skin. Under the past regime it was a common occurrence to sacrifice human being or to bury live cows for their political and business success. Thus it was not a strange sight to discover a child with her private organs missing. "We have been watching a lot of them coming here to throw juju in the sea. Since the overthrow" one observer at the government wharf told the Globe. (*Globe*, August 22, 1992)

Like the human leopard accusations of the legitimate trade, such rumors concerning the use of human body parts (especially reproductive organs, and especially those of children and young women) make powerful statements about the appropriation of others' productive and reproductive capacities. In the *Globe* article, this ritual appropriation of victims' lives is said to have taken place through diviners' prescriptions of human sacrifice and the use of body parts for the enrichment and political success of their "big" clients. Members of the APC government itself, the journalist implies, derived their power from such hidden acts of ritual murder and thereby promoted the conditions in which these grotesque appropriations flourished (cf. Meyer 1998b: 28–29).

Closely linked to these tropes of perverted production are tropes of excessive consumption. In his writings on the "banality of power" in postcolonies, Mbembe examines how grotesque appetites for food, drink, sex, and other pleasures are used both by those who wield political power *and* by those subordinated to them in multivocal images that go beyond such simple dichotomies as popular "resistance" or "compliance" to regimes of domination (1992). These tropes of ingestion, digestion, and penetration are, as Mbembe makes clear, not restricted to Africa but are characteristic of regimes of power more generally: witness recurring stories of the greedy or lascivious behavior of European kings and princes (both past and present), as well as recent political scandals about sex or alcohol that have involved Bill Clinton, the Kennedys, Yeltsin, and countless others.

Similar images have been a prominent feature of popular Sierra Leonean critiques of corruption and domination. In 1987, for instance, a popular nickname for President Momoh was "Zanghaliwa," the title of a hit record that came to stand for a popular rumor (Fyle 1997: 173). One night, according to the version of the rumor I heard, Momoh stayed inappropriately late at a party: fading older diplomats were unable to escape because the head of state was enjoying himself and refused to leave. When his aides finally insisted on his departure, Momoh got up to leave but was unable to resist dancing yet again when someone put "Zanghaliwa" on the turntable. "The implication here," as Fyle observes, "is of fickle character, given more to ephemeral pleasures and incapable of maintaining the dignity of being president" (173).

During the 1980s, the APC government's clampdown on public criticism in the press meant that political critiques were expressed indirectly, often in the form of songs, rumors, and nicknames such as "Zanghaliwa" (Fyle 1997). They thus became "public secrets" that sought to expose what lay beneath the official rhetoric and surface appearances of those in power (Meyer 1998b: 25). After the 1992 regime change, however, the "public secrets" that had circulated informally for years about the gluttonous and womanizing proclivities of the former president now became public revelations in the print media, often in political cartoons. One such cartoon (plate 19), which appeared in the *New Shaft* newspaper (July 28–August 3, 1992) in Freetown three months after the coup, combines the idiom of unregulated consumption with that of the supernatural. Here a man wearing the professional male attire of the Western suit and tie sits on a mat, surrounded by several wads of money. Next to him a man in a long white gown usually identified as Muslim dress sits on a mat with Muslim prayer beads to his right, gazing into a book that lies open in front of him: this is a Muslim diviner consulting one of his Arabic divination texts. *"Tell me alphaman,"* says the man in the Western suit, *"I still believe in you, why did you deceive Momoh?"* *"I did my best,"* the diviner replies, *"but he broke one of my laws not to drink palmwine for one day."* These "laws" are prohibitions that accompany the use of powerful medicines, and that, if not observed, can either make the medicine ineffective or turn its power against its user. The former president, the cartoon suggests, was not only in the habit of using diviners and their ominous medicines to maintain his position but was also so incapable of bodily restraint—even for a single day—that in the end he undermined his own sources of supernatural support.

After Sierra Leone's 1992 regime change, then, both the forces of the old APC government and the forces that threatened to overthrow the new one were crystallized in popular (and occasionally official) images that reworked a vividly remembered colonial-era discourse of ritually mediated rapacity. If the obscene appetites and grotesque forms of consumption examined by Mbembe embody the banality of power in postcolonies, these demonizing images of mercenary diviners with cryptic texts, of the insurgency of *"illiterate herbalists,"* man-eating spirit-snakes, human sacrifice, and the ritual plunder of human bodies are, in contrast, anything but banal.[3] They too, as I shall detail in the next section, refer to forms of excessive consumption that identify postcolonial domination, but they do so as lurid supernatural counterparts of Mbembe's examples, underscoring the harm such consumption does rather than merely deriding it.

Living with One's Sorcerer

> But . . . during the reign of a despicable government that had embarrassed him by jailing its critics and hanging some of its opponents, General Masimiara had wondered at the docility of the people, and at their ability to receive the endless instruments of pain.   Syl Cheney-Coker, *The Last Harmattan of Alusine Dunbar*

In Sierra Leone, processes of "eating" and incorporation—especially the incorporation of medicines (often prepared by diviners and related ritual specialists)—are central to the constitution of power, both within and outside the arena of state politics. Writing of understandings of power and hierarchy in a community in southeastern Sierra Leone, Ferme (1992: 229–81) describes the importance of a "big person's" capacity for expansion and circulation beyond the boundaries of the body through, for instance, the generous distribution of food and money among dependents. These and other forms of agency through extrabodily extension derive, she emphasizes, from processes of incorporation such as the assimilation of dependents (and their labor) into one's household, and the bodily absorption of hidden sources of power in medicines. As long as the latter processes of consumption are balanced by generosity and other benevolent forms of extension to their dependents and supporters, big persons are understood as acting within moral limits. Yet as we have seen, both in the colonial human leopard scare and in the tropes of "demonic insurgency" following the 1992 coup, many stories circulate that attribute the power of big persons to the most extreme form of "consumption" of all: the ritual use of body parts in the preparation of medicines that confer power and wealth. In these stories, medicines derived from vital organs are described as making political leaders "shine" (Richards 1996a: 143–45), such that "when politicians . . . displayed unusual oratorical skills, when they seemed particularly charming and persuasive, . . . bystanders often wondered what made them so attractive" (Ferme 1999: 170).

Similar claims about the derivation of power are widespread elsewhere, especially in relation to the modern state, its apparatus, its leaders, and its urban elites (Austen 1993; Bastian 1993; Geschiere 1997; Geschiere with Fisiy 1994; Meyer 1998b; Rowlands and Warnier 1988; White 2000). In contemporary Cameroon, according to Rowlands and Warnier, "the public recognition of personal possession of (socialised) occult powers is an integral component in the evaluation of success and achievement . . . to the extent that the acquisition of wealth, achievement of high office and the possession of high status consumable goods cannot be conceived without them" (1988: 129). The socialization of occult powers referred to consists, once again, in acts of generosity and the circulation of benefits by the wealthy and powerful (124). Such occult capacities may indeed be approved of because of the "positive value [perceived] in the fact that some figures of authority have the mystical power to ward off the malignancy of others" (Austen 1993: 91). Control of such forces gives powerful patrons the very necessary capacity to defend their dependents *against* witchcraft. Part of the advantage of living with one's own sorcerer, then, is that he (or she) can defend you from other sorcerers.

In Sierra Leone, a skilled balancing act is thus required of most political contenders. While the capacity for political power necessarily entails control over hidden forces, one's own mystical powers must be cast as "benevolent" in contrast to those of others: as Ferme (1999: 171) observes, certain politicians seek to enhance their reputations by hinting at their own hidden powers while at the same time spreading rumors about the far more malignant occult activities of their rivals. Yet because occult forces have also been rendered incommensurable with "modern," "rational" government in formal political discourse, politicians have both to claim and not claim mystical powers, sometimes alluding to these powers obliquely, and at other times disclaiming any belief in such "superstitions."[4]

The Politician and the Diviner   Like politicians, diviners in Sierra Leone have to tread a fine line between claiming occult powers and yet disclaiming the malefic use of such powers. The diviners I knew were specialists who, as we have already seen, not only practiced divination but also healed and prepared medicines for their clients. Some affirmed that they prepared medicines to create or sustain the power of big persons, the ingredients for which were revealed by their tutelary spirit through divination or in dreams. Once prepared, such medicines could be applied by eating or drinking them, washing with them, boiling them and inhaling the steam, rubbing them into incisions in the skin, dropping them in the eyes, wearing an undershirt soaked in them, sewing them inside a belt tied around the waist, or enclosing them in an amulet hung around the neck.

Even diviners themselves make use of stereotyped images of "bad" ritual specialists in order to underscore the differences between the latter and themselves. Pa Yamba put it this way during my 1992 visit:

> PY: *What I do is the work of God* (K-uru). *I have seen them* [the politicians and other leaders] *call big Muslim diviners* (aŋ-ləfa) *to come to this country. He says he wants power; he tells the diviner. Ah, Satan* (Sethani)! *The diviner says "I want blood." Well, I who have power, now, I call the members who are behind me, if I'm a minister. Any power I get, they will get it too. They will go and find a person to kill.*
>
> RS: *Where do the diviners come from?*
>
> PY: *Some come from Guinea, some from other countries. This work, I don't want it. It's the money of Hell* (aŋ-kala ŋa ro-yanama).

Pa Yamba thus appropriated the discourse that demonizes diviners for the purpose of his own castigation of other specialists, using it to condemn powerful foreign diviners outside Sierra Leone's borders. The latter, he suggested, are an external evil drawn in from beyond the nation's boundaries by an internal corruption within the government. These foreign diviners from Guinea (especially, he added, from the Futa Jallon area) are the modern counterparts of the Muslim strangers I discuss in chapter 3, who came and settled as ritual advisors to Temne chiefs. The "wonderful" literate Islamic knowledge of these specialists is still recognized as superior, but it is now indelibly associated with the excesses of the most corrupt and nefarious political leaders. A strong moral dualism distinguished Pa Yamba's own divinely-derived work (*"the work of God"*) from their "Satanic" activity and its diabolic reward (*"the money of Hell"*). But even these "Satanic" strangers, he pointed out, were driven by the (literally) consuming ambitions of local politicians and their followers.

Politicians and other big persons, he also explained, consume the foreign aid intended for the poorest people of Sierra Leone, diverting it for the exclusive use of their own families. *"When they send money to this country from outside for the poor people,"* he complained, *"it goes to the big people. They sit on it, and their families eat it."* Thus instead of channeling the flow of benefits to their communities, they arrest it by *"sitting on it,"* limiting its distribution to their families alone and thereby turning proper circulation into improper accumulation. For Pa Yamba, as in Bayart's (1993) and Geschiere's (1997) writings on respectively "the politics of the belly" and "the eating of the state" in contemporary Cameroon, this pattern of insatiable accumulation and consumption by politicians is itself a sign of sinister occult predation.

Pa Yamba added that although *"you can be in the government without killing"* (and claimed that he had himself enabled some politicians to do so) the government *(aŋ-koamɛŋt)* was, in fact, the source of ritual murder for medicines of power and enrichment: *"They didn't kill people before the government came. It was different, different. The first time, they didn't kill because the chief would name his successor. The competition brought the killing."* As I discuss in the previous chapter, precolonial Temne chiefs nominated their successors according to principles of rotation among ruling lineages (see Dorjahn 1960b). Ritual killing, Pa Yamba maintained, was formerly only practiced by warriors (aŋ-kurgba): *"In those days, they will ask if you have a child, and that child is given as a sacrifice* (s-athka)." The nature of contemporary political competition, by implication, makes modern politicians more like predatory warriors than like the chiefs of "the first time."

Pa Yamba, while acutely aware of his own potential as a target for suspicion, thus viewed the topic of diviners' political sacrifices through memories of warriors' predations during the nineteenth-century trade wars and of historical transformations in chiefly power and succession during the Protectorate era. He thereby added his own voice to those of others whose stories connected the APC's "eating" of the nation to the human leopards' "eating" of their dependents' futures.

Because of these memory-mediated images of diviners who perform human sacrifice and extract vital organs for their powerful clients, diviners have to use discretion in establishing and maintaining links with politicians and other big persons. On the one hand, they actively seek political patronage. During the reign of the APC regime, a government minister told me that he kept a file, labeled "Dreamers and Diviners," full of letters to the president from diviners who recounted dreams and oracular predictions of coups, assassination attempts, and other crises about which they wished to warn the head of state, and which only their professional services could avert. On the other hand, a diviner hired by a politician is in an awkward position: if he broadcasts the identity of his important client, the latter's position will be undermined; yet if no-one knows about this patronage, the diviner will not gain the reputation he seeks. The successful diviners I knew therefore displayed their accomplishments in the form of material property and modern commodities acquired with the money from a grateful client, these possessions standing metonymically for the diviner's success in his work for unnamed clients of substance. During one of my stays in Freetown, a businesswoman who had called a diviner from the Republic of Guinea to perform a sacrifice (s-athka) for her told me that I should attend because this was the head of state's diviner. *"Look at his car!"* she urged me when I asked how she knew, and parked outside the house was indeed a car so spectacular that it would have stood out on the streets of the most affluent cities in the world, let alone Freetown, where most vehicles have been ruined by years of punishment on streets filled with car-eating potholes. *"Chiefs, Ministers, Presidents,"* the diviner answered when I later asked him about his clientele, his response sufficiently vague as to conceal specific identities but sufficiently clear as to confirm his eminently successful standing.

During my first period of research, I came to know another diviner with a wide regional reputation, "Pa Ahmadu" (a pseudonym), whose success in attracting a clientele of big persons was registered in his ownership of two cemented and painted houses on the same road in a provincial town. On one of my visits to him, both of his houses had a Mercedes-Benz parked outside, flying the national flag, and inside each house was a government minister who had coincidentally come to see him at the same time. Pa Ahmadu was constantly moving from one house to the other, his pockets stuffed with banknotes, trying to keep each of his powerful clients unaware of the other's presence. One minister had come, Pa Ahmadu told me later, because he was worried about an impending government reshuffle and wanted to ensure that he would not be moved from his "fat" ministry to a "low" one.[5] The other minister, "X," emerged and, seeing me as I stood wondering whether I should go inside or not, came up to introduce himself and to find out what I was doing there. I told him that I was doing research on Temne divination, and he told me that he was merely there to accompany his brother and uncle. My unexpected presence as a European of uncertain identity—especially one who claimed an academic affiliation—necessarily invoked a context in which government and divination were antithetical. *"They believe in it,"* the minister said, referring to his brother and uncle, *"but I don't."* Afterwards, Pa Ahmadu told me that he had enabled minister X to achieve his position and that in gratitude this minister had arranged for Pa Ahmadu's street on the periphery of town to be connected to the electrical grid. A line of new electrical poles carried cables along the street and into his two houses, channelling to Pa Ahmadu and his extended family a form of power that has come to carry meanings of urban prosperity and progress.[6]

For Pa Ahmadu, as for the diviner in Freetown with the spectacular car, the connection of his houses to the power grid was a concrete realization of his own connections to power as a diviner—his ability to convert divinatory flows from powerful spirits into monetary and commodity flows from big men. But in the eyes of those who tell stories about diviners who perform human sacrifice or make "bad" medicine from body parts on behalf of politicians, such prestigious houses and cars materialize a double process of illicit and destructive "eating." Through these evil forms of sacrifice and medicine, the ritual consumption of a human being's life and potential gives the politician—and through him, the diviner "behind" his power—access to the consumption of the wealth of the state. Thus "eating" people ritually, through the mediation of a diviner, confers the capacity to "eat" people politically, through the apparatus of the state.

Conclusion   The events following Sierra Leone's 1992 change of regime focus our attention on two contrasting forms of popular memory. As Sierra Leonean youth celebrated the NPRC's 1992 takeover through their commemoration of the *Amistad* revolt, they and their parents also castigated the ousted APC regime through the lens of memories of colonial "cannibalism." Mnemonic images of links among diviners, politicians, and violent occult consumption were affirmed even by diviners as they sought to distinguish themselves from their "demonic" counterparts and to locate themselves within a frame of positive ritual power. Such images form part of a historical imagination that draws upon critiques of excesses of power and wealth from Sierra Leone's slave-trading and colonial past.

If the public memory of Sengbe Pieh and the other *Amistad* captives was defined by the standpoint and concerns of the present, the less discursively mnemonic images of predatory postcolonial leaders and their demonic diviners involved a more recursive relationship between past and present. While memories of "cannibalistic" power from earlier epochs of Sierra Leone's history mediated the experience and evaluation of postcolonial power, these memories were also reworked into late-twentieth-century images of "demonic insurgency." Instead of the appropriation of the past by the present, the very dichotomy between past and present was subverted by their mutual interpenetration, their reciprocal fashioning through memory.

In contrast to the long-forgotten *Amistad* triumph bursting into public consciousness, the less discursive memories of a modernity crystallized in the image of "cannibalistic" politicians and diviners exhibit a continuity through time even as they are continually reconfigured. Memories of violence, Sturken (1997) tells us, seem to be remembered differently from those of triumph; quoting Nietzsche, she suggests that if cultural memories are to endure they must be "burned in" (1997: 15–16; and see Cole 2001). Memories of the violence of Atlantic and colonial modernity are, I suggest, "burned into" non-discursive memories that structure the agency of postcolonial subjects as they experience the opacity and dangers of national politics and reflect upon the opportunities the modern state provides for its own forms of extraction.

These forms of memory have, unfortunately, been rendered tragically relevant during the rebel war, in which rumors circulate of the "cannibalism" of the rebels and of human sacrifices made by militia leaders.[7] Once again, such rumors are fitting expressions of the human costs of a war financed by diamonds and fought with the extracted labor of young people who are treated—by all sides—as commodified resources (Richards 1996b; 2000). Richards suggests, in fact, that the moral critique developed in "cannibalism" stories might provide a useful basis for local debates about how to limit abuses of patronage and rethink patrimonial political culture in Sierra Leone (1996b: 160–61). Whether or not such debates take place, we would do well to listen to what the discourse of "cannibalism" tells us about the memory of Atlantic commodities and the modernity of a twenty-first-century war.

Remembering Modernity

> The Governor-General then dreamt of a luxurious road over the ocean, a
> road that was fed from all parts of Africa. A macadam road of fine crushed
> diamonds and sprinkled silver and laminated topaz. A road that gave off
> the sweet songs of mermaids and nereids. Beneath this marvellous road
> there were dead children and barbarous fetishes, savage masks and bro-
> ken spines, threaded veins and matted brains, decayed men and embalmed
> women. It was a road made from the teeth and skulls of slaves, made
> from their flesh and woven intestines. . . . It was indeed a splendid road.
> It had been built by the natives, supervised by the Governor-General. . . .
> He dreamt that the natives would transport . . . resources tangible and
> intangible, on their heads, or on litters, walking on the great road, in an
> orderly single file, across the Atlantic Ocean, for three thousand miles.
> Ben Okri, *Infinite Riches*

In the above excerpt, Ben Okri's "famished road," the all-consuming road that
began as a river, now extends across the Atlantic. More than a route connecting Africa to America, it has become a chronotope that links "here" and
"there" at different points in time, a gathering-place of extractive mobility
that folds together the Atlantic slave trade, colonialism's corvée labor, and the
mining of African minerals into a palimpsest of many pasts. Like Okri's fantas-

tic road, the forms of memory I have explored in this book construct a historical imaginary in which phantoms from different layers of time flow into each
other and make hitherto invisible realities apparent.

Through the ritual memories explored in the preceding chapters, I have
tried to recover a past that differs from that delineated in positivist histories of
the slave trade. Along with others who are currently exploring historiographic
alternatives to apparently "neutral" empirical studies of human traffic (e.g.,
Austen 2001; Isichei forthcoming; Palmie 2002), I have sought to focus on
memory as social and moral practice (Lambek 1996). This, in turn, has entailed my paying attention to ritual images, rumors, dreams, visionary experiences, and other forms of expression that, to borrow Palmie's apt term, constitute "spectral evidence." Such "spectral" entities as spirit raiders from the bush,
amulets of Darkness and Closure, human crocodiles, and the invisible witch
city are, as Palmie argues for other ghostly presences in the Atlantic world,
vehicles for the "release of versions of history that . . . otherwise remain not
just 'unevidenced,' but actively rendered . . . unspeakable . . . because such a
relation goes beyond the limits of what is representable within the discursive
formation we call 'history'" (2002:12). Unlike the allegedly impartial character of a positivistically conceived history, moreover, the "versions of history"
generated by these spectral forms of memory are ineluctably moral constructions.

Speaking as they do to cultural ideas of power and its abuses, of social
community and its failures, of moral values and their transgression, such presences as witches and human leopards locate the slave trade in a moral universe that reveals the nightmarish character of the traffic in human commodities. Contrary, as Austen (2001) notes, to the recurring claim that Africans felt
(and still feel) no sense of moral responsibility concerning the sale of slaves,
the association found in parts of Africa between witchcraft and the slave trade
bespeaks the presence of a profound moral antipathy toward this trade. If we
look, for example, beyond the understandable awkwardness of Edward Ball's
Sierra Leonean interlocutors when suddenly confronted with direct questions
about their ancestors' participation in the slave trade (1998: 421–43), we find
that four centuries of slave trade have neither been erased from memory nor
insulated from critical moral scrutiny. In the Temne-speaking communities I
knew in Sierra Leone, the slave-trading past was vividly and often disturbingly
present in such practical forms of remembering as spirits of the landscape,
diviners' tutelary spirits, ritual protection, divinatory images, strereotypes of
wives as channels of incursion, practices of witchfinding, images of the witch

city, stories of human leopards, and rumors of sinister ritual ties between politicians and diviners.

These forms of remembering differ, as we have seen, from those suggested by analyses of public memory in terms of "the politics of the past in the present." Thus I have argued that memories of the Atlantic trade and European cannibals mediated the nineteenth- century experience of colonialism and human leopards, "produc[ing] history on the basis of history" (Bourdieu 1990: 56), just as memories of colonialism and human leopards mediate the experience of postcolonial violence in Sierra Leone today. This is not the unidirectional process suggested by "presentist" approaches, in which a sovereign present continually stamps its impress upon an infinitely malleable past. Instead, both past and present interfuse, shape, and mutually fashion each other, such that memories form a prism through which the present is configured even as present experience reconfigures those memories. Memory, then, works both forward and backward.

Through the forms of memory explored here, modernities past—successively, those of the Atlantic trade, the legitimate trade, and the British Protectorate—have formed a lens through which modernities present and modernities future are experienced. On this part of the west Atlantic coast of Africa, such processes of modernity as world markets, increasing social inequalities, commodity production (first slaves, then cash crops, then minerals), and the consumption of foreign imports have unfolded over the course of several centuries. These "old" forms of modernity are remembered through such forms as human leopards, witch guns, contractual relationships with river spirits, and divinatory images of roads—forms that have been taken for "tradition." That these images and ideas may not appear to be signs of modernity and its global currents is, as Piot (1999) observes, a function of an implicit neo-evolutionism in our conceptions of the modern and the global. Witch guns and divinatory roads are nevertheless the products of a history in which Atlantic circulation, Muslim Mande commerce, colonial transformation, and local cultural meanings and practices have long interfused in mutually creolizing processes that have made the Sierra Leone hinterland "as cosmopolitan as the metropole itself" (Piot 1999: 23).

Such processes of simultaneous localizing and Atlanticizing both integrated Sierra Leone into a transcontinental political-economic region and transformed this Atlantic integration through local practices and discourses (new forms of leadership, predatory warfare, indebtedness, witchfinding divination, cannibalism rumors) that shaped, defined, and commented on modernity. This latter work was not merely a local appropriation of a monolithically conceived modernity (Ong 1999: 4; Rofel 1999: 10–17). Just as "the cultures of industrial capitalism have never existed in the singular" (Comaroff and Comaroff 1993: xi), neither has any single, all-encompassing form of Atlantic modernity: Western modernities were (and are) no less culturally specific than those of Cuba, Suriname, and the Sierra Leone hinterland.

This mutability—the fact that "the institutional configuration of modernity cannot be defined in advance" (Englund and Leach 2000: 228)—is troubling for those who prefer an invariant concept of modernity against which to understand all other variations (which would be, in consequence, reduced to the status of "deviations" from a single norm). But as Bastian points out, any attempt to generate a standardized "laundry list" of features of modernity is a futile exercise, destined, like modernity itself, to be "necessarily incomplete" (forthcoming). Not only would such a classification be polythetic, with constituent elements that overlap but are not constant, highlighted in some places and minimized (or absent) in others. But the constituent elements themselves would also be inconstant: processes of commodification, to take just one example, have not shared a common trajectory in different parts of the world. In Sierra Leone, the commodification of persons as slaves usually involved their disappearance; in Cuba, commodified people became part of the "machinery" for the proto-industrial production of the commodity of sugar (Palmie 2002); and in England, mill and factory workers' consumption of the imported commodity of sugar provided the "empty calories" for the industrial production of manufactured commodities (Mintz 1985). Among these interconnected Atlantic spaces, experiences of commodities have had little more in common than a loosely shared family resemblance.

In Sierra Leone, I have argued, experiences of modernity have been configured through four hundred years of external and internal slave-trading. Even without the slave trade and its memories, it is hardly surprising in Sierra Leone's current predicament of state collapse and rebel war that the accumulation of wealth, the consumption of scarce commodities, the exchange of products on global markets, and the rise and fall of leaders who control (at least to a limited degree) these processes should be regarded with ambivalence at best. But the images that Sierra Leoneans tend to use again and again to express this ambivalence—of the political "cannibal," the diabolic diviner, the witch, and the invisible witch city—recapitulate historical connections between witchcraft and the production of human commodities, long-standing representations of slave traders as cannibals, and the human leopards and crocodiles of the legitimate trade. The remembered modernity of the slave trade, I suggest, forms a prism through which current experiences of a damaged world are refracted, revealing modernity itself in the image of the witch.

Yet modernity is never simply criticized; it is also appropriated. Because of this, some suggest that to write at all of modernity's malcontents, immoral economies, and critiques of capitalism is to impose a spurious opposition between a global capitalist juggernaut and local, oppositional cultures. Such an opposition, it is argued, fails to confront the fact that Western forms are desired and domesticated, and that histories of capitalist and colonial encounters are creatively incorporated into local cultural worlds. African agency is better served, the argument goes, by focusing on the ways in which capitalism, colonialism, or Christianity are appropriated, transformed, and rendered African.

At first sight, this is confirmed by Temne diviners' appropriations of the powerful transactions of Sierra Leone's slave-trading past. In their contractual relationships with spirit tutors, their visionary experiences of being seized, bound, and made to work, their use of Islamic techniques and literacy from powerful northern states, and their divinatory manipulation of Roads and Crossroads, diviners harness the powerful transactions of the slave-trading past. Thus dangerous but wealth-producing processes linking slave-raiding and ambush, mobility and transport, indebtedness and labor, and African hosts and European traders have been rewritten in a different script, empowering diviners to tap the power of these processes for divination. We could end on this note: through ritual memory, a violent capitalist past has been locally appropriated, domesticated, converted into power and efficacy.

But look again. Consider other memories explored in this book: the landscape of spirit raiders, men's suspicions that wives may be channels for incursion, images of the witch city, and rumors of big persons' involvement in ritual cannibalism. These tell different stories—of terror and depredation, and of the consumption of human life through its exchange for power, commodities, and money. The fact that cannibals and witches are sometimes admired (especially if they distribute some of their wealth and protect us from other predators) does not make them into unambiguously moral beings, and it does not make stories about them simple celebrations of modern wealth and power; it simply renders them morally ambivalent.

We can see, then, a duality of incorporation in which the modernity of the slave trade becomes both a source of ritual potency and a source of moral commentary. In diviners' visionary experiences and in divination techniques themselves, the violence and charged exchanges of the slave trade become memories that are harnessed for ritual power. At the same time, more popular memories realized in phantasmagoric images of diviners and politicians, witches and cannibals, subsume the processes of the slave trade within a framework of moral values, providing a basis for the critique of both these and subsequent processes—the colonial legitimate trade, the British Protectorate, the abuses of postcolonial politicians, and the depredations of the RUF rebels and other fighters in Sierra Leone. Each of these uses of memory entails the creative subsumption of global capitalist processes into local discourses, through African agency—and such agency is surely not reduced by the fact that some of these discourses are critical.

The past, Lambek (1996) points out, is imperfect. This is not only so grammatically but also in its essential incompleteness, in the sense that it is never completely over: "it continues to shape the present, even as it is distinct from it, and at the same time it is available to be addressed by the present" (Lambek 1996: 243). Over the past ten years, as Sierra Leone's rebel war spread from the Liberian border to every corner of the country, it became clear that the slave-trading past was not over. It did not end with Abolition, but continued in another form through the nineteenth-century legitimate trade, and in the invisible raids of bush spirits through the twentieth century. During the rebel war, it was brought back again in concrete form, through the plunder of towns and villages, ambushes at roads and crossroads, the seizure of (especially) young people as captives, and the use of their labor to produce commodities (diamonds, this time) to be sold on the global market (Richards 1996b). In this latest recapitulation of the slave trade, practices of Darkness and Closure, images of the cannibal, and techniques of divination form mnemonic threads tying together past and present experiences of capitalism and warfare, commodification and violence.

Yet from that imperfect past ordinary Sierra Leoneans have also recovered techniques of living with war, making it habitable from within (Richards 1996b: 152–63) and eventually undermining it. Especially notable in the current context of reconciliation in Sierra Leone are grassroots initiatives for the rehabilitation of ex-combatants. Working with NGOs, local communities in many parts of the country are reworking practices of divination and sacrifice, composing ritual processes for the cleansing, healing, and reintegration of young ex-combatants. In so doing, they create their social and moral world anew as they re-member it through ritual.[1]

Notes

Introduction

1   Bunce Island's inarticulacy as a commemorative site also forms a poignant contrast to well-publicized international projects initiated by Joseph Opala and others that connect Sierra Leone to Gullah communities in South Carolina and Georgia in the U.S.A. The Gullah creole language includes a large number of African words and names, 25 percent of which derive from languages spoken in Sierra Leone (Hair 1965); moreover, a Gullah song—a Mende funeral song whose words, remarkably, are remembered on both sides of the Atlantic—is the longest African text recorded from an African-American source in the U.S.A. (Opala 1987: 34–35). Through the medium of a booklet on the Gullah (ibid.) published in Sierra Leone by the United States Information Services, through two visits to Sierra Leone by a Gullah delegation and by Mary Moran, the singer of the Gullah version of the Gullah/Mende song, and through two moving documentary videos of these visits (South Carolina ETV: 1991; INKO Productions: 1998), Opala has promoted the development of what Yoneyama (1999: 188) calls a mnemonic community linking Sierra Leone, South Carolina, and Georgia.

2   One exception, however, is that of elite nineteenth-century oral traditions concerning the slave trade in Ouidah, in which both descendants of wealthy slave-trading Ouidah merchants and successful ex-slave returnees from Bahia celebrated the trade as a source of beneficial transatlantic connections (Law forthcoming).

3   Notable exceptions, however, include Sahlins (1985), Schoffeleers (1992), and Spyer (2000).

4   White suggests, for instance, that in East and Central Africa, "vampire stories may well play off as yet unrecovered imaginings about earlier extractive states" (2000: 22, n. 49; see also 18).

5   Modernities are plural, then, because of the particular histories through which they have been constituted among different people in different regions. Such alternate, historically constituted modernities may, moreover, provide an oppositional space, as Gilroy asserts when he argues that memories of slavery have been drawn upon to create a counterculture of modernity in the African diaspora (1993; and see Piot 1999: 21). "The distinctive historical experiences of this diaspora's populations," Gilroy writes, "have created a unique body of reflections on modernity and its discontents which is an enduring presence in the cultural and political struggles of their descendants today" (1993: 45). Gilroy thus locates Black Atlantic memory in the very modernity of slavery (see also 71).

6   See Inikori (1982) for a critique of these positions.

7   This binary logic has been most evident in critiques of the Comaroffs' work, e.g. Englund 1996; Englund and Leach 2000; Gable 1995.

Chapter 1   The Atlanticizing of Sierra Leone

1   From the late fifteenth century to 1808, "Sierra Leone" refers to the part of the upper Guinea coast that the Portuguese named "Serra Lyoa." From 1808 it refers to the British Crown Colony established on that coast, based in Freetown; and from 1896, it was also used of the British Protectorate of Sierra Leone, which was imposed on what was formerly termed the "hinterland." From 1961 it refers to the nation-state of Sierra Leone.

2   As with all peoples in this region, the name "Temne" represented a language group rather than a fixed ethnic identity.

3   Fernandes also tells us that both Temne- and Bullom-speakers recognized, in addition to the king of each village, a figure called "the lord of these Bolones [Bullom]," but that this lord had no more authority than other "lords" (1951 [1506–10]: 80–83; trans. Alice Clemente).

4   This term possibly derives from *tangomaas*, the Temne name for priests of a cult that controlled the kola trade (Brooks 1993: 191–92). It is cognate with terms for "priest" and "diviner" (*ngoma, sangoma,* etc.) in Bantu-speaking parts of Africa.

5   Fage (1969), in fact, acknowledged that his conclusions about the insignificant impact of the slave trade on West Africa do not necessarily hold for the upper Guinea coast. He appears to attribute this to the fact that this part of West Africa was, in his characterization, "an economically little developed and backward region" (1969: 397), by which he basically seemed to mean that its peoples were not organized into a large state.

6   Neither did they, however, create an ethnic identification as "the Temne": the latter affiliation seems to have been catalyzed by British colonial action in the late nineteenth century (Ijagbemi 1968: 21).

7   These lineages controlled the labor and services of others, largely through their dominance within the (men's) Poro and (women's) Bondo cult associations (see Bledsoe [1980] and Murphy [1980] for the Kpelle). Rodney describes the Poro as "an instrument in the hands of slave-raiding chiefs" (1970: 258), as it was through the Poro that these ruling lineages had an important role in the regulation of warfare, trade, and agriculture (see Little 1965 and 1966 on the Mende Poro).

Chapter 2   Spirit Memoryscape

1   I shall use "Closed" or "Closure" with a capital "C" to distinguish ritual Closure from the ordinary closing of a door or window shutter.

2   See, e.g., Boddy 1989; Lambek 1996; Masquelier 1995 and 2001; Rosenthal 1998; Stoller 1995.

3   Both Masquelier (1993 and 2001) and Schoffeleers (1992), however, provide remarkable exceptions.

4   In northwestern Temne-speaking towns, where Islam is more strongly established, there are even fewer.

5   They consulted diviners, for example. Manuel Alvares complained that "certain relics of the spiritual edifice of the church militant, that is, the *lançados* (run-aways) and *tangomaos*, employ . . . forms of divination themselves, and encourage others to do so, to the great scandal of the faith" (1990 [c. 1615], 2, chap. 5: 10).

6   Report by Her Majesty's Commissioner and Correspondence on the Subject of the Insurrection in the Sierra Leone Protectorate. Appendix I: Oral Evidence. PRO, CO 879/54, 1898: 373–74.

7   I am grateful to Adeline Masquelier for her observation that the recomposition of space-time-being that Soja (1989) and others have marked out as characteristic of modernity existed some time ago in the Sierra Leone hinterland. Yet what Ijagbemi describes here is not the "time-space compression" that Harvey (1989) identifies as a key feature of (post)modernity; instead, the spatiotemporal experience of ordinary people during both the Atlantic and legitimate trades was rather one of increasing "time-space dilation," in which five miles stretches out endlessly to become a hazardous two-day journey. It is significant, in contrast, that Korombo the warrior was described as having been able to fly, for it was in warriors' capacities for rapid road- and water-borne travel and for sudden appearances and disappearances during raids that time-space compression was realized in particularly brutal form.

8   As with Closure, I will use a capital "D" to distinguish this ritual condition from ordinary darkness.

9   Similar concepts of Darkness are found in the Mande heartland to the northeast. According to McNaughton, for instance, the Bamana term *dibi*, "is an abstract concept denoting 'darkness, obscurity, a very dangerous place.' Sorcerers, thieves, murderers and spirits *(jinew)* can be found lurking there in abundance. . . . *Komo* masks are believed to bear a special relationship to *dibi*. They are 'an affair of obscurity,' *a ye dibi la ko ye*. With their blacksmith-wearers, they are able to enter that murky, dangerous place to light fire with fire" (1988: 143–44).

   Temne-speakers may, in fact, have assimilated Darkness medicines from initially dominant Mande-speaking peoples. Alvares mentions the use of one such medicine called *nebrina*, brought by the sixteenth and seventeenth century Mane rulers, as having the following effect: "A village is approached by those bent on war. A fog then arises which prevents one man seeing another, and hence, God willing, the attackers have the victory" (1990, 2, chap. 12: 5).

10 The Colony's authorities perceived the "war fences" that defended stockaded towns as a "barbaric" embodiment of the "warlike" character of those who inhabited them. T. J. Alldridge, a colonial official based in the south, described the transformation of the town of Pendembu from 1892 to 1908 in these terms: "In those days Pendembu consisted of three towns, each surrounded by dense war-fences. On my recent visit all was changed. The squalid huts with their barbaric war fences had given place to a town with a fine open quadrangle containing some of the best native homes in the country" (1910: 175).

11 It seems likely that the story Schlenker—a missionary—recorded may also have incorporated biblical themes.

Chapter 3 Roads to Life, Roads to Death

1 Sometimes—as in the Susu occupation of Port Loko, described in chapter 1—the development of Mande and Islamic cultural practices arose out of struggles to control the slave trade.

2 De Boeck (1998) argues that whereas divination techniques in Congo/Zaire used to (and some, indeed, still do) draw upon enduring, life-giving connections to matrilineal ancestors through a cosmogonic ritual process, divination has undergone a radical rupture in the postcolonial present. In a context in which life is experienced as having become "cadavéré, sinistré, déclassé, épavé" (1998: 25), he describes certain new divination techniques in Congo/Zaire as materializing fragmentation, hybridity, and the dislocated mingling of dead and living. In contrast, instead of presenting a vision of continuity with an unchanging ancestral order, established forms of Temne divination *already* materialize the troubled and often violent past during which they took hold.

3 This technique is similar to that described by D. T. Niane (1965: 9) in his version of the Mande epic of Sundiata, the twelfth-century founder of the Mali Empire. Sundiata's birth is foretold through the cowrie divination of a visiting hunter and seer.

4 Like "the cowries," this form of divination is also similar to that described in Niane's version of the Sundiata epic (1965: 12). Sundiata's father, Nare Maghan, uses sand divination to overcome his wife Sogolon, the buffalo woman (and future mother of Sundiata) who transforms herself into her animal form when her husband attempts to consummate their marriage.

5 This was a less usual technique among the Temne diviners I knew, and may have been more common in Mandinka communities. A vivid account of its use is given in *The Spirit of Badenia*, Sheikh Gibril Kamara's novel about a Mandinka community in southern Sierra Leone (1996: 156).

6 I do not know whether the name "Accaron" refers to either the diviner ("the sorcerer") or the spirit consulted through divination. The root *-roŋ* is used for particularly powerful spirits, including *aŋ-roŋ a ra-baŋ,* the bronze-masked spirit of the chiefdom; *aŋ-roŋson,* the hunter-spirit of the forest; and *aŋ-yaroŋ,* the mermaid spirit of the sea and rivers.

7 It is interesting, however, that both in this technique and in that of the boiling water, the diviner interprets the movement in a vessel of water. In both techniques, moreover, a sinking movement—suggesting depth and the cooling of heat—is given a positive significance.

8 South of Temne-speaking areas, in the Galinhas part of the coast toward Cape Mount, early-nineteenth-century sources describe Muslim specialists as using ritual techniques to attract ships engaged in the Atlantic commerce ("'doing Muslim work so that ships would come to trade'"), while "others were asked to perform sacrifices before a military attack was made" (Jones 1983: 178).

9 Yet while Temne chiefs used these specialists as channels through which to assimilate the power of Islamic knowledge, they also used the male cult associations of *aŋ-Pɔrɔ* and *ra-Gbeŋle* as ritual buffers, holding important meetings in the sacred Poro or Ragbenle forest grove to keep knowledge of important decisions from their powerful Muslim "strangers."

10 See Farias (1990) for a parallel use of the same hadith as a Yoruba narrative for the origin of *Ifa* divination. This story presents an interpretive problem for both Western and pious Muslim readers because the diviners in the narrative are working for the unbelievers (or, in Pa Biyare's version below, for the "bad" warriors). It may be that the story was originally used as part of an anti-divination message. The diviners I knew, however, ignored the story's moral message and instead used the narrative to highlight the revelatory power of their divination techniques. This story is not, in any case, for public consumption and is thus not subject to the moral scrutiny of the community: it is something that diviners tell their own students.

11 Although these three techniques are widespread among Temne diviners, my focus on them is not based on their "representativeness." My interest in them derived originally from the fact that the diviners I knew best—Pa Koroma in Petbana, Ya Yebu in Malal and Petbana, Pa Fonah in Rokirfi, Pa Biyare in Makeni, Pa Yamba in Freetown, Ya Bay in Freetown, and Pa Ibrahim in Wellington—used these techniques.

12 The technique of river pebble divination *(beresigele)* as practiced by a Kuranko diviner with whom Jackson worked would appear, however, to be closer to Temne cowrie shell divination (ta-faŋt) than to aŋ-bɛrɛ. In the technique that Jackson describes (1989: 57–61), the pebbles are not arranged into the straight parallel lines of aŋ-bɛrɛ; instead, the diviner throws them and interprets the pattern of their fall.

13 Cowries are also seen as being eye-shaped and are thereby emblematic of the all-seeing spirits who animate them.

14 This interpretation might correspond to the sign in khatt ar-raml called *al-jama'a,* "group" or "assembly," denoted by four pairs of marks (Brenner 2000: 15).

15 There is, however, a close resonance with such European devices as the scrying glass, the crystal ball, and with popular understandings of vampires as soulless beings who cast no reflection in the mirror, all of which became part of a sphere of magic that formed the dark underbelly of Enlightenment rationality.

16 The influence of such a technology of individuation may perhaps be seen in certain witchfinding movements in southern Africa, where mirrors are used to capture an image of the witch's inner moral state (Auslander 1993).

17 We have seen above, however, that Pa Alfa Koroma referred to aŋ-yina Musa as *"a Muslim spirit"* who *"transferred his knowledge to the Qur'an"* and *"showed his knowledge of divination to some of the Muslim people."* And as we will see below, Pa Koroma also described aŋ-yina Musa's face as filled with flames. These could be implicit references to Musa (Moses) the prophet (aŋ-nabi Musa), who is a powerful wonder-worker in the Qur'an. Musa predates Muhammad's recitation of the Qur'an, and hence could be understood as "transferring" his knowledge to it. I am grateful to Richard Allen for this suggestion.

18 It should be noted here that Pa Fonah's West African Muslim ideas about white and black people cannot be equated in any simple or direct way with European and North American categories of race. The former grew out of a different history, in which the spread of Islamic hegemony in this part of West Africa (largely, as we have seen, through political influence and trade) did not give rise to sharp, immutable Euro-American racial distinctions. Moreover, the category of "slave" in West African contexts has not—as in the Sudan—become equated with that of "black person." Both "slave" and "black person" have, in any case, been more fluid and polysemous categories in Muslim West Africa than have

the corresponding categories in the New World, being understood as much in terms of religious identity, cultural practice, and language as of skin color. This being said, nevertheless, it is very clear that Pa Fonah asserts a connection between superior spiritual qualities and paleness of complexion. Given the long presence of European slave traders and colonial officials in this region, European ideologies of white superiority may themselves have had an impact upon Muslim meanings of "whiteness."

19 I am greatly indebted to my colleague Muhammad Mahmoud for his translation of—and insights in relation to—the Writing presented below. I shall distinguish Writing from ordinary pieces of writing by using a capital "W."

20 It is possible that they might be keys, recalling references in the Qur'an to Allah and Muhammad as the keys to spiritual and worldly life.

Chapter 4 Diviners' Knowledge, Diviners' Lives

1 Since the spread of the rebel war from 1991, moreover, seizure once again became horrifyingly concrete, with the RUF's widespread abduction of civilians—especially teenagers and children—as fighters, sex-slaves, and diamond diggers.

2 Spirits have been seizing diviners in this region for a long time. Cube, for example, the early seventeenth-century diviner who became a Christian convert in Manuel Alvares's mission, told the missionary of a frightening visionary episode of seizure by his tutelary spirit: "Cube told me that the devil had appeared to him and had squeezed his upper arm, so that his whole body shook with fright. I ask him, what is the matter? He says nothing. Go back, fear not, if you want to serve me I will make you a great herbalist. The devil showed Cube various herbs, and made him so distinguished that he gained for him a good number of souls. This spirit always went about with Cube" (Alvares 1990 [c. 1615] 2, chap. 5: 4–5, note [c]). While Cube's seizure took place after the Atlantic trade had been established for more than a century, we should not assume that similar initiatory encounters were absent before this trade's introduction.

3 A "swear" is a powerful ritual object or collection of medicines activated by verbal curses in order to take action against an unknown witch, thief, or adulterer. When "caught" by a swear, the miscreant may (depending on the particular capacities of the swear) be seized by sickness or paralysis, struck by lightning, or killed in a car accident. See Littlejohn 1960a.

4 Miers and Kopytoff write: "In most African societies, 'freedom' lay not in a withdrawal into a meaningless and dangerous autonomy but in attachment to a kin-group, to a patron, to power—an attachment that occurred within a well-defined hierarchical framework. It was in this direction that the acquired outsider had to move if he was to reduce his initial marginality. Here, the antithesis of 'slavery' is not 'freedom' qua autonomy but rather 'belonging.'" (1977: 17). In her near-kinless marriage, Ya Bay lacked such attachments.

5 Ya Bay's relationship with her spirit husband will probably sound familiar to those acquainted with the literature on spirit-possession. Here, surely, is a classic example of Ioan Lewis's "deprivation hypothesis" (1971), in which a hard-pressed wife uses a spirit affliction as a strategy enabling her both to voice complaints against her husband and to make demands upon him that would otherwise be impossible for her to verbalize. We might thus be tempted to see Ya Bay's spirit abduction as a deliberate strategy that allowed her

to leave her first husband, draw the attention of her kin to her plight, mobilize their support, find an independent source of income as a ritual specialist, and make certain demands on her second (human) husband. But Ya Bay's horrifying stay in the bush, the death of her child, and her long periods of "work" in a liminal state when taking up the "loads" of all her ritual specializations can hardly be said to have made Ya Bay's visionary path an attractive one.

I believe that Ya Bay probably did use her relationship with her spirit strategically: my aim is not to discount her agency but to argue that her agency is considerably more complex than that of a woman who constructs a relationship with a spirit as an act of conscious instrumentalism. If we accept the skeptical distance that Lewis's model seems to suggest, how do we then take seriously the reality of Ya Bay's relationship with her spirit-husband?

Boddy's interpretation of the *zar* cult in Northern Sudan as providing a spirit "antilanguage" (1989) provides an attractive alternative: instead of using spirit possession as an instrumental strategy, women experience their relationships with *zar* spirits as a powerful reality—and one that, Boddy argues, counters hegemonic but disadvantageous discourses about women. Yet, as I discuss in chapter 5, Temne women as wives do not lack for means of expressing their complaints and demands. And neither Temne women's ritual relationships with their personal water spirits enshrined in pebbles, nor with the spirits of their Bondo cult association, normally involve the spirit seizure that Ya Bay experienced. While spirit possession—even as an "affliction"—has a certain regularity and predictability for Northern Sudanese women, this is not the case among Temne women. Thus if we place Ya Bay's story in the context of the agency of Temne women as wives and as ritual actors, there is far less congruence between Ya Bay's experience and that of Northern Sudanese *zar* women than first appears.

6   This is manifest in the narrative that Schlenker recorded, which continues as follows: "But it is not proper for any one to act wrong; because eight persons surround him; two are at his right hand; two are at his left hand; two are before (him); (and) two are behind him, when he is walking. These are telling God every thing which man does; they are helping the white people in the war, and in every danger. Therefore white people do not use country fashion [do not use divination], they do not set up a Krifi [spirit], they do not tie on amulets, (and) they have no Greegree for war; but they are victorious in battle" (Schlenker 1861: 34–35).

7   This key of access, however, has itself been historically inaccessible to most of those in the north of the country, in which Temne-speakers are located. Although missionary organizations established schools in the nineteenth-century Colony of Sierra Leone, and Freetown boasted the first university in West Africa, missionary education was slow to spread to the hinterland. When it did spread, moreover, it established itself more easily in the south, where there was less competition with Islam. This pattern was replicated during the Protectorate stage of colonialism: by 1922, there were fifty-five primary and ten secondary schools in the colony, of which thirty-six primary and two secondary schools were in the Southern Province, and only eight primary schools were in the entire Northern Province (Ojukutu-Macauley 1997: 96). In the postcolonial period, however, this north-south regional disparity in the distribution of schools was eliminated. From 1988 to 1991, enrollment in primary and secondary schools was actually highest for boys

(although not for girls) in the Northern Province (see Ojukutu-Macauley 1997: 102–3, tables 1.7 and 1.8). But by that time, Sierra Leone was in a state of economic freefall that, together with rampant corruption in the Ministry of Education, was already causing the country's education system to disintegrate.

Chapter 5   A Thing under the Water

1   "Despatch from the Administrator-in-Chief Enclosing Information Regarding the Different Districts and Tribes of Sierra Leone and its Vicinity." Memoranda supplied by T. G. Lawson and arranged and carried out by J. C. E. Parkes. PRO, CO 879/25, 1887: 23.

2   Development projects did not seem to have changed this situation. In Petbana and its environs, agricultural development projects were mostly focused upon loans for men to develop swamp rice cultivation, the main consequence of which seemed to have been increased indebtedness for all but the wealthiest farmers.

Chapter 7   The Production of Witchcraft

1   Rutherford (1999) further argues that scholars writing about witchcraft in Africa should focus on competing discourses *about* witchcraft. On this basis, he criticizes those who analyze witchcraft and sorcery as commentaries on modernity, claiming that such scholars attend only rarely to the ways in which sorcery and witchcraft have been constituted (in terms of concepts of "backwardness," fraudulence, exploitation, injustice, anxiety reduction, etc.) through government projects and moral debates among colonial authorities, local government, Christian churches, and anthropologists (1999: 98–105). The significance of such discourses is not in doubt. But to claim that studies of witchcraft and sorcery should be focused primarily on these competing discourses is to risk privileging the standpoints of everyone except those for whom sorcery is a reality. Thus in Rutherford's otherwise careful unpacking of the competing social projects that shaped a witch-finding ceremony on a commercial farm in northwest Zimbabwe, the meanings and experiences that constituted witchcraft for the farm workers and the witchfinders are left largely unexamined (1999: 93–96 and 104).

2   Crick argues that the English word "witchcraft" should not be used to translate terms such as *ra-ser* at all: "English witchcraft existed in a culture which possessed such categories as 'natural philosophy' and a theological system upon which witch beliefs were partly parasitic. Great violence must be done to the conceptual structures of another culture in speaking of witchcraft if it lacks those environing categories which defined it in our own" (1976: 112). Yet the English word "witchcraft" is more fluid than Crick suggests: in contemporary Britain and North America, for instance, it is more likely to suggest New Age rituals and Harry Potter than seventeenth-and eighteenth-century categories of evil. We should also remember that translation is not only the prerogative of Western scholars. African appropriations of such English terms as "witchcraft" and "sorcery" themselves developed in historical contexts that were hardly free of European words and meanings. Today, *witchman* is part of the vocabulary of Krio, Sierra Leone's lingua franca, which is spoken not only by the Krio but also by most urban Temne.

3   Rotating credit associations *(ε-susu)* are mutual aid groups formed to help members save money on a regular basis. For each meeting, members are required to bring a certain sum of money and, once these contributions have been allowed to accumulate, a lump sum is given to one member. This process of contribution and accumulation is repeated so

that each member in turn builds up an investment for either long-term goals (such as starting a business) or emergencies (such as funeral expenses). In witches' ε-susu, each member in turn is required to bring a human victim to the meeting; if no victim is contributed, the group falls on and consumes the delinquent member instead. Thus it is specifically the kind of association that supports people in acquiring habits of capital accumulation that provides the ties connecting witches together.

4 "Lanterns" are elaborate art forms carried in a parade in towns and cities during an annual festival called *aŋ-wuthpa,* marking the end of Ramadan.

5 Writing of peoples further north, Alvares describes how herbalists give offerings to "the idols" *(china)* in ritual requests to intercede for them with the witches who consume the sick and dying: "If an illness is unknown to them and they will not run the risk of treating it, they obtain from the sick man something to give to the *china,* since they have persuaded the people that (when they are sick) witches are devouring them. By this trickery these priests make the man believe that they will go to the idol and will demand that it does not permit this to happen, by causing that person (? the witch) to feel regret and sorrow for the ill he has done, so that he then leaves the victim alone. But if the sick wretch dies, they say that witches ate him up. No-one dies here, for to die is to be 'eaten up.' 'They have eaten him' means 'they have killed him.'" (1990, 1, chap. 7: 10–11)

6 It was also used to detect other wrongdoers, such as poisoners and adulterers.

7 Alvares gives a similar account of the divinatory interrogation of the corpse and its litter among the "Sonequei" (Soninke). This interrogation, however, may (literally) take a different path if the bearers of the litter pass by the "famous idol Manga Jata": instead of disclosing the human agents who "ate" the deceased, this reveals that the deceased was a witch killed by this "idol" (1990, 1, chap. 3: 4). The name "Manga Jata"—"King Jata"— presumably invokes Sundiata (or "Mari Djata," or "Djata"), the founder of the Malinke Empire.

8 Piot's work on the slave trade among the Kabre in present-day Togo (1996) raises an interesting question about possible interrelationships among the different slave-producing practices in Sierra Leone. In the eighteenth century, the Kabre dwelt in noncentralized communities on the watershed of the two great slave-trading states of Asante and Dahomey. In a context in which Kabre communities were subject to considerable slave raiding from these powerful states, Kabre men responded by selling their sisters' children in the marketplace—a strategy that gave them more control over the inevitable fact of slaving and that was ultimately "successful" in that it eventually replaced the raids. Although the sale of slaves through witchfinding and pawnship cannot be seen as parallel strategies for reducing raids and wars in the Sierra Leone hinterland—for unlike the Kabre, those who bought slaves from elites were not usually those who raided and waged wars against them—the issue of possible interrelationships among warfare, raiding, witchfinding, indebtedness, and pawnships deserves further investigation.

9 There seem to have been regional differences, however, in the numbers of slaves produced through divination and ordeals. Christopher Fyfe writes: "Slaves not taken in war were usually criminals: in coastal areas, at least, it was rare for anyone to be sold without being charged with a crime. . . . Only in Muslim areas, where adulterers were flogged, and charges of witchcraft less frequent, were slaves regularly obtained by kidnapping" (1962: 9; and see 1964: 75–76).

10 Jones (1983) notes similar consistencies among ordeals and witchfinding further south in Galhinas country from the mid-seventeenth century to the early nineteenth century. He writes: "Continuity may also be traced in methods of detecting a 'witch' when a big man died. A nineteenth-century witness described the procedure as follows:

> The man who pretends to make the dead speak will cut off the hair of the forehead, and the nail of the great toe, and of the thumb, and, tying these into a mat, will put it on the head of a person selected for that purpose; then with a stick in his hand, he will strike the mat lightly, and ask, 'Who killed you? your brother or sister? or any of the family?' If the mat should slide from the man's head at the moment that any particular name is mentioned (for a great many names are called over), they . . . fix upon the person last named as the murderer. (*6th Report of the African Institution*, London, 1812: 129)

This description is extraordinarily close to that given by Dapper 150 years earlier" (1983: 185).

11 Report by Her Majesty's Commissioner and Correspondence on the Subject of the Insurrection in the Sierra Leone Protectorate. Appendix I: Oral Evidence. PRO, CO 879/54, 1898: 142.

12 In contrasting "Mohammedan courts" and "pagan courts" in terms of the "degenerative" tendencies of the latter, Parkes draws upon an evolutionary idiom that often framed British (and French) colonial attitudes towards Muslims. Islam was commonly viewed by colonial officials, both in Sierra Leone and elsewhere in West Africa, as a "civilizing" influence that was more accessible to Africans than the heights of Western civilization that these officials believed themselves to embody.

13 Many different forms of public divination are available. First, there are what Dorjahn (1962: 5–6) calls "moving vehicle" techniques in which a single diviner uses an object charged with medicines that control the movements of one or several ritually treated bearers. As well as the "corpse-interrogation" techniques of "the funeral litter" (*aŋ-saŋka*) and "the coffin" (*aŋ-beŋthɔ*) (divination methods similar to those that proliferated during the slave trade), moving vehicle methods also include "the broom" (*aŋ-gbalɔ*), "the pestle" (*ka-roŋp*), and "the whip" (*aŋ-rakɛt*), all of which compel their bearers to beat an accused person who is thereby identified as the culprit. Second, spirit embodiments from certain male cult associations—*ma-nekɛ* spirits of the *ra-Gbeŋle* society in eastern Temneland (see Dalby and Kamara 1964; Dorjahn 1959), the masked *ka-yogbo* spirit of the (originally Yoruba/Aku Krio) *Oje* society in western Temneland, and *aŋ-Gbaŋgbani*, the spirit of the Limba Gbangbani society along the Temne/Limba borderland—are extrahuman agents that disclose the guilt of witches and other wrongdoers through verbal interrogations, accusations, and pronouncements (see Shaw 1985; 1991). Finally, there are also ordeals (rarely used now, to my knowledge, but vividly remembered), including "the ax" (*ka-bap*), whose blade is placed on the suspect's tongue after being heated in a fire until it glows; "boiling oil" (*ma-kobe*), into a pot of which the suspect reaches to bring out a piece of iron within; "the needle" (*aŋ-seni*), which is threaded and passed through the skin along the suspect's forearm; and the infamous "red water" (*ma-kɔn*); cf. "the bark of *macone*," used for the same purpose in the early 1600s (Alvares 1990, 2, chap. 3: 5).

14 In order to do so, they had to pass a test known as "the concealment" (*aŋ-maŋk*): a small object such as a coin was hidden and had to be found through divination in order to demonstrate the capacity to discover what is concealed.

15 What about gender? In the historical sources I have examined, the gender of those accused of witchcraft is not usually specified (although Winterbottom [1803: 139–43] gives
a remarkable account of witchcraft accusations against newly inducted novices by officials
of the women's Bondo society at the end of the eighteenth century; those who confessed
or failed a medicine ordeal were sold into the Atlantic trade). Today, however, not only
do understandings of witchcraft represent women as the majority of witches, but these
understandings also resonate in telling ways with some of the strongly gendered consequences of the slave trade for Temne marriage that I explore in chapters 5 and 6.

Chapter 8   Cannibal Transformations

1 And although the upper Guinea coast had been exploited for slaves by the Portuguese
since the 1460s, the volume of the trade and its impact upon local peoples grew exponen-
tially with the involvement of the Mane. According to Rodney: "When the Manes led the
invasion into Sierra Leone in 1545, they sparked off a period of unprecedented slaving.
The Portuguese seized the opportunity to profit from the rout of the Sapes. The ocean-
going slavers remained in the coastal bays and estuaries, while the boats of the *lançados*
hovered like vultures in every river, waiting to take hold of the victims of the struggles.
So numerous were the unfortunates, that the boats sometimes rejected further offers of
slaves after they had gorged themselves until full" (Rodney 1970: 102).

2 The explorer Mungo Park, for example, encountered a group of slaves when traveling
through Mandinka country: "they viewed me at first with looks of horror," he wrote,
explaining that "a deeply rooted idea that the whites purchase Negroes for the purpose
of devouring them ... naturally makes the slaves contemplate a journey towards the
coast with great terror" (1817, 1: 484).

3 I acknowledge a debt here to the work of Auslander (1993), Bastian (1992: 148–208),
Masquelier (2000), Weiss (1996: 179–219), and White (2000: 122–47) on the interconnections among spatiotemporal dislocations of roads and transport, transformations in
commodities and labor, and bodily dismemberment and extraction.

4 They did, however, return from Brazil to nineteenth-century Ouidah and Lagos (Law
forthcoming; Matory 1999). They also returned to Freetown in the late eighteenth and
nineteenth centuries, where they became Krio ("Creole"). Yet most Krio in Freetown had
originally come not from the Sierra Leone hinterland but from elsewhere in Africa; in
any case a sharp disjuncture developed between Krio in Freetown and peoples in the hinterland.
   Many accounts of Atlantic cannibalism were recorded in Freetown during the first
half of the nineteenth century, when the incoming flow of recaptives from other parts of
Africa made Freetown a crossroads for the circulation of such stories. A former slave from
Bornu called Ali Eisami Gazirmabe (later renamed William Harding), for example, described his encounter in 1818 with "a white man ... whose name was Mr. Decker" in
one of the new towns beyond Freetown: "he ... drew me into his house, and I did not
fear him; but I heard inside the house that my people without were talking, and saying,
'The white man has taken Ali ... in order to slaughter him'" (Curtin 1967: 215).
   Eighteen years later, the English traveler Rankin bemoaned the fact that when crews
of English naval vessels captured slave ships and took them to Sierra Leone for adjudica-
tion, the recaptive slaves had the "strong impression ... that they will be eaten by the
British—a belief carefully instilled by the Spanish and Portuguese; and one which has

caused many a negro to throw himself into the sea, that he might escape being devoured" (Rankin 1836, 2: 104).

5 See, e.g., Curtin 1967: 313, "The Narrative of Samuel Ajayi Crowther."

    During the Middle Passage, cannibalism stories sometimes catalyzed African captives' resistance to the process of their own commodification. Some threw themselves into the sea, and by so doing not only avoided being consumed by their captors but also acted upon another circulating Atlantic idea: that the spirits of those who drowned in the sea would fly back to Africa (Gomez 1998: 117–20; Law forthcoming). Others organized shipboard rebellions. While Stephen Spielberg's film has made the story of the *Amistad* famous, it is less well known that this 1839 uprising was sparked by a rumor of European cannibalism: the Mende captive Sengbe Pieh organized and led the revolt after being told by the ship's cook that the white men planned to eat the slaves that day. While European slavers and their crews sometimes fuelled Atlantic cannibalism stories (often in order to incite their slaves to resist capture by English vessels after the slave trade's abolition), these stories could also bring about the slavers' demise when desperate Africans decided that being killed in an uprising was preferable to being eaten (see also Ceyssens 1975: 527, n. 147, and 529).

6 The two uses of human victims that Matthews gives do not, of course, preclude each other: today in Sierra Leone, as in most parts of Africa, sacrificing an animal usually (although not always) entails eating it.

7 There were, however, local differences. Accounts from the (predominantly Temne-speaking) northwest were more likely than those from the south to implicate forms of witchcraft in which those accused either consume their victims in the spirit or shape-shift into predatory animals (Kalous 1974: 50, 79, 89, 230–31).

8 We should not assume, however, that the capacity to metamorphose into a wild animal is (or was) always viewed as an unambiguously negative quality (see Jackson 1989: 102–18). In twentieth-century Temne oral traditions, for example, great nineteenth-century warriors (*aŋ-kurgba*) and warrior chiefs (*aŋ-bay a-rəfa*) were often admired for their capacities for metamorphosis: thus Bay Simera—a chief who actively opposed the British and fought for control of the legitimate trade on the Rokel river in the 1870s and 1880s—is described as having been able to change into animal forms (Ijagbemi 1968: 221). During my fieldwork I was often told that, like the great warrior chiefs who had used their powers to benefit their chiefdoms, the best hunters (*aŋ-kapra*) are able to turn into elephants or bush-cows. While some claimed that such powers constitute a form of witchcraft (ra-ser), others argued that those with these capacities (called *poŋine* or *thekre* in Temne) are so accomplished that they do not need to use their witchcraft to destroy others. Thus a hunter who embodies the strength and senses of dangerous animals appropriates the forces of the bush in order to provide valued bushmeat for the community, while a witch merely acts out of greed or revenge: the moral or immoral qualities of capacities for animal transformation are modified by the destructive, protective, or redistributive uses to which it is put.

9 Although the external trade in slaves was reduced, it did not disappear: the coastal Galin-has area to the south was an important site for the Atlantic slave trade for most of the nineteenth century (Jones 1983). Susu, Mandinka, and Fula traders, moreover, smuggled slaves north, into what is now the Republic of Guinea, both to grow groundnuts on the coast (ibid., 83–85) and for use on the farms or in the armies of military leaders (Wylie 1977: 83–84). And as late as 1875 (just before the human leopard and alligator scare

exploded), an episode of enslavement through witchfinding in the Temne-speaking chiefdom of Koya attracted the attention of the colonial government nearby. What happened there is significant because it illustrates why witchfinding could no longer be sustained as a technique for the production of slaves. According to the Government Interpreter, the Regent Chief and certain subchiefs of Koya took "a large quantity of rum and other goods" from Susu slave dealers, but "the time for paying having arrived and they having no slaves on hand to meet their demands, charged several persons . . . with witchcraft," accusing them "of being possessed of the Art of witchcraft and can transform themselves . . . into leopards and alligators" (Kalous 1974: 185). Significantly, these chiefs also claimed that their actions had "the consent of [the colonial] Government" (185). Although there was no such consent, the very fact that these chiefs felt constrained to authorize their actions by claims of government approval tells us a great deal about the colonial presence at this place and time. In fact, the chiefs' transaction with the slave traders was not completed due to the intervention of a senior female chief who managed to obtain the release of eight of the thirteen (or twelve) charged, and who appealed to the colonial government to intervene in the conflict that broke out as a result (186). Thus although ideas of shape-shifting witchcraft persisted (and do still), the ritual processes through which these ideas were linked to the export slave trade were no longer viable, due largely to the Colony's proximity and its practices of surveillance and intervention.

10 Because these reports include numerous references to the use of body parts to make "bad" medicines, and do not depict murders committed simply to provide a meal, some scholars have argued that the English term "cannibalism" is a misnomer here (see, e.g., Abraham 1975; Jones 1983: 185). But in fact several of the human leopard accounts *do* include descriptions of cooking, distributing, and eating human meat (e.g., Kalous 1974: 89–90, 96, 104–5, 168, 255, to cite but a few)—processes that clearly correspond to the division, preparation, and consumption of the victim of an animal sacrifice. Animal sacrifice is not performed simply to provide a meal either; and more importantly, the provision of a meal—whether sacrificial or not—is never in any case a simple matter of ingesting calories (Ferme 1992; Weiss 1996). In human leopard accounts, the participants' consumption of human meat is part of a ritual process that is depicted, I argue below, as a transgressive parallel to animal sacrifice. This depiction does not correspond to English representations of "African cannibalism," but it does evoke, I suggest, *African* representations of "European cannibalism."

11 Thirteen years after the end of colonial rule, Milan Kalous published 315 accounts of "Cannibalism and Tongo Players" from the colonial archives in order to demonstrate that "British colonialism at least, was a positive chapter of African history" (1974: x): Human leopard stories were thus resurrected in the service of colonial nostalgia. The consequences of this publication have been very different from those intended by Kalous, however. Ironically, by making a large number of these documents readily available, he facilitated the study of human leopard accounts in their colonial contexts, thereby unintentionally assisting in the development of interpretations that direct critical scrutiny upon colonialism itself (Abraham 1976; MacCormack 1983b; Jackson 1989: 112–114; Richards 1996a, 2000).

12 Thus Abraham (1976) argues that human leopard accusations should be understood in terms of the social and political tensions and insecurities generated by colonialism. Jackson (1989), developing Abraham's point, observes that Sherbro—the location of the

most frequent reports of human leopard killings—was beset by acute political conflicts over control of the legitimate trade, the sale of land to Creole traders, chiefs' authority over their subjects, and slave-trading. He also notes that the "earliest reports of leopard societies date from . . . British annexation . . . after a dubious treaty was signed with *some* local chiefs" (1989: 114). This was also the period, we might add, when the Sherbro region became the key area for the trade in palm kernels (Mitchell 1962: 205).

13 Through these interventions, Wylie suggests (1977: 184), the colonial government gradually created a de facto protectorate even before one was formally declared in 1896.

14 In 1890, for example, a member of the colonial administration complained to Bay Simerah in Rokon that "you have made a law compelling traders to pay heavy fees before they can come to Freetown . . . and impose heavy fines, seize their canoes and confiscate their property when they do not obey the law" (quoted in Wylie 1977: 178). It is surely no coincidence that two years later, Bay Simera called a diviner to identify those responsible for human alligator killings in Rokon, and that those accused were "well-to-do" people (Kalous 1977: 217–19).

15 In keeping with its abolitionist goals, the colonial government had made treaties prohibiting the internal traffic in slaves (Wylie 1977: 139), and refused to return slaves who escaped to Freetown, thereby posing a threat to chiefs' control over labor (see Jones 1983: 154; Rashid 1999: 213–15). Then, with the imposition of the Protectorate in 1896, the British tried to abolish internal slavery. While the uprising that followed in 1898—the Hut Tax War—is commonly attributed to the introduction of a house tax, Rashid (1999: 215) points out that the chiefs cited British attempts to dismantle domestic slavery as a major reason for their having taken up arms to fight the government.

16 In 1917, for example, when a number of "alligator society" accusations were leveled against Bay Sherbro of Samu in Karene District, the District Commissioner noted that "apart from being mixed up in the alligator society [Bay Sherbro] has been oppressing his people to such extent that some of them have been deprived of a considerable quantity of land" (Kalous 1974: 81). For some of Bay Sherbro's subjects, moreover, the seizure of their land and the seizure of victims by human crocodiles were directly linked: "Kuni Lamina complained . . . that his child . . . had been eaten by an alligator. . . . On enquiry one Lahai Sebu stated that he had been employed by Pa Nain, nephew of the Paramount Chief Bai Sherbro, to catch the child. The child was caught to frighten Lamina so that he would leave the chiefdom and Pa Nain could take his farm. Lamina was fined £4 in the Chief's court, and as he only paid £2 he was flogged and the farm was taken away from him and given to Pa Nain. The farm has now been restored to Lamina" (Kalous 1974: 81–82).

17 Sometimes this colonially mediated "fighting for the chieftaincy" was manifested in cannibalism accusations: in Karene District in 1910, for instance, Paramount Chief Alimamy Noah claimed that his kinsman "Bundu wanted a crown" and had, after consulting a "murry man," sacrificed his first cousin in order to obtain it (Kalous 1974: 137). Such accusations were also made against chiefs who did not have popular support. Witnesses for a human leopard case in Timdale Chiefdom in 1909, for instance, stated that two sections of the chiefdom "did not agree to the crowning of Humpa Peah Yambo," that "after he was crowned some of the people did not obey [him]," and that the chief sacrificed "a crazy man" in order "to make the people of one mind in the country" (Kalous

1974: 161–66). An especially infamous case was that against Daniel Wilberforce of Bon-the, a minister of the United Brethren Mission who had been educated in the U.S.A. He became Paramount Chief of Imperri in 1899, was arrested and acquitted for a leopard murder in 1905, and was later arrested and convicted on a second charge in 1912 (Kalous 1974: 239–64).

18 In 1954, the chiefs' persistent "eating" of their chiefdoms gave rise to "Disturbances" in the form of an uprising of youth in the Northern Province (Dorjahn 1960b: 111, 139).

19 See Kalous 1974: 13, 32, 55–56, 78, 82, 85, 88, 89, 102, 107, 118, 121, 133, 139, 161, and 277.

20 See also Kalous 1974: 60, 67, 83, 129, 130, 133–37, 141–42, 148, 161–72.

21 Raiders did not, of course, bite captives on their genitals. They did, however, "mutilate" the reproductive capacity of the families whose young people they stole by severing them from their next generation.

22 In Imperri chiefdom in the southwest, these diviners were known as "Tongo Players." Their name, *tongomo* in Mende (Richards 2000: 90), seems to be closely related to the sixteenth-century Temne or Bullom term for "priest," *tangomao*, that was applied to those European lançados who adopted African cultural practices with particular enthusiasm.

23 Kiyelleh the trader, for instance, was one of eighteen "well-to-do" people accused in 1892 of crocodile killings in Rokon by "Chief Bey Simerah and people" (Kalous 1977: 217). Bay Simera had called "a medicine man, who could point out such persons" to Rokon, and those accused by this diviner were placed in stocks (219). But shortly after, the colonial authorities sent a contingent of Frontier Police to Rokon to intervene, and Bay Simera was forced to release those accused (Wylie 1977: 184).

24 Some accusations were, in fact, made by chiefs and big men against domestic slaves (Kalous 1974: 63, 89). Yet such accusations tended to rebound upon the accusers: in one of these cases, for instance—a human chimpanzee case in Mange—a number of slaves confessed, but later claimed "that their confessions were extracted by torture" (91). The District Commissioner for the area asserted that the real culprits—of both the human chimpanzee killings and the slaves' torture—were "the gentry of the country," comment-ing that "the slaves would admit the acts . . . having been whipped up [to] the admitting point by means of the lash." (91).

25 This raises the question of how many of the accusations and confessions in the colonial records are dream narratives. Baum (1983), for instance, documents colonial trials of Diola witches in the Casamance region of Senegal that were based on French misreadings of dream narratives as confessions of murder in the waking world.

Chapter 9   The Politician and the Diviner

1 Quoted in Opala 1994: 25.

2 The political scientist A. B. Zack-Williams describes the economic legacy of this OAU summit as follows: "In the midst of this international potlatch, the Sierra Leone bourgeoi-sie had to be reminded by the Governor of the Bank of Sierra Leone that: '[the] economy has continued to flag badly, and 1980 was one of the worst years for a long time. The costs of hosting the OAU summit conference seriously skewed Budgetary spending and development investment . . . direct spending on the summit was Le123m.'"

To the ordinary Sierra Leonean who picked up the cost for hosting the Conference, the sacrifice demanded of him was always clear to him as can be seen from this aphorism which spread throughout the country, 'OAU for you, IOU for me'" (1989: 127–28). For Sierra Leoneans, the everyday consequences of bearing this collective "IOU" were that by 1984 motor transport ground to a halt as petrol supplies in the country dried up. The government had not paid its fuel bills, and overseas suppliers refused to extend credit (Fyle 1997: 169).

3   Van Dijk and Pels (1996: 253) are right to emphasize that "magic" often has a banality and matter-of-factness that we should beware of exoticizing. As we have seen, divination and ritual healing are in many contexts taken-for-granted realities in Sierra Leone. But accounts of the occult partnerships of politicians and diviners have an explicitly sensa-tional quality that signals a departure from more ordinary ritual contexts.

4   Such disclaimers do not protect politicians from ritual attack by their rivals. In 1988 an alleged attempt by one government minister to eliminate another involved a fake "warn-ing" to the potential victim that his political enemy had hired a diviner to attack him. This enemy, according to the newspaper coverage of the ensuing court case, *"had hired an 'alphaman' from Gbinti in north-western Sierra Leone to cast a spell . . . with a view to get him 'paralysed' so that he may be sent into political limbo"* ("Court Told: Big Plot to Kill Dr. AKT," *The Vision,* Freetown, December 16, 1988). The aim of the plot, according to the minister it allegedly targeted, had been to scare him into seeking ritual protection from a second diviner—sent to him on the secret instructions of his political rival—whose supposedly "protective" countermedicines would then have been used to poison him.

5   According to Pa Ahmadu, four other "big men" consulted him that weekend. A former minister sought his help in a court case in which he was on trial over his use of violence during the elections, which had resulted in a man's death; a new chief called for a divina-tion prior to his coronation (he would be very powerful and wealthy, said Pa Ahmadu, but would not live long); a headmaster sought success in his fight with another headmas-ter for a government position; and a prominent lawyer whose wife had left him and taken their children sought medicine to compel her to return the children. This last client spontaneously gave me the same account himself when I met him by chance, several months later.

6   For rural (and now even urban) Sierra Leoneans, as for those in the Tanzanian Haya communities Weiss (1996: 202–19) discusses, electricity is experienced as a privileged resource of the state and of big men that is inaccessible to ordinary people. Correspond-ingly, the loss of electric power in many provincial towns in Sierra Leone from the 1980s onward was experienced as a tangible sign of disconnection and national failure (Fergu-son 1999: 234–54).

7   See Ellis (1999) for parallel accounts from the Liberian civil war.

Conclusion   Remembering Modernity

1   These rituals of rehabilitation form a remarkable parallel to those that local communities developed under similar circumstances in Mozambique (Honwana 1997; Nordstrom 1997).

Bibliography

Abbreviation
PRO, CO   Public Records Office, London, Colonial Office Records

Sierra Leonean Newspapers
Globe
New Shaft .
The Vision
We Yone

Films
Family Across the Sea. 1991. South Carolina Educational Television (SCETV), Columbia, South Carolina.
The Language You Cry In. 1998. INKO Productions and the Image Workshop (film school), University of Alicante, Spain.

Books and Articles
Abraham, Arthur. 1975. "The Pattern of Warfare and Settlement among the Mende of Sierra Leone in the Second Half of the Nineteenth Century." *Kroniek van Africa* 2: 130–40. Reprinted as Occasional Paper No. 1, Institute of African Studies, Fourah Bay College.
———. 1976. *Topics in Sierra Leone History: A Counter-Colonial Interpretation*. Freetown: Leone Publishers.
———. 1978. *Mende Government and Politics under Colonial Rule: A Historical Study of Political Change in Sierra Leone 1890–1937*. Freetown: Sierra Leone University Press.

285

Abu-Lughod, Lila. 1990. "The Romance of Resistance: Tracing Transformations of Power through Bedouin Women." *American Ethnologist* 17: 41–55.

Adler, Alfred, and Andras Zemplini. 1972. *Le Baton de l'aveugle: Divination, maladie et pouvoir chez les Moundang du Tchad.* Paris: Hermann.

Alldridge, T. J. 1910. *A Transformed Colony: Sierra Leone As It was, and As It Is. Its Progess, Peoples, Native Customs, and Undeveloped Wealth.* London: Seeley and Co.

Alvares, Manuel. 1990 [c. 1615]. "Ethiopia Minor and a Geographical Account of the Province of Sierra Leone." Translated and edited by P. E. H. Hair. Department of History, University of Liverpool. Photocopy.

Amadiume, Ifi. 1987. *Male Daughters, Female Husbands: Gender and Sex in an African Society.* London: Zed Books.

Apter, Andrew. 1993. "Atinga Revisited: Yoruba Witchcraft and the Cocoa Economy, 1950–1951." In Jean and John Comaroff, eds., *Modernity and Its Malcontents,* 111–28. Chicago: Chicago University Press.

Arazu, R. C. 1978. "Ezenwadeyi of Ihembosi." In E. Isichei, ed., *Igbo Worlds: An Anthology of Oral Histories and Historical Description,* 171–77. Philadelphia: Institute for the Study of Human Issues.

Ardener, Shirley. 1981. "Ground Rules and Social Maps for Women: An Introduction." In S. Ardener, ed., *Women and Space: Ground Rules and Social Maps,* 11–34. London: Croom Helm.

Aretxaga, Begona. 1997. *Shattering Silence: Women, Nationalism, and Political Subjectivity in Northern Ireland.* Princeton, N.J.: Princeton University Press.

Asad, Talal. 1993. *Genealogies of Religion: Discipline and Reasons of Power in Christianity and Islam.* Baltimore: Johns Hopkins University Press.

Auslander, Mark. 1993. "'Open the Wombs!': The Symbolic Politics of Modern Ngoni Witchfinding." In Jean and John Comaroff, eds., *Modernity and Its Malcontents: Ritual and Power in Postcolonial Africa,* 167–92. Chicago: University of Chicago Press.

Austen, Ralph A. 1993. "The Moral Economy of Witchcraft: An Essay in Comparative History," in Jean and John Comaroff, eds., *Modernity and Its Malcontents: Ritual and Power in Postcolonial Africa,* 89–110. Chicago: University of Chicago Press.

———. 2001. "The Slave Trade as History and Memory: Confrontations of Slaving Voyage Documents and Communal Traditions." *William and Mary Quarterly* 58: 229–44.

Ball, Edward. 1998. *Slaves in the Family.* New York: Ballantine Books.

Bangura, Abdul Karim. 1997. "The Effects of Arab Foreign Aid on Sierra Leone's Economic Growth: A Quantitative Analysis." In Alusine Jalloh and David E. Skinner, eds., *Islam and Trade in Sierra Leone,* 179–95. Trenton, N.J., and Asmara, Eritrea: Africa World Press.

Banton, Michael. 1957. *West African City: A Study of Tribal Life in Freetown.* London: Oxford University Press.

Barber, Karin. 1982. "Popular Reactions to the Petro-Naira." *Journal of Modern African Studies* 20: 431–50.

———. 1991. *I Could Speak Until Tomorrow: Oriki, Women, and the Past in a Yoruba Town.* Washington, D.C.: Smithsonian Institution Press.

Bastian, Misty. 1992. "The World as Marketplace: Cosmological, Historical and Popular Constructions of the Onitsha Market." Ph.D. diss., University of Chicago.

———. 1993. "'Bloodhounds Who Have No Friends': Witchcraft and Locality in the Nigerian Popular Press." In Jean and John Comaroff, eds., *Modernity and Its Malcontents: Ritual and Power in Postcolonial Africa,* 129–66. Chicago: University of Chicago Press.

———. Forthcoming. "Vulture Men, Campus Cultists and Teenaged Witches: Modern Magics in Nigerian Popular Media." In Henrietta Moore and Todd Sanders, eds., *Rethinking Witchcraft and Development in Postcolonial Africa.* London and New York: Routledge.

Battaglia, Debbora. 1992. "The Body in the Gift: Memory and Forgetting in Sabarl Mortuary Exchange." *American Ethnologist* 19: 3–18.

Baum, Robert M. 1983. "Crimes of the Dream World: French Trials of Diola Witches." Paper presented at the University of Warwick's conference on the History of Law, Labor, and Crime.

———. 1999. *Shrines of the Slave Trade: Diola Religion and Society in Precolonial Senegambia.* Oxford and New York: Oxford University Press.

Bayart, Jean-François. 1993. *The State in Africa: The Politics of the Belly.* London: Verso.

Beidelman, T. O. 1986. *Moral Imagination in Kaguru Modes of Thought.* Bloomington: Indiana University Press.

Bellman, Beryl. 1984. *The Language of Secrecy: Symbols and Metaphors in Poro Ritual.* New Brunswick: Rutgers University Press.

van Binsbergen, Wim. 1995. "Four-tablet Divination as Trans-regional Medical Technology in Southern Africa." *Journal of Religion in Africa* 25: 114–40.

———. 1996. "Regional and Historical Connections of Four-tablet Divination in Southern Africa." *Journal of Religion in Africa* 26: 2–29.

Bledsoe, Caroline H. 1980. *Women and Marriage in Kpelle Society.* Stanford: Stanford University Press.

———. 1984. "The Political Use of Sande Ideology and Symbolism." *American Ethnologist* 11: 455–72.

Bledsoe, Caroline H., and Kenneth M. Robey. 1986. "Arabic Literacy and Secrecy among the Mende of Sierra Leone." *Man* 21: 202–26.

Blier, Suzanne Preston. 1995. *African Vodun: Art, Psychology, and Power.* Chicago: University of Chicago Press.

Boddy, Janice. 1989. *Wombs and Alien Spirits: Women, Men, and the Zar Cult in Northern Sudan.* Madison: University of Wisconsin Press.

Boone, Sylvia A. 1986. *Radiance from the Waters: Ideals of Feminine Beauty in Mende Art.* New Haven: Yale University Press.

Bordo, Susan. 1993. *Unbearable Weight: Feminism, Western Culture, and the Body.* Berkeley: University of California Press.

Bourdieu, Pierre. 1990. *The Logic of Practice.* Stanford: Stanford University Press.

Bravmann, Rene A. 1983. *African Islam.* Washington, D.C.: Smithsonian Institution Press.

Brenner, Louis. 2000. "Histories of Religion in Africa." Published Inaugural Lecture delivered on March 25, 1999, School of Oriental and African Studies, University of London.

Brooks, George E. 1993. *Landlords and Strangers: Ecology, Society and Trade in Western Africa, 1000–1630.* Boulder: Westview Press

Callaway, Helen. 1981. "Spatial Domains and Women's Mobility in Yorubaland, Nigeria." In S. Ardener, ed., *Women and Space: Ground Rules and Social Maps,* 168–86. London: Croom Helm.

Ceyssens, Rik. 1975. "Mutumbula: Mythe de l'opprimé," *Cultures et developpement* 7: 483–550.

Cheney-Coker, Syl. 1990. *The Last Harmattan of Alusine Dunbar.* Oxford: Heinemann.

Ciekawy, Diane. 1992. "Witchcraft Eradication as Political Process in Kilifi District, Kenya, 1955–1988." Ph.D. diss., Columbia University.

———. 1998. "Witchcraft in Statecraft: Five Technologies of Power in Coastal Kenya." *African Studies Review* 41: 119–41.

Ciekawy, Diane, and Peter Geschiere. 1998. "Containing Witchcraft: Conflicting Scenarios in Postcolonial Africa." *African Studies Review* 41: 1–14.

Cole, Jennifer. 1998. "The Work of Memory in Madagascar." *American Ethnologist* 25: 610–33.

———. 2001. *Forget Colonialism? Sacrifice and the Art of Memory in Madagascar.* Berkeley: University of California Press.

Comaroff, Jean. 1985. *Body of Power, Spirit of Resistance: The Culture and History of a South African People.* Chicago: University of Chicago Press.

———. 1994. "Defying Disenchantment: Reflections on Ritual, Power, and History." In Charles F. Kayes, Lauren Kendall, and Helen Hardacre, eds., *Asian Visions and Authority: Religion and the Modern States of East and Southeast Asia* 301–14. Honolulu: University of Hawaii Press.

Comaroff, Jean, and John L. Comaroff. 1991. *Of Revelation and Revolution.* Vol. 1, *Christianity, Colonialism, and Consciousness in South Africa.* Chicago: University of Chicago Press.

———. 1992. *Ethnography and the Historical Imagination.* Boulder, Colo.: Westview Press.

———. 1993. "Introduction " to J. and J. Comaroff, eds., *Modernity and Its Malcontents: Ritual and Power in Postcolonial Africa,* xi–xxxvii. Chicago: University of Chicago Press.

———. 1999. "Occult Economies and the Violence of Abstraction: Notes from the South African Postcolony." *American Ethnologist* 26: 279–303.

Comaroff, John L. and Jean Comaroff. 1987. "The Madman and the Migrant: Work and Labor in the Historical Consciousness of a South African People," *American Ethnologist* 14: 191–209.

———. 1997. *Of Revelation and Revolution.* Vol. 2, *The Dialectics of Modernity on a South African Frontier.* Chicago: University of Chicago Press.

Connerton, Paul. 1989. *How Societies Remember.* Cambridge: Cambridge University Press.

Crick, Malcolm. 1976. *Explorations in Language and Meaning: Towards a Semantic Anthropology.* London: Malaby Press.

Curtin, Philip, ed. 1967. *Africa Remembered: Narratives by West Africans from the Era of the Slave Trade.* Prospect Heights, Ill.: Waveland Press.

———. 1975. *Economic Change in Precolonial Africa: Senegambia in the Era of the Slave Trade.* Madison: University of Wisconsin Press.

Dalby, David. 1965. "The Mel Languages: A Reclassification of Southern 'West Atlantic.'" *African Language Studies* 6: 1–17.

———. 1970–71. "The Place of Africa and Afro-America in the History of the English Language." *African Language Review* 9: 280–98.

Dalby, David, and Abdul Kamara. 1964. "Vocabulary of the Temne Ragbenle Society." *Sierra Leone Language Review* 3: 35–42.

Dantzig, Albert van. 1982 [1975]. "Effects of the Atlantic Slave Trade on some West African Societies." In J. E. Inikori, ed., *Forced Migrations: The Impact of the Export Slave Trade on African Societies,* 187–201. New York: Africana Publishing Company.

De Boeck, Filip. 1995. "Bodies of Remembrance: Knowledge, Experience and the Growing of Memory in Luunda Ritual Performance." In G. Thines and L. de Heusch, eds., *Rites et ritualisation*, 113–38. Paris: Librairie Philosophique J. Vrin.

———. 1998. "Beyond the Grave: History, Memory and Death in Postcolonial Congo/ Zaire." In Richard Werbner, ed., *Memory and the Postcolony: African Anthropology and the Critique of Power*, 21–57. London: Zed Books.

Denzer, La Ray. 1971. "Sierra Leone—Bai Bureh." In M. Crowder, ed., *West African Resistance: The Military Response to Colonial Occupation*, 233–67. New York: Hutchinson.

Dirks, Nicholas B. 1992a. "Introduction." In Nicholas B. Dirks, ed., *Colonialism and Culture*, 1–25. Ann Arbor: University of Michigan Press.

———. 1992b. "Castes of Mind." *Representations* 37: 56–78.

Dirks, Nicholas B., Geoff Eley, and Sherry B. Ortner. 1994. "Introduction." In *Culture/Power/History: A Reader in Contemporary Social Theory*, 3–46. Princeton: Princeton University Press.

Donelha, Andre. 1977. *Descrião da Serra Leoa e dos Rios de Guiné do Cabo Verde (1625): An Account of Sierra Leone and the Rivers of Guinea of Cape Verde (1625)*. Editing of Portuguese text, introduction, notes, and appendices by A. Teixera da Mota; notes and English translation by P. E. H. Hair. Lisbon: Centro de Estudos de Cartografia Antiga.

Dorjahn, V. R. 1959. "The Organization and Functions of the Ragbenle Society of the Temne." *Africa* 29: 156–70.

———. 1960a. "A Brief History of the Temne of Yoni." *Sierra Leone Studies*, n. s., 14: 80–89.

———. 1960b. "The Changing Political System of the Temne." *Africa* 30: 110–40.

———. 1961. "The Initiation of Temne *Poro* Officials." *Man*, o.s., 61: 36–40.

———. 1962. "Some Aspects of Temne Divination." *Sierra Leone Bulletin of Religion* 4: 1–9.

Dorjahn, V. R., and C. Fyfe. 1962. "Landlord and Stranger: Change in Tenancy Relations in Sierra Leone." *Journal of African History* 3: 391–97.

Doutté, Edmond. 1910. *Magie et religion dans l'Afrique du Nord*. Algiers: Typographie Adolphe Jourdan.

Ellis, Stephen. 1999. *The Mask of Anarchy: The Destruction of Liberia and the Religious Dimension of an African Civil War*. New York: New York University Press.

Englund, Harri. 1996. "Witchcraft, Modernity and the Person." *Critique of Anthropology* 16: 257–79.

Englund, Harri, and James Leach. 2000. "Ethnography and the Meta-Narratives of Modernity." *Current Anthropology* 41: 225–39.

Equiano, Olaudah. 1969 [1789]. *The Interesting Narrative of the Life of Olaudah Equiano, or, Gustavus Vassa the African*. Vol. 1. Edited by Paul Edwards. London: Dawson of Pall Mall.

Evans-Pritchard, E. E. 1937. *Witchcraft, Oracles and Magic Among the Azande*. Oxford: Clarendon Press.

———. 1965. *Theories of Primitive Religion*. Oxford: Clarendon Press.

Fage, J. D. 1969. "Slavery and the Slave Trade in the Context of West African History." *Journal of African History* 10: 393–404.

Falconbridge, Anna Maria. 2000 [1802]. *Narrative of Two Voyages to the River Sierra Leone during the Years 1791–1792–1793*. Edited by Christopher Fyfe. Liverpool: Liverpool University Press.

Ferguson, James. 1999. *Expectations of Modernity: Myths and Meanings of Urban Life on the Zambian Copperbelt*. Berkeley: University of California Press.

Ferme, Mariane C. 1992. "'Hammocks belong to Men, Stools to Women': Constructing and Contesting Gender Domains in a Mende Village (Sierra Leone, West Africa)." Ph.D. diss., Department of Anthropology, University of Chicago.

———. 1994. "What 'Alhaji Airplane' Saw in Mecca, and What Happened When He Came Home." In Charles Stewart and Rosalind Shaw, eds., Syncretism/Anti-Syncretism: The Politics of Religious Synthesis. London and New York: Routledge.

———. 1999. "Staging Politisi: The Dialogics of Publicity and Secrecy in Sierra Leone." In John L. Comaroff and Jean Comaroff, eds., Civil Society and the Political Imagination in Africa, 160–91. Chicago: University of Chicago Press.

Fernandes, Valentim. 1951 [1506–10]. Description de la Côte Occidentale d'Afrique (Sénégal au Cap de Monte. Archipels). Translated and annotated by Th. Monod, A. Teixera da Mota, and R. Mauny. Bissau, Portugal: Centro de Estudios da Guine Portuguesa, no. 11.

Fisiy, Cyprian F. 1998. "Containing Occult Practices: Witchcraft Trials in Cameroon." African Studies Review 41: 143–63.

Foucault, Michel. 1979. Discipline and Punish: The Birth of the Prison. New York: Vintage Books.

Fyfe, Christopher. 1962. A History of Sierra Leone. London: Oxford University Press.

———. 1964. Sierra Leone Inheritance. London, Ibadan, and Accra: Oxford University Press.

Fyle, C. Magbaily. 1979a. "Precolonial Commerce in Northeastern Sierra Leone." Working Paper no. 10, African Studies Center, Boston University.

———. 1979b. The Solima Yalunka Kingdom: Pre-Colonial Politics. Economics and Society. Freetown: Nyakon.

———. 1981. The History of Sierra Leone. London: Evans Brothers.

———. 1988. History and Socio-Economic Development in Sierra Leone. Freetown: Sierra Leone Adult Education Association.

———. 1997. "Popular Islam and Political Expression in Sierra Leone." In Alusine Jalloh and David E. Skinner, eds., Islam and Trade in Sierra Leone, 161–77. Trenton, N.J., and Asmara, Eritrea: Africa World Press.

Gable, Eric. 1995. "The Decolonization of Consciousness: Local Sceptics and the 'Will to be Modern' in a West African Village." American Ethnologist 22: 242–57.

Geschiere, Peter. 1997. The Modernity of Witchcraft: Politics and the Occult in Postcolonial Africa. Charlotteville: University of Virginia Press.

Geschiere, Peter, with Cyprian Fisiy. 1994. "Domesticating Personal Violence: Witchcraft, Courts and Confessions in Cameroon." Africa 64: 323–41.

Geschiere, Peter, and Francis Nyamnjoh. 1998. "Witchcraft in the 'Politics of Belonging.'" African Studies Review 41: 69–91.

Giddens, Anthony. 1984. The Constitution of Society. Berkeley: University of California Press.

Gilroy, Paul. 1993. The Black Atlantic: Modernity and Double Consciousness. Cambridge, Mass.: Harvard University Press.

Gilsenan, Michael. 1982. Recognizing Islam: Religion and Society in the Modern Arab World. New York: Pantheon.

Ginsberg, Carlo. 1983. The Night Battles. New York: Penguin Books.

Gluckman, Max. 1956. Custom and Conflict in Africa. Oxford: Blackwell.

Gomez, Michael A. 1998. Exchanging Our Country Marks: The Transformation of African Identities in the Colonial and Antebellum South. Chapel Hill: The University of North Carolina Press.

Green, Maia. 1997. "Witchcraft Suppression Practices and Movements: Public Politics and the Logic of Purification." *Comparative Studies in Society and History* 39: 319–45.

Gupta, Akhil, and James Ferguson. 1992. "Beyond 'Culture': Space, Identity, and the Politics of Difference." *Cultural Anthropology* 7: 6–23.

Guyer, Jane. 1995. "Wealth in People as Wealth in Knowledge: Accumulation and Composition in Equatorial Africa." *Journal of African History* 36: 121–40.

Hair, P. E. H. 1965. "Sierra Leone Items in the Gullah Dialect of American English." *Sierra Leone Language Review* 4: 79–84.

———. 1967. "Ethnolinguistic Continuity on the Guinea Coast." *Journal of African History* 8: 247–68.

———. 1978. "Hamlet in an Afro-Portuguese Setting: New Perspectives on Sierra Leone in 1607." *History in Africa* 5: 21–42.

Halbwachs, Maurice. 1992. *On Collective Memory.* Edited, translated, and with an Introduction by Lewis A. Coser. Chicago: University of Chicago Press.

Harvey, David. 1989. *The Condition of Postmodernity: An Enquiry into the Origins of Cultural Change.* Oxford: Blackwell.

Hinchman, Mark. Forthcoming. 1997. "The Maison des Esclaves of Gorée: History, Memory, and Tourism." In Ralph Austen and Kenneth Warren, eds. *The Slave Trade in African and African American Memory.* Durham, N.C.: Duke University Press.

Hogendorn, Jan, and Marion Johnson. 1986. *The Shell Money of the Slave Trade.* Cambridge: Cambridge University Press.

Honwana, Aleinda Manuel. 1997. "Healing for Peace: Traditional Healers and Post-War Reconstruction in Southern Mozambique." *Peace and Conflict* 3: 293–305.

Horton, Robin. 1967. "African Traditional Thought and Western Science." *Africa* 37: 155–87.

———. 1984. "Judeo-Christian Spectacles: Boon or Bane to the Study of African Religions?" *Cahiers d'études Africaines* 96: 391–436.

Howard, Allen M. 1997. "Trade and Islam in Sierra Leone, 18th–20th Centuries." In Alusine Jalloh and David E. Skinner, eds., *Islam and Trade in Sierra Leone,* 21–63. Trenton, N.J., and Asmara, Eritrea: Africa World Press.

Hunt, Nancy Rose. 1999. *A Colonial Lexicon of Birth Ritual, Medicalization, and Mobility in the Congo.* Durham, N.C.: Duke Univeristy Press.

Ijagbemi, E. Ade. 1968. "A History of the Temne in the Nineteenth Century." Ph.D. diss., Department of History, University of Edinburgh.

———. 1973. *Gbanka of Yoni.* Freetown: Sierra Leone University Press.

Inikori, J. E. 1982. "Introduction." In J. E. Inikori, ed., *Forced Migrations: The Impact of the Export Slave Trade on African Societies,* 13–60. New York: Africana Publishing Company.

Isichei, Elizabeth. Forthcoming. "Cowries, Statues, and Zombis: Some African Representations of Wealth and Death from the Sea." In Ralph Austen and Kenneth Warren, eds., *The Slave Trade in African and African American Memory.* Durham, N.C.: Duke University Press.

Jackson, Michael. 1977. *The Kuranko: Dimensions of Social Reality in a West African Society.* London: C. Hurst & Co.

———. 1982. *Allegories of the Wilderness: Ethics and Ambiguity in Kuranko Narratives.* Bloomington: Indiana University Press.

———. 1983. "Knowledge of the Body." *Man* 18: 327–45.

———. 1989. *Paths Toward a Clearing: Radical Empiricism and Ethnographic Inquiry.* Bloomington: Indiana University Press.

Jackson, Michael, and Ivan Karp. 1990. "Introduction." In *Personhood and Agency: The Experience of Self and Other in African Cultures*, 15–30. Stockholm: Almqvist and Wiksell International, and Washington, D.C.: Smithsonian Institution Press.

James, Wendy. 1988. *The Listening Ebony: Moral Knowledge, Religion and Power among the Uduk of Sudan*. Oxford: Oxford University Press.

Jones, Adam. 1981. "Who were the Vai?" *Journal of African History* 22: 159–78.

———. 1983. *From Slaves to Palm Kernels: A History of the Galinhas Country (West Africa) 1730–1890*. Wiesbaden: Franz Steiner Verlag.

Kalous, Milan. 1974. *Cannibals and Tongo Players of Sierra Leone*. Aukland, New Zealand: Wright and Carman.

Kamara, Sheikh Gibril. 1996. *The Spirit of Badenia*. London: Minerva Press.

Karp, Ivan. 1988. "Laughter at Marriage: Subversion in Performance." *Journal of Folklore Research* 25: 35–52.

———. 1995. "Agency, Agency, Who's Got the Agency?" Paper presented at the annual meetings of the American Anthropological Association, Washington, D.C.

Kearney, Michael. 1995. "The Local and the Global: An Anthropology of Globalization and Transnationalism." *Annual Review of Anthropology* 24: 547–65.

Klein, Herbert S. 1983. "African Women in the Atlantic Slave Trade." In C. C. Robertson and M. A. Klein, eds., *Women and Slavery in Africa*, 29–38. Madison: University of Wisconsin Press.

Kleinman, Arthur, and Joan Kleinman. 1994. "How Bodies Remember: Social Memory and Bodily Experience of Criticism, Resistance and Delegitimation following China's Cultural Revolution." *New Literary History* 25: 708–23.

Laing, Major Alexander Gordon. 1825. *Travels in the Timmannee, Kooranko and Soolima Countries in Western Africa*. London: John Murray.

Lambek, Michael. 1990. "The Practice of Islamic Experts in a Village in Mayotte." *Journal of Religion in Africa* 20: 20–40.

———. 1993. *Knowledge and Practice in Mayotte: Local Discourses of Islam, Sorcery, and Spirit Possession*. Toronto: University of Toronto Press.

———. 1996. "The Past Imperfect: Remembering as Moral Practice." In Paul Antze and Michael Lambek, eds., *Tense Past: Cultural Essays in Trauma and Memory*, 235–54. London: Routledge.

Lamp, Frederick. 1978. "Frogs into Princes: The Temne Rabai Initiation." *African Arts* 11, no. 2: 38–49.

———. 1983. "Balancing the Lopsided Load: Dimension and Sequence in the Arts of the Temne." Unpublished manuscript.

———. 1985. "Cosmos, Cosmetics, and the Spirit of Bondo." *African Arts* 18, no. 3: 28–43, 98–99.

Latour, Bruno. 1993. *We Have Never Been Modern*. Cambridge, Mass.: Harvard University Press.

Launay, Robert. 1992. *Beyond the Stream: Islam and Society in a West African Town*. Berkeley: University of California Press.

Law, Robin. Forthcoming. "Commemoration of the Atlantic Slave Trade in West Africa (with special reference to Ouidah)." In Ralph Austen and Kenneth Warren, eds. *The Slave Trade in African and African American Memory*. Durham, N.C.: Duke University Press.

Leach, Melissa. 1992. "Women's Crops in Women's Spaces: Gender Relations in Mende Rice

Farming." In E. Croll and D. Parkin, eds., *Bush Base, Forest Farm: Culture, Environment and Development*, 76–96. London: Routledge.

Lenga-Kroma, James Samuel. 1978. "A History of the Southern Temne in the Late Nineteenth and Early Twentieth Centuries." 2 vols. Ph.D. diss., Department of History, University of Edinburgh.

Lewis, I. M. 1971. *Ecstatic Religion.* Harmondsworth: Penguin.

Little, Kenneth. 1965. The Political Functions of the Poro." Part 1. *Africa* 35: 349–65.

———. 1966. The Political Functions of the Poro." Part 2. *Africa* 36: 62–72.

Littlejohn, James. 1960a. "The Temne Ansasa." *Sierra Leone Studies*, n.s., 14: 32–35.

———. 1960b. "The Temne House." *Sierra Leone Studies*, n.s., 14: 63–79.

———. 1963. "Temne Space." *Anthropological Quarterly* 36: 1–17.

———. 1973. "Temne Right and Left: An Essay on the Choreography of Everyday Life." In R. Needham, ed., *Right and Left: Essays on Dual Symbolic Classification*, 288–98. Chicago: University of Chicago Press.

———. 1978. *Aspects of Medicine among the Temne of Sierra Leone.* London: Social Science Research Council Report no. HR 4873, British Library Lending Division.

MacCormack, Carol. 1979. "The Sande: Public Face of a Secret Society." In B. Jules-Rosette, ed., *The New Religions of Africa*, 27–37. Norwood, N.J.: Ablex.

———. 1983a. "Slaves, Slave Owners, and Slave Dealers: Sherbro Coast and Hinterland." In C. C. Robertson and M. A. Klein, eds., *Women and Slavery in Africa*, 271–94. Madison: University of Wisconsin Press.

———. 1983b. "Human Leopards and Crocodiles: Political Meanings of Categorical Anomalies." In Paula Brown and Donald Tuzin, eds., *The Ethnography of Cannibalism*, 51–60. Washington, D.C.: Society for Psychological Anthropology.

MacGaffey, Wyatt. 1986. *Religion and Society in Central Africa: The Bakongo of Lower Zaire.* Chicago: University of Chicago Press.

Manning, Patrick. 1990. *Slavery and African Life: Occidental, Oriental, and African Slave Trades.* Cambridge: Cambridge University Press.

Marshall, Ruth. 1995. "'God is not a Democrat': Pentecostalism and Democratization in Nigeria." In Paul Gifford, ed., *The Christian Churches and the Democratization of Africa*, 239–60. Leiden: E. J. Brill.

Masolo, D. A. 1994. *African Philosophy in Search of Identity.* Bloomington: Indiana University Press.

Masquelier, Adeline. 1992. "Encounter With a Road Siren: Machines, Bodies, and Commodities in the Imagination of a Mawri Healer." *Visual Anthropology Review* 8: 56–69.

———. 1993. "Narratives of Power, Images of Wealth: The Ritual Economy of Bori in the Market." In Jean and John Comaroff, eds., *Modernity and Its Malcontents: Ritual and Power in Postcolonial Africa*, 3–33. Chicago: University of Chicago Press.

———. 1995. "Consumption, Prostitution, and Reproduction: The Poetics and Power of Sweetness in Bori." *American Ethnologist* 22: 883–906.

———. 2000. "Of Headhunters and Cannibals: Migrancy, Labor, and Consumption in the Mawri Imagination." *Cultural Anthropology* 15: 84–126.

———. 2001. *"Prayer Has Spoiled Everything": Possession, Power, and Identity in an Islamic Town of Niger.* Durham, N.C.: Duke University Press.

Matory, J. Lorand. 1994. *Sex and the Empire That Is No More: Gender and the Politics of Metaphor in Oyo Yoruba Religion.* Minneapolis: University of Minnesota Press.

———. 1999. "The English Professors of Brazil: On the Diasporic Roots of the Yoruba Nation." *Comparative Studies in Society and History* 41: 72–103.

Matthews, John. 1966 [1788]. *A Voyage to the River Sierra Leone, on the Coast of Africa: Containing an Account of the Trade and Productions of the Country, and of the Civil and Religious Customs and Manners of the People: In a Series of Letters to a Friend in England.* London: B. White and Son.

Mbembe, Achille. 1992. "Provisional Notes on the Postcolony." *Africa* 62: 3–37.

McNaughton, Patrick. 1988. *The Mande Blacksmiths: Knowledge, Power and Art in West Africa.* Bloomington: Indiana University Press.

Meyer, Birgit. 1995. "'Delivered from the Powers of Darkness.' Confessions about Satanic Riches in Christian Ghana." *Africa* 65: 236–55.

———. 1998a. "'Make a Complete Break with the Past': Memory and Postcolonial Modernity in Ghanaian Pentecostal Discourse." In Richard Werbner, ed., *Memory and the Postcolony: African Anthropology and the Critique of Power,* 182–208. London: Zed Books.

———. 1998b. "The Power of Money: Politics, Occult Forces, and Pentecostalism in Ghana." *African Studies Review* 41: 15–37.

———. 1999. *Translating the Devil: Religion and Modernity among the Ewe in Ghana.* Trenton, N.J. and Asmara, Eritrea: Africa World Press.

Middleton, Karen. 1996. "The Memory in the Marriage." Paper presented at the workshop on "Substantiating Memory." European Association of Social Anthropologists, Fourth Biennial Conference, Barcelona, July 12–15, 1996.

Miers, Suzanne, and Igor Kopytoff, eds.. 1977. *Slavery in Africa: Historical and Anthropological Perspectives.* Madison: University of Wisconsin Press.

Miller, Daniel. 1994. *Modernity: An Ethnographic Approach.* Oxford: Berg.

Miller, Joseph C. 1976. *Kings and Kinsmen: Early Mbundu States in Angola.* Oxford: Clarendon Press.

———. *Way of Death: Merchant Capitalism and the Angolan Slave Trade, 1730–1830.* Madison: University of Wisconsin Press.

Mitchell, P. K. 1962. "Trade Routes of the Early Sierra Leone Protectorate." *Sierra Leone Studies,* n. s., 16: 204–17.

Moore, Henrietta. 1988. *Feminism and Anthropology.* London: Polity Press.

Morphy, Howard. 1995. "Landscape and the Reproduction of the Ancestral Past." In Eric Hirsch and Michael O'Hanlon, eds., *The Anthropology of Landscape: Perspectives on Place and Space,* 184–209. Oxford: Clarendon Press.

Mudimbe, V. Y. 1988. *The Invention of Africa.* Bloomington: Indiana University Press.

Mullen Kreamer, Christine. Forthcoming. "Contested Terrain: Cultural Negotiation and Ghana's Capa Coast Castle Exhibition, 'Crossroads of People, Crossroads of Trade.'" In Ralph Austen and Kenneth Warren, eds. *The Slave Trade in African and African American Memory.* Durham, N.C.: Duke University Press.

Munn, Nancy D. 1990. "Constructing Regional Worlds in Experience: Kula Exchange, Witchcraft and Gawan Local Events." *Man* 25: 1–17.

Murphy, William. 1980. "Secret Knowledge as Property and Power in Kpelle Society." *Africa* 50: 193–207.

Niane, D. T. 1965 [1960]. *Sundiata: An Epic of Old Mali.* Harlow, U.K.: Longman.

Niehaus, Isak A. 1998. "The ANC's Dilemma: The Symbolic Politics of Three Witch-Hunts in the South African Lowveld, 1990–1995" *African Studies Review* 41: 93–118.

Nora, Pierre. 1989. "Between Memory and History: *les lieux de memoire.*" *Representations* 26: 7–25.

Nordstrom, Carolyn. 1997. *A Different Kind of War Story.* Philadelphia: University of Pennsylvania Press.

Nylander, G. R. 1819. "West-Africa Superstitions: Trial by Red-Water, Among the Bulloms." *The Missionary Register,* 496–99.

Ojukutu-Macauley, Sylvia. 1997. "Religion, Gender, and Education in Northern Sierra Leone, 1896–1992." In Alusine Jalloh and David E. Skinner, eds., *Islam and Trade in Sierra Leone,* 87–117. Trenton, N.J. and Asmara, Eritrea: Africa World Press.

Okri, Ben. 1991. *The Famished Road.* London and New York: Doubleday.

———. 1993. *Songs of Enchantment.* London: Jonathan Cape (Vintage Edition).

———. 1998. *Infinite Riches.* London: Phoenix.

Ong, Aihwa. 1999. *Flexible Citizenship: The Cultural Logics of Transnationality.* Durham, N.C.: Duke University Press.

Opala, Joseph. 1977. "Archaeological Resources on Bunce Island: A Preliminary Survey." Sierra Leone National Museum, Freetown.

———. 1982. "The Limba *hu-ronko.*" Seminar paper presented at the Department of Africa, School of Oriental and African Studies, University of London, March 4, 1982.

———. 1987. *The Gullah: Rice, Slavery, and the Sierra Leone-American Connection.* Freetown, Sierra Leone: United States Information Service.

———. 1994. *Ecstatic Renovation! Street Art Celebrating Sierra Leone's 1992 Revolution.* Freetown: Sierra Leone Adult Education Association. (See also *African Affairs* 93: 221–36.)

Ortner, Sherry B. 1984. "Theory in Anthropology since the Sixties." *Comparative Studies in Society and History* 26: 126–66.

———. 1989. *High Religion: A Cultural and Political History of Sherpa Buddhism.* Princeton: Princeton University Press.

———. 1995. "Resistance and the Problem of Ethnographic Refusal." *Comparative Studies in Society and History* 37: 173–93.

Osagie, Iyunolu. 1997. "Historical Memory and a New National Consciousness: The Amistad Revolt Revisited in Sierra Leone." *The Massachussetts Review* 38: 63–83.

Palmie, Stephan. 1995. "The Taste of Human Commodities: Experiencing the Atlantic System." In Stephan Palmie, ed., *Slave Cultures and the Cultures of Slavery,* 40–54. Knoxville: University of Tennessee Press.

———. 2002. *Wizards and Scientists: Explorations in Modernity and Afro-Cuban Tradition.* Durham, N.C.: Duke University Press.

Park, Mungo. 1817. *Travels in the Interior Districts of Africa.* Vol. 1. London: J. Murray.

Parkin, David. 1991. "Simultaneity and Sequencing in the Oracular Speech of Kenyan Diviners." In P. Peek, ed., *African Divination Systems: Ways of Knowing,* 173–89. Bloomington: Indiana University Press.

Peek, Philip M., ed. 1991. *African Divination Systems: Ways of Knowing.* Bloomington: Indiana University Press.

Phillips, Ruth B. 1995. *Representing Women: Sande Masquerades of the Mende of Sierra Leone.* Los Angeles: UCLA Fowler Museum of Cultural History.

Piot, Charles. 1996. "Of Slaves and the Gift: Kabre Sale of Kin During the Era of the Slave Trade." *Journal of African History* 37: 31–49.

———. 1999. *Remotely Global: Village Modernity in West Africa*. Chicago: University of Chicago Press.

Prussin, Labelle. 1986. *Hatumere: Islamic Design in West Africa*. Berkeley: University of California Press.

Ranger, Terence. 1996. "Postscript: Colonial and Postcolonial Identities." In Richard Werbner and Terence Ranger, eds., *Postcolonial Identities in Africa*, 271–81. London and New Jersey: Zed Books.

Rankin, F. Harrison. 1836. *The White Man's Grave: A Visit to Sierra Leone in 1834*. Vol. 2. London: Richard Bentley.

Rashid, Ismail. 1999. "'Do Dady nor Lef me Make dem Carry me': Slave Resistance and Emancipation in Sierra Leone, 1894–1928." In Suzanne Miers and Martin Klein, eds., *Slavery and Colonial Rule in Africa*, 208–31. London and Portland, Ore.: Frank Cass.

Rathbone, Richard. 1996. "Resistance to Enslavement in West Africa." In Patrick Manning, ed., *Slave Trades, 1500–1800: Globalization of Forced Labour*, 183–94. Aldershot, England: Variorum.

Reno, William. 1995. *Corruption and State Politics in Sierra Leone*. Cambridge: Cambridge University Press.

Richards, Paul. 1986. *Coping with Hunger: Hazard and Experiment in an African Rice-Farming System*. London: Allen and Unwin.

———. 1996a. "Chimpanzees, Diamonds and War: The Discourses of Global Environmental Change and Local Violence on the Liberia-Sierra Leone Border." In H. Moore, ed., *The Changing Nature of Anthropological Knowledge*, 139–55. London and New York: Routledge.

———. 1996b. *Fighting for the Rain Forest: War, Youth and Resources in Sierra Leone*. Oxford: James Currey.

———. 2000. "Chimpanzees as Political Animals in Sierra Leone." In John Knight, ed., *Natural Enemies: People-Wildlife Conflicts in Anthropological Perspective*, 78–103. London and New York: Routledge.

Robertson, Claire C., and Martin A. Klein. 1983. "Women's Importance in African Slave Systems." In C. C. Robertson and M. A. Klein, eds., *Women and Slavery in Africa*, 3–25. Madison: University of Wisconsin Press.

Rodney, Walter. 1970. *A History of the Upper Guinea Coast 1545 to 1800*. London: Oxford University Press.

Rofel, Lisa. 1999. *Other Modernities: Gendered Yearnings in China after Socialism*. Berkeley: University of California Press.

Rosenthal, Judy. 1998. *Possession, Ecstasy, and Law in Ewe Voodoo*. Charlottesville and London: University Press of Virginia.

Rowlands, Michael, and Jean-Pierre Warnier. 1988. "Sorcery, Power and the Modern State in Cameroon." *Man* 23: 118–32.

Rutherford, Blair. 1999. "To Find an African Witch: Anthropology, Modernity, and Witch-Finding in North-West Zimbabwe." *Critique of Anthropology* 19: 89–109.

Sacks, Karen. 1979. *Sisters and Wives: The Past and Future of Sexual Equality*. Westport, Conn.: Greenwood Press.

Sahlins, Marshall D. 1985. *Islands of History*. Chicago: University of Chicago Press.

———. 1988. "Cosmologies of Capitalism: The Trans-Pacific Sector of 'the World-System." *Proceedings of the British Academy* 74: 1–51.

Sayers, E. F. 1927. "Notes on the Clan or Family Names Common in the Area Inhabited by Temne-speaking People." *Sierra Leone Studies*, o. s., 10: 14–108.

Schlenker, C. F. 1861. *A Collection of Temne Traditions, Fables and Proverbs.* London: Church Missionary Society.

Schoffeleers, J. Matthew. 1992. *River of Blood: The Genesis of a Martyr Cult in Southern Malawi. c. A. D. 1600.* Madison: University of Wisconsin Press.

Scott, James C. 1990. *Domination and the Arts of Resistance: Hidden Transcripts.* New Haven: Yale University Press.

Shaw, Rosalind. 1982. "Temne Divination: The Management of Secrecy and Revelation." Ph.D. diss., Department of Anthropology and Sociology, School of Oriental and African Studies, University of London.

———. 1985. "Gender and the Structuring of Reality in Temne Divination." *Africa* 55: 286–303.

———. 1990. "The Invention of 'African Traditional Religion.'" *Religion* 20: 339–53.

———. 1991. "Splitting Truths from Darkness: Epistemological Aspects of Temne Divination." In P. Peek, ed., *African Divination Systems: Ways of Knowing,* 138–52. Bloomington: Indiana University Press.

———. 1992. "Dreaming as Accomplishment: Power, the Individual and Temne Divination." In M. C. Jędrej and Rosalind Shaw, eds., *Dreaming, Religion and Society in Africa.* Leiden: E. J. Brill.

———. 1995. "Mami Wata and the Sierra Leone Diamonds: Wealth and Enslavement in Men's Dreams and the State Economy." Paper presented in the panel on "The Global Mermaid and Her Mercantile Mirror: Transnational Icons and Embodiments of Consumption." American Anthropological Association's Annual Meetings, Washington, D.C., November 15–19, 1995.

———. 1997. "The Production of Witchcraft/Witchcraft as Production: Memory, Modernity, and the Slave Trade in Sierra Leone." *American Ethnologist* 24: 856–76.

———. 2000. "*Tok Af, Lef Af:* A Political Economy of Temne Techniques of Secrecy and Self." In I. Karp and D. Masolo, eds., *African Philosophy and Critical Inquiry,* 25–49. Bloomington: Indiana University Press.

Shaw, Rosalind, and Charles Stewart. 1994. "Introduction: Problematizing Syncretism." In Charles Stewart and Rosalind Shaw, eds., *Syncretism/Anti-Syncretism: The Politics of Religious Synthesis,* 1–26. London and New York: Routledge.

Skinner, David E. 1976. "Islam and Education in the Colony and Hinterland of Sierra Leone (1750–1914)." *Canadian Journal of African Studies* 10: 499–520.

———. 1978. "Mande Settlement and the Development of Islamic Institutions in Sierra Leone." *International Journal of African Historical Studies* 11: 32–62.

———. 1989. "Sierra Leone Relations with the Northern Rivers and the Influence of Islam in the Colony." *International Journal of Sierra Leone Studies* 1: 91–113.

———. 1997a. "Islam in the Northern Hinterland and Its Influence on the Development of the Sierra Leone Colony." In Alusine Jalloh and David E. Skinner, eds., *Islam and Trade in Sierra Leone,* 1–20. Trenton, N.J., and Asmara, Eritrea: Africa World Press.

———. 1997b. "Islamic Organization and Influence in Sierra Leone 1930–1990." In Alusine Jalloh and David E. Skinner, eds., *Islam and Trade in Sierra Leone,* 137–160. Trenton, N.J., and Asmara, Eritrea: Africa World Press.

Soares, Benjamin. 1997. "The Spiritual Economy of Nioro du Sahel: Islamic Discourses and Practices in a Malian Religious Center." Ph.D. diss., Northwestern University.

Soja, Edward W. 1989. *Postmodern Geographies: The Reassertion of Space in Critical Social Theory.* London and New York: Verso.

Sommers, Marc. 1997. *The Children's War: Toward Peace in Sierra Leone.* New York: Women's Commission for Refugee Women and Children.

Spyer, Patricia. 1997. "The Eroticism of Debt: Pearl Divers, Traders, and Sea Wives in the Aru Islands, Eastern Indonesia." *American Ethnologist* 24: 515–38.

———. 2000. *The Memory of Trade: Modernity's Entanglements on an Eastern Indonesian Island.* Durham, N.C.: Duke University Press.

Steedly, Mary Margaret. 1993. *Hanging without a Rope: Narrative Experience in Colonial and Post-colonial Karoland.* Princeton, N.J.: Princeton University Press.

Stewart, Charles. 1991. *Demons and the Devil: Moral Imagination in Modern Greek Culture.* Princeton: Princeton University Press.

Stoller, Paul. 1995. *Embodying Colonial Memories: Spirit Possession, Power and the Hauka in West Africa.* London and New York: Routledge.

Sturken, Marita. 1997. *Tangled Memories: The Vietnam War, the AIDS Epidemic, and the Politics of Remembering.* Berkeley: University of California Press.

Taussig, Michael. 1987. *Shamanism, Colonialism and the Wild Man: A Study in Terror and Healing.* Chicago: University of Chicago Press.

———. 1992. "Culture of Terror—Space of Death: Roger Casement's Putumayo Report and the Explanation of Torture." In Nicholas B. Dirks, ed., *Colonialism and Culture,* 135–73. Ann Arbor: University of Michigan Press.

Taylor, E. R., ed. 1957. *The Troublesome Voyage of Captain Edward Fenton.* Hakluyt Society, no. 113, 2d series.

Thayer, James Steel. 1983. "Nature, Culture, and the Supernatural Among the Susu." *American Ethnologist* 10: 116–32.

Thomas, Hugh. 1997. *The Slave Trade: The Story of the Atlantic Slave Trade, 1440–1870.* New York: Simon and Schuster.

Thornton, John. 1996. "Sexual Demography: The Impact of the Slave Trade on Family Structure." In Patrick Manning, ed., *Slave Trades, 1500–1800: Globalization of Forced Labour,* 39–48. Brookfield, Vermont: Ashgate Publishing Co.

el-Tom, Abdullahi Osman. 1983. "Religious Men and Literacy in Berti Society." Ph.D. diss., Department of Social Anthropology, University of St. Andrews, Scotland.

———. 1987. "Berti Qur'anic Amulets." *Journal of Religion in Africa* 17: 224–44.

Tonkin, Elizabeth. 1992. *Narrating Our Pasts: The Social Construction of Oral History.* Cambridge: Cambridge University Press.

Trimingham, J. Spencer. 1959. *Islam in West Africa.* Oxford: Clarendon Press.

Tsing, Anna. 1993. *In the Realm of the Diamond Queen: Marginality in an Out-of-the-Way Place.* Princeton, N.J.: Princeton University Press.

Turay, Abdul Karim. 1971. "Loanwords in Temne: A Study of the Sources and Processes of Lexical Borrowing in a Sierra Leonean Language." Ph.D. diss., School of Oriental and African Studies, University of London.

———. 1976. "The Portuguese in Temneland: An Ethnolinguistic Perspective." *The Journal of the Historical Society of Sierra Leone* 3, nos. 1 and 2: 27–35.

Turner, Victor. 1957. *Schism and Continuity in an African Society: A Study of Ndembu Village Life.* Manchester: Manchester University Press.

———. 1975. *Revelation and Divination in Ndembu Ritual.* Ithaca, N.Y.: Cornell University Press.

van Dijk, Rijk, and Peter Pels. 1996. "Contested Authorities and the Politics of Perception: Deconstructing the Study of Religion in Africa." In Richard Werbner and Terence Ranger, eds., *Postcolonial Identities in Africa,* 245–70. London and New Jersey: Zed Books.

Vansina, Jan. 1974. "Comment: Traditions of Genesis." *Journal of African History* 15: 317–22.

Weiss, Brad. 1996. *The Making and Unmaking of the Haya Lived World.* Durham, N.C.: Duke University Press.

Werbner, Richard P. 1989. *Ritual Passage, Sacred Journey.* Manchester: Manchester University Press and Washington, D.C.: Smithsonian Institution Press.

———. 1998. "Beyond Oblivion: Confronting Memory Crisis." In Richard Werbner, ed., *Memory and the Postcolony: African Anthropology and the Critique of Power,* 1–17. London: Zed Books.

White, Luise. 1990. "Bodily Fluids and Usufruct: Controlling Property in Nairobi." *Canadian Journal of African Studies* 24: 418–38.

———. 1993. "Cars out of Place: Vampires, Technology, and Labor in East and Central Africa." *Representations* 43: 27–50.

———. 2000. *Speaking With Vampires: Rumor and History in Colonial Africa.* Berkeley: University of California Press.

Wilmsen, Edwin. 1989. *Land Filled with Flies: A Political Economy of the Kalahari.* Chicago: University of Chicago Press.

Winterbottom, Thomas. 1969 [1803]. *An Account of the Native Africans in the Neighbourhood of Sierra Leone to Which is added an Account of the Present State of Medicine among Them.* Vol. 1. 2d edition. London: Frank Cass.

Wylie, Kenneth C. 1977. *The Political Kingdoms of the Temne: Temne Government in Sierra Leone, 1825–1910.* New York and London: Africana Publishing Company.

Yoneyama, Lisa. 1999. *Hiroshima Traces: Time, Space, and the Dialectics of Memory.* Berkeley: University of California Press.

Zack-Williams, A. B. 1989. "Sierra Leone 1968–85: The Decline of Politics and the Politics of Decline." *International Journal of Sierra Leone Studies* 1: 122–30.

Index

abduction, 113; of children, 239–40, 241, 245, 282n. 16, 283n. 21
Abdul, Pa, 43, 105, 110–11, 112
Abraham, Arthur, 234, 237, 281n. 12
Abu Bakr, 81
Accaron, 73, 272n. 6
al-Adhami, 89
adultery, 165, 172, 173, 179, 196–200. *See also* marriage
"Afro-Portuguese Ivories," 28
agency: African, in slave trade, 17–20, 36, 116, 267, 268; among diviners, 188; among diviners' clients, 180–81; vs. hegemony, 20–21; vs. resistance, 18–19. *See also* history
Ahmadiyya, 146
Aldridge, T. J., 271–72n. 10
Allah, 86, 100, 130, 274n. 20. *See also* Islam; Muslims; Qur'an
Allen, Richard, 273n. 17
All People's Congress (APC), 249, 250, 251, 253, 254, 259
Alvares, Manuel, 28, 29, 34, 53–54, 57, 62, 108–9, 213, 216, 271n. 5, 274n. 2, 277n. 5; on Mane domination, 212–15, 228, 229
Americans: as influence on spirits, 112. *See also* British; Europeans
Amistad, 250–51, 280n. 5
amulets(aŋ-sɛbɛ), 48, 60, 61, 62, 74, 76, 77, 78, 80, 90, 238; Muslim supersede Temne, 77, 78. *See also individual categories*
ancestors (aŋ-baki): contacted through divination, 97, 130; importance to Temne, 48, 49–50, 54–56, 63, 66–67; pebbles as, 85; as protectors, 173–74, 217. *See also* history; lineage; memory
animals: alligator, 243, 244, 282n. 14; as alternate forms of witches, 208, 216, 245, 280n. 8; and cannibalism, 226, 232, 233, 240, 252, 280n. 7, 283n. 23; chimpanzees, 241–42; crocodiles, 241; human leopards, 234, 240–41, 243, 244, 245, 253, 254, 256, 259, 281nn. 10, 11, 12; leopard/crocodile/chimpanzee, 225,